CW00481388

ZEN JUNGLE

THE
HOLISTIC MASTERCLASS
IN HOW TO TRULY
LOVE LIFE

From the Author

I have been privileged enough in writing this book to both
take and experience the transformational journey it represents.

How I started this journey, is certainly not how I emerged from it.
This book reflects a profound process of growth and learning for me and the rest of the
team involved in its creation. The wisdoms it contains and evolved from,
were received by us during that process and are not *all* of our invention.

With that in mind, I have taken reference to my name from the cover
and wish for the book to be a wholly owned creation of
The Zen Jungle Organisation.

We can change the world, by helping one person at a time
to realise who they really are and to finally love life.

Jason Tyldesley

The ZenJungle.org mission

to help the whole of humanity to love life, free from overthinking,
re-connected to the power and peace of nature.

The Zen Jungle Vision

An awakened, unpolluted world at peace, free of mind and ego.

Table of Contents

By way of introduction

Our personal journey of life is often very mixed, full of twists and turns. The world is thrust upon us the moment we're born; and as we grow we accumulate a multitude of thoughts, experiences, opinions and expectations. At first, the world is an exciting adventure – but all too often, and for most of us, things slowly start to feel more difficult as we grow and age.

This masterclass, course, transformational journey – call it what you will – is the culmination of some very personal experiences of a group of people, including me, who shared that all too common perspective. Some time ago, we had a sort of collective realisation that for whatever reason we and almost everybody we met were struggling to keep things together, to think clear thoughts and navigate the endless mental dialogue that seems to accompany life in the modern world. We decided we needed to change things. The fact that you're reading this now suggests you might be feeling the same.

Our own journeys certainly didn't begin with the thought of building a masterclass, so let's start with a bit about how we all got here. In this introduction I'll recount a little of my own story, just the basics, to show that something that felt so lonely and personal to me proved far more commonplace than I could ever have imagined. Every member of the Zen Jungle team has their own story, personal to them but including similar themes and conclusions. It was recognising those similarities and our shared search for purpose and meaning that brought us all together.

The patterns in life and the experiences we all have seem on the surface to form a unique and personal set of problems, expectations, fears and thoughts that we must deal with individually as we transit through life. It can seem that we are each of us the only person who sees and feels the things we do, so we learn to live with what sometimes feels like internal chaos and hide it from the world. We're told and conditioned to believe that the world is the world and that we should be grateful, happy, successful, generous, great parents, good husbands and wives, great at our jobs... The list goes on but the message is clear: that's how life is. We just need to get on with it.

We are here to tell you two things. First, that you are not alone. And second, that there is a fundamentally better way to live – that you can actually love life in ways you might never have thought possible.

Just about everyone we speak to seems to recognise the sequence of early-childhood excitement slowly giving way to repetition, fight for status, survival, competition, money and comparison. Somehow life events, relationships, business, careers, family and more become a cycle of unending stress and challenges. It happens earlier for some than it does for others but it happens to almost all of us at some point. You wake up one morning (if you've slept at all the night before, that is) and all you know is constant thought. Life seems like an endless series of decisions and worry, underpinned by perpetual demands that you perform, conform, play your part or do something in the world that makes a difference before you die. On the face of it, this seems to be totally unrelated to whether you're privileged or poor, popular or not, apparently successful or failing. The battles exist for most of us, and we see around us only a few who appear to have conquered these demons. The skewed and filtered version of the world presented in the media and on social networks only makes matters worse.

My own journey was much like this. I grew up in what might be considered a greatly loving and lucky family. A rebel since early on, I had the suspensions from school and the complex little incidents that come with having a risk-taking character. My parents were strongly entrepreneurial and really believed in the "life is what you make it" motto, so from an early age I was indoctrinated with the value of hard work. I worked in all areas of the family business, progressing to the roles best suited to me as permitted by my age; so one day I'd be on a production line, the next driving trucks, the next selling in a shop. You get the picture. It all seemed to go pretty well... In summary, my life soon became one of ambition and chasing dreams of wealth. Before I knew it I had a failed marriage, and two children who I realised not long ago are clever, beautiful and amazing (until recently, I didn't have time to stop, look and consider that). Then it was on to a series of failed relationships as I sought the perfect life partner, while enjoying an intensely adrenalin-fuelled lifestyle that included becoming a pilot, motor racing, skydiving, some questionable over-friendly parties and more. All in the name of finding fulfilment, contentment and peace.

Along the way, over the course of twenty-five tumultuous years, I built a very large business. By tumultuous I mean that the experience was often rewarding and endlessly stressful and provided few of the benefits that people looking on from outside might have expected it to. Following a few years of real challenges, when fast expansion saw me repeatedly needing to raise finance, I eventually sold the business (which by then had 1,300 employees) to my largest competitor in order to stop the cycle. I was pleased to be out.

Interestingly, it was then that I really began to learn how to live. I wouldn't have thought of it this way at the time but everything I've just described was part of a pattern of searching for something to make life worth living, to give it the purpose and meaning it never seemed to have. Up until this point I'd been endlessly chasing – chasing things that would make me happy, that would make it feel exciting to wake up in the morning and that would make me into a person I and everyone else could love. Needless to say, my quest failed. Looking back, this seems unsurprising – clearly the approach was fundamentally flawed. But one thing's for certain: we're most of us not taught "fulfilled life" in school; I had no idea. For me, that watershed moment after selling the business, when the emails had stopped and the phone no longer rang, was the first time I'd had the opportunity to pause and consider everything more deeply. There was more time to live, more time to contemplate and more time for some much-needed self-reflection. It was then that I discovered just how little peace I had and how unfulfilled I really was; it was also when I began to understand that the source of my disquiet was much deeper than could be resolved by all the stuff I was chasing.

Having lots of time is scary, as is solitude and constant reflection. Being alone with your own thoughts is hard when you're busy but they become deafening when life is quiet. It can feel desperate, painful, relentless and impossible. My life became one of perennial dog walks and reading book after book to find answers, starting with the success manuals and progressing to things much deeper and more philosophical. While I see now that this process was part of my growth and healing, at the time it was a seemingly endless search for answers and I believe it nearly broke me. There was some drinking, some drugs and lots of attempts to escape – which is something most of us are doing in one way or another and to differing degrees.

I was starting to find out much more about myself, but I was also often becoming more self-critical. The voice in my head seemed to get louder, not quieter – as was my aim – to a point where it was deafening; this felt like a crisis and nothing like the growth I was seeking and hoped for. The failed relationships continued and the patterns of my life, though now far less audacious, were centred on sadness and depression, tears and virtual collapse. I'd experienced moments of sadness before but these feelings were heightened as I relentlessly searched for what I know now was fulfilment but at the time certainly felt was a reason to carry on.

Add to the mix a life coach, some counselling and the purchase of a house in Ibiza, where I planned to go wild and relax equally, and you have a great picture of where all this went. My life situation looked ideal from the outside but to me it felt bleak. The audio books built interminably in number but the voice in my head just got even louder, debating why I was like this, attacking me, applying guilt and more. You know the drill, I'm sure. Would there ever be any break or peace? Then things started to change.

Having reached the bottom, my mind was now more open than ever – open to trying anything at all, with nothing whatsoever off limits. Serendipity had me choose the perfect life coach (thank you, Rebecca), who was fully aligned and well versed in the ways of raising the spirit, aligning with the universe and making the much talked about Law of Attraction start to work for real. The book recommendations began to make a difference and the answers that came, while not actionable or totally coherent, felt right at their core, so I continued with vigour. It was then that my climb from the tunnel started. It has since only gathered in pace and I now see progress every single day. Peace is now almost permanent and I have a feeling inside that I never, ever thought I'd achieve.

The more of the right books I read, the more I wanted to read. I was consuming hundreds of hours of texts old and new and progressing on my self-built positive path. The information I needed was in this book, then in another, and as I embedded each one in turn the process then became all about implementing technique after technique. There were some that worked and some that didn't; I found that I would understand and believe in many things I read, but that making them actionable and bridging to what I actually needed to *do* was much harder. Frequently the most prominent thought in my mind was, "Yes, but what does that actually look like in real life?" Then there'd be the not knowing when and how to apply things and I'd become confused and frustrated. I'd know something was right but would find myself questioning whether or not it was applicable to my situation.

Serendipity then also became a way of life. There were people entering my life with projects and perspectives who not only had the same sorts of thoughts and challenges, albeit stemming from very different experiences, but who were also feeling the same way and wanting the same actionable answers. That's when, unknown to us, we unconsciously embarked on the journey of bringing together the things that would really change our own lives and those of others; things that were actionable and in conjunction with each other profoundly impactful. We began to retrain our minds and change our perspectives, to learn new things from many different sources and to realise that the answers were *there* but just needed extracting.

In fact, many things we learned felt more like lost memories than unfamiliar ideas. Like we'd always known them but had forgotten them at some point along the way. We simply knew the truth when we saw it – and when we saw it, we knew it didn't need further investigation or validation. There was something very uncomplicated about this process of unfolding, a kind of emerging trust in the truthfulness of stuff that can't be fully understood or proved. If a principle serves you, use it; if not, don't. Like that. The fact is, in the short time it's taken to build this masterclass all these things have been more impactful than I could even begin to describe – so they work in practice and that's really what matters.

What we all agreed, though, was that the content itself was generally hard to consume and even more difficult to action. Understanding isn't enough; we're talking about things that have to be embedded into your very being and in these texts we were reading, the route to that was often very unclear or clothed in science or religious dogma. Many of the ideas were ancient, written over thousands of years, and they all needed to be brought together from different sources in order to make them coherent and simple to understand and use. However, their combined effect on all of us was intense and always clear; so we knew that if we could bring them together they'd work in a similarly profound way for the many people everywhere who are ready for better things. People searching for peace, purpose, an end to anxiety, or for sleep, awakening or enlightenment, long-lasting happiness and a love of life.

We knew that if we could make it all more coherent, place it in a sequence that was easy to consume and learn, help people to truly believe in it and to absorb it through practices and techniques, then this would be a game-changer. By stripping back the language and delivering it in an exciting, accessible and modern way, we'd also minimise the potential for subconscious resistance and allow people to help themselves, without getting in their own way – as of course we all do, unfortunately.

We humans search for happiness in the strangest places. The world around us suggests that it will be found in external things – material objects, places, people and so on – and so we often find ourselves, as I certainly did in my earlier life, veering from one thing to another in hot pursuit. Generally, though, we find on reaching each one that our sense of happiness is only fleeting, so we move on in search of the next "fix"; we're never able to feel truly satisfied and remain perpetually unfulfilled. Happiness in every moment of every day is a big ask but it's certainly possible to achieve. And where happiness is elusive, by living openly and without resistance you can maintain a bare minimum of peace – and I'm sure you'll agree that peace is an amazing start.

The Zen Jungle masterclass is a clear, eleven-step recipe for peace and happiness that just *works*. It's essentially a course in life, thought, perspective, love and self-realisation. We didn't invent all of the content; we just curated it then made it easier to find, digest and action. It's a transformational journey towards quieting the inner voice and transcending the mind to bring ultimate freedom. It begins by explaining why we are where we are in our thoughts. It then builds on that foundation of understanding to start to change thinking and stop it from being an involuntary act. It transforms that voice in your head into a beautiful friend, rather than one who won't stop chattering, considering, competing, comparing and scaring you; a friend who brings you peace and happiness and allows you to see life more as a game than the stressful battle it often becomes.

The masterclass takes time but not a lot. It is written for the digital age and so has written, video and digital content that's easy to consume and easy to visit and revisit until it embeds as ongoing habits. It teaches you lots of exciting new things; it may satisfy or ignite a thirst for learning and will reshape both your thinking and the way you see the world. Read this book, or do it digitally and online – follow it in the way you like and at your own pace. It will immediately feel right, and you'll understand. This journey requires commitment, but you'll find it almost instantly life-changing and rewarding.

As a team our aim is to help the whole of humanity to love life again and to reconnect to the power and peace of nature. With your dedication, this transformational journey will quickly yield results and have the profound effect on you that it has had on everyone who's been exposed to it so far. The concepts it contains have given us a purpose in life and I for one now enjoy almost every minute of every day, deeply and with joy. This is why we're sharing it with you.

In reading this far, you've made the first step. We truly wish you well in your journey and in reaching the point where you'll soon truly love life again. Open your mind as wide as possible to everything that follows and try to relax. The masterclass starts with basics – foundations are built and then developed – so you may find you're already familiar with some of the content. Please follow it all regardless and allow the masterclass to unfold so you have the fullest, clearest picture before you move on and can really make some amazing changes to your life.

With all of our love, Jason, Dan and Saskia and everyone at Zen Jungle.

Online Content

By joining the free online members area of zenjungle.org,
you will gain access to a growing number of resources, free downloads and
helpful learning materials to compliment your transformational journey.

. Infographics can be detailed and often need to be viewed in a larger format than
can be printed in the book. There will also be a wider range of content added over
time, based both on the online course and on the feedback of others
who take the journey before you do today.

Visit zenjungle.org/new-member

ZEN JUNGLE

Step 1 : Who Am I?

Chapter 1: Endless mental dialogue

It's the middle of the night and you're wide awake. There's a seemingly important debate going on in your mind about something you need to do tomorrow: a decision that you need to make; how you should feel about something someone said – someone who is "supposed to be" a good friend. It's 4 a.m. and you need to go to sleep but your mind just won't shut up. This issue will most likely seem totally inconsequential tomorrow but is currently feeling like life or death – and even when you tell yourself that it's not, and that you need to get some sleep, you can hear the debate go on and now added to it is the thought of what will happen if you don't get enough sleep... *Please let me sleep!*

The truth is that this kind of scenario is not confined to the 4 a.m. debate. It's an ongoing deliberation in whatever you are doing. It's the voice in your head. "I don't have that voice," some of you just heard in your head, while others heard, "I can't believe he knows what happens to me at night." This "voice" is clearly your mind and it's clearly very busy thinking, constantly processing things and talking to you about it as it goes. Thank you, mind.

You have probably joined the Zen Jungle masterclass in part because you, like almost all of us, appear to have very little control of this voice. Over time, the overthinking has become less than funny and now creeps in to almost every part of your life. True, there are hotspots of intensity when there is guilt, relationship issues, career, family or money stuff but the voice is permanent and generally loud and the overthinking behind it seems totally out of your control. It's easy to get sucked in – almost unavoidable – and the thoughts aren't even of your choosing most of the time, which is super strange in itself.

The thoughts and the voice seem to be considering different options around almost everything you do and every part of life. They are also speaking to you about what you like and don't like and will get deeply ingrained with how you feel at this moment too, or about every person you meet and every situation you are in. There are things that might happen in the future if you do or don't do what you "should". There are the things that have just happened that you wish hadn't and would like to change. Then there are the things long gone that you are sad about and regret. Sometimes you're feeling guilt, sometimes regret, sometimes fear, but it's probably clear that generally your mind is endlessly and actively trying to reason things out for you. Maybe it has to do it and just wants to make things easier, but if this is natural it's hard to see why it does it like this and makes you feel this way.

It actually seems to have arguments without you ever getting involved. The voice will play both sides, trying to find the right answers in never-ending debate. Should you, shouldn't you, why did you, what could you have done differently and what if... It's all going on in there and it must be totally necessary if you are to make sure everything in your life goes well and right, mustn't it?

Your own personal pet voice also seems to impact on you, way more than anyone else's version of the voice seems to affects them. To that point, one of the debates playing on loop usually goes along the lines of: "Why am I not like John? John seems so calm and quiet; I wish I was laidback like John. I feel like there are all these things to think about. Maybe there's something wrong with me – maybe I need help!" Truth is, John probably has the same voice and feels a similar way; it's just not something he's sharing with you or anyone else because he too feels like it's just him and it's his own scary little problem to keep secret, exactly as you are doing.

What's interesting is that often when people say that they are looking for peace, they mean freedom from their thoughts. It's about the fact that this endless internal dialogue is exhausting. Everything seems hard and everything seems to involve lots of debate and decision-making, to require lots of emotion and have a very *crucial* feel. Once it starts, even remembering to take the clothes out of the washing machine can be built into a problem. Is it? Probably not. But it's like bad things will happen if you don't indulge in the process.

Overthinking must be obligatory, then, and is clearly a part of being human. In order for us to be successful in life and to compare well to others, to conform or to compete, the voice seems like a very necessary part of things. The 4 a.m. debate is something that can't be avoided and when the overthinking becomes anxiety about a future or past event, well, that's sort of expected too. In reality, anxiety is usually just another form of overthinking and can be a reaction with or without the voice. It often does have the voice, and physical symptoms too – a panic attack or heart palpitations – but in any case it's all part of the same response mechanism. It's the same thing in another form.

So what is peace? For most people it is (yes, you guessed it) freedom from overthinking. It's freedom from the voice in your head and the endless internal dialogue that comes with it. We often expect that peace would come if only we didn't have all these life-related things to think about. We truly believe that there'll come a moment when our mind runs out of things to consider and then peace will arrive as if by magic.

The question is, will it ever really stop and why is it even like that anyway? Save that thought for later... This masterclass is a journey through some concepts and ways to change your habits and life, at its core, that for most will create a state of freedom. Thinking when it's wanted and not as something involuntary or with inappropriate impact on your life – an end result you probably never thought possible, the idea of which maybe just prompted your inner voice to say, "I'll believe that when I see it." The end result means peace is there permanently, with or without life happening around you as it invariably and relentlessly does.

Can you imagine a time where your sleep is sound and deep, all the way through the night? Where the things that you feel guilt about have disappeared into the past for good and need no further consideration, ever. And where the things you fear in the future – those that may go wrong or may go right – have become things you no longer need to expend your energy on or ever think about again. Even better, what if the expectations that are placed on you by yourself and others simply melted away? What would be the impact of that across the whole of your life? That time is coming; it is now more than a hope or possibility. You are now, already, on the journey that with a little staying power will help all this happen and so much more.

First, let's look at *why* you overthink. This starts with the simple question "Who are you?" How would you answer that? With your name? A short life history? "I'm Jason. I have two children, I'm divorced..." etc. Or would you talk about where you're from, your experiences, profession, status or titles? Have you ever actually been asked this slightly strange and challenging question and considered it deeply enough to answer truthfully? Doing that might also involve the question "Why are you who you are?"

One quick way to get a glimpse of the answers is to first ask, "Who am I?" – and then follow every response with a simple "Why?" So: "I am Jason. Why? Because that's the name my parents gave me. Why? Because..." and so on. Keep going. In fact keep going until you can go no more. Interestingly, you will see that the final answers often end in some subjective idea, not with a truth or any real final conclusion. This little exercise gives only a glimpse or at best a partial answer but is a great way for you to start thinking more deeply. And if it all started to sound a little philosophical and has you wondering where the discussion may lead, that's intentional. Soon it will help you better understand why our minds overthink as much as they do, and in the specific ways they do.

Who you are, once we get past the simple answer of name and maybe a peripheral history, is something that you have been working to build since you were born (and, yes, likely before that too). Your identity – for ease, let's use that term to refer to "who you are" – is actually not ever a finished article and it forms, grows and changes over time as you live your life, experience, learn and judge the world. Let me explain...

When you were born, a process began that is common to almost all of us. You started incrementally absorbing and learning certain things about the world. These things then formed the basis of who you are, how you think, how you act and the expectations you create and place on yourself in an ever-growing number. As a baby, you may have learned to love or fear your parents, what you liked and disliked, to fear hot water and to hate the cold; you may have seen things that scared you – in fact the list of influences is diverse and endless. These are all things that quite possibly have stayed with you since then and remain true as your likes, dislikes, fear and more today. They, along with everything that has happened since, have likely become part of how you describe yourself as a person. "I hate the cold, the rain", "I'm scared of getting burned, heights", "I don't like cats, spiders, birds, noises…" and so on. This process deepens as we grow older and our minds then become like some super vacuum cleaner, taking in lots of experiences, perceptions, likes, dislikes, judgements about what's right and what's wrong, concepts we were told to believe and opinions that we "think" we now have. We have a complex storage system of memory and we identify with a huge range of the elements now stored inside it.

As a child, almost before we can speak or process words, we are being told what to believe and being influenced by what we see others do and how they react; much of it is in the disguise of learning, where preferences and beliefs are embedded and simply accumulate over time. We are literally brainwashed and conditioned, told what to think and how, then told how to experience the world around us. Rain is bad and sunshine is good. Oh, OK, I believe you; not sure that the plants would agree when they need water but fine. The grass is grass because it's grass and boys are boys and girls are girls; girls behave like this and boys do this. We realise that we are male or female and we understand very early on what part we must play in either role.

In fact, there are so many influences on who we deem ourselves to be, the labels we're given, our likes and dislikes, what scares us and what we accept, that no two people have the same influences and so no two people have the same resulting mind identity. The programming of what *you* think and who you are is never the same as *my* programming and what I think. The combinations of ingredients for identity and how we process them give unlimited combinations – so the great news is that you are most definitely unique at the created-identity level. Yay, we're all complex and different! Well, maybe.

All that said, the ingredient list is in many ways always the same. Things we feel guilty about or were made to feel guilty about bring us sadness and low self-esteem, while things that were celebrated bring us confidence. The illnesses we had in the past are often a real badge of honour, just like the trophies we won at school sports days or our exam results. They are all pointers to who we are. "I'm good at this", "I'm rubbish at that", "I love speaking on stage" or "That scares me to death". We build this mental picture of the person we are and we live by it in an ever-increasing way, happily embedding something that happened once in our past as a permanent feature of our constantly developing personality.

Everything that happens, every day, is diligently stored by the mind, as it busily catalogues and remembers as best it can. Later, we can proudly point to these pieces of stored information as defining proof of who we are, and use them as evidence to defend our definition of ourselves whenever we are asked or challenged. "I could never bungee jump; do you remember the time I froze on the garden wall and that wasn't even high..." What a great reason to be scared of heights! These points of reference are all so convenient and useful, providing us with ways to say, "That's me and that's why." The question we couldn't answer before – "Who am I?" – is actually the question we are answering constantly, to anyone who will listen. We define ourselves with the good and bad, using statements like "I hate this" or "I love that", and even "I'm a bad husband" or "I am good parent".

We wear our experiences and beliefs like badges that we display to show off who we are in all different circumstances; even though many of them are based on a weak memory of an event or outcome, we attach to them strongly and can easily recall the proof. One significant aspect of life that creates a truly deep impact is pain. Both physical and (often more so) mental pain are real drivers of the turmoil we carry inside and of the identity and behaviours we exhibit outside, day in and day out. It may be something big or small that creates a major or minor trauma for us, but the belief we etch about it into our minds and hearts means we constantly fear ever reliving it or being in the same situation again.

This is one great and obvious reason why your mind is constantly working so hard: it is trying to avoid the situations that you don't want, with those that caused you pain at the top of its list. The underlying thought is, "Let's not do that again." It's for this reason that many people who have bad experiences in relationships later go on to have many more; they are trying to avoid previous pain rather than committing openly to new experiences. Fear changes our behaviour in ways that can realise our worst fears.

This internal storage department of who you are also really loves to listen to what others say about you. The comments that praise or hurt you, and the boxes other people put you in – "He's terrible with girls", "He's not an academic" – burn into your mind and become totally real to you. If you think about it, you are being judged and labelled permanently. The impact is obvious. You will even and often hear yourself repeat other people's judgements of and labels for you when a relevant subject comes up. The impact of this is even more profound when the person giving you the label is held in high regard. If you trust them or respect their views then you'll take their judgement on board and identify with it more easily.

Your internal judgement engine may have just gone into a slightly higher gear, in fact, anticipating that we are about to dig deeply into psychology. You can be assured that is not the case. This is an important area of coverage but predictable psychology or counselling it certainly is not.

Getting back to the identity. To consider all the many different ways in which you have been building who you "think" you are is quite incredible, and is an important precursor to making the much needed changes you want in your life. So let's look at a few more specifically before we move on. Labels for instance. Few influences on identity are more significant than the many labels and roles that are applied so readily in almost every area of human life. Your identification with them becomes embedded into you and always forms a multidimensional part of who you are. Roles like "I'm a boy", "I'm a father", "I'm a husband", "I'm a solicitor", or "a joiner", "a mother", "a daughter", "a runner", "a christian", "an atheist", "rich", "poor", "a victim", "a success"... You play these roles like a Hollywood actor. Even your age is a role that you carry and must play diligently. "I'm forty-six and therefore I behave this way."

As a child you could play the role of a child but later must become mature and more serious in your actions; as you take the role of adult, you must then be more responsible and set an example. These are all societal expectations, not natural occurrences in nature. The roles are well defined and we are conditioned to understand and play them. In the end, your identity is an incredible mash-up of parts you play and the expectations that come with them.

It's no wonder, then, that over time you have decided that you like or dislike certain things. You've decided that this person is good and that one is bad. This one is good-looking and that one isn't. You hate being at work and you love being on holiday. You don't like rich people and you love being a liberal. These are all simply subjective *ideas* that at some point became who you believe you are as a person. Many are inherited from those around you, or educated into you. They are also *judgements*. Judgement is at the heart of almost everything we humans do. The voice in your head is busy doing it all the time.

Maybe you're judging what you're reading right now: "What has this got to do with sorting my life out...?" Over time, our judgements about people, situations and things amass, becoming a huge load of things and preferences that we must consider in order to *do* or *avoid* almost everything. The labels discussed above are the result of the judgements we're discussing here. Right and wrong, good and bad, likes and dislikes, who you've forgiven and who you haven't and the guilt associated with your own actions and those of others... All these play a part in who you have become. Even your simple opinions and preferences about everything and everybody are judgements – more subtle judgements, but judgements nevertheless.

The vacuum cleaner of the mind and the past is not the whole story on identity, though. Now enter the future. Imagination is a wonderfully creative thing. As part of its rich harvest of fruit, it brings us really believable and immersive, cinematic alternate versions of the future. These are amazingly effective if overthinking was an aim when we were made. These future scenarios often create strong parts of your identity for you in a time that hasn't yet even happened. Your mind spends lots of time building what may happen in the future in order to allow you to worry about it now, and for some people this becomes an endless pastime. Your identity really cares about your legacy and who you may or "should" become, in order that you can do the work to build it now. It is in fact always concerned with the *somebody* that it feels you should become.

Your goals and who you will become someday therefore form another aspect of your identity. The decisions to be successful, to achieve certain ambitions, to be respected or to care for your family mean that you have to *be* that person too, and all the expectations that go with it. This means that the future brings expectation and fear in huge quantity to the present, becoming a great source of further anxiety and inner voice. Add this to the personality that has been created from history, and the one being created right now for a future that hasn't yet happened, and we have more of an idea of who you actually might be. Wow! This stuff is huge. I bet life was way easier when you thought you were just your name…

Chapter 2 : Fear, expectation, regret, preferences

So what does this all mean? How does it contribute to the waking up and needlessly thinking at 4 a.m.? To keep things simple, it's good to consider that all of these things result mainly in fears, expectations, regret and lots of preferences. If knowing that doesn't make dealing with it easier, remember that the mind has needed over generations to become the ultimate defence mechanism against this simple list of seemingly innocuous words and the patterns they represent. Humans are uniquely burdened by these patterns, as they are conditioned and deeply embedded, so un-doing them will always be a huge challenge.

Behind the scenes, this drama that you have called your life has become something that your mind feels the need to fully protect you from. In fact, that has become your mind's primary function. It has taken on the role of sole protector and now considers everything that happens or may happen to you in minute detail and incredibly deeply. It is narrating every aspect of your world before, during and after it happens in a way that is both unmanageable and unimaginable. It is doing the impossible task of reasoning it all out for you. Specifically, it is trying to avoid making decisions that may hurt you and situations and things you may not like, while trying to control the world, almost in its entirety, to make you happy. Magically, this also means that it is predicting the future, second-guessing what will happen next so it can decide whether or not to protect you from the imagined event or move toward it and chase it as something you want. Amazing really, isn't it?

The endless debates and ongoing mental dialogue are actually forms of love and protection, so this is a great point to mention that your mind is your very best friend. Believe me? Well, please don't hate it for trying to do what it has come to perceive as its job. All those constant considerations represent an amazing challenge for it. "What is the best way forward to avoid pain?", "What will meet all the expectations?", "How can we stay with things you like rather than dislike and protect you from mistakes, pain and regret..." Ironically, the voice that takes so much of your peace away is tirelessly trying to make your life easier. Odd, then, that it has evolved into a much bigger problem for you than the world outside could ever be. So much so that it has become the major cause of suicide and the key reason people are choosing therapy, mindfulness, more anxiety medications than ever before, sleep remedies and so on. We are navigating a world full of incessant demand for decisions, reasoning, consideration and acceptance, and meeting expectations forced on us by ourselves and others. Comparisons and competitions abound and our minds are understandably overactive; but unfortunately this means we often feel we've lost control and can't stop the inner voice from doing its thing.

One of the primary causes of the activity in your head is expectations. They are literally everywhere. All of your roles, labels, likes and dislikes result in extensive expectations that pose an impossible challenge to your mind. For example: "I am a man, and history tells me I will provide for my family" or "I am a woman, so I will be a great mother..." These are just two of the (sexist) stereotypes that hold true as real underlying expectations in the West; but you are dealing every day with layer upon layer of expectations, the volume and contradictions of which are mind-blowing. For example, a woman might also be expected to have a career, to be independent, caring, feminine, loving, beautiful... Expectations come at us from all sides, formed among other things by conditioning and what we learn from the world around us, experience, comparison and competition. One of the problems of social media is that it serves as a powerful amplifier for expectation: we see the curated and unreal highlights of other people's lives, then try to make every day of our own life match the impossible expectations we've been shown.

Every one of the roles and labels we assume comes with more expectations to add – and we know how many roles and labels can make up a single identity! It would be great if we just had one. The expectations that came with it would be annoying but probably more manageable than the reality our huge list of roles presents for each of us. As it is, even the roles and labels we don't want, come with expectations and internal battles, and have us creating further expectations of ourselves just to defy them. It's amazing. But is it any wonder that you are waking up at night or experiencing anxiety when just meeting expectations is a full-time job for both you and your mind?

It is worth mentioning at this point that money – which is closely related to status, your roles and, ultimately, power and independence – has now become a synonym or metaphor for much of the above list. The very fabric of your being is often defined by how much or how little money you may have. It's a badge of success, your self-worth and a key driver of expectation, competition and comparison. It may also, as a result, be a key underlying driver in chasing things to make you happy or to visibly display your status, which we often believe will make us happy in itself.

We spoke about how labels, roles, judgements and expectations relate to identity, but there are other, more hidden parts to identity too – parts that we often don't even know exist. To make the whole thing even more complex, some of the roles, labels and expectations we don't instantly see are created secretly, in the background, by pain and fear. These are often purposefully hidden from us by the mind. In Chapter 1 we discussed how the mind works hard to avoid situations that cause pain. When pain creates fear then often, in much the same way, the mind will hide the cause deep in our subconscious to help keep us in a happy state. Your trusty mind diligently keeps it out of view, making sure that you are not affected and attacked by it in the future. This creates the odd effect of having a role or the expectation without actually knowing where it comes from or what caused it – and yet experiencing the same reactions to and anxieties about it as if you did know. Pain and fear create a ball of sensitivity that prompts an aggressive reaction when it's touched. This is the effect when hidden fears and expectations come to the surface.

The overthinking mind, then, is hardly surprising but it's also who you are; you attach to it and (hopefully) you love it. In any case it's interesting to see just how much time you spend defending its elements. To see the real awe and splendour of your mind-identity in action, to see what it's really made of and what it does when it is threatened. What if someone questions one of your beliefs – says, "You like carrots!" when you *know* you don't – or stirs up the thoughts that cause you pain? Your mind will vehemently defend anything and everything that you have ever judged as right or wrong, as good or bad; your beliefs, opinions, attachments and expectations. When challenged, your mind will fight to preserve these judgements as if they are who you actually are and not simply a subjective point of view. This is essentially the cause of all arguments, wars and conflicts. "I believe this" and "You challenge my belief or disagree" has started every major war. That's how aggressive the identity response can be.

The voice in your head is actually a superb defence mechanism. It is way more interested than you think in making sure that this vacuum-cleaner bag full of thoughts, beliefs, expectations, ways of living, roles, expertise, experiences and illnesses and more – the stuff that says who you *are* – is allowed to define you unchallenged. It keeps it all within an impregnable fortress that cannot easily be impacted. It's like a vicious animal in a cage, just waiting for those poking fingers of attack to come through the bars. See how fast it reacts when any of part of your identity is questioned and see how powerless you are to stop it. It's literally in the core of your being.

So, by now you know that the answer to the question "Who am I?" is as deep and diverse and rich with detail as the entirety of your every experience, influence, belief, ambition and more. Further, this wonderful concoction that is your identity is kept safe by your brilliant overthinking mind. Given all that, you'd be forgiven for wondering at this point whether overthinking really is a necessary fact of life. We'll get to that question shortly... but – spoiler alert – this is only the beginning of the masterclass that will remove it.

Chapter 3 : But first let's think: what is actually real and true?

Is any of this real? Clearly it must be. Your identity was built in exactly the way I said. Hopefully that is an obvious fact and an inner feeling tells you it's true. Moving forward, then, the next question is more about understanding the way your identity was built in the context of a slightly bigger picture. This takes a bit of explanation, so stay with me.

Our discussion of who you are simply concluded that that is related to every experience and influence in your life; that your beliefs and what you have been told are important, the things you like and dislike and your judgements and roles too are all wrapped up in the middle of your identity. All very real and all very much part of who you are. Yes? Good. Hold that thought, because we're now going slightly off subject for a moment for reasons that will become clear as we go...

Do you know how long the earth has been in existence? When I googled it today, it said it was 4.543 billion years old, which means that it will still be approximately the same age if you read this even 30 or 40 years from now. This must be true because it said it on Google. I asked the same question about the universe and it told me that it was 13.8 billion years old. Wow – that's a long time. I then googled "How many planets in the universe?" and the answer that came back blew my mind. There are over 200 billion galaxies and they each have lots of planets, so the best guess is 1,000,000,000,000,000,000,000,000 planets in total. There's a reason that I didn't try to write that in words. Is that even a real number? Anyway, so that's a lot then.

Out of interest, I then asked how many species there have ever been on earth. I have to say that the answer was a bit vague by Google's standards. It said "something like 8.7 million" – and I quote the next part so you can try it yourself – "give or take 1.3 million". Which again is a lot. All this inspired me to think a bit philosophically about the fact that humanity is just one of 8.3 million species on an earth that's been around for 4.543 billion years. So how long has humanity been around? Well, if we stick with modern man (from troglodytes onwards, I believe), it's thought to be around 200,000 years. Now I think that's 0.004 per cent of the lifespan of earth.

What does that mean? It means that most of the earth's lifespan so far was spent without any humans at all and that there have been lots of species coming and going forever in the relative sense of forever. The point being that the universe and galaxies seemed to do just fine with the other 8.3 million species (interestingly, it's the same number even when I take the humans out) on earth before the humans arrived. So, the reason for this interlude? We left the idea of how your identity was built at the point of asking, "Is any of it real?" We've just googled the answers to everything and you're about to see why that's apt. Let's review some of the constructs that went into building who you are, just to help us think about all that again.

You were born; let's start there. You started to accumulate a version of the world that later became embedded in your mind as the things that would define "who you are". Your experiences and the things you were told were key to this. Experiences are often driven by what people – humans – do and think and what we're told is a simple culmination of what humans think or have thought. In fact, what we're told has been being passed on for thousands of years and has been formed from the core of what humans thought about and decided may be true since the beginning of their time on this planet. Let's forget the bit where the earth was flat and you could fall off it, and stick with what we know or think we know to be "true and right". With some necessary revisions, what humans decided was right and wrong, good and bad, what should be liked and disliked, feared and not feared has been accumulating and communicated over many, many thousands of years.

Almost everything you have ever experienced and almost everything that you have been told originated from thoughts and these same accumulated beliefs that humans have been progressively absorbing over the course of time. Your dad told you stuff, his mum told him stuff, her mum told her stuff and so on. Weirdly, it's probably all the same stuff too.

From the moment humans could make sound, they felt the need to communicate what they judged to be right or wrong, good or bad, interesting and boring and so on. At some point they actually had to invent the words themselves in order to pass on these concepts. As they did so, they analysed the sh** out of the world and tried to make deeper sense of its mysteries, inventing maths and numbers just because some bright spark wanted to create a way to describe some things better than they could already do with the words they already had. This has enabled even more layers of thoughts, opinions, fears and expectations to be added into the human world and to accumulate and be passed from generation to generation. Great – how clever are we?

This, however and interestingly, is something that the other 8.3 million species haven't managed to do for themselves because they're not as "advanced" as we are. They just start life with a will to live, go with the flow and generally enjoy life, then die at the right moment and move on to the next life (maybe).

The whole human world we live in, and everything that your mind has been using to build who you are, is actually the product of what is, in effect, popular opinion, all passed down through the ages and accepted as right through subsequent generations. The good, the bad, the ugly and the beautiful were all defined somewhere along the way and have been taught in our schools and by our parents ever since. Granted, there were some pretty big mistakes made in right and wrong and how we thought things work, and maybe there will be a realisation soon that even more of what we know is wrong; but for now it's considered correct.

What is notable is that we have become so conditioned to receive it all that we grow up simply accepting and taking for granted much of the world we live in without ever thinking more deeply or questioning what we are told. We just get on with living in the life that has been presented with its thought-provoking structures and experiences giving us a reason to overthink along the way.

As a special case in point, the wonder and beauty of nature is often taken as a given with no deeper consideration than that. That's a tree, grass is grass, water looks like this and feels wet and the sun keeps us all nice and warm. Trees are trees because we said so and let's forget why they are there or how they got there because that is simply something we don't understand at all... The truth is that no amount of analysis has ever provided answers to the mysteries of life and the universe or the reason *why* it all exists. I mention this because it shows how invested we really are in the illusion and societal framework of subjectivity that we have created as a species. So much so that most of us now ignore the biggest questions, present all around us.

When was the last time you really considered the amazing beauty of the world we live in? When was the last time you stepped outside of the commercialised, structured existence that humans have and are creating and took in the wonder of just how perfectly everything that we didn't make actually works? How the plants grow in cycles, the rain waters them, the sun feeds them and us and so on for 8.3 million species whose ecosystems interrelate with and support each other, just because they do. It all interacts so beautifully, yet we often see only the illusion that has been created by people, with its rules, structures, beliefs, ownerships, money, competition, comparison, governments, societies, technology and more.

This understanding or perspective is important on this masterclass because it helps us to consider and look at what is actually real and what is not; what we have invented and what is simply part of a human illusion that we have been born into and accepted without question. The life we live is wholly based on a society that is building its own version of knowledge and the world. It is creating structures, setting beliefs, suggesting what your preferences should be and even, underlying it all, giving you a way to think.

The media and social media serve to strengthen these patterns and constructs and their influence is now stronger than ever. They are inescapable, giving us relentless directives about what to think and how to feel, creating expectations and imposing belief in rules – all thrown at us everywhere we go and in every waking moment. The whole "idea" of life for our species is communicated rather than learned, with little opportunity to ask or even to find the right questions to ask. We are simply told and passively exposed to what to believe.

A great example of the human illusory construct is government. The whole idea demonstrates just how much our preferences and beliefs are embedded, with fixed ideas of right and wrong, life and death, good and bad built into extensive rules and the imposition of authority. As I write, there has been a global pandemic, and by order of governments the population of almost every country in the world has been *confined* to their homes "for their own safety". Almost an entire species has been told what to believe and what to do – and do it they must, irrespective of whether or not they agree. The concept of being born free seems ultimately and easily questionable at this moment.

Control on this level is unprecedented and while it has been taken essentially in the name of progress, I'm sure that we are unlikely to see the same thing happen elsewhere in nature; certainly it is not something that has ever happened before, across all 8.3 million species. The human illusion grows stronger every day and the effects of this fact on the natural course of things are dramatic. What nature intended for us is defied and avoided. Our views on life and death, certainly in Western society, are ever more strongly programmed; fear of death and the wish to prolong life have together become an all-consuming force, causing overpopulation, disease and pollution of the planet and upsetting the natural balance of how things were supposed to be. Not least among the visible and highly impactful consequences of all this is our mindset, mental health and confinement to endless, invasive thought.

This is by no means a tree-hugging, anti-establishment address. Rather, it's a simple pointer to the fact that this human illusion is what causes your identity and is responsible for the ever-growing epidemic of anxiety and overthinking. Our institutions, parents, experiences and everything we are exposed to simply re-enforce the endless expectations of who we should be and why but importantly, it is all itself created by human thought at its core.

Is the human illusion good or bad? There is no need to add further judgement or imagination to a world already full of it. Awareness is all we need, together with an acceptance of the reality we live in and the symptoms it creates. If our aim is to help you to love life, we must first help you accept the causes as our basis for change. Reaching our end goal does not involve changing the world! (Well, it might, but not like this.)

It's now time to prepare your mind to start some positive changes. As you will soon learn, you are a product not of your *external* environment but of your *internal* environment. As the 1999 film suggested, perhaps living in the Matrix is more a choice than a necessity – and just maybe it's more about unlearning what you *think* you know, than learning something profoundly new.

ZEN JUNGLE

Step 2 : Escaping the Judgement Loop

Chapter 4 : It's time for change

So this is where it all really does start to "get real". The previous chapters will serve as a great foundation to create a base level of understanding so we can now begin to make some important changes. From this point on, change is the name of the game.

Assuming that you really do want to "love life", now is a good time to set some expectations to help you to move into the right mindset. As we now move forward, you'll find that the content and information is not only conceptual but will also require your commitment and action. This masterclass is for those who are ready to live life differently, open-minded enough to receive and committed enough to take action – the reward being permanent peace and almost permanent happiness. If that's you, let's go.

This is a learning process; we will start slow and progress because this stuff takes practice. You may find you instantly recognise and change your habits, behaviours and thinking, or it may take you a while. That's OK: make peace with what happens and enjoy the process. This is a masterclass based on simple truth; it's not magic. It's about forming a deeper understanding of the causes of overthinking, unhappiness and anxiety at their core and starting to undo what years of habit-building has created. The goal is not to chase the idea of "loving life"; the goal is to understand and adopt some key principles that before you know it will have you in just the place you want to be.

Over the next few chapters, we'll look at a handful of the things that have a major influence on your peace and start the process of retracting from the ones that don't serve you; increasing the dominance of the ones that do. You'll find that some improvements happen very quickly and easily; other things will require more effort and practice, using techniques found deeper into the masterclass to help embed your new habits. The great news is that you'll soon have a clear picture of where you are going and why...

Judgement

Our story starts, as it should, with the cause – the *seed* – allowing you to see both that and the flowers (or weeds) that grow from it. Our seed is judgement. As we've discussed, almost every thought you have is some form of a judgement. "I like this", "I don't like that", "This is the right thing to do" – all obvious judgments. In reality, though, we judge almost everything we see, hear, smell, touch and feel. We immediately judge every person we meet, our inner voice saying, "She's nice", "He's an idiot", "pretty", "ugly", "clever"... You get the picture. We also judge every situation: "This is fun", "This is boring", "This is interesting" and so on. In fact our judgements are endless and we're busy making them much of the time, automatically without knowing or thinking. We even judge things like the weather, without any real aim or outcome: "It's nice", "It's horrible" – in reality it's just the weather. At the start of this paragraph I said *almost* every thought is a judgement but in truth *every* thought is fundamentally a judgement.

I'm going to say that judgement may have come before even the first person could speak and before the first language and words were created. That may or may not be true but I don't know and I don't care. Look, I even judged what I just said and what you may have said in response. Judgement is everywhere. In modern life, with the illusory framework of humanity to refer to, we have so much more to judge. Popular opinions have become collective judgements that we now all adopt as our own. There are so many things that we don't need to judge for ourselves but instead are simply *told* are good or bad, right or wrong, easy or hard, to like or dislike and so on. How *convenient* that we all understand what's what and from an early age can be programmed with what to believe so we all start from a common base. It's as if these judgements were facts and not simply opinion.

Added to that, the machine of our amazing memory and mind is a machine that not only makes judgements at lightning speed, but also retains our personal judgements from birth and over our lifetime, holding on to the things we decided we liked or disliked when we were six years old, just as if we'd made those judgements yesterday. Experiences, thoughts and emotions from a whole lifetime then result in judgements and expectations about how we "think" the world should be, or what box it should fit into, in super microscopic detail. We know what we want and what we "should" and "can" expect.

Going back to Chapter 1, that beautiful identity we have all created for ourselves is actually this big ball of judgements. It "knows" what you like and what you don't, what you fear, love, are good at and so much more. It knows because you stored everything away as it happened or as you were told what to believe, and it's been doing this your whole life. Some of these were "snap" judgements, made quickly on a little information or "instinct"; others were slow-burn judgements, where a seed was planted and you watched it develop before deciding to store it as a full-blown judgement. Others still arose from you feeling emotion around a particular situation or experience – things that hurt you, made you sad, excited you, scared you and so on. These were stored as special, stronger judgements that could be deeper, conscious or subconscious desires or fears; if allowed, they will cause you to feel the same emotions they stemmed from whenever you're reminded or think of them again. What an amazing and wonderful thing the human mind is. It is constantly building a framework of filters for the way you see the world, creating the boxes that everything must fit into and perpetually refining those boxes, shrinking them, as more judgments get added along the way.

At the core of judgement is attachment. This is the simple process of you giving a personal meaning to anything, including people, places things or events. Attachment is part of judgement but is also the deeper reason that we store and retain these subjective events forever. Once something has a personal meaning, it is embedded within you and within your identity. In reality, nothing at all in life actually needs to be given a meaning at all, though humans seem to do it as a matter of course. In earlier chapters we spoke of the immense universe and the billions of years it has been in the making. The fact that we are one of over 8 million species and as an individual, you are currently one of over 7.8 billion on this planet, one planet of billions, in billions of galaxies, seems to be lost on us. Why? Judging and giving meaning to the most inconsequential of events in human life is one of our most common, moment-to-moment activities. Then, what we give meaning to becomes embedded within. In the grander scheme of things, how could anything or anyone you experience ever truly have a consequential meaning? Something to think about and retain for later.

Judgements dictate grudges and guilt, and they are at the heart of all expectations too. A judgement of what is right or wrong, of what you and others should or shouldn't be, is embedded into you by almost all influences in the modern world. It's actually like the world was made to create and totally support judgements. The media love it, social media is a soapbox for it and the idea of free speech would be nothing without the endless judgements that underpin it. You could say that humanity has created a framework of judgement as the basis of everything. Whether we like that or not, I guess that's just the way it is. Or is it?

At this point, it is worth considering the possibility of living without judgement in your life, or at least without personal, focused judgements of people, situations and things. The ones that become part of your identity. How would your life change if you never judged in this way? What would it be like if you never adopted the judgements of others, just because everyone else had them? Do you need to adopt them or not? Is judgement serving you or not? What if you decided not to remain part of the popular movement after all? After all, does it work for everyone else?

Preferences

To go a little deeper, let's have a think about the (not so) beautiful sequence of events that begins with judgement and snowballs to include several other things of interest in our transformational journey towards "loving life". From judgements, our mind diligently creates our preferences. I judge a situation as bad and I now prefer not to be in that situation at all or ever again. Judgement essentially creates polarities. Before a final judgement of this kind was established, a thing could have been described as varying degrees of good; everything could start as good and get better until it was amazing. But now that we have invented a polarity the scale goes from bad through neutral to good. Judgement creates very specific and compartmentalised likes and dislikes, ideas about right and wrong, good and bad, things I want in life (goals) and things I don't (fears and failures). It makes things easy or hard and it dictates what I want, where I want or don't want to be and lots of other important things too.

Judgements and preferences become quite a fundamental part of life and once we've made them we cling to them and defend them because they are part of *us* – or part of our mind-created identity, to be more specific.

The strange thing about them all is that they are simply thoughts that we've stored and are holding in our head. They are totally subjective: one person may love something while another may hate that very same thing. This means that judgements and preferences are certainly not truths. They are not facts but rather simply opinions that we decide to embed over time. They are things we adopt and keep for our own as part of "who we are" in our self-made identity. Great, isn't it? You can love being somewhere or doing something and the same place or activity can be my worst nightmare. The only difference between us is the thought we "chose" to have about it. Taking this a step further, this means you are happy in that place or doing that thing and I am not – so our relative happiness has been defined by a voluntary choice. Wow: did you see that strong link to happiness? Realisation is coming fast now, isn't it?

Our preferences are something very precious to us. We think they define "who we actually are", so once we've created them we essentially *become* them, even though they are at their core just thoughts, and defend them strongly. That's because my likes and dislikes, loves and fears are what make me different from you and that difference is what we have been told and conditioned to seek. "Be an individual," they say, and off we go making sure we don't want what everyone else wants and don't always like what everyone else likes. In consumer societies difference is a currency; so the more limited or exclusive the edition, the more individual we feel when we own it – which is of course great news for fashion brands and the retail industry. Ironically, we are all the sheep that were brainwashed into believing what would make us an individual and we'll pay a premium for this pleasure.

Culturally, even though our beliefs about what is right and wrong have been conditioned, and therefore "free choice" is something of an illusion, as a perfect contradiction we are also told to be our own person, think our own thoughts and have our own opinions. How cool is that for irony? We should do our own thing and do what we like, avoiding what we don't like and not even realising that many of the preferences we have are not even our own. It's become a cultural right to be unique, so it's no wonder we have embedded "our" preferences so hard into "our" mind identity. If they are what makes me "me" and you "you", then any threat to them is a threat to our whole identity. If you love the mind identity you've created and those defences serve you, great. If the preferences you had were all your own and having them makes life better, fantastic. Well, maybe...

Resistance

We now know that judgement leads to preferences. In turn, preferences then lead to resistance – and, as we're about to find out, resistance is where the true hard work starts. Having experienced, seen or heard something, judged it, created and stored my personal preferences and embedded myself in defending them as if my life depends on it, I have now developed a duty of resistance. This is manifest as proactively taking a stand against everything I don't like, or flying the flag for the things I do (or think I do). We all know how much we fight for our preferences.

Don't believe me? My mother doesn't like onions and it falls to me to sneak them into whatever I cook, just to see the detective-style "Are there onions in here?" search followed by the "I can't eat onions" speech. That's a simple example but it shows both the act of resistance and the nature of it too. Is "I *can't* eat onions" a fact or an opinion? Looks like a real fact, but would it be true on a desert island where the only food was onions?

There are thousands of common forms of resistance. "I hate work", so I complain all day, every day before, during and after it. "I hate the rain", so I'm bored and unhappy on rainy days. "I love being on holiday", so every day when I'm not on holiday I post shots of Ibiza on my Instagram with phrases like, "I wish I was in Ibiza now." In reality we have so many preferences, many of which go much deeper than simple likes or dislikes, that resistance becomes almost a full-time job. "I love the weekend", "I'm bored", "I can't go near a dog"... Our abundance of preferences means that resistance is always rearing its head in a time-consuming and high-effort sort of way throughout every day for the whole of our lives.

Your preferences and the resistance needed to defend them are fully woven into your life. The beautiful activities of that voice in your head in respect of these things are off the charts. It is intense. The overthinking required when you're outside your "comfort zone" – which is basically the box you've created for things, where all your preferences are satisfied – is, to quote the film *Armageddon*, "a life-sucking bitch".

Scary, then, isn't it, that we spend almost all of our lives outside of where our preferences are trying to keep us. We are rarely on holiday, rarely eating our favourite food, rarely in a place we like and rarely with the people who we've judged as the ones we like. In fact, we spend most of our time where our preferences say we don't want to be, with the people we don't want to be with and doing what we don't want to do. They say 80 per cent of our time is spent at work and for a lot of us that means 80 per cent of our time spent on the list of things they don't want. What a playground for effort, resistance, complaint and ultimately general unhappiness. Our lives have become a journey between fleeting moments of the happiness that comes to us when all of our preferences are met, and differing levels of self-made misery in between. Well done us!

When you feed the preferences into resistance and avoidance of what you don't want, you would appear to have arrived in a pure hell. The product of all these preferences mixed together is a situation in which your mind is constantly trying to ensure that, wherever you go and whatever you do and whomever you're with, your ever-growing list of preferences is met. Add to that your expectations and fears, the things that make you scared and emotional, the things that you want to avoid forever and you have the world you and most others are living in. It is a precariously balanced ball of comfort zone, fear, expectations and life that needs to perfectly conform to what you want or you'll be honour-bound to resistance. It's always only a breath away.

Chasing happiness

As I hope is already clear, these patterns are not focused only on your bad experiences and complaining about or avoiding the things you don't like. They are sometimes even more intense around the things that you love or the things you think you want. This is a far more important pattern too, because it represents the beginning of seeking happiness in the outside world and in the places that you believe will bring you fulfilment.

Let's look at that a little more deeply. It's understandable that we avoid the things we "think" we dislike but sometimes even more intensely we chase the things we "think" will make us happy. The new house, the new car, the new husband, the new dog, the handbag, the new job... The list goes on. What do all these things have in common? They are driven by judgements and preferences, but they are also all synonymous with chasing happiness. We are addicted to feeling happy, loved, good and more – and because (as we've already discussed) we spend most of our time in between the things that make us happy, we chase those things aggressively. How long the happiness lasts when we get to them is debatable and we'll look at that later; at this point, though, it's just good for us to acknowledge firstly that we chase and secondly that what we want is never the *thing* but rather the *feeling* we hope that thing will give us. This is consumerism at its best.

Essentially, once we have established all our preferences, we start to look to them in search of the happiness that almost all of us are missing. What a wonderful thing, to know in such detail what you like or dislike and for it to be something you can go out and seek. This "shopping list" means you can focus on some future event that will bring you your comfort zone or joy and transcend the moment you are currently living in, which in all likelihood is just a means to an end or a waiting game until you get to your next, joyous, happy milestone. You can even build your life around these events, living from one focused initiative to be somewhere, do something or buy something to the next. Your judgements and preferences have now enabled you to constantly chase the things you want, like and love, the things that are better than what you have or where you currently are. Believe me, it is endless and most of us are doing it permanently.

Relationships are a great place to see these patterns at work. Over time and after failed relationships, the box into which our prospective partners must fit becomes smaller as we find that the list of things we like and don't like, want and don't want – our "shopping list" for the perfect partner – gets longer and longer. The longer and more specific the list, the harder this perfect partner is to find – and when we see someone who looks suitable we're straight in to try them out. We might even leave someone we're already in a relationship with to do this: perhaps because our current partner no longer meets our requirements, or they don't fit inside the box we've created, or we have a new and improved box as defined by this relationship. Once we're together with our new partner we'll scrutinise them closely, checking whether they fit inside our preferences box and watching for "red flag" behaviours we've seen before – behaviours that simply raise the alarm if it looks like the box will soon explode and this partner isn't "right". Often we'll press the ejector-seat button well before we're actually disappointed and well before the preferences box breaks, just to avoid the pain and suffering.

Wonderful that our past has given us these very detailed specifications and things to watch for, so that we can get rid of each partner way faster and earlier than we did the last! The fact that our preferences are extending while the box gets smaller, making the next person even harder to find, means there are more ways to fail next time too. This pattern has us chase, find, experience and eject in an ever-quickening cycle, bringing moments of early optimism and rich experience, which develop to become signs of the things we don't like and ultimately avoid. Are our preferences, judgements and fantastic memory and identity making us happier? Mmm...

The same pattern of happiness-chasing is repeated in almost every area of our lives. As our preferences develop, we find ourselves harder and harder to please and consequently fewer things make us happy. We want to be on holiday permanently because that's where we are happy but when we get there we find that it's not as good as last time. We remember the details that we loved and, even though they were never going to be precisely replicated this time, we judge the place we loved so much last time, take it off the list and complain about it, wishing it was better.

Throughout our lives, all the preference boxes into which things must fit become increasingly smaller, and our scrutiny and our application of preferences and resistance become increasingly aggressive. We chase, find and have a fleeting moment of happiness before returning to the endless misery that we feel in between

the few things that we can do that bring us joy. It is like the highs ¡
(which, perhaps unsurprisingly, often feature too). The euphoric higl
and we forget the come-downs. The highs get shorter and the lows
we can't continue and at some point don't remember why we were do…y it in the first
place. Everything that we love in life is now slowly following this pattern and as we age
we progressively lose hope of true and deep, long-lasting fulfilment.

Preferences lead us to chase happiness, resulting in fleeting moments of joy with
everything in between becoming a subject of deeper and deeper resistance and
complaint that takes up more and more energy. Relationships, places, possessions,
family, jobs and careers are all part of this cycle. The chasing gets more focused as
the highs become shorter and the lows deeper. Chasing happiness means spending
our whole time chasing somewhere we are not, to be with someone we're not, to have
something we don't have. It means we're left in an almost permanent state of non-
fulfilment and an endless want. Does that sound familiar? Oh, judgement, preferences
and resistance, what have you done?

The fight for control

As discussed in previous chapters, our minds are engaged in a battle to control our
surroundings and everything we experience. And what a battle it is! As you'll know
from listening to the voice in your head, your mind is busy *all* the time, trying to ensure
that the world meets your detailed list of expectations and preferences because it's
learned by bitter experience that you will be unhappy if it doesn't. It is dutifully working
on your behalf to make the world around you work in the way you want it to – and so it
should; why wouldn't you want that? Surely our super clever minds can easily make
the world conform to our preferences? That might be things like "If only I had money",
"I need to get one of those", "I'd be happy if I was on safari right now (until the spiders
come, anyway)", "I want a promotion", "I don't like my husband", "I hate my house", "I
don't want to work"... Let's stop: this is getting a bit too real.

So, some understandable mind noise and a few sleepless nights along the way, and
lots of decisions to make – but it's all worth it, isn't it? Surely, once you reach the goal
and get the things you want and like and avoid everything you don't like or fear, life will

e perfect won't it? Well, not if your previous experiences of happiness-chasing comes to pass. Have you ever been satisfied by the chasing? Have you ever successfully avoided what you don't like? Has the world ever been predictable before? Are your preferences realistic? Have you ever had a sense of control? What *can* you effectively control? Spoiler alert: the answer is nothing outside of your own thinking. You cannot in any way control anything, anyone or the world outside you. But more of that later.

Before then, it needs to get a little bit worse. This fight for control involves an inherent extra layer of frustration and stress. What happens when our perfect plans and preferences aren't delivered? What happens when the world throws you the long list of inevitable curveballs; when people don't behave as you wanted or when things aren't as you wanted them to be? What then? Well, then you're back outside your comfort zone and way outside your preferences box. You're back in one of those situations you fear or don't like. You know: the ones that you've judged and created your preferences from? This feels complicated now, because you've created one of the things you don't like by trying to create a world that only does what you do like. Head fully mashed!

And what happens *then*? It isn't pretty, let me tell you. All those sleepless nights and all that mind noise didn't work, so you've failed and you're not good enough to manage this situation to your own satisfaction. You chose the wrong partner again, hated the holiday that was going to solve all your problems, got the car and it was great for the first day but now it's just a car again. You have the cash, you're on the super yacht... but you feel the same as you did before and you now need a private island to be happy – super yachts are so yesterday, after all. *How has this even happened?*

This may be a great time to step back a little. Hopefully I have adequately explained the beautiful relationships between judgement, preferences, resistance, chasing happiness and, finally, the fight to control your whole world. Does it all make sense so far? If the answer is yes, then the elephant in the room might be: what is the alternative? Does it have to be that way? Are we bound to an existence where we fall in line and judge, create preferences, resist, chase, and seek control? Are all these things unavoidable? The answer to that is in a simple question: do you have any choice in whether you do any or all of them? Great news: yes, you do!

Let's review them individually and look at what you need to do to change them. You should consider whether or not they serve you in some way; and if they don't you should look at how you can just remove them from your life.

1. Does judgement serve you?

So, we are going through life making decisions about what we like, want, need, hate, etc., and building an endless list of preferences from them. We're even taking some on from the world and other people: from our culture, media and social groups. And we create a preferences box that all of life must fit into and that gets smaller and smaller as our experiences build. It gets so small, in fact, that almost nothing fits in at all and we spend our lives unhappy on the outside of our comfort zone, chasing the things we judged that we want.

So, what would happen if we dropped judgement? Could we just stop deciding to like and dislike everything and attaching to all these thoughts and opinions as if they were real facts and as if our life depended on it? Does doing this serve us or should we decide to see rain and sunshine not as bad or good but just as the weather? To take no view on everything we see and everyone we meet and to let go of those thoughts as soon as they arrive? Would that be OK? If it would, maybe we should just drop the judgement. So let's drop it. Yes, it's really that easy.

2. Does your long and elaborate list of preferences serve you?

Clearly, the more preferences we create the more we must make everything fit them. As we try to fit them all into what's essentially an increasingly smaller box, more things break the box and more things make us unhappy because they are not what we like, love and want. Added to that, as the number of preferences we have increases so does our sense of disappointment that things don't fit. We must then give things more scrutiny to ensure that everything meets our preferences and still fits inside our ever-diminishing box.

Importantly, our preferences are just opinions and thoughts and that means it's possible for me to be totally unhappy in the very same situation in which you are totally happy. A simple judgement resulted in a preference that then resulted in my needless unhappiness. How silly is that? At some point I chose a huge list of things that can make me sad, along with an equally huge list of things I now need to seek endlessly in order to be happy. I'm not willing to do *un*happy for no reason and I'm not willing to limit my potential for finding and being happy to a really small number of things. Let's drop preferences too.

3.   Is resistance serving you?

How are you feeling about the endless resistance and the energy taken in defending preferences and complaining? Not great? The good news is that if we drop judgement and preferences there's nothing left to resist – so we've basically dropped that too. It feels better already, doesn't it?

4.   Does chasing happiness serve you?

It follows that we should stop chasing happiness in external things, because we know that what we're seeking is never the things themselves but the feeling they give us. How many of the things we chase deliver a permanent result? None. Why? Because you wanted the *feeling*, and nothing at all ever continues to deliver once we've got it because we're all set up to judge and prefer, to chase and resist. Remove those obstacles, though, and suddenly your happiness is under our own control. Externally generated happiness is always temporary and fleeting, if it exists at all. This series of things that are currently embedded into our lives and act as happiness milestones is at best noise and at worst the anarchist of the mind at work. It creates so many decisions, so much thinking, so much anticipation, so much waiting and so much disappointment. The kicker is, it's all totally unnecessary. We can drop happiness-chasing too. No more focus on externalities as a vehicle to influence how we feel inside; that starts right now.

5.   Does control serve you?

Control is the final straw in this mad way that we live life. Control is a fantastic illusion of the human mind; even though it never works, it's something we dwell on and keep trying in vain to retain. Life will do what life will do and our huge effort to keep ourselves within our ever-shrinking comfort zone is futile at best. The stress we cause when life doesn't go our way is also a difficult pill to swallow. The best-laid plans are often hit by a curveball and life is full of curveballs. We optimistically create a path that keeps us safe and happy and are endlessly surprised when things *never* go to plan, despite the fact that that plan relies on people, places, situations and things – really, the whole world – totally conforming to our detailed expectations.

Control is clearly a happiness-management exercise, yet we entrust it with all of our happiness by attaching to a totally unpredictable outside world, where we have literally no control, and to people whose mind identity was built and is manifest totally differently to our own and is hence also totally unpredictable! The outside world brings us all of the experience and trauma that we're trying to avoid – but only because we didn't expect what we got. If we understand that, and accept that our attempts to control rarely if ever succeed, we can perhaps stop constantly risking our whole wellbeing in this way. This will be easier now we've lost the other things that don't serve us so let's drop control too.

So there we have it: a really clean list of things that you can and should remove from your life in order to free yourself from endless stress and overthinking. More to the point, doing this marks the beginning of you being free to be happy in whatever situation and doing so many more things. This is a magical hit-list and the process is very simple: drop judgement, preferences, resistance, happiness-chasing and control and you'll start profound change in your life; keep them and experience a never-ending cycle of disappointments and fleeting happiness. As always, the choice is yours.

Chapter 5 : If control doesn't work then what does?

To answer this, it's worth revisiting the discussion in Chapter 2 and thinking about the part we play in life and our ability to control, understand and participate in what matters. You'll recall that we found out that the universe is 13.8 billion years old and that humans have been around for only a tiny fraction of that time.

Watching the news and social media and listening to the people around you, it's easy to forget that the version of life that we live in and choose to see is almost entirely an illusion created by humans. Everything we learn and are programmed to believe seems to bring answers about how things work, why things happen and the best ways to live, including what to eat, drink, look like and more. In reality (and you'll perhaps find yourself instantly resisting this, if it challenges your beliefs or preferences), we know literally nothing about life itself. For instance, while we may look outside and feel content in the knowledge that we know what a tree is – or grass, or flowers, air, water, and more – this is actually mainly because they were given a name and we accepted what we were told about them.

We have, for instance, been told and taught and have blindly accepted that trees and grass grow from seeds and "practice" photosynthesis. We don't question the fact that what they *do* tells us nothing about what they *are*, why they are here or where they came from. Over time, science-type people have watched and analysed them and we've read the books or listened to what they said, and now we think that both they and we know how they work, how they were created and why they exist. We don't. We also might believe that we have some sort of control over them – after all, it is clearly true that we can take the seeds, plant them and grow a new tree or some new grass wherever and whenever we want to.

Time to get real. We have simply observed and analysed the patterns across the whole of nature. The whole of science is about discovering how things work and seeing if we, as humans, can use the phenomenon to human advantage; but the question of how it all comes together this way, why it's here or what causes things to happen the way they do will in all likelihood remain unanswered forever. A seed could start as a single cell and over the course of time will, with water and some things in the soil, become a beautiful tree. It will grow a trunk, branches and leaves. It will be the beautiful material we know as wood and it will flower in summer and drop leaves in winter, only to re-grow them again in spring. Why? Who knows? It is literally part of the amazing mystery of life itself.

More than that, every flower, insect, animal, the light, the gases, the minerals, the water, the cycles – in fact everything in the universe – work together as a system. They are interrelated and each is a part of the cause of everything else. How it could be designed and built this way is beyond our understanding – and it's incomprehensible that it has taken 13.8 billion years to reach where we currently are. From there being nothing, or maybe a single atom, to the Big Bang, which is now the unilaterally agreed truth and not a theory, there is now the universe, the stars, the planets, the earth, then life and the systems we see. It is not even worth us thinking about, other than to wonder at the complexity and perfection, but here we are, experiencing the result now and in every moment. We are ourselves part of that miracle and we are the only part that is visibly and truly consciousness and experiencing it. It is magical and we are lucky to be involved in our miniscule way, experiencing it in every moment we live.

Interestingly, as a race, we mostly accept and take it all for granted. We even take credit for the magical nature of it, thinking that we actually "make our own babies" or "grow our food" or "create our reality". We really don't. At best and in reality, we are almost insignificant participants in this dance of life, with millions of other life forms sharing it with us. Babies grow from a single cell and then form a heart, lungs, skin, bone... In fact, millions of things come together, and it then carries human life. I mean, where on earth would you start actually "making a baby"? *We* simply do what we are programmed to do, having sex and procreating; but *life* – nature, the universe, god or whatever you feel most comfortable calling it – does the rest and we have no clue how at all.

Really, to call it "the rest" doesn't even begin to describe it. In reality, it is everything. The fact is, we are observers and bystanders in the play of life and we have no understanding of why or how anything happens or why it really works. We have analysed and observed our environment and found some reasons and patterns that we have documented and sometimes used to our advantage. That's all.

Why is all this important here? So that we can more realistically consider the level of control that we truly have in the world and over life itself. Bottom line: everything that happens in the universe will happen whether you are here or not. The series of events leading up to and playing into what happens to you in this moment have been going on for billions of years. They are not visible to you; there are way too many contributing factors to count, the interrelationships are incomprehensible and it's totally outside of your ability to predict or control what happens next. Surely that's unsurprising and totally understandable to you?

Your importance to the whole is absolutely negligible and while you can maybe have status in the human world your influence on life itself – yours included – is essentially even less than nothing. In contrast to our misguided beliefs, life is certainly not about humans; it's not dependent *on* us in any way and nor is it happening *for* us. It is beautifully unpredictable and beautifully exciting but only if you relax for long enough to see the bigger picture. If you can start to see life as an amazing series of uncontrollable experiences and not something to resist and try to control, that is when everything changes. This includes the mystery of every other person, life and every life situation that presents itself to you or indeed doesn't. All are just as unpredictable, as will become strangely apparent as you start to consider your experiences so far. Outside of your own mind, you are in control of nothing; life itself has been guiding you, giving you every person, place and situation as part of that unpredictable adventure since you were born. Everything has been a beautiful learning experience and not for a single moment have you been in control.

This arrives at a simple truth. You are always where you're supposed to be and your purpose in this moment is to do whatever you're doing and to be wherever you are. Once you realise this, life gets so much easier and much more fun. It was never going to happen any another way – and all of that resistance and control you've been working so hard at is, simply and needlessly, making your life *so* much harder than it needs to be. If you drop all resistance and accept that life is fundamentally and wonderfully unpredictable, it will from this point forward always be beautifully exciting. *This* is the alternative to control.

By surrendering to the idea that life will always take you where life wants to take you, you can dramatically change and improve your relationship with it. It simply will not fit into a box and comply with your endless preferences, so your resistance and attempts to control it will prove eternally disappointing. This is not to say that you can't choose a general direction, set goals and take actions that are designed to create an outcome. It is saying *don't get attached to those outcomes* because they will often veer off course; if you take time to see them, new paths will open up and the mystery that is life will take you to a very different (often better) destination. But only if you allow it to do so. It really is only peripherally up to you anyway. Surrender to life, expect everything to sit outside of your preferences and ultimately lose your preferences entirely. Become attached to nothing and enjoy every experience while it lasts.

When we talk about attachment, we mean the act of taking a person, experience, preference or feeling and starting to attach meaning to and identify with it. This creates a form of dependency: you essentially develop a need for whatever it is. That need in turn means that if the person or experience or whatever does not meet your expectations, you will feel loss; it means that if you attach to a positive feeling, you will endlessly crave it, and that if you attach to a person in this preference-based, control-driven way, you will become dependent not only on their presence but how they behave too. Furthermore, should they ever do something that hits your attachment – which is perfectly possible, given that they're as unpredictable and uncontrollable as the universe itself – they'll create needless pain in your life. This is about all you should expect.

Now is the time to become ultimately flexible, to embrace the adventure and require zero control. It's time to prefer nothing. See the signs when things are changing and, without attachment to a specific outcome, be fluid and open to a new path without disappointment, fear, preferences or unhappiness. These are just experiences, and you are so lucky to have them all.

With surrender, adventure and excitement in your heart you can simply accept each moment as it comes, whether or not it fits your box. Lose the box entirely and you'll remove all of your resistance and the effort associated with it – the sleepless nights, the endless thinking. Acceptance is about looking at what *is* and embracing it fully, whether it fits your preferences or not. Lose the preferences and see each moment as a wonderful adventure of new experiences and opportunities. Attachment brings disappointment and unhappiness; non-attachment brings adventure and helps you to experience the joy and wonder of everything in life.

This is true freedom. Freedom is not delivered by money or a super yacht, the big house or the status; it is created when the mind is willing to accept and enjoy every moment without judgement, preference, attachment or a need to control. It is when you are going with the flow of life, not demanding or expecting that only specific, rigid outcomes will make you happy. It is when you are at peace with whatever happens, whether it is planned or unplanned, liked or disliked, wanted or not wanted, loved or feared.

Surrender of this nature has no effect at all on your ability to make plans, create a vision or set goals but it does have an effect on how rigidly attached to them you are. This is about how flexible you are and how much you understand that enjoying the journey is always going to be far more important than arriving at the destination; after all, as you know by now, the thrill of the destination will fade but the journey can continue endlessly. Our purpose in life is to reach a state of being where we enjoy the journey without any attachment to the destination at all. To be permanently happy and at peace, rather than constantly seeking.

This is important, so I'm going to say it super clearly: surrender to the fact that life is wonderfully unpredictable. Remove the resistance of trying to make it conform to your expectations and realise that your judgements, expectations, resistance and attempts to control are simply making things feel more difficult than they really are. Now is the time to embrace and start to love the unpredictability of life because whether you love it or not unpredictable is what it is. It gives you signs and synchronicities, though; look for them and be willing to change direction fast and frequently. It's fun. Above all, remember that resisting and seeking a degree of control that simply doesn't exist simply creates something to waste effort on – you are only fighting yourself.

As a final point here, we should really consider what creates the peace and happiness in life that we want so much and that is the objective of this class and also what creates the overthinking and anxiety we want so much to avoid. Before the human illusion appeared, we were presumably here living life the way that nature suggested. Just like the animals, trees and everything else, we essentially trusted life to take us where we needed to go – without resistance and without believing in an illusion of control. This is still possible; and in some cultures outside of what's known as Western or "developed" countries it remains a perfect way of life. Ironically, the more "progress" we make, the more the human illusion distracts us and takes control. The more we are exposed to collective expectations of control, and the more we live outside of what nature intended. Does that bring peace and happiness? You can decide that. Is there a better way? Having begun to experience it, I can certainly say yes – yes, yes, yes. Hopefully you are now on the path to finding it too.

The great news is that when you start to surrender, the magic is visible. You will begin to see and be guided by the signs because they are everywhere; synchronicities and nonstop serendipitous moments that seem to have your best interests at heart – moments that with preference, judgements and resistance you would never have even seen or experienced. The journey itself now becomes your goal and your ability to experience and feel aware of the joy in every moment exponentially increases. Surrender to it and let go, because this is the start of a whole new life.

ZEN JUNGLE

Step 3 : Let It All Go, Bring the Joy

Chapter 6 : The past has gone; let it go

We are now starting to make real progress towards the act of dropping parts of this mind-created identity that we've built over time. The parts that don't serve us; the somebody that has throughout your life vacuumed everything up and identified with subjectivity, experiences, thoughts, judgements and emotions, then formed a box of preferences, fears and expectations into which it would like your whole world to fit. You may already have begun to feel the freedom. The more we practice the steps, the more freedom we start to feel. This is freedom from the prison of that identity and all the rules, preferences, wants and likes it has been locking you into and constantly forcing you to resist. This is the start of fundamental change. It is about really "loving life" and not just feeling better or placing a bandage over an open wound, hoping it will heal. Happiness and peace are completely internal concepts and cannot be found outside. Hopefully this is all starting to become clear.

We're now going to look more deeply at how we take the experiences of life and create a box or framework of control from them, and how as we age, we then make that box smaller by the exact same process. The following example demonstrates well how all this eventually ends if we don't wake up to it – which is essentially with a box so small that nothing fits into it at all, and anything that did once make it in simply gets squeezed out over time so we're left without fulfilment, peace or happiness.

Relationships provide a great way to explain this process and of course often have a massive impact on our lives and overall happiness. So, we're going to take a life journey through some relationship stuff and out the other side, seeing the wonderful result that your mind will create if you allow it to do so. Your own life may or may not resemble what's being discussed but you'll almost certainly know or have heard of someone whose life does. I can safely say that there was a time when I could relate to parts of this very strongly.

So, let's start when we are young, maybe just a teenager, and have begun to think about getting a girlfriend or boyfriend and feel stirred by the idea of a relationship. That's of course if you can call teenage love that; maybe at this point it's more a testing phase, but either way... We experience the idea of deciding to like someone or finding them attractive and we then get to the point of asking them out.

Our early experiences in romance can definitely go a few ways. But in the first instance, when we're ready to give it a try, we can essentially be successful or we can be rejected. Both have a significant impact on our identity. What a great moment, then, to highlight the development of insecurity or confidence, of feeling good-looking or feeling ugly, attractive or not. Clearly – because we now understand how these things work – these rejections and acceptances can be carried throughout our whole lives. Indeed, if our first romantic experience was of being accepted, a seed of confidence is sown: we know we can ask and will be well-received; this reduces our fear of future rejection, gives us higher self-esteem and different experiences of the dating game as a whole, moving forward. Conversely, if rejection is our first experience this may lower our opinion of ourselves and create a lack of confidence or a lower standard in terms of who we feel able to ask out in the future.

Obviously, none of these outcomes are actually valid reasons why we should create a change in our identity, but we nonetheless do just that. So off we go. We're now building elements of our identity from a sample of one event; I think most people would agree that this happens – and often proves profoundly impactful later on in life.

Most of us then embark on a series of relationships of increasing gravity and importance. "Is she *the one*?" perhaps comes to mind at some point after "playing the field", for example. Over time, the list of things we like about girls or boys starts to grow (this was certainly the case for me). And all the while, as we spend time with different people and judge what they do and say, the list of things we *don't* like grows too. Some things also creep into the more specific likes and dislikes box. For instance, maybe we had a real crush on someone and for that reason attached to a certain thing they often said or an action they did; we liked it, and the experience of liking it then made that thing a characteristic that became *our thing*. A personal preference. It wasn't actually our true preference but was driven by attachment to the person and the overall way they made us feel, so we made it into something to look for in the next person.

Anyway, our list of the qualities that we're looking for in someone develops and becomes longer and longer, albeit very slowly to begin with. The preferences box into which "the one" needs to fit is still quite large because the list of preferences is still relatively small, since the commitment has been lower and the painful experiences have been few. Life hasn't yet delivered our perfect person and the comings and goings, while slightly traumatic, have not been marriages or life partners; so no major shake-ups at this point. This means we're still flexible about who we "like" and the fact that our experiences, expectations, thoughts and emotions about this area are limited, means we don't fear or anticipate dramatic issues when things in relationships go wrong.

Then it gets real. We find "the one". They are everything we want in a person! Much of this is aesthetic but they're ticking all the boxes and because of the emotions they stir within us we feel that underlying all the surface attractions is the "fact" that this person is the one who'll *make us happy*. After all, that's what it's all about, isn't it? The things that we can accumulate in our outer world that will make us permanently happy. Obviously there are many external things to chase – money, freedoms, relationships, possessions; the list is truly endless – but number one (or close to it) among them must be our romantic partners. So, this person is *the one*; they fit into the box and we go in with both feet. First it's moving in together, then it's engagement and next it's marriage. What could possibly go wrong? We are young and we are free, we need each other and it's all going to make both of us happy. We're super focused on it and it is "certainly" the "right" thing to do.

We're married. The wedding was amazing, although planning it could have been easier. The honeymoon was OK too. Time passes and that feeling of butterflies we give each other fades a bit and a few annoyances build but all will be OK. More time passes and there's just us together and neither of us is sure that we're getting everything we need now, so having kids is the next thing to be chased. Then pregnancy was fun; the birth was traumatic but then they came – babies, nappies and all that stuff. Aren't they beautiful? Now we need some freedom and time to ourselves, so let's chase that. Holidays, things, money and essentially escape because the marriage and the kids have now lost a bit of the shine for both of us. They've become more boring and normal, and fail to satisfy those wants and needs that seem to keep coming back. One of us then fails to get the required and "expected" attention and decides to "chase" it elsewhere... To cut a long story short, what happens next is divorce and horrible pain and suffering for all. This is true crisis and the pain is being attached to and stored, really effectively. Everything is given disproportionate meaning, so the attachment is deep and strong.

So, what's happening to the preferences box all this time? Well, it's being filled with pain, with things we know we don't want to talk about, things we can't handle, things we never want to happen again; with patterns we can look for in the future, trust issues, regrets and more. What a wonderful shopping list we now have for when we're looking for the next life partner, and it is all becoming part of our identity. That said, our fear is now so great and the memories so painful that avoiding relationships and commitment altogether has become the whole box, at least for a while. Dating is hard and trust of anyone is now non-existent. Add to that the drop in self-esteem and you've got a perfect recipe for seeking precisely the *wrong* partners with the totally wrong preferences box.

The box is now either too small for anyone to fit in, or small enough that the list of requirements to get in is way too big for anyone to meet it. It's now a disaster, totally driven by history. "This moment is not influenced at all by history," I hear you say. "But I remember it all as if it were yesterday," I retort... The reality is, of course, that the process is the same for relationships as it is for everything else; thus we apply everything from our relationship history to every subsequent romantic encounter, seeing patterns in them that we've seen before. So if we've been cheated on we'll expect to be cheated on again and will consequently become incredibly insecure and suspicious. This is all based on the past and has nothing to do with this moment, but because we chose to store it all for future use we're now stuck with the result.

Our new relationships are then fraught with difficulty, driven by that history and pain manifest as preferences. This creates huge resistance and a need for unrealistic control. Seemingly good people are treated like criminals and nobody can fit the mould; everyone fails sequentially and is eventually stamped with a similar pattern.

Partner after partner gives us more and more likes and dislikes, needs and wants; and as they do and our experiences build we form even more preferences and need even more control. The box that a partner must fit into is now not only so small that it's like searching for a needle in a haystack but it is super rigid too. We now think we "really know" the kind of person we want and will not deviate at all. We will also observe anyone we're with so closely that they can't breathe, and even the slightest sign of a problematic pattern will ring a super loud alarm bell. A few alarm bells later and we pull the ejector handle once again and the search continues – this time with an even smaller and more rigid box.

This pattern is of course true for the whole of and every aspect of life. As we accumulate the elements of our identity and build our judgements, preferences, expectations and need for control, we simply reduce the size of the box into which every aspect of our lives and (importantly) our own self too must fit. It becomes even more rigid and increasingly takes away our peace as we overthink the perceived need for control. Our opportunity to be happy and without stress has now all but gone, and we cannot relax or function normally. Life feels generally bad and unfulfilled; we are almost in an existential crisis. It is all way too much to think about – and that's before we start on the comparison and competition and the status we have to maintain in the world.

This situation is driven more than anything else by our ability and predisposition to memorise and retain things from our personal past, rather than letting them go. Our wonderfully capable mind is endlessly processing judgements, creating preferences, looking at experiences, events, thoughts and feelings or emotions, which all come together moment by moment. The ones that hit us, the ones that seem to matter, are essentially attached to and stored as important for use later.

Interestingly, we store what hits us emotionally more often than we do anything else because we give them more meaning. Previously "important" things that caused us pain, love, fear or anxiety get stirred up by certain triggers and are increasingly amplified each time, so their effect is disproportionately compounded. "From small acorns, oak trees grow," is the saying that comes to mind: little things can become big things in your mind, incredibly fast.

Unfortunately, it's often the case that we store only snippets of information from each experience. We might keep just the scary bit, the painful bit, the offensive bit, etc., because that's what impacted us at the time. This means that experiences are remembered very badly by the mind, though we conversely always believe things are better than they are at the time. Most of our memories are distorted and saturated with emotions before we apply them as preferences and control filters to new moments later on. It is these frightening unreliable fragments that we use for what amounts to two simple purposes: worrying and trying to control the world so it gives us what we want; and worrying and trying to control the world so it *doesn't* give us what we *don't* want. Anxiety and control: that's actually all these stockpiled memories are used for. Ouch.

Clearly, in addition to these personal-mind thoughts we have the work of the intellectual mind, which has learned and memorised more practical things, such as maths and reason, for future application. But the primary purpose of our memory of personal experiences is to filter the world and try to make it conform to our imagined or expected future, leading to disappointment after disappointment – because, as we know, everything is really so beautifully unpredictable.

So, what do we do about all that? The good news is that there's an alternative to the futility of this storage process. We can simply drop all attachment to those personal experiences, in real time and as they happen, knowing that if the end result will be preferences or attempts to control, we don't want it.

This moment, right now, is simply a rich experience and it will be the past almost instantly. It will have no influence on the next moment or any subsequent moment in our lives – unless we keep it and taint our whole perspective with it every time something resonates in the future, that is. Let's call what we need to do *experience and release*. This is simply the act of surrendering to the unpredictability of the universe and life and is actually what we and our minds are designed to do. If we agree that it is not useful to save the events of this moment because they will not help us to control a future moment, then it stands to reason that anything saved from a relationship twenty years ago will likewise have no positive bearing on the relationship we're in today. We can let that go too.

To recap: the past is a gift that only we, as humans, experience because unlike other living things we have a clever memory to retain the present and review it later. This is actually the only way in which time itself exists. Unfortunately, most of us now use that gift and our minds to collate those experiences in our past and – by turning judgements of them into preferences – then try to use our memories to filter and control our future. It doesn't work because, as we know, people, places and situations have always been unpredictable and likely always will be because that seems to be the nature of things. If we attach to things and become dependent on the behaviour as dictated by our preferences and ideas of control, we will be repeatedly disappointed when things don't go as planned. The alternative is to have experiences but not attach to them, no matter what they are; to let them go, embracing and surrendering to the fact that life is completely unpredictable. Are you up for that?

What if you went through life knowing a few important things that are always true? First: you can't change what is or has been; so you can never change the past. Second: this moment is a new moment and does not depend on any previous moment from your past. Finally: everything we experience is simply just that – an experience – and, whether good, bad, scary or beautiful, experiences all take our lives forward.

Accepting and noticing how experiences make us feel is a good thing, but making judgements of them and giving them deeper meaning as good or bad or whatever is not; judging them essentially means attaching to them. Experiences all serve a purpose, will always make life richer and more of an adventure, and will teach you something in their own given moment; then they can be let go. The key learning here is that the only reason you retain ideas about them at all is because they didn't go as *expected* and they made you feel a certain way. If you expect something and are disappointed or distressed because your expectation wasn't met, that is all on you. Why did you predict in the first place? If you're going to predict at all, be realistic and flexible enough to know that anything can happen and always does. If you attached to the feeling instead of observing and experiencing the moment, then you *became* the feeling so that you could want or avoid it in the future. That never goes well.

The degree to which we hold on to or to let go of the past is a direct result of how much we attach to the things we're trying to control or that we've decided will make us happy. Once we realise that happiness is not brought about by these things that we search for or cling to, we are no longer attached to them; and once we realise that more peace and happiness is lost by attachment, preferences, resistance and control than by anything else, deciding to drop those things – and the past – becomes easy.

To make this point in the most actionable and practical way: again, this moment will be the past almost instantly. Experiencing it, and the people, things and thoughts it involves, without attaching to any of it will serve and reward you with peace and no need for future resistance. Realise that what is, just *is*. The past has gone, can never be changed and serves no purpose in your future. Let it go, together with judgements, choices and preferences.

Let it go immediately and as you do, relax about the unpredictable nature of the world. The universe has your back: whatever happens will deepen your existence rather than making it worse. Your resistance to what is, to the past and to the unknown will certainly take away your peace and in its place create a journey full of endless disappointing destinations that may offer fleeting gratification but will soon need to be replaced by a new destination and a new focus for happiness when this one, like the last, fails to really deliver. Focus only on the journey itself. No moment is ever permanent unless you hold on to it; even uncomfortable moments will pass if you don't attach to their outcomes or expect to control the world.

Let the past go and each moment is a new adventure. This is the only freedom that truly exists.

Chapter 7 : Blame, guilt and becoming a victim

Letting go of the past has some really interesting practical outcomes that will form part of a truly life-changing experience. As we go deeper into what we mean by "the past" and what letting go means, we'll clearly see some amazing underlying truths. On this masterclass, "the past" is defined as anything and everything that happened in any moment before the present moment. So now is now but that moment has just ended and entered "the past" and thus now is the new now. And now, and now... You get the picture. The present endlessly becomes the past, as each moment expires and disappears into history, which only exists in your mind and books. (Unless of course you have the car from *Back to the Future*.)

The aim of this transformational journey is to help you to make tangible changes to your perception of the world and to fundamentally change your life. Hopefully you'll see that the learnings so far are simple truths, requiring no resistance. One of these is that we only have the present moment. This is essential to your future peace and happiness. It would be easy to mistake this truth for some sort of philosophical idea or to think of it as very deep and complicated but really the point is simple: you only ever live the present moment. That's it.

The only reason the past exists at all is because you have a memory and the only reason the future exists is because you have a creative imagination and can envisage one or more futures. In fact, you can quite magically imagine multiple futures, some scary, some wonderful, but they are all a mind-created illusion. As soon as the present moment becomes the past, there's no longer anything you or anyone else can do to change or access it. Likewise there's no way to access anything that you imagine as a future – because the future, like the past, doesn't exist. Does that make sense? Then now we can move on and build on it.

It may or may not be that the universe itself experiences a series of present moments in the same way, with each moment following the last in a simple succession. How long is a moment? It may be a second, a millisecond, or some small amount of what we'll call "human time" but it is essentially the now or the present. There's actually no concept of time in the present moment because it's simply the now. Now, now, now... Remember? Each moment is explicit and unique and experienced universally. However, we only experience this moment by seeing what comes into our awareness during it. A moment is what we see, feel, smell, touch, hear, think, taste. An infinite number of moments occur from the countless perspectives other than our own and in every point in the universe, every one of them out of your view or reach. But yours belongs to you and is totally unique, which is nice.

The thing to take away from this is that without memory, the moments we experience and keep a version of in our mind memories have no impact on this moment, or this one or this one... Got it? Good. This is where it all gets interesting.

We now know how we make our own identity, based on judgements, emotions, experiences, what we are told, etc., and we know that it is predominantly identity that creates our overthinking. We also know that the past is unrelated to the future and that whatever we've created and kept stored from it – such as our judgements, preferences and control framework – simply does not serve us at all. In fact it is making us resist the past, present and future, complain and experience never-ending disappointment. This is what's taking away our peace and happiness.

We also know that we should apply total acceptance to the present moment, no matter what it is and how it makes you feel. This gives us total and permanent control over the way we feel. We know we should embrace the unpredictable nature of things by surrendering to the flow, rather than trying to control and resist – neither of which work anyway. These are not suggestions or theories; they are reality and truth. Accepting what *is* is fundamental, not because someone said so but because we simply cannot change what *is* or the past.

We're now going to look at how all of that comes together in our relationships with people, circumstances and life itself. The ways in which we respond to other people and what governs our relationships are important because the action of full acceptance and surrender applies to literally everything..

So, in previous chapters we've discussed the fact that we judge people and situations in the same way as we judge literally everything else. We instantly make a judgement about a person before, during and after we meet them; and the way we perceive them forms a place in our own identity, around like or dislike, attraction or repulsion and so on. We then go on to create a totally separate identity for them in our minds – a culmination of our thoughts, assumptions, what we've heard about and experiences of them, and (especially) how we feel about what they say to and about us. This becomes something like our very own version of the person. It's certainly the one we think we *know*.

Interestingly, and as a slight aside, this person of course has their own mind-created identity of themselves in addition to the one we built for them. Lucky them: two identities. These two identities are always totally different. One is based on almost everything that has ever happened in their lives (theirs) and the other is based on a fraction of that and only what we know (ours). Neither is who they really are, but that is for later. For now suffice it to say that both are a ball of thoughts and opinions that have been embedded in the past and over varying amounts of time, and each just as unreliable as the other. Naturally it follows that everyone you know has their own identity version of you too, none of which bears even a passing resemblance to the identity you've created for yourself. Worth a mention, just to disturb your own identity a little...

That's a lot of identities flying around! This creates a weird melting pot of potential misperception, misunderstanding, conflict and offence as all these identities – with their specific expectations and aims to control the world around them – interact precariously with each other and hope to meet all the respective expectations. To make matters a bit more complex, let's say you speak to a friend: it's your identity speaking to the identity you made for them in your own mind; and it's their identity speaking to the identity they made for you. Remember, though, that everything here is simply mind-made human illusion of identity, built from thoughts and created since birth. So really when you speak to your friend you've got four interacting balls of thoughts and opinions that are neither truth nor fact, just subjective opinion and belief. What a mess.

Now we get to the blame game. This is a favourite of mine, though for many it can be a bit challenging. To further add to the mayhem, mind identities (sometimes called egos) do not like to take responsibility for anything at all – and hence we love the human ego go-to of blame because it makes someone other than ourselves responsible for everything. Clearly all these interactions between constructed identities create the perfect conditions for blame and guilt – all those expectations, preferences and sensitivities, some of them deeply hidden and driven by emotion and pain. At any time, any identity might react and become emotional or *offended*, prompted by their desire to control their whole world and for it to meet their expectations and preferences.

Yes, there are many other things that cause bad reactions in people too. Other people, places, events, situations and emotions; society-invented rules and crimes that we've collectively agreed are "wrong or right"... Everything. This means that even life itself can become the subject of blame when things don't go our way – or, more specifically, when things don't go the way our controlling framework expected or wanted them to. This can be very uncomfortable and very "offensive". The very definition of offensive is someone or something behaving in a way you did not expect and do not like. Essentially, the breaking of a subjective preference box can make you *offended*.

I am going to start this next discussion with a statement: we are always where we placed ourselves and we always have a choice of how to react to everything that we experience. We can perceive that things just happen and are just experiences; or we can perceive that things are done or happen *to* us, taking the position that we've been attacked. The latter is the most usual choice and as such blame is not just inherent but is also the common result of many of the things we do and experience. We seem to want to believe that things happen *to* us whenever our expectations are not met and therefore become easily offended by situations, people, events or life itself, instantly blaming and shifting the burden of responsibility away from ourselves.

So, applying the lessons of acceptance and surrender is truly significant to these situations, people and events that may hurt, offend or disgust us. What does this mean in terms of responsibility and blame? Unsurprisingly, it means letting go of the past immediately so that blame cannot exist at all in our lives. It also means accepting responsibility for our lives and how we feel – and doing this by ourselves and for ourselves, in every single moment. But before we look at that more closely we need to understand more about the specifics and merits of blame itself.

This masterclass is partly about losing the things that don't serve us: the things that ultimately take away our peace and/or create endless overthinking, anxiety and lack of fulfilment. In many ways this masterclass will be about willingly losing an old mind-created identity and replacing it with a better and more conscious way to think and live. We need to look at blame, guilt and forgiveness – and how they serve us and why –in real detail because they really, really matter in this process.

Firstly, and to get this out of the way (I know how embedded this idea can become so let's address any loud chatter from those internal voices): there's no denying that sometimes in life things happen that are not your fault. There will be many situations, experiences and interactions that you could, if you so wanted, say were nothing to do with you but were caused by someone or something out of your control; and you could easily find them offensive, hurtful and so many more things that require you to blame. So, yes: they were not your fault, other than because you were there and may or may not have chosen to be there at the time. Hold that thought, just for a moment.

Some of us go through life thinking that things are literally happening *to* us, that we are inherently unlucky and "being made to feel" a certain way by forces external to ourselves. But the adventure and unpredictability of life most certainly applies to people, situations and events; if the experiences we have offend us in some way it is almost always because something didn't go according to our preferences or expectations. After all, how could we be offended, hurt or anything else if all we ever expected were unpredictable life experiences? It wouldn't happen.

If, however, we've attached our own version, or the subjective worldly version, of what is "right" and "wrong" to our expectations, then unfortunately what we get – and how disappointed or offended we are – is clearly down to only us and we are certainly responsible for how it may make us feel as a result. This is because what is real in nature and the truth does not play by those arbitrary rules of right and wrong created by humankind. It just *is*, and will be whatever it is without morals or respect to what we think it should or want it to be. That's simply wanting control.

If it rains on your wedding day, you could blame the universe or say it doesn't like you. If someone says something that you don't like, you could blame them for saying it because you decided it was something nobody *should* ever say. You can actually blame anything and anybody for not fitting with your expectations of the world. Maybe you're thinking, "That's right, though: there *is* right and wrong." Yes, in the human illusion, but is it reality and truth? Is that how the world really is, how the universe works? Not in my experience, though I can't speak for yours.

Perhaps we should consider this in the context of some real and common examples of emotive situations. Your husband cheats on you; you catch him and he leaves you for someone else. Or a child in your family dies. Surely blame belongs here: you can blame your husband for his actions; or, if you consider that the death of a child is always "too early", you could blame life, a doctor, the other driver, a murderer and the universe for it. We might blame ourselves in some way too, so there's clear potential for complex layers of blame and or guilt.

In our methodology so far, we would see anything that happens of this nature as having happened in the past, which means we would have to accept it and let it go. We would also have gone into this knowing that the universe and life do not play by our rules; that we should be thankful for the experience with the husband or child while it lasted, but should have expected that it would end at some unpredictable point without us ever having attached to it. Surely that's not a good approach when something is not our fault, when something or someone else *is* at fault? Blame is then natural and valid, isn't it?

Well, to answer that, we should look at what immediately happens when we blame and the different approaches and options we can take. So, your husband cheats and leaves you or, worse still, your child dies. Blame is totally understandable, isn't it?

Both situations are certainty high impact and sad for you. The husband committed to be married forever; he has not only broken the promise of marriage but has also cheated. As for the death of a child, surely the universe, doctors, the other driver or someone else must be responsible. Yes or no? It is certainly not "right" for a child to die young, is it? (My answer to that is, incidentally, "Not if *you* say it's not." But we'll get to that a bit later.)

At this point, the death remains a sad problem of expectation and preferences. In reality, people do die at any and all ages all over the world. It is "normal". If your identity believes that there's a minimum age for death and doesn't expect it any other way, then you'll certainly think you're within your rights to believe that someone or something is to blame. If, on the other hand, you accepted every moment and surrendered to the truth and what *is*, you'd view the world not in relation to your expectations but as reality has it: out of your control and totally unpredictable. Would you still blame?

You may well be wondering how anyone could anyone possibly experience either of these things and respond by simply accepting them and letting go, even if they embraced unpredictability.

It is super important, then, to consider the sequence of events that follow when we blame. In both of the examples above, we blame and we have immediately become a victim of something or someone. There can't be blame without a victim and there also can't be blame without a guilty party. We are the victim and someone else is guilty: fact. Importantly, we have also instantly made someone or something else responsible for how we now feel and opened the door to a range of our own victim-identity responses and behaviours.

When we blame, we agree wholeheartedly to take on the additional role of victim. This compounds our inability to take responsibility for ourselves and how we feel because it is adopted as part of our identity – and will therefore be lived, defended and upheld aggressively, just like any other part of our identity. We all know that victims do this.

As a victim, we become someone with whom others can empathise or sympathise. We also deepen our attachment to our mind identity and create something else to hold on to from the past – something we can relate to and project on to our future, using it to define who we are and to gain a form of status and attention. Now that we've stored it and have *become* it in this way, we can also use it to validate our fears – so in the examples above this might be fear of future relationships or overprotection of our children. Victimhood offers a great opportunity to hide from life somehow, to perpetually regret, retaliate, bear a grudge and overthink. This is a multi-purpose piece of our past, to be kept alive in our mind and used in ways that will never serve us.

Let's deal with the question of responsibility before we move on. Our aim here is to change your world so you can eventually choose what, when and how to think, feel and respond; if you want to love and understand life, this is where you need to be. This masterclass is about changing your state of being to one of peace, purpose and permanent happiness. That's not peculiar to when life is going well – in fact it's even more important that you're at peace, happy and fulfilled when life is at its worst too. Part of the fundamental learning to that end is taking full responsibility for how you think, feel and act.

So, the first rule is that you must take full responsibility for how you think and feel, at all times, because that is actually the only thing in the whole universe that you are truly in control of (though it may not have felt like that before you began your transformational journey). We'll be exploring how that happens throughout the whole masterclass but here's how it applies to our current example... By apportioning blame we lose all responsibility for our own feelings and responses and in doing so also lose all power and control over ourselves. You can see that as a victim we lose all power over how you feel or act – because the victim is simply not the responsible party. By applying guilt we create a whole extra world of involuntary thinking. And by treating life as anything other than a series of unpredictable experiences, we become offended when experiences don't meet our unrealistic expectations. Ultimately blame strips us of any ability to choose our thoughts and quiet our mind without preferences, judgements and expectations. After all, blame is simply an intense form of judgement.

Let's now give deeper consideration to the act of removing all blame, and accepting ultimate and unconditional responsibility for our life and how we feel. Blame, guilt and forgiveness are deeply related. If you remove blame from your life, from now and in the future, the need to forgive anything will immediately evaporate; if you never blame again, there can never again be anything that needs your forgiveness. No grudges at all. It's true: if you cease to create blame, the need for you to forgive will also cease.

Forgiving everything that we've previously blamed for has a profound effect on the stored pains, expectations, preferences and sensitivities that we already carry around in our mind identity. It's like a cleansing exercise, creating a huge amount of space and peace. Imagine if you had never blamed anyone or anything for any experience you have ever had, accepting it as simply the nature of life, just another unpredictable experience. How much lighter would you feel? How much energy have you wasted up to this point in your life on carrying blame, on grudges, on complaining about what someone did or said or something that happened? Blame is super heavy and forgiveness is the antidote.

So, what happens when all the blame is removed and we replace it with forgiveness? Without blame as a concept in your life, there can be no guilt at all. That means for you and for everyone else. Yes: removing your blame of the outside world and in effect, the whole concept of blame; eliminates all of your own guilt about anything and everything. After all, if you no longer believe in blame, how could you ever feel guilty? With the concept of blame totally removed from *your* life, and unconditional forgiveness living in its place, guilt disappears forever. That includes the guilt you yourself feel, as well as the guilt you place on others and that they place on you. You then unconditionally accept and forgive them for blaming you too, your peace no longer disturbed by it. This has a really cool effect – and it's easy to try it out. The results are almost immediate, or at least way quicker than you might think.

But why would you unconditionally accept everything anyone does "to you"? Well, after you've learned and accepted that you, and everyone else, has a mind-made identity, it becomes clear that you must and can; after all, you know from your own experiences that the mind-made identity makes us all do and say some strange things from time to time. Every identity is built from a different set of life experiences, conditions, thoughts and feelings but none are the real self. Yours is not you; there is no them. As we break down the elements of those identities, we find that they are simply a ball of subjective stored thoughts, all in a unique combination. As such, they'll all respond very differently to any given situation or experience. At our core and beneath that thought identity, we all start out the same, and it is this foundational similarity that we must now choose to see in others; not the false, thought-based product of their accumulated life circumstances and influences. Accept that and you will develop the super power to both accept and forgive anything.

The truth is that people, places and circumstances are all totally unpredictable. They are part of an unpredictable and beautiful universal adventure. Every experience is learning and it would always serve you well to feel lucky to be having them all, whatever their nature. By not judging any of them you can learn to love them all, even the ones you may previously have wanted to blame. You are then enabled to love everything and everyone truly unconditionally because without blame why wouldn't you?

As soon as blame is removed from everything and everyone, a new and interesting dynamic evolves between you and the world – a dynamic without fight and resistance, and full of acceptance. This changes your relationship with almost everything, immediately placing you at peace with people, places and situations. Grudges are always for things in the past, guilt too; and for you, letting go of the past is now happening in real time, moment to moment. Your peace is now permanent and your perception has started to change.

You may currently be dwelling on the example of the death of the child; perhaps you're wondering if removing all blame and guilt from an event like that, and simply letting it go, is something anyone could really be expected to do. The answer will develop in multidimensional ways as we progress through further steps. This relates to many areas of our perception; our identity, how we see nature and, ultimately, how the universe really works underneath it all. As we move forward new perceptions are likely to develop, changing our foundational thoughts and allowing us to see a world in a new and contrasting way. This won't make the death of a child any less sad, but it may well mean we see life and death very differently and that in turn may alter our responses to some of the things we experience as it all plays out.

Chapter 8 : So what have you got to lose?

We've covered a lot in the last few chapters, so it's probably worth consolidating everything and summarising some simple action points. These represent the first steps towards creating permanent peace and happiness.

Keeping it *really* simple... Removing the seven items on the following list from your life will bring about transformative change:

- Judgement
- Preferences
- Resistance
- Seeking happiness endlessly, external to yourself and in all the wrong places
- The fight to control the uncontrollable
- Attachment to the past and past experiences
- Blame, guilt and the role of victim

Hopefully by now you've developed a real appetite for freedom and will understand the benefits of this action. The content we've covered in these early chapters will be developed much more over the following steps of the masterclass. You may or may not find yourself agreeing with everything just yet, but the coming chapters are designed to offer deeper insight and perspective, activities and practices that will bring it all to life and help you to see the real, tangible benefits in action.

If you're feeling resistance or challenge so far, don't worry; this is to be fully expected. At this time you have a strong mind identity that has come to believe lots of things – some that serve you and many that don't. If you're still here and willing, then change will come.

We've covered a lot in a short space of time – some really deep and important concepts that challenge what most of us have come to know as our way of life. For me, this raises a huge question: how is it that human culture has essentially been built with judgement, popular opinion and preferences at its core? How is it that almost everyone, and society itself, is charging the whole world with the energy of ego and mind-created identity, with all its incumbent insecurity, need to chase things to bring happiness, low self-esteem and the false view that peace and happiness come from things outside and not within?

Almost everything in human culture is designed to make us believe that we will somehow be happier and more fulfilled when we buy this, go to that destination, look like this, find true love and so on and so on and so on. This encourages people to believe that they need to "attach" to all of those things and more if they're to stand any chance of ever being happy. It's a recipe for disaster yet we teach it to our children from birth and embed it as they grow. It feels real, like there is no other way. After all, if the whole world believes that peace and happiness is fundamentally an external thing, why wouldn't we adopt that same belief without exception or question? Everyone we know has bought into it so no wonder we have too. After all, what alternative are we being shown we can believe in? Peace and happiness can be bought or found on a website or by travelling the world, by buying a bigger house or an amazing car, dressing in the designer clothes and looking like a supermodel with perfect skin and six-pack abs. It really seems to be that simple.

In reality, however, that's all simply a creation of the ego identity and attachments, this endless search for what we *think* makes us feel good. We try each thing in succession, failing to notice that whatever we get is just a stepping stone to the thing after that – in constant pursuit of all these things we "need" that will "hopefully" make us feel better. Really, it's a perpetual and total waste of our time, energy and stint here on the planet as human beings.

The cynic in me does notice that in this comparison-rich and identity-driven culture, commercialism thrives. If this way of life works for anything, it certainly works to keep everyone busy thinking and sell lots more stuff. You can constantly chase and buy what you don't have and dream of going to the place you've never been. The next place that you believe is heaven on a long list of places. What you do have must be better and bigger, to give us more status and fancier badges; otherwise it's simply too old and makes us look bad, or poor or like a loser or someone who doesn't compete with their friends. Even love – the single biggest external we chase – can be bought and paid for, on dating websites, thus turning that incredibly personal thing into one of the biggest industries there is on earth.

Setting conspiracy aside (theories don't matter anyway), the absolute truth is that *every* war there has ever been was a result of a person or a group of people judging, creating preferences and opinions, that then lead to them trying to control the world in order to impose their views on a wider group. This human-created mind identity affects literally everything we see and do. The judgements and preferences of a single person become the judgements and preferences of whole societies; they decide to "know" what's best and impose it on everyone else.

Imagine a world where children were taught in kindergarten how to understand their ego identity, learning techniques to avoid judgement, attachment and blame and so on. Where the universe was understood to be the unfathomable truth and life was defined as it really is: a beautiful, unpredictable and moment-to-moment adventure of experiences and learning; not as a thing we should try to control and feel disappointed in when things don't go as planned. Most importantly, what if kids were taught to see people as just one part of that unpredictable adventure, and learned to love them all and have joy without attachment or ownership or chasing and clinging? Or if they knew their sadness and their fear, as beautiful and necessary experiences that should be let go of as they happen, to prevent them projecting them into their futures? What then? I wonder if we'd need all the police, the psychiatrists, the medications, the weapons of war...

This short detour is designed to show you that *your* progress, here today in your transformational journey, is really progress for the whole world. As you take the next steps towards acceptance, losing judgement, preferences and resistance and stopping the struggle for control that is simply not available to you, it is not just your life you're changing. These are next steps in the evolution of humanity and you're taking your place at the leading edge of that. To me that feels special; and if this book has a bigger and more important purpose than helping just you to "love life", then it is to change the world one person at a time until we're all living without the mind identity and ego that currently drives every negative in the world.

Chapter 9: Bring the joy

Now to get back to the focus of your deep learning. There has always been another way to live and it starts with a simple and fundamental realisation. If we seek peace and happiness in people, things, situations and places, we will live life on an endless and unhappy search. When we attach to anything outside of ourselves in the expectation that it will make us feel good inside, we are entrusting our peace and happiness to what may be a totally amazing and totally beautiful universe but is also a fundamentally and unpredictable force. This will inevitably lead to disappointment because it takes how we feel out of our own hands and sphere of control.

It also means we are seeking only the peaks: the things that we found, judged and chased because they gave us the best feeling and we're trying to dodge the troughs. The troughs are the things we found, judged and disliked or feared; the stuff we've decided we don't want in our lives. Of course, the bad news is that the peaks are both short-lived and few and far between, so they'll never deliver the sustained feeling of peace or happiness we're looking for. Plus, for every peak there's always a new trough. It's an eternal wave of ups and downs.

The troughs are unfortunately unavoidable and the universe will bring that home to us in some beautifully high-impact way each time we think we've managed not to be brought down again. Ironically, we usually don't see this for the perpetual unpredictability that it is and keep trying to control anyway. Someone close to us dies or gets ill, we lose a job or a partner leaves, there's an earthquake, a tidal wave, a car crash or the dog dies... All these things happen again and again, all over the place and to everyone; they are varied and common and there's always another lower, more surprising one just around the corner.

This means that living life while trying to avoid them usually brings endless and pointless resistance, followed by a familiar or new and improved trough that should have been anticipated but nevertheless appears to be an unexpected curveball. The tragedy is it's not the troughs themselves that cause us pain but the fact that we choose to believe they won't happen, fail to expect them and so feel maximum impact when they do. We all seem to spend a whole lifetime failing to learn that we are perpetuating this pattern, so don't feel bad just yet if you forget; you're certainly not alone.

Then suddenly it happens. Life becomes an endless journey of contrasting preferences. Since we're only happy at the peaks, the rest is just not enough for us. This is a perpetual cycle of complaint, lack of fulfilment and waiting for the next peak until yet again a trough arrives instead (how rude and unexpected). Who is to blame? Who did this? You. You willingly created the whole problem.

I have to say, when I write this stuff down it seems so obvious and so super easy to solve. Like everyone should know it, see it and solve it without ever needing to be told how. Of course, while I find it confusing that we don't, having been there and got the T-shirt I do *know* that we don't – and that the "we" referred to throughout this masterclass includes almost every human on the planet (or close enough for statistical relevance). That changes for you now, so we should return to work on the best and most effective plan of action to change these patterns forever.

It all starts with a deep and respectful understanding of the fact that we live life in this moment. It is the only one we ever have. The past has gone, the future can only be imagined and the only real moment we have and can access is this moment right now. The following exercise helps us see what that means.

I'd like you to take a piece of paper and draw yourself a picture. Create a horizontal timeline of your life. It starts at birth on the left and it ends at death, represented to the right as some unpredictable moment in the future. As you're looking at the line, focus on a point in between those moments, maybe around the centre, and to the left of that point draw a vertical line. Then draw another vertical line to the right of the centre point. You should be left with a space between the two vertical lines. Are you with me so far? Good. If not, have another read and get familiar.

The space to the left of the left-hand vertical line is the past; and the space to the right of the right-hand vertical line is the future. The space in between those vertical lines is right now, the present. As we move through this transformational journey it will help us greatly to have a think about what is in the past and what should therefore go to the left of the vertical line on the left. We should categorise here rather than listing too many specific things – we don't want your whole life spelled out in full.

So, to keep things simple we're going to list everything as three interrelated groups. First, *experiences* (things you've been told, things you've seen, feelings, thoughts, relationships, things you loved, things that scared you, things you never want to speak of again). Then *practical learnings* (things like maths and languages, hand-eye co-ordination, typing, writing, that hot burns and you can lose a leg when it's too cold and so on). Then things you've learned that are totally subjective and may be either personal to you or representative of a collective view – we'll call them *subjective learnings*. This includes everything you've experienced and made a judgement on then turned into a personal preference; and things you were told to believe or value because they exist in your culture or religion or society, company or peer group. In any case they're things you adopted because they seemed to fit at the time or seemed right in some way. Essentially, these are opinions and beliefs.

We now need to look at these things in a way that will serve us moving forward. Remember: we've already floated the need to let go of the past; to clarify what this means we'll consider what you need to carry with you from the past into the present and what you really, really don't. Using the diagram to illustrate this should help things click into place.

From the list above, all *practical learnings* become *skills*; skills clearly exist and serve us in the present and so they get to come with us as simply factual "content", which has no attachment. Next, if we work on the basic principle I've been pushing in the last few chapters, that "Life is a series of beautiful, unpredictable, present-moment experiences that we should be grateful to have without judgement or preference", we can see that life builds *memories*. How wonderful, to store the things that have enriched your life. Memories are like photographs, and testimony to the unpredictability and beauty of life, so of course they come too – but on one condition: that they are inert and do not carry attachment or deep emotion. They too are simply content. We leave the *experiences* themselves in the past and take our memories of them with us as a simple means to hold them fondly. This means they now hold no emotional "meaning". We drop the meaning and the emotion that came with them.

That now leaves us with *subjective learnings*. When we talk about letting go of the past, this specifically means letting go of any residual judgements, preferences, emotions and collective opinions – forever, in real time, as and when the experience that would have created them is actually happening. Because when we remove all judgment and the related emotion, we also let go of associated preferences (likes, dislikes, wants, expectations, and so on) that have caused our attachments to subjective views and beliefs as well as to things, people, situations and places.

Importantly, this involves letting go of the emotions of fear, hate and regret that cause very deep attachment and negative attachment. This is the essence of the "meaning" we give that creates attachment. It's these judgements, preferences and emotions that together drive our fruitless will for control over the present and the future; we will never be free until they have gone and have been replaced by a simple love for every unpredictable experience, good, bad or anything, throughout our lives. *Subjective learnings* and opinions must all remain in the past so we let go of them forever.

We now have a really clear picture of what's in the past and know that what comes with us into the present moment are *practical learnings* and simple *memories* that hold no emotion or preference. We have nothing subjective at all and have nothing left to attach to. We have lost or subjective likes, dislikes, opinions, loves and fears. Even what we decided or *judged* was "right" or "wrong" has gone, or at least, we are flexible and as with all opinion will be dynamic in letting it go or changing it as needed. We are now in the present moment and have *skills* and *memories* and what just *is* and cannot be changed.

Importantly, there is no future in the present moment either; the present is "where we are" and not "where we want to be" at some later point. If we accept it as it is and accept that it cannot be changed, without bringing the past or future into it, this moment is almost always utterly peaceful. Yet it is not a moment that many of us have experienced much of in our lives. Why? Our "time" is generally and commonly spent more in the past or the imagined future. After all, how would we dwell on guilt, regret and sadness or create so much anxiety if we spent our time in the present? You get the picture.

Great news, we've now dispensed with the past. We've taken forward all that we need and we don't have to go there again dragging anything up that we gave false meaning to. That was all the mind-created identity or ego anyway and we've taken that part out. What a relief to lose all of those fears, likes, dislikes, attachments and expectations. What a difference this will make to life...

But we do still need to finish our diagram and deal with the space we've left for the future. If we do a similar exercise to the one we did for the past, what will we write on this list? I'm guessing you might think it'll be all your goals, dreams, aspirations, expectations, fears, purpose and stuff like that. This is interesting because actually all we can list is *an unlimited number of futures created by your imagination*. What goes in this space is a set of creative-mind illusions. I say a set because there are many and they're constantly in flux: sometimes the future is bright; sometimes it's dark.

Sometimes you're heading towards a peak and sometimes you're at the bottom of a trough. Your mind tells stories and creates a future to suit every occasion, all totally dependent on the emotion you feel at the time of imagining. It then layers the past – recent or distant; the mind doesn't care – on top of the future; it essentially uses the past as a filter to guide your creative imagination. If everything is going wrong, the future may look like it's going to continue that way; if things have been good, the future might be full of optimism. In any case it's just imagination, tainted with one emotion or another and a set of fears, wants, and preferences.

There's more to say about the future and how it relates to the past and the present, but before we expand on that let's look at our finished diagram (an example is available online in the members area). Whether you drew it or just visualised it, the only things you should have in the present are inert content: *skills*, non-attached *memories* and what *is*. As we move through the masterclass you might find it useful to refer back to this, so maybe stick it on your fridge or wherever you can easily find it.

So, back to the future, so to speak... The awful thing about it is that it's always uncertain. This is where that pesky desire to control life lives. It's also what brings about repeated disappointment, as an "unexpected" part of the beautiful, unpredictable, adventure that life would be without it. No matter what future we're imagining, we are basically saying, "Will I get what I want?" or "I hope I don't get what I don't want!" while trying to create the right conditions in the belief that the future is under our control. Guess what? It really isn't! Stop all that and see it all for what it is: imagination from a beautifully clever mind; a recipe for fear and anxiety based on something that is fundamentally not real and varies wildly with emotion.

When I say this, the most common and super strong reaction raised by ego is around goals, success and taking direct action towards creating the future you want. I have been the poster child for that too and fully believe in taking action; the great news is that taking action really isn't impacted by what I'm about to say, so stay with me and see this thing through. Attaching to and making things creatively, in an imagined future part of who you are, is totally pointless. To one degree or another it will always end in disappointment. It's possible that this fact will really hit a nerve with anyone who's been reading the success books, so please hold on. Those books are all about setting goals, perseverance, adapting and overcoming, aren't they? Well, here's the newsflash: following that method is setting yourself up for a life full of needless resistance and achieving less; it is the definition of attachment and will result in you chasing one specific "achievement" after another as you mistake your purpose for struggle and persuade yourself to become addicted to that instead of the real effective, efficient and enjoyable progress that is nature's way.

Imagine for the moment that we have a different approach to "success" and we play the "game of life" in the terms we've already discussed in depth: that is, understanding it to be a beautifully unpredictable adventure. We surrender to what is and we remove all resistance by accepting that statement and we are fluid and flexible as a result. We set our goal but we do not attach to it specifically. Instead of believing that it's the only thing that will offer fulfilment, we believe that there are many goals and are prepared for surprises, unpredictability and to adapt and change our path. Our goal now becomes a present-moment goal that exists in the now, for the now, and importantly is not chasing an imagined future state that we suppose will make us happy, peaceful or fulfilled.

The success books may define such states in terms of being rich or earning money "that brings freedom"; but our goal is freedom now and fulfilment now, so imagined future states will no longer work for us. They are a focus on externals again and we now *know* that's not the *future*. Accepting this allows us to then choose to take a different kind of action. This is *fulfilled* action towards our goal in every present moment, our aim being to accept and enjoy that action as much as when we reach the goal itself and to the very maximum. This makes our actions full of intent and love. It keeps us flexible, and without attachment to a specific outcome, it allows us to be fluid in delivering the best possible end result. It also means that, whatever the outcome – which will be great because of the inspired actions and love we have injected to create it – we have been deeply fulfilled all the way on the journey, changing direction as necessary along the way and being unconcerned with the specifics of the result. We have simply loved and done our best with every moment of the action towards the goal, enjoying fulfilment in every moment. Wow!

What I'm leading back around to here is that – as we learned in our recent exercise – we have a clear place where all of the best outcomes will always be created, where it is always peaceful and where we can always be happy. That place is of course the present moment. Equipped with our skills and blessed by our memories, we can live and take action there without the baggage of the past or the imagined future. As with any good strategy, you need to know where you are and where you'd like to be and then take steps towards it. As described above, this is all available without ever leaving this present moment.

What a beautifully simple world this is. It all happens in the now. There is no past and there is no future. We have skills. We have unpredictable and beautiful experiences in every moment, which we carry as wonderful memories. We don't need to attach to anything and can then love everything equally without judgement, preferences or the risk of losing something to which we're attached.

We must simply choose to accept each and every moment as it comes, to embrace experiences, to let go of the associated emotions as they happen and to live the adventure in *this* moment, not the moments of the past or future. If we attach or identify with things, people, situations or places, we will be hit emotionally when they are removed or change unpredictably – which will always and inevitably happen. This is about accepting that we can live free to experience the whole adventure, without the resistance of judging it or deciding to like or dislike it, only then do we find that we have no need to control it. Without judgement, preferences and the resulting attachments, every experience has a base of neutrality. None is good, bad, right or wrong and all are ready to have our own joy and love applied to them so they become rich and fulfilling.

This concept is huge and should not be underestimated. Have you realised what this means for your life, starting right now, if you can and do action all of the principles here so far? Taking this forward will literally bring about a new state of being in which you can lose all resistance and ditch the fight for control and instead be at peace in every moment and almost permanently happy. We're only on Step 3 of the masterclass but already the possible outcome is profound.

The cool thing is that by stopping the judgement, you start a chain reaction that will remove subjective preferences and give you neutrality of feeling in almost any place, with anything and anybody. You no longer need to complain about the bad weather, talk about the rude person you met at Starbucks, attach to the car you want as if it will make you into someone or hate your work and everything you do all day – because without judgement, they are just weather, a person, a car, a place you go to earn money and so on. They are essentially just experiences that you can now be broadly thankful to have. More than that, you have now made them all neutral and accepted the unpredictability of the universe to throw you curveballs, so how hard is it to add your own joy and turn them all from neutral to enjoyable?

One thing to note as an underlying thread here is the total disregard for your mind-built identity, all of its judgements and the meaningless ball of thoughts that make it up. Why? Because it's essentially incapable of making good decisions; its judgements take away your peace and bring unhappiness. But mostly because doing things the way *it* wants to hasn't worked so far. The suggestion here is not that you become neutral in everything, have no ability to choose or become numb to the world. Rather, this is the start of a process: we're raising the issue that your mind is not the right vehicle to drive your choices.

For the moment, this method allows for your peace and happiness in all situations; as you read on you'll find a way to make the choices that serve you best. This is a step-by-step process; finish the masterclass and you'll find the differences between mind decisions and knowing the right choices. For now, though, you can simply implement what you've learned so far and wallow in the peace and happiness it gradually starts to bring to you.

The simple message of this chapter is that external things do not bring you consistent joy. If you want that, you need first to accept what is and then add your own joy from within. This idea is reliant on you knowing and embracing the truth that the universe is totally unpredictable and that nothing will ever consistently be as you want or expect it to be, no matter how you try to control it. So don't try; just embrace the adventure. Love it and enjoy the beautiful unpredictability and be grateful for every experience it gives you, not sad when it ends. Through acceptance and the addition of your own joy, there is a failsafe resistance-free route to happiness with you taking responsibility for how you feel, all the time and no matter what. It is all in you. This is the only route to real freedom, peace and happiness; nothing else will or can ever work. Anything else is just endlessly chasing external attachments.

In summary: love every experience without feeling the need to judge it. It need not be "right" or "wrong"; you need not decide if you "like" or "dislike" it. Experiences just *are*. They are *what is* (or was). They cannot be changed and need not be resisted. Feel the emotions of the experience without feeling the need to attach to the experience. Let the past go, let the future go and live permanently in the present – because there is no other moment you can change or access. That right there is the beginning of the rest of your life; the old way just doesn't work. If you're still feeling resistance, have a judgement or a conflicting opinion but don't want to because you really want the dream of happiness, that's OK; it's to be expected. Read on to find out how to make all this happen or take a moment to let those opinions go; accept, and come back later when you've found how much that acceptance really works.

ZEN JUNGLE

Step 4: Finding Presence

Chapter 10: Introducing presence

So far we've introduced some core principles and the totally life-changing potential of putting them into action. You're possibly now fully understanding of and believe in those principles but also left wondering that while it all *sounds* great, you've no idea how on earth to actually *do* it. Relax, stay in the present and take your time. This is a process; it may take some repetition and more than one read of each step to fully absorb the information. Breaking habits and creating new ones never happens instantly, though your mind may hope and expect that it could. The great news is that we're now moving on to one of the most useful techniques to help you achieve real progress.

We've now reached a clear point where our aim is to start to live life from the present, to dispense with the past for all non-practical purposes and to remove all thought of imagined futures from our world. However, living in the present is a real skill – and perhaps easier said than done with that wonderful voice in our head likely still very much on full volume. That's why new techniques and new habits will really help and will serve you as you begin to implement the ideas we've already covered as well as those yet to come.

The first of these is the practice of *presence*, which is distinct from the all-encompassing concept of living in the present. Presence essentially creates the same end result as living in the present but in a very momentary and specific way. In other words, presence creates moments without past or future but is more of a progressive support towards really living in the present than an immediate magical solution to being there. The practice of presence is incredibly important to the success of your transformational journey and will progressively create profound results in relation to mind activity, the voice in your head and your ability to avoid reacting to the many involuntary thoughts and emotions that you have almost endlessly at the moment. Its primary function, though, is to help you to become the "watcher of your thoughts" so you're no longer entangled in them as if they're who you are.

This chapter will deal with what presence actually is, and with the benefits and progressive improvements it will bring to your life. We'll also look at why it's necessary to practice presence as much as possible in everyday life in order to make true progress and achieve the other key elements of the masterclass. Presence is fundamental to this masterclass and as such will be continually developed throughout it. This is merely the beginning.

For those who are familiar with presence to some degree, or those who relate it to meditation and are familiar with that, the strong advice here would be to read this chapter in full and with interest because the differences and definitions here will be important. Meditation and presence are related but are not the same; we'll be making use of both in this masterclass, often for very independent reasons. There's much misunderstanding and confusion around both meditation and presence, the benefits they bring and how to practice them in ways that maximise their impact. We're going to massively simplify all of this so they become the great easy-to-use tools that they really are.

Entire bestselling books have been written about presence, yet it is in fact a very simple concept and very simple to action. It's often complicated by being needlessly intermingled with "living in the moment", "acceptance of what is" and the act of "dispensing with past and future". Clearly, all these have been the focus of our previous chapters, and will be the effect of this practice, but are not especially relevant to *how* you take the actions you need to take. So, for the purposes of simplicity and helping you to quickly utilise the practice, we're going to stick to the core of what presence is and how to attain it.

Presence is essentially you being here now, focusing your attention on something in this moment with zero thought about it and with no other thoughts in your mind. The aim of presence is to give your consciousness and mind a simple, single point of focus that reduces your mind's ability to think about anything else and requires no thought in itself. To clarify what presence means, it is helpful to associate the definition with the aim.

Words can be confusing. Often when presence is described, people expect some sort of altered state of being or for something to actually happen. This seems to create a sense that presence is a challenging or complex technique. It really isn't. Presence is simply the act of focusing your consciousness and mind on something that is here and now, in front of you or imagined, and creating the right conditions for your mind to stay quiet and without thought for as long as possible. Eckhart Tolle, the most famous and well-regarded author on living in the now and the state of presence, often defines presence as "intense, thoughtless attention", which is a great description for our purposes here.

To help join up the dots, here's a simple explanation of what presence may be and feel like. Imagine for a second that you're sitting in the garden at this moment and you simply watch the view outside, the landscape or broad vista in front of you. You are conscious of it all at once and you're not analysing it or intending in any way for your mind to commentate on it. This means there's no need for that voice in your head to say: "That's a tree", "Look at the bird", "It's raining again", "How beautiful" and so on – the kind of narration that the mind loves to do so much and so often. We're now primarily using awareness, not mind, and as such we take in everything in front of us without needing to define each item we see in the way the mind normally does. It's worth noting that this is an amazing way to realise just how powerful your conscious awareness actually is. It takes in everything that is in front of you, instantly. You actually "know" everything that is there, in its entirety, and without any need of a single thought. In this state, you are giving the whole landscape intense, thoughtless attention and have created a gap in your thoughts where the mind is quiet. That is presence. That is you simply being here now.

Does it sound easy? It really is, but it takes time to develop the skill. To begin with as you practice presence you'll likely find that thoughts quickly become active again whether you like it or not. It's that voice in your head again, doing its thing. We can deal with that next. It's strange that presence isn't our base state, the one we're in lots of the time; but really this is because no matter what we're doing, we're usually doing it while constantly thinking about something totally unrelated. The practice of presence will slowly change all that.

To understand what presence is it can also be helpful to discuss what it is not. Presence is not you doing something and thinking about something else. It is also not you even "thinking" about the thing you are currently doing, seeing or imagining. On the contrary, it is placing your full attention on something with the aim of being completely aware but completely thought*less*.

Think of those times when you're driving and literally arrive at your destination with no recollection of how you got there. You've been driving all the way, yes, but you've actually been thinking nonstop about something else. The reason that you don't remember how you got to your destination is that you have been driving subconsciously, and using the time to think about all the things you need to do, all your problems and anything else that your mind decided to bring up from the past or future. Your thoughts can't be from the present, because the only thing in the present is you driving. In reality, you weren't there for the driving.

It's the same when you're in a conversation and using the time while the other person is speaking to second-guess what they're trying to say, forming your response and quite likely then interrupting them before they've finished. Come on, don't pretend you don't do this – we all do. It's OK. But it is not presence.

In this example, presence would be you listening to the other person with your entire, focused and conscious attention. Your thinking mind would not be busy making assumptions and preparing an answer to those assumptions; in fact, you would not be thinking *at all* while they speak. Once they'd done talking and not before, presence would be you formulating your reply to what they'd *actually said* and not whatever you'd been busy assuming they were going to say.

When you're driving, presence would be intense thoughtless awareness of the road in front of you. This is *thoughtless* because our awareness processes information many times faster than our minds can. That's why we can drive and think about things other than the driving: our awareness is on driving and our mind is thinking about the past or the future or a combination of both. Presence while driving, on the other hand, is a kind of peaceful, aware, meditation.

There are thousands more examples we could use but these illustrate well that presence is simply and thoughtlessly being in the here and now. It is the act and practice of being intensely aware but without feeling the need for internal narration or comment. Importantly, these examples show that presence can and should be practiced anywhere, at any time; every waking moment is an opportunity for you to be present and to develop and practice presence. Why does that matter? Because the more you do it, the more life-changing it is.

When you find presence you'll know you've found it. It is peaceful and special. It connects you with the now and often brings a new level of vibrancy to everything that's perhaps gone unnoticed before because your mind has always been on something else. Presence means becoming intensely aware of what is in front of you with all of your senses and with no mind voice at all to distract you. All is quiet but feels more alive and more real than before – that is, until the mind voice chirps up to say, "So that was presence – I did it!" or something equally pointless and interrupting. Fortunately, the time before that happens generally increases with practice. Remember: the aim of presence is a simple moment where your attention is on the here and now and the mind is totally quiet.

The most commonly used technique to achieve presence, and especially in meditation, is to focus on your breathing. Becoming aware of your breath, all the way in and all the way out, takes the focus of your consciousness and allows less opportunity for mind noise to creep in. In meditation, you do this with your eyes open or closed and you will simply be aware of – or watch – your whole breath in and out. All of your attention is thus given to something that needs no thought at all; if you continue to watch the breath, you will remain without thought while doing it for a prolonged period. For now, our focus here remains on presence and not meditation.

For presence, becoming intensely aware of where you are and looking at what is in front of you is more important. However, adding to this the action of becoming aware of your breath, as just described, is incredibly powerful because it compounds the effect of both. So, from this moment forward on our transformational journey we're going to use this as our highly effective way of becoming and staying present: first, becoming intensely aware of what's in front of us, without the need to define or describe it in thoughts, and then adding awareness of the full breath.

If for some reason you need or want an alternative focus to breath, you can do the same practice but giving your attention to the way the ground feels under your feet while you walk or to different parts of your inner body. For our purposes it is all the same and can be equally effective. The main thing is that you achieve a state where all of your attention is on something and your mind is quiet with no thoughts. The more varied the places you practice presence the better, but all presence has the same benefit.

Presence is an incredibly powerful state. It is you being consciously and fully aware of the here and now, with no mind activity taking you into the past or the future. In fact while you're fully present you simply cannot *have* a past or future – which has really obvious benefits for worry and anxiety, sadness and guilt, as we know from our discussion in previous chapters. The state of presence is far more powerful than just that, though, and we'll keep developing it throughout this masterclass for several reasons. The practice can be life-changing in itself and produces almost immediate results for anyone who over thinks and has a generally overactive mind.

Before I go on to the benefits in more detail, it is important to discuss why presence is a "practice" and not just a simple activity or state of being. That's because in order to do it effectively, you'll need to practice it very regularly. As already mentioned – and you'll know this if you've already tried meditation, which involves a large element of presence – your "intense, thoughtless attention" is frequently and rudely interrupted by your mind, coming in and breaking the thoughtless silence. Please don't blame the excited little mind for this; remember, you've had it very busy diligently trying to control the whole universe, so it's bound to "think" it needs to consult or debate with you on a very regular basis. Imagine being given that job and having to do it without debate. Hell no! This is all more than normal and totally understandable so don't worry. Presence is a practice: when you notice that the mind has taken you off into thought, your practice is to watch the thought, get back to presence, reset and stay there as long as you can... Until it does it all over again, which it invariably will.

The benefits of presence are actually huge. At this stage, we'll focus on just a few – the ones I'm sure you'll agree you really want and need right now. These are centred around reducing overthinking and creating an ability to watch rather than become your thoughts.

So, over time, you'll develop your ability to become present and it will get much easier. With practice, you'll find that the time you experience thoughtlessness will extend and your rude interruptions from the voice in your head get progressively less frequent. Importantly, this is not you fighting the mind. This is you taking no interest in it and it in turn losing interest in speaking to someone who doesn't want to listen or respond. What does that mean for you? It means that this quieter mind will begin to exist even when you're not actively aiming to be present. It means that by practicing presence you are slowly training your mind to stay a little quieter day by day. Sound good?

A quieter mind isn't even really the best part of this! Yes, really. Ironically, the annoying interruptions may well be the most important part of practicing presence. How cool is that? As explained, the rude interruptions are to be expected; they do reduce over time but they rarely disappear – or it takes some time for them to do so. This is actually great news, because each interruption is an opportunity to see the mind thought and *watch* it rather than *becoming* it. So, let's say today you sit and practice presence. If you're like most of us when we start the process, you won't realise that your mind has taken you on a joy ride until you've been there, bought ice cream and are on the way home feeling sick. The last thing you knew, you were totally present; and then suddenly you notice that for the past ten minutes you've been considering what colour balloons to get for your daughter's birthday party without even knowing it. How did that happen?

As you practice presence, slowly and surely these detours into thought will get shorter and shorter and you'll start to realise earlier and earlier that you're on one. This is important because over time you'll become aware of them in real time, as they happen – the very moment they begin, in fact. This will be the moment when you're becoming fully conscious and it will be consciousness not only of thoughts as they begin but of emotions too. As soon as the mind starts up out of the quietness, or the early sensation of an emotion begins, you'll see it, be able to accept it happening and watch it. This allows you to observe your thinking rather than believing you actually *are* your thoughts. It also allows you to immediately calm the mind and reset, returning to presence almost instantly and at will. Now that is a skill we all need for peace, isn't it.

In addition to having a quieter mind and starting to become the watcher of your mind and thoughts, you'll find there's a further related and profound benefit to presence. This is the one you'll fall in love with the first time it happens. Not only will you now be thinking less, and have the ability to return quickly and easily to presence when you get interrupted by the mind, but you'll also start to see the thoughts at their inception, in real time, and can choose whether or not to act on them or even to have them. If you're a smoker who finds themselves with a cigarette in their mouth without even realising, you can now quit – because you can see the thought about having one without believing that the thought *is you*. Smoking then becomes your choice. This covers almost all addictions and all other reactions and impulses that start in thought. As the watcher of thought, you can choose the thoughts that serve you and reject the ones that don't.

Most importantly, those who master this process and have the correct training (like this masterclass provides) soon see from their position of thought observer that the mind offers very little of use in their world. This is a profound truth that must be experienced to be realised. The mind is not as clever or useful as we give it credit for. The way it makes decisions is totally flawed and the results it achieves on its own are rarely good. Big choices and anything that matters are better left to other things that we'll discover later in the masterclass. The practice of presence, though, is the first important step.

Clearly, presence also provides a much-needed rest from the past and the future, which are the home of guilt, regret, sadness and all worry and anxiety. The more time we spend without them, the more we realise the power of removing them. Our attachments then decrease and our minds grow increasingly clear. Fundamental to this transformational journey is the removal of the elements that create mind identity, the pain and emotions of the past and the focus on the future; all are equally important. Presence may not help with the choices you need to make or the commitment you need to give these actions, but it will embed and facilitate them in clever ways that are difficult to imagine.

There are many more benefits to presence but they're generally far more related to mediation and we're keeping things simple for now. Please take away from this that you can practice presence anywhere at any time. You can find things to thoughtlessly focus your attention on everywhere and you can reset your mind to those things repeatedly when it wanders off. This is a practice that you need to be doing as often as possible, so from this moment forward practice whenever and wherever you can. It takes no additional time and the method here builds the potential to live from a base of total presence too. This is an amazing place to be.

This is a good juncture to discuss the relationship between thought creativity and finding practical solutions. One of the more common questions about becoming increasingly thoughtless is whether it in some way reduces your ability to complete tasks, achieve goals and compete in the world. This is an interesting and understandable thought that as I sit here writing this book I can give a very specific answer to.

As I write, I am not actually thinking and the words are coming out in an almost automatic way. That's because both creativity and practical tasks rarely rely on the thinking mind but are instead often a result of a subconscious connection to a higher state in which they simply flow. This phenomenon is often referred to as the "flow state" or as being "in the flow" (or "zone") and is when analysed not a thinking state. Thinking is the mind activity that we've been discussing as generally involuntary. If I say, "Don't think of a blue whale," what do you do? That's mind activity and thought. Yet I say to drive me somewhere and you don't need thought at all. I write this book and the words appear on the page faster than I can actually think them anyway. They are not thought; they are created somewhere else and simply arrive here but thought is not involved.

Some of the most famous masterminds in history, such as Einstein, Thomas Edison, Nikola Tesla, along with almost every artistic and literary genius, have made clear in their descriptions that their creative flair has never originated in thought. In fact, most have made clear that the more you think or try to think, the more you become blocked. We have all experienced this to some degree. This is an important concept and reality. The mind would have you believe otherwise (and you may or may not have resistance to the idea) but it is important to understand that this reality has you create less and of a lower quality when directly employing thought than you do when you simply connect directly to the power of consciousness. In the flow state, things just come without thought; you have an objective and the answers simply arrive, rather than being forced into existence.

If you're aligned with this concept and believe it, then the contents and practice in this chapter gain in significance. They'll serve to facilitate as you reduce your reliance on direct thoughts, allowing the flow state and connection to what appears to be your boundless, creative consciousness or intelligence. The difference between geniuses and the more average among us appears to be in their ability to motivate and connect to this state of consciousness, releasing unlimited potential when we do. As someone now practiced in invoking flow state at will – and who's seen the part presence plays in that – I can only confirm that it is profound and exciting. I'm often amazed when I read things back, having been unaware of the content I've written (though the grammar is sometimes less satisfying).

Hopefully we now have a good basis for the practice of presence. For some of you, practicing presence already forms part of your daily routine. If that's you and you're happy with what you're doing and can remain present effectively for long periods, feel free to continue in your existing method. If you have a time-based routine, then add this process to it and develop a more permanent base of presence – because that's the fundamental aim of this practice here.

The most common mistake people make is to view meditation and presence as a sort of challenge to prevent thought or to gain overall control of the mind. This practice is neither! It is also not designed to kick-start your frustration with or hate and blame of your mind for doing what it does. The mind is a beautiful instrument and capable of many amazing things. Remember that you tasked yours with control of your world and all its doing is meticulously trying to carry out that order. Over the course of your whole life, your mind has worked hard to make the world meet your preferences, expectations and responses to pain and pleasure and you should deeply love and embrace it for doing so.

Taking this position allows you to relax and understand that the way your mind thinks and the relentless barrage of thought it creates are actually OK. You can accept and learn to watch them rather than going into battle about anything. Really, we've all been in conflict with our minds for almost all of our lives. And we've found to our detriment struggling to make it perform only compounds our problems; the things we resist serve only to fuel what we don't want.

Presence and meditation are all about that acceptance. They both involve a gentle process that progressively reduces the overthinking and, more importantly, lets us see and watch our thoughts. Remember: with practice we begin to realise more quickly when we've been sucked into thought, and at some point we're able to see a thought at the moment it occurs, in real time; so it is these very thoughts we want to avoid that will eventually set us free from our minds. Take every opportunity to realise and watch a thought or a pattern that you've been taken into, because this represents learning and another step closer to freedom. Smile at the thinking and accept whatever it is. None of these thoughts matter and they should be allowed to pass by like clouds in the sky, without your attention or reaction.

Soon, as we begin to develop our consciousness, we realise that almost all thoughts are meaningless, which is essentially the final teaching of presence. Once we learn this, we achieve the ultimate freedom.

Our action plan: be present as often as you can. In the shower, on the toilet, while tying your shoes, brushing your hair, walking the dog, making and drinking your coffee, driving... You get the picture. Anywhere and everywhere. Watch the moment, be aware of the breath, feel the inner body, feel the ground under your feet. Presence is the act of being here now without thought of what you're doing or the past and future. The more you do it, the less you think and the more you can watch your thoughts. That's it. Presence is easy. Now practice it, a lot.

Chapter 11 : A safe haven and a way to release what is trapped

As soon as you've begun to practice presence as described, you will very quickly realise that you can enter the state almost instantly and at will. Once there, you'll have few or no thoughts at all and will simply experience the peace and vibrancy of this moment. There can be no future or past and whatever is in the moment will usually bring peace and, commonly, a feeling of joy and love. That's because when we are in this moment we are connected to our purpose. We've escaped the mind and entered a new realm that represents the truth of what actually is. This is you being aligned with what is in effect the core of your being. It is your present experience and adventure.

That feeling can be all-consuming and for many brings a near-instant feeling of connection and wellbeing. As we practice presence and become more proficient in achieving it, either remaining thoughtless or able to stand back and observe our thoughts, we eventually become untouchable by them.

This means that the state of presence can be called upon in situations of overthinking, stress and anxiety. In fact, if we're self-aware enough to invoke presence during any deep emotional response – say, fear or guilt – those feelings will almost immediately reduce and disappear. Clearly, the main challenge here is to become aware that you are lost in your mind or emotions and to be conscious enough to start the process of presence instantly. If you are, you'll find that presence brings instantaneous peace and comfort and will provide you with time to relax and consider your reactions to whatever life situation stimulated your thoughts and emotions to a degree that affected your peace. Of course, for most of us these intrusions happen all too often.

Together with the opportunity to watch our thoughts, the stillness that presence provides allows us to see the overactive mind for what it is and limits the occurrence of anxiety or emotional response. This makes presence a great tool. For many people presence brings a huge sense of freedom from the mind and creates a sense of real control over thoughts and feelings.

As you practice presence, make it your "go-to" state whenever you feel an upturn in emotions or anxiety. You will see immediate benefits. There's another very significant way to put presence to use too. You'll recall that Steps 1 and 2 discussed in great detail how thoughts, experiences and emotions from the past become trapped in our bodies and act as a filter to what we see in the present and imagine in the future. As part of its efforts to control our universe, our dutiful little mind suppresses and stores these things in the hope that it can either cling to or avoid the same feelings happening again. If it's something we loved, it clings to it; if it's fear or pain then it avoids it. Almost everything is tainted by them; really, they dictate our whole perception of the world. This is particularly true of events that at the time stimulated emotions of fear, love, guilt, and so on, so we end up carrying trapped and often invisible sensitivities throughout our whole lives.

It is these that cause the most stark and involuntary reactions when they're reawakened. The accomplished yogi and gurus of India call them samskaras and define them as trapped energy, held in the body just waiting to be reignited and to raise the same feeling and emotion that occurred the first time they were experienced, over and over again. We all have these sensitivities; and, as we've discussed previously, the experiences and emotions behind them must be fully accepted and let go if we're to gain relief from the involuntary reactions they create.

We don't need too much detail here but your new-found skill and practice of presence will heighten your awareness of samskaras when they rise. With practice and presence, each time a situation presents itself that creates an emotional reaction based on something from your past you will see that reaction more and more quickly until finally you're aware of it at the very moment it begins. This awareness will allow you to take the required next action in order to release that energy and become free of future reactions generated by the same samskara. In time, this will come to have a profound effect on your whole life.

Our stored experiences can be inert and insignificant, and manifest simply as, say, strong preferences, or they can be deep and traumatic. The fact that there's so many of them means we can be triggered very easily in a broad range of situations. Really, when reaction events rise in us we can do one of three things. We can suppress them again, stopping any expression and pushing them back down to become even stronger and effectively under even higher pressure, only to have them rise again with even more vigour the next time we're triggered. Or we can express them and show a heightened and seemingly disproportionate sense of emotion when we're triggered. We've all had moments when our response is way stronger than we'd have liked it to be but we're unsure why – or we know why but are unwilling to think deeply about it. That is the expression of a samskara. These are really personal too; after all, they stem from our own subjective fears and emotions from the past.

Expression can often increase in intensity with time, becoming a very ugly symptom of this pent-up energy. It is highly likely that the very same event would not trigger the same emotion in anyone else in the same situation, which is why our behaviour around certain triggers might seem irrational, or to indicate some anger-management issue, etc.

The third option that we have available to us is my recommendation here. This is to become present, allow ourselves to feel the response, welcome it and accept it in order to let it go. This process is simple. When we're present, we can shower the feeling in love and acceptance, reducing it and ultimately making it disappear completely. In essence we're making peace with the feeling and giving it no power over us in the future. This conscious decision can remove it forever.

As a practice, using your presence to let go of your samskaras on an as-needed and daily basis will slowly free you of all your stored pain and the reactions it causes. It will rebalance your internal energy and bring you a sense of wellbeing, peace and freedom over time. All you need to do is practice presence and work to recognise those feelings rising, then let them go without expression or suppression. While you will have many of them to begin with, they will slowly but surely reduce in number to zero.

That is, of course, if you've taken the advice from earlier chapters to accept and let go of every experience as it happens, good or bad, and are now simply experiencing in the present without judgment, attachment and without building preference. If so, that means that you are now essentially having your moment-to-moment experiences without giving them any personal meaning, which leaves them inert and stored simply as content or memories. By doing so, you are now operating on both creation and release of the samskaras, preventing storage of new ones, and releasing and removing old ones that were stored previously. This is now slowly clearing your whole energy system.

So that's presence, for now. Steps 2 and 3 gave you a way to live and removed patterns that don't serve you. Now this step, Step 4, has given you an incredibly powerful technique that will help you to embed and use what you have learned. If up to this the point you've been diligently practicing what's been covered, then you're already seeing huge benefit. If not, now is a great time to start in a truly motivated way.

You might choose this moment to pause the masterclass and temporarily move into focused implementation of what you have learned so far, even if only for a few days or a week. This is because experiencing the benefits will be incredibly valuable to your understanding of the more advanced concepts that follow as we move forward. Life really is changing now for those who have committed and this journey only gets more exciting from here on in.

ZEN JUNGLE

Step 5 : Becoming the Real You

Chapter 12 : Moving the "I am"

I am truly excited that you have come this far in the masterclass. Hopefully you are now starting to change your state of being and have been practicing the previous chapter content on a daily, if not minute-by-minute basis. As you've moved through the masterclass you may have already found that you have a feeling you already know the content; that the thought and feeling of "That's right" or "Of course that's true" is becoming a recurring thread for you. How strange, then, if you "know" the content and feel it to be instantly true, that you've only just found it as a way of being and are just beginning to use the practices. I know that for me this was a strange subject of fascination; I felt like I'd known and forgotten this content, because the reality was that even though I felt I *knew* it I'd never formally heard it or been taught it at any point in my life. Maybe that's something that we should start to understand and consider as we move forward.

Up until this moment, we have deeply discussed the voice in your head, the creation of your mind identity over time and how your judgements became preferences. We went on to learn how those preferences result in endless mind resistance and in attempts for your mind to control everything in your world. Essentially, all of this highlights that we're constantly collecting the past and projecting it on to the future, meaning that we're consequently spending most of our time living in the past and the future without even seeing the present. We've now seen that we're living with a mind that is almost out of our control. Now that it is visible, it should be clear that this mind-created identity or ego is something we should work hard to make quieter and to become the observer of, rather than effectively becoming further identified with it. The ego is an endless thought stream of noise and debate that's perpetually attempting to control our unpredictable world and it is both meaningless and futile.

This masterclass so far has been dedicated to your understanding of how this ego has been built and showing you how you can both change its behaviour and become the watcher of it. It's important to remember that for as long as we allow it to do so the ego will constantly create involuntary dramas in our lives. Yet it appears that we are born without the weight of this thought ball and its determined filtering of the world we see;

in fact we begin with just awareness and presence and gradually build the weight and concede to its filter. Immediately after birth we enter a collective conditioning process, created by humanity over time. In it we're told what to believe and how to behave and have numerous collective preferences installed. This means that ego or mind identity is akin to a social institution, something that everybody has and most of us believe is real; who we are is not simply a product of our own objective and subjective experiences. Married with our own personal experiences, this collective identity becomes part of who we "think" we are and something we identify with and attach to on so many levels during our lifetime. In fact, generally we come to conclude that who we are at our core comprises a combination of our own roles, preferences, likes, dislikes, experiences and beliefs and the collective experiences and beliefs we've had installed. That's quite scary really. It's just a thought ball.

This entity, created largely by popular opinion, is active nonstop. It debates and plays two or more sides of every argument, it judges almost everything incessantly, it stores things that emotionally affect us and it converts everything into a control mechanism of things to cling to and things to avoid if we're to be happy and at peace. All the while, it in fact takes away our peace, almost every minute of every day. This is ironic to say the least. What's more, almost everyone we know is submerged in – or rather suffering from – the same process and until now there's never appeared to be a viable way out or possible alternative. This ego or mind identity contains *everything* about the way we've been viewing the whole world. It collects from the past and overlays its hoard as a filter on everything we see in the present and for the future too. It is the source of every limiting belief, creating a world that we continually resist, fear and try to control. It generates the infinite series of things to chase because we perceive they'll bring happiness but that instead without exception simply bring temporary highs, inevitable lows and perpetual disappointments that give rise to the next chase. Given all that, the unending futile optimism that most of us demonstrate is both admirable and painful to see.

The great news is that this masterclass has already taken us forward significantly. We can now all see the ego for what it is and begin the process of removing the control we've allowed the mind identity to have so far. We already know enough to plot a very different and more peaceful and fulfilling path – one that progressively allows us to see thoughts without taking action, to understand that almost all thoughts are meaningless and to create ever-increasing moments of vibrant and joyful thoughtless awareness. We can now, at will, create peaceful moments when the mind is quiet and we're simply aware, seeing thoughts as they appear like clouds passing in the sky and choosing whether or how to react to them.

This is the only true form of freedom because the only peace we're ever seeking is the peace that comes from a quiet mind. This is the peace of surrendering to the flow of the unpredictable universe rather than attempting to control it through rigid attachment to our wants, goals and wished-for destinations. This flexibility and flow naturally and always brings what's in our best interests. To become the watcher of the mind is the only true peace, freedom and fulfilment. Add your own joy and you are now permanently happy too.

Threaded through every part of this masterclass so far is a clear understanding that the identity you have created within your mind is a ball of thoughts, opinions, experiences, fears, likes and preferences that you have kept and become identified with over time. Everyone we know has done it and we've all come to believe that it is who we are, relating to this mass of thought to give ourselves uniqueness and meaning. We've essentially attached to lots of arbitrary things over time and started to play a part based upon them. We have already learned that this identity is truly an illusion and a series of subjective choices, arrived at more by chance than planning. We are not bound by any of it and, most importantly, it is fundamentally *not* who we are at all.

We now have a progressive method to unpick it and change our relationship with it, to become the watcher, to change its patterns and to react or not to react, based on a new set of rules and perspective. We are now starting to liberate from it and play by our own rules and we have a new life ahead.

So, that's of course a very detailed recap. That is because the question that now rises to the surface is the big one: if you are not this mind identity and you are the watcher of it, then who are you really? Wow. This is a cool thing, isn't it? We are now looking at ourselves from a totally different perspective and realising that our "self", the watcher, is able to see the mind almost from above and simply observe it – and, more to the point, can choose to completely disregard and ignore it at will. It has become the annoying friend who won't be quiet but who we can listen to fully or totally disregard, humouring it and smiling but without needing any consideration of the content.

So, who or what *is* the watcher? If you are not your ball of thoughts and mind-created identity – which you clearly are not – then who are you? Another great question now is, "Who do you feel like you are?" Before you have a deep think about that on the deepest level possible, it might help if I answer that question for myself. Sitting here writing this book, I am just here being. I am alive and in this moment; I am simply experiencing the moment while typing on a keyboard. I am doing this in "flow state", without truly knowing what words will come out until I see them on the page in front of me.

If I go a little deeper into "who I am", I can feel temperature; there are smells and the sound of birds; I feel at peace and calm and I am not thinking as such in any way. I can sense and feel my environment around me and, although it is hard to describe, in this moment I simply feel alive. While I guess I am somehow in my body, I'm not totally sure that I truly feel that is where I am. I look at what I am doing and because my eyes and ears are located in my head I seem to have a bias of feeling in that area, but on closer inspection that feeling of awareness and aliveness seems to be around and all over my body too. The me that is here doesn't feel like any particular part of my body; it feels like I'm in the general vicinity of my body. To be truthful it's weird and it's difficult to articulate. Maybe you should do the same while reading or listening, so that we can compare our notes. After all, direct experience is always the best judge and is what we need for this part of the masterclass.

One interesting aspect of this feeling of aliveness is that as I write this I am forty-seven years old, yet I can't ever remember that anything felt any different than it does today at any point in my life. In becoming present and taking away all thoughts; I simply feel like I just *am*. I am here. I am aware and I am certainly alive. I know it. I also believe that I felt just the same present aliveness when I was a child. This feeling of awareness and aliveness hasn't got older or changed with the age of my body; it appears unrelated and unaltered by the fact that my mind has grown in its collection of thoughts, knowledge, skills and experiences. I think the feeling of "just being" has been the same forever. In fact, I can't ever remember not "being" or imagine the idea of not "being" at some point in the future either. This "being" part is definitely the watcher for me and it seems very constant and always there – except of course when I'm asleep, when I suppose it's present only in my dreams.

Obviously the mind activity isn't involved in the being part, so when we set that to one side we seem to be left with the bit that is simply aware of where it is and how that looks and feels. The mind may comment on every situation we're in, but we know the situation before the mind gets round to narrating it. If it's cold we don't need the mind to tell us; we're just cold. Then the mind says, "It's cold." Our awareness sees everything in front of us before the one-by-one observations begin. Whether that's the "There's a car", "a tree", "a bird", "a table" type of narration or the kind based in judgement, like "That's beautiful", "she's pretty", "I don't like that" and so on. This watcher, awareness or aliveness – call it what you will – seems to be directly plugged into the five bodily senses and is directly "experiencing" what we see, hear, smell, touch and taste. It appears to be the immediate experiencer of everything and that includes emotions too.

Maybe that's a great way to define and think of it as we move forward – *immediate situational awareness*. It is constant and is allowing us to experience our world before and actually in substitution of any and all need to think. It is just being and it uses the senses of the body and the emotions to create the endless series of experiences that we are and have. I say "are" and "have" because there's little difference between being the experience and having the experience; you're always part of the experiences you have and they cannot happen without us. The "you" that's aware of those experiences, that is.

The important thing here is that those experiences happen well before the mind gets involved. They are always complete, in real time; a live experience of the true present moment. They have no judgement attached and have no thought; they are pure and rich and, without the distraction of mind activity, often intense. That, for me, seems to be what the watcher is: my aliveness in and awareness of the present moment in all of its sensory forms. I really don't have to think about it at all to "know" and experience it; experience happens across my whole body and the aliveness is in and around it all. Of course, it may or may not be different for you.

The idea of being has been studied, described and analysed for thousands of years and across almost all cultures on the globe – and interestingly nearly all of these explorations arrive in a similar place with similar conclusions. Many cultures have made being the centre point of their existence. This is especially true of the yogis of India and the Buddhists, who have over time – and without any distorted religious thought or constructs – really analysed the nature and operation of this conscious watcher, with some amazing results. One common finding that it's pertinent to mention right now is that this watcher is also the seat of instinct and knowing. This may or may not be one of a number of further senses, or it may well be something distinctly different; but as it is relevant to peaceful decision-making it's certainly worth deeper consideration here.

Over the course of the last few chapters, I have discussed my writing in the context of the flow state in which I've learned to operate – as I've suggested, this state means that I don't see the need for thought in order to create these words and find myself fascinated by what arrives on the page. We've also discussed the deeper "knowing" that is inherent in you reading this book and, more to the point, the concepts within it. How we can somehow *know* what is right, and feel familiar with something without ever having come across it before – so it feels more like something you knew and forgot than something you're only just learning.

This is a form of what we may well have come to call instinct or intuition, which I'm guessing is a concept we're all familiar with and agree on: the notion that you "just know" when something is right or wrong when exposed to almost any given situation. We've also discussed the idea of surrendering to what is and to the flow of the universe; of being fluid and going where that instinct or knowing takes you, even if it's not where your planning said you would go. This relies wholly on the sense of "knowing" in order to follow a path presented to you by life and constitutes a form of trust that the universe has your back. This knowing is instinct and it comes before thought as part of the watcher and awareness present within it.

This watcher or awareness is the one that is going to watch our thoughts and allow us time to decide upon our reactions, if any; the one that is the only thing in play when we're truly present and aware and the one that is guiding our best decisions. "Knowing" is literally the same awareness that is seeing, smelling, tasting, touching and hearing. Just as importantly, this awareness is the one that "knows" instinctively without the addition of needless thought and debate and it is the one that feels on an emotional level too, giving us the most fully rounded experience. It is the leading edge of our reality, creating the experiences, putting all of the information together instantly in the present moment and is the one with the ultimate intelligence to take us forward on the best and right path. It is a state found when you are truly present. It is also the one that is, unfortunately, in the background to the mind until the mind identity is removed.

Furthermore, the watcher appears to be the driver of the body too; and while we go about our lives thinking and doing, it seems to be there making everything work and allowing us to sense, experience, be alive and self-repair. Intriguingly – and I don't know if this is just my own strange thought – it also appears to be totally independent of the body on almost every level. What I mean by that is that I'm pretty certain this awareness and watcher is not related to any one part of the body – and thus *the* body – in any way. The reason I believe this is that it has felt the same whether I was seven or forty-seven in vastly different and totally regenerated bodies. It has not changed at all with the body. There are people out there losing arms, legs, vital organs and more, and it seems to remain constant and unchanged, no matter what parts of the body are lost or remain. It appears to be "just there" in all things that are alive.

Indeed, this same awareness seems to exist until the body itself dies; it may lose sight or hearing if those sensors go, but otherwise its nature or function appears uninterrupted. It is the me I have come to know – and while I have been distracted for much of my life by thought, this essence of aliveness and awareness is always me and always constant. Maybe you agree or maybe you don't. Again, this feels like something I "just know" to be true; and I for one have come to trust that "knowing" entirely and very much more than I've trusted any thought that has ever entered my head.

Chapter 13: Is this life itself?

In Douglas Adams's *The Hitchhiker's Guide to the Galaxy* a supercomputer takes several years to work out the "Answer to the ultimate question of life, the universe and everything" – which turns out to be 42. We're going to explore our own version of the same question in a little more detail, which should not only bring about a more useful answer but also help anyone who's still experiencing resistance at the moment.

This is a great juncture to reiterate that we're in this to help you to truly "love life" and the purpose of this masterclass is to show you the things that will best serve you moving forward. If you are experiencing resistance, remember that "proof" is not essential to "knowing"; the scientific theories in this chapter are just part of a much deeper learning. That said, I'm happily anticipating that for the majority the concept of knowing is becoming increasingly loud, meaning that resistance is at this point all but gone. If that's the case for you, then you're in great shape for profound change. If not, that's OK too. The mind likes to think about everything too much but it will be impossible for it to rationalise a lot of the content here without the knowing part kicking in. It does also hate to give up control in favour of a greater intelligence, though, so hang on for a bumpy ride until it finally goes quiet. Believe me, it will in the end.

In our quest to become the watcher and observer of our mind, we have now considered what that entity is and where it lives. In my world it is somewhere in and around the whole body; it is the aliveness and awareness that basically produces every experience and it is the part of me that "does" before my mind has time to add its relatively slow thinking to everything. It is what we use during the flow state and it's the seat of knowing and instinct, co-ordinating all of your senses and into a more complete picture or interpretation of the present moment. It requires no thought and seems to be the ultimate difference in being alive or not. With it, we can just be here in the present; without it, well, we wouldn't be anywhere.

Before we directly address the question in the chapter title, there are a few things that it would really help us to think about or know deeply as a starting point or foundation. The question of what the universe is and what makes it all work in the wonderful way it does is relevant but warrants a complete book of its own; so for now it's better to consider a smaller subset of that huge conundrum. Since its inception the purpose of physics has been specifically to answer that massive question and it's done a pretty good job, arriving at many useful conclusions that provide some interesting insight into what drives the universe and what it's actually made of. There's a long answer to this and a much shorter one that rests on the conclusions. Here we're going to try to give enough detail without anyone needing to become a physicist to understand it. Note that to this end we're going to rely predominantly on Einstein for the science, as this has become the accepted and pretty much unified scientific version of what we believe is our reality.

Since the science of physics was created it has been investigating the base particle, the thing that everything else is made from. Early on, there were those who loved the idea that the universe was all brought together by chance and explained to some degree by chaos theory; but the fact that everything is too perfectly ordered and organised to be the product of chance or probability has all but dispensed with that school of thought. Consequently there came the quest to split the atom and split what was found within it again and again in order to find out what is underlying everything – the theory being that there must be a basic building block and it must have some form of intelligence. So off they go, smashing the atom over and over, trying to find out what everything is made of. They have often called this the search for the god particle: the base substance or thing that is behind the creation of everything.

These physicists have done well! Between them all and using huge cyclotrons, lots of brain power and maths, they have smashed the atoms to find the smallest of the smallest particles, things or whatever words one should use to describe them. (These so-called god particles are actually not a "thing" and have been described as "waves", "possibilities" and more.) The work is ongoing but the question of what the universe is made of appears to have been largely answered and they've found some pretty complex and quirky results around the subject too. For the non-physicists among us, Einstein's theory of relativity essentially declares that the universe is made of energy that is itself fundamentally based on light. In other words, a form of light was the basis of everything and depending on its vibrational frequency it would manifest as all of the differing things, substances, gases and so on in the universe. This conclusion is now pretty much agreed and means that on some level the universe is simply a projection of light. For many this translates into the notion that life and the universe is in effect like a movie that we're all actually of and living in, which is an interesting way to look at it. When we consider that that the universe is also like a mathematical equation then us mere-mortal non-genius types have some real food for thought.

Here, however, we should stick to what is useful and what will serve us in our quest to "love life" moving forward. Bear in mind that this is an extremely simplified summary, but... The fact that the whole of everything is at its core made from one base thing is a great place to start. The base thing is also essentially light, so that's great too. That one thing then vibrates at differing frequencies to produce protons and electrons and then molecules, creating the different "things" in the universe. When I say everything is made of the same thing I really do mean everything. There is no end to this stuff and the gases, the air, the life, the elements, you, me, our cars and our houses, the planets, space and *everything* are all made from a sea of it vibrating at various different frequencies. (Physicists please forgive me.)

In addition to all that, it's useful to discuss something known as the "observer effect", which was discovered by physicists observing electrons to try to establish what they actually were – whether they were a mass, energy, a product of light, etc. Very simply explained, the observer effect means that the act of observing the electrons actually changed their behaviour and whether, how and as what they presented themselves. It showed that they could literally come into and out of existence as if at will and could be a wave, a particle, a probability or some other physics stuff just like that.

Further, and really weirdly, there was also some sort of relationship between the nature of the experiment being performed (in terms of what it was looking for) and the behaviour of the electrons. The suggestion seemed to be that they were affected by the conscious awareness itself and the findings that were being sought. If the scientists were looking for a mass, they found mass; if they were looking for light, they found light, and so on. The fact that electrons could also be manifest and unmanifest showed that they could instantaneously change form from one frequency to another, becoming invisible again at the higher frequencies. All I can say is that this seems super clever.

These conclusions seem to be the most relevant to us here; and (without decreeing anything true or proven) they also seem to imply a few other things that conveniently serve our purpose on the masterclass. Firstly, that everything is essentially made of the same basic thing and we live in a sea of that with no beginnings and no ends. This means there are no true edges to anything. The table you see in your room, sat within the space around it, is simply a change in frequency of light particles from higher to lower, where they make up and manifest as molecules of a gas or solids and different substances. Secondly, the idea that the whole world is a projection of light at different frequencies also appears to hold true – and that means that we're each actually and intrinsically very much part of the space around us, as well as the body we see. We and the space are all just a continuum of light presenting at differing frequencies.

Our perception of the world is then based on our senses, which are designed to interpret these projections as solids, gases, life, sound, light, colour, heat, cold and so on. I know some of this frequency stuff sounds strange, so maybe it is useful to understand how frequency can perceivably change a solid to a gas and how that same frequency can affect everything about our perception. To explain this, I can use the example of a simple fan. If the blades spin slowly – i.e. have a low frequency – we can poke our fingers between the gaps and perceive only space and nothing solid. As the blades spin faster and faster, we gain an increasingly solid perspective of the fan until at super high speed (faster than any fan really goes) the blades would be perceived as a solid, offering us the ability to touch them and feeling like a surface rather than spinning blades. Yet when the fan is not spinning we can see that the circle the blades sit within is as much space as it is blades.

So, we are all part of this "endless" sea of light and we none of us begin and end; there are no edges, just changes in frequency – and they manifest as the elements we see and perceive. This concept has wide-reaching implications because it essentially means that we do not *live* in the universe but rather we *are* the universe. We are simply a part of this sea of the same thing and we are not just connected to it but actually part of a singular whole and indeterminable from the rest of it on just about every level. And you thought you were an individual...?

As Einstein's theory of relativity seems to indicate, the whole universe is energy and the whole universe is light. What's important to us on the masterclass, over and above the fact that we're here in a sea of light with no beginning or end, is the deeper consideration that light energy is also intelligently organised and itself intelligent. It is affected by awareness and consciousness and very likely to actually *be* a sea of consciousness. After all, when we contemplate the behaviours of the electrons being observed and then changing their manifestation and behaviour according to the observation, this probably shows some sort of intelligence and on a conceptual level perhaps a direct connection with consciousness.

For instance, think about the cells of the human body: autonomously repairing themselves, healing wounds, killing disease and so on. In these we can see that autonomous intelligence exists in the smallest of things. All of these cells work together to make the whole and play their part in this universal miracle that is created from them. Likewise experiments in modern physics make clear that electrons and their smaller composites can change their form instantaneously and can manifest as any form they "choose". This question of choice and connection to the bigger organism is complex but seems to be becoming the best answer to what we can see. It means that the whole universe and everything in it is in reality a single organism made up of parts that all work together to be what it is and quite probably to experience itself from an endless number of perspectives.

Why does this all matter? Well, because it means that consciousness appears to be life itself. It seems to be a form of intelligent energy, shared by the whole universe and ultimately pliable in the sense of becoming anything at all almost instantaneously. What an amazing idea. This means that we do not have "a life"; we *are* life. A pool of infinitely intelligent energy that has created the whole universe and *is* also everything in it – including you. Are you with me so far?

OK. We should now return to the idea that there is our mind identity, our awareness and essentially our body too. That everything is made from conscious intelligent light and that within that we have created thoughts as a form for ourselves too, which are also just another form of light with yet another frequency. These thoughts make up our mind identity but our connected consciousness is our aliveness and is clearly in the driving seat. This is the awareness, consciousness or "you" that is simply alive and aware. It is the field of consciousness that is the watcher and the experiencer we've been discussing. It is the one taking all of the senses and turning them into perception and it is the one that operates well before thought.

Most importantly, it is the you and awareness that is connected to everything else. It is a direct part of the whole – the sea of consciousness – and it is connected to all of the other intelligent consciousness in the universe as a part of a singular, universal organism. An organism that's apparently aiming to experience itself from an endless number of perspectives; hence the number of things and living things in existence. These are big ideas, I know, but please stay with me.

Perhaps you wish to resist this line of enquiry on the basis that it conflicts with long-held beliefs in the depths of your mind identity, or perhaps it "feels totally true" to you. In any case the conclusions it brings are incredibly visible in life and give rise to much that we all experience and see day in, day out and from moment to moment. We don't in fact need to rely on science for complex proof of it all, because the truth of it can be seen, felt and experienced by each and every one of us almost constantly in everyday life and with a greater awareness of nature itself.

We also now see that we can function without thought; that once we become the watcher, we can feel and "know" our way through life. We can connect with what nature wants and deliver intelligence at different and higher levels than thought alone could ever provide. As I write in this state of flow it is through connection, not mind energy. As we've already discussed, creativity is found without thought, not by trying to think about a problem; answers come with little or no effort if we allow them to. When we're plugged into the universal-consciousness grid, the "I am" is more like the "we are", giving us access to unlimited universal intelligence if we so decide. It requires no force or effort, just a quietness of mind that gives unobstructed access to our abundant, true creativity.

We spend our lives identifying with the wrong part of us – a voice in our head made of meaningless thought, experience, the past and fear – when alongside it is our awareness, waiting to take over but drowned out by the constant chatter. If this is a sea of consciousness and that consciousness is life itself, then we have been sidetracked and distracted by mind noise, reason and an illusion of self and identity. Truth is everywhere; it takes only a moment's consideration of nature around us to be totally convinced of that. And then scientific theory converges with what we instinctively know: that the whole of the universe and everything in and of it is this wonderfully organised, incomprehensible but intelligent system. We are part of it and we are inseparable from any other part too.

So "I am" consciousness and you are consciousness. If that is life itself, then great. If not, it has to be close. We don't have our own consciousness because we are part of a single consciousness. We are all the same thing, connected and aware, and we offer this universal organism different perspectives of itself. We are life and we don't have life. Interestingly, science now to some degree reflects the understanding at the root of almost all religions (though religions have throughout history been misinterpreted, misrepresented and dogmatised so they now barely resemble their foundations).

Certainly the sea of consciousness or intelligent energy we're discussing here could easily be interpreted as the god figure seen across any and all religions. It is in everything and pervades everything; it is what everything is made of and it is eternal. While it serves no purpose here to debate or define religion, if we see god as this basic consciousness and everything created from it as the "son of god", this picture of our universe seems to fit the basis of most religions perfectly. No rules, no figure head, no personification, and no need for imposed thought structures.

The term "spiritual" is much misunderstood but has a very simple meaning. It is not religious or even related to religion in any way. Rather, it is a description of the movement of our identification away from our body and mind, which are both temporal, towards identification with our conscious being, spirit, intelligent energy or consciousness, whichever word suits you best. That means moving from past and future to the present; to a state of flow, and to becoming the watcher and the experiencer not the thinker and reflector. It means staying out of the past and not imaginatively creating and attaching to the future and it means releasing the trapped energies that make life so hard and full of overthinking. As already noted, the Buddhists and Indian spiritualists are especially focused on the discovery of and connection with this conscious intelligence. In fact many of the ways in which they seek to utilise it are echoed within the principles in this masterclass, so through them we can see how useful so much of it really is when it's lived to the maximum.

What matters for the masterclass is that we're clear that there is mind and there is consciousness; that intelligence lies in neither the latter nor the former and that we can connect and use it to our advantage to bring us true peace. How we see it is of little importance, but consciousness is everywhere and it is the "I am" that changes everything if we identify with it. This is a masterclass in how to truly love life, but it also represents many of the same concepts held in the idea of spiritual awakening plus a few more besides. Call it what you will but this is the route to the only freedom that truly exists: the freedom from the mind illusion of identity and entry in to your real identity; when you *become* the intelligent consciousness that you are.

Chapter 14: My body as a vehicle

Our focus so far has been on this mind, the ego, the illusion of our self that won't be quiet and the false identity that rules our lives. We have been moving towards becoming the conscious experiencer instead, and making a transition to being able to watch and choose our thoughts, and our reactions to thoughts and emotions, rather than identifying with and becoming them in an inescapable hell of meaningless mind noise.

In the previous chapters we have also touched upon the relationship between the mind, body and consciousness. This relationship is truly important if we're to reach our goal and truly love life. We have already looked at where consciousness lives and where the "I am" in us is. Is it in our head or the whole body, around it or outside it? We've considered how much control we have, and how the body works to allow us to experience our surroundings, how it repairs itself and manages itself without any of our conscious input. So how does all that relate to who we are and how we can be happy, or to our purpose and to life itself?

This is where the "knowing" of the consciousness will grow louder and stronger for most of you. Consider now how you're feeling about the discovery that everything in the universe is made of the same thing, varying only in frequency, and about the idea that this base thing is light, life or consciousness itself. Have you looked within at your perception of actually just being in the world? Have you considered where your awareness lives and how it feels to be alive, perceiving the world around you? Are you now regularly present and are you starting to feel the ultimate vibrancy of the world, which grows stronger in that state of conscious present focus? If so, do you accept the connection of all things and the sea of consciousness being a single organism, simply trying to experience itself from the perspective of a tree, a plant, the grass, the sea, the animals, the birds and humanity among millions of other things, including you and everyone you know? Well, it's now time now to consider what the body actually is and what part it really plays in that idea of the universe.

In fact it makes little difference whether you accept the above idea as true. The body appears to be a simple vehicle for consciousness to experience itself. It has at least five senses that are interpretable by your consciousness in order to experience everything around it. It has feelings and emotions and is a system by which the ultimate experience is possible. It can travel and move in this sea of universe and can perceive everything within it through feeling and deep awareness. It has also developed a clever mind where it stores the past and creates versions of the future, continually applying them to new scenarios and trying to control its environment.

This body is an amazing machine controlled by a field of intelligence all around it, like a remote-control, fully automatic, self-repairing vehicle that works at a subatomic level to manage its ability to richly experience every moment. If it gets cut, it heals. If it's attacked by disease (which is another form of the universe experiencing itself), then it defends itself and generally recovers. The old saying that doctors don't heal you but your body does is eternally true. A doctor may set the bones straight but it is the body that works the healing magic. It grows and gets stronger, gaining broader different experiences, then peaks and retracts, moving elegantly towards death. All the while the same exact consciousness, unchanging and un-aging, is the ultimate experiencer, often dictating direction and instinctively finding new and varied experiences.

This body is complex and as well as senses has an intricate heart (in the sense of centre, not organ) made of systems that measure energy as emotion that it stores and works with to deepen each and every experience. In previous chapters we've spoken about the freeing of energy and the holding of pain and attachments that come with doing so. The body works to experience in depth and detail that is impossible to describe; overall, though, it seems really clear that everything it is and does serves its fundamental impetus as a vehicle for experience.

In our search for purpose we need to give this only slight consideration to see that this body was clearly made to experience and to do so in the richest and deepest ways possible. Senses, thoughts, feelings and emotions are all in there; love and pain, joy and sadness – in fact everything, because this is the splendour of the universe and nothing is to be preferred and nothing avoided. The body is there to reason and to figure things out, to calculate and to make use of its findings. This vehicle was built for the ultimate experience; to take consciousness on an adventure and to feel all the knocks and, without interference from mind and memory, to experience then let go of it all as fast as it happens. It's perfectly built and it is truly amazing. If consciousness is life then the body is its vehicle to take (and richly feel) the amazing ride.

The picture I'm creating is one of consciousness driving each and every body and mind through a series of the richest possible experiences. Of us taking a body at birth, it taking its first breath and then taking us on a full and unpredictable journey of experiences and perceptions, happiness and sadness in a purposeful aim to experience the whole universe – of which it is an inseparable part, just like the consciousness itself. This all makes total sense to me. It's reasonable and logical; it stacks up and it all fits and what feels right usually is. It makes sense to a growing number of other people too – and hopefully by the end of this masterclass it will make the same sense to you. I say hopefully because if it does, you will have removed fear and installed clear purpose and have the ultimate source of freedom and peace. I really can't wait to show you.

This amazing body and mind may appear to be who you are. After all, this is what you can see and feel. It's the conduit for every experience you have and it's not surprising that most of humanity has gotten lost in it and identified with the body or the mind or a little bit of both in some way or another. The consequence of that, though, is that most of us feel individual within the universe. We see our minds and bodies as a separate entity from the whole, and often place ourselves in competition with it, rather than existing in its obvious flow. This is understandable, given that we can't see this sea of consciousness and everything looks like lots of separate elements outside us being brought together with space in between them. But in reality, as we know now, there is no space and there's no such thing as nothing. There's only an endless sea of a single thing vibrating at different frequencies all over the universe, a sea we are just a part of and not separate from at all.

A confusing factor in this is that humanity has been slowly making discovery after discovery. There have been versions of the truth throughout all of human time and they have changed and been reset time and time again. We have been searching for proof and analysis, and getting so deeply involved in it that most of us have failed to simply look outside and see the complexity and wonder of nature and the world as it really is. The truth is there – it's obvious and visible; we just need to leave the past and future for long enough to see it in the present.

Of these many scientific discoveries, one in particular looked like real proof of our separateness and uniqueness. Thanks to genetics we have seen our differences and know that we are all uniquely programmed with a genetic strand that contains everything we are and defines us all as totally distinct from each other. In fact we believed it was so unique that we made it into a way of proving identity beyond any doubt. It was believed to be that complex; that there are sufficient combinations to make us all totally unique.

The assumption was that we're born with a certain genetic sequence or pattern and remain that forever. A genius, a painter, a plumber, a writer... You get the picture. Spoiler alert: this assumption has since changed in some really key ways and our understanding is now starkly different. We now know that we are all born with every single gene: the gene for genius, artist, dancer and runner... All of them, for everything – and there are millions. They are all there in all of us but when we're born only some are expressive and some are recessive, meaning that we show some traits and are deficient in others. Originally it was thought that the code endured forever but numerous more recent experiments are now proving that it can be purposefully or accidentally changed over time.

It has been found and proven that a combination of thought, emotion, changes of behaviour and patterns and the movement of energy, coupled with a purposeful intent to change, can cause new parts of your genes to express and others to become recessive. You can literally reprogram yourself by means of intent, mind and emotion. Now, if ever there was an opportunity for change, maybe that really is it. It's well worth reading the books from Dr Joe Dispenza to see this in action.

What does this mean? It means that our bodies have a start point inherited from our parents. We are not locked into any of it, though, and have ultimate choice about who or what we want to be and become. Nothing is cast in stone and we can exercise our choice to vary our behaviour, set an intention and feel our way into a new pattern and expression. This matters to us at this point in the masterclass because it supports the reality of consciousness being life and the body and mind comprising a vehicle for experience. If we can start with a pre-programmed body and mind but reprogram it with certain "conscious" actions, then it would appear to be a simple tool to be used as we wish during its lifetime and with unlimited possibilities.

Much of this masterclass is and has been about our identification with a mind-created identity and ultimately with our body too. The current step is all about giving this context and gaining an understanding of who you are and what you can and should identify with and as. The human condition seems to love to get trapped in the overthinking mind – in fact you're possibly here for that reason – but it also gets trapped in the body too. All too often it comes to believe that who you are is a product of the two together. This equates to the statement: "I am actually a product of my experiences and my history and I am also in part the body that facilitated those experiences, even though what is true is that I have been the same awareness, having conscious experiences, for all the time I can remember." There's a clear mistake in there somewhere.

I was about to say that when we buy and drive a car we don't become and identify with it. But interestingly that's exactly what you do. As part of that mind-created ego identity, we identify with anything and everything we pick up along the way or experience. It often actually is a car, a house, a boat or our designer clothes, handbags, badges and "things" in general. Not surprising then that we make the same mistake with our mind and body: they are simply a vehicle for experience but we've failed to see the much bigger picture – that being of course that we are essentially consciousness and part of an almost endless sea of connected consciousness that is riding around in bodies and things, simply to experience itself.

This is a pivotal moment in our transformational journey and more life-changing than any other. Right now there's a fork in the road that relates to our choice to identify with mind and body or to identify fully and wholly with our conscious awareness, intelligent life energy or spirit. What we call it is irrelevant but the extent to which we accept and identify with it is everything. I for one have come to know that consciousness is who I am at the core. I see the ego identity that I created and I watch it always. I see it overthinking; I hear the endless voice and, as the watcher, I choose to react or not to react. It has been transformative to see my own ego for what it is and also to consider my body as my own personal vehicle.

My personal body is a 1973 model and while it's not perfect it does seem to get me to the places and the broad range of experiences that come to me endlessly. It enables me to keenly see, hear, feel, taste and smell what I need in order that I can experience the amazing, unpredictable adventures that life continues to throw at me moment by moment. It has deep emotions and a heart full of energies that make the feeling of life so much richer and my experiences run much deeper than I suspect they would otherwise do. This is an experiencing machine of the highest calibre; it could not have been built better for that specific purpose – or at least not in a way that I can think of anyway. Though who knows what upgrades a year-3000 model will have.

By this method I have also learned not only to abstract myself from the thought ball of my past experiences, pains, thoughts, experiences and attachments but also to clearly see the human illusion that caused it all, exactly for what it is: an illusion. That in no way represents a decision to exit the world as it currently is; it's simply a firm understanding that my *purpose* is not in that illusion – but the illusion can be played as a really fun game without nearly as much anxiety, pain or consequence.

This means that my contextual understanding of where I identify, and with what, is definitely now within the consciousness. It means that I clearly see my purpose in life as simply to experience without preference or holding on to things that I arbitrarily call good or bad, or that I like or dislike. This is a "spirit" driving seat for the body and mind that allows for joy in all situations. It has no preferences or judgements. It works for me; it makes total sense and it has been transformative in terms of peace, love, fear and happiness.

You might be wondering right now what that looks like. Happy? No overthinking? From this seat we watch and we don't need to react. It is not a Get Out of Jail Free card – the mind still takes over once in a while. Rather it is a state of being where we can become centred again and see the mind, body and world around us for what they really are. There, we can inhabit a constant series of present-moment adventures and they can all be fun, even the sad and scary ones. There is no rigid attempt to control the universe, although some goals and actions make the game great fun. It's about enjoying every situation and every action taken more than chasing destinations or imagined futures. It's about realising that this is a choice and how we feel is our own responsibility; and it allows us to have the experiences that don't go as planned or create fear or sadness because we can immediately drop the memory and leave it inert and fully let go of, never to be relived or seen again.

I said that this was a watershed in the masterclass and it really is. At this point you either have a clear appetite to make the change or you don't. We're at that fork in the road and you have the choice. You've already begun to move your identification away from the ego and the mind-created identity driven by the past; if you take the leap you'll undoubtedly still carry some of it for a while because the process is not instant. It really is worth the practice and effort though. You have the basic principles you need in order to take this action. The practice of presence is of course pivotal and the understanding of identity, the human illusion, the way to live and approach judgement and the conceptual understanding of the universe are all key too. You can choose to believe and take action or to resist and remain where you are. So: are you in or out?

Chapter 15: A relationship game-changer

I'm now really excited for you. If you have come this far, you are taking the whole journey and have committed to changing your whole life for the better. Well done to you for making the best decision possible. Quite probably, you have made that decision from a seat of "knowing" rather than in your mind, and without all of the evaluation and debate that the mind brings with it. As a little indulgence, I am also pleased with myself for having explained things well enough to gain your buy-in and understanding. These concepts really can be a challenge to take in and make peace with. As you'll have already seen, the mind dwells on insignificant details that it seems to want not to understand or that challenge what it "thinks" it knows. All the while, the consciousness watches and knows but doesn't get a look in, drowned out by all the mind noise.

You are now part of the ever-growing number taking this step. Don't be fearful of the term but part of this process, if actioned well, will result in the real meaning of spiritual awakening. Remember: this is not a religious term; it's simply defined as the movement of you, and what you identify with, away from body and mind and towards consciousness itself. It really is that uncomplicated yet is the ultimate liberation.

As someone who now has a fundamental and actually fairly deep understanding of ego and how it was created, you are now moving towards spirit and becoming increasingly close to living in the seat of consciousness. Consequently, and as we continue, you will likely start to see some profound and significant effects on your experiences and life. These may well create some flux within you and give you a very different perspective on the world and the people around you. It's worth us spending some time to discuss this because there'll likely be some interesting and possibly difficult moments ahead. If they've already begun, just know that this is great news because it says that you're learning and that your practice has been diligent and committed.

Having seen and understood the ego for what it is, knowing how it was created, you're now likely to be very committed to moving your identification away from it and towards your seat of consciousness. As you start to do this, seeing and understanding your own ego even more, the ego in others will become increasingly and often starkly visible to you.

As you begin to see yourself essentially as three components – the mind, body and consciousness or spirit – you will also begin to see those same components in others. This will inevitably change your perspective on many of the people you know and meet. As you make the irreversible transition to consciousness yourself, you'll begin to see that almost everyone with whom you come into contact speaks directly from the ego and is not in touch with consciousness at all. Some of the symptoms you'll notice are that they find it hard to listen, they have lots of mind activity, many subjective opinions and they react emotionally and involuntarily to almost everything.

Progressively, as you practice and improve the ability to see your own ego in action, you will then see more and more of the ego dominance in others. This will be most visible in the stored energies that cause them to react slightly or completely irrationally when triggered by the things that happened previously in their lives or the subject of a conversation. You'll see the adversarial nature of the ego and the need for it to be "right", to judge or vehemently defend what it has come to subjectively believe as if it were defending the individual personally.

This is of course because people and their opinions have a tendency to merge, often to the extent that they perceive someone disagreeing with them as a personal attack they must defend. Importantly, they are defending "who they are" and not a simple thought or mind-created view. The fact that all this will become so visible to you will fuel your understanding and progress, so really it's a great thing; nevertheless it can initially be a little shocking to find yourself bombarded by very noticeable and high-impact egos.

You will also begin to see that on a consciousness level we are all the same; from the seat of consciousness and as the observer and experiencer, this becomes increasingly obvious. This awareness and feeling of oneness will really help when your mind is tempted to judge others, as it always does and will for some time yet. In reality, and up until this point in time, you have always been conversing as an ego to the ego in others. As your presence grows, though, you'll begin to converse from a state of consciousness while the majority of others continue to speak with the mind-created identity – conscious individuals are, after all, few and far between. However, please don't run away with that and make it a part of a whole new ego identity to replace the old one.

This is not a destination; it is a state of mind while in life's journey. You will be happily conscious until you suddenly wake up during a conversation or activity and realise that you got lost in mind once again. So there is no judgment of others who speak from ego and it must not be allowed to become frustrating either. Focus on being present yourself and the conscious awareness of others and simply accept their involuntary ego reactions. The Bible phrase "Forgive them for they know not what they do" is a great motto to apply here.

Your newfound sight makes forgiveness inherent and easy – because when you can see the ego entity with all its history and pain for what it is, how could you not forgive it for anything it says or does? After all, it is not the being of the person in front of you in any way, it's a thought illusion made of the past and pain and experiences. Our earlier principle of unconditional forgiveness is now incredibly important and far easier to live and action. There simply is no place for blame in your life.

Remember that we are all connected entities and essentially the same. If you have really understood and identified with the concepts around the sea of consciousness or life in which we exist and the connected nature of everything, you will now be very clear that you really are not a separate being. You are not all alone as a separate entity in a great big universe; you are inseparable from any and all parts of it, at one with all of it and every other being in it. It is a unity.

For a great comparative example we can once again consider the cells in your body. They are seemingly individual and they all have their own purpose. They are running around living that purpose as part of the bigger organism and when they're required to do something they move to the appropriate part of the body and they do it. They are intelligent and in order to make the whole thing work they do things that you don't ever know about and could never understand or comprehend. Are they part of your body? Yes. Are they sort of independent? Yes. Separate, no, but do they work independently on their own purpose, it seems so.

This is just like you operating within the universe. You are moving around serving your purpose (which is of course simply to experience) and while doing so you are clearly and essentially also being an integral part of the whole singular organism. Remember: you do not *have* life, you *are* life. You are not *in* the universe; you *are* the universe. You are not separate from it, you are it. That is the crucial thing and by the way it all just works perfectly. Everything plays a part in the whole but is equally one with the whole too.

This connectedness clearly means that you are no more separate from other people than you are separate from the universe. You are one with everything. They are you and you are them and the sea of conscious energy is clearly without edges or boundaries between you and them.

Within this fact are the most interesting consequences and reality, which strongly relate to our previous discussions on blame and judgement. How? When you judge others or any situation, place or event as part of the singularity, you are simply judging yourself, whether directly or indirectly. Because you are connected and part of the same organism, when you blame others you are directly or indirectly also blaming yourself. In a world where everyone was separate, your blame would move from you to "them"; but in this reality, where there really is no "them" but just a single organism, putting your blame on anything at all is simply putting guilt-inducing blame on yourself.

Removing blame from your life really is a fundamental of your transformational journey. Hard for anyone who's been wronged and bears grudges, but necessary nevertheless. The principle of unity now starts to demonstrate another reason why the process of removing blame on others will always remove all blame from ourselves, much of which is a weight we feel subconsciously if not consciously. This relates to blame for anything, major and minor, no matter how small. In a world where you don't accept or believe in blame, you will never feel guilt of any kind. You will have removed guilt from the world. It is that simple.

We are all part of the same endless, edgeless sea of consciousness. We are all one. This means that if we love unconditionally, we love everyone and everything, ourselves included. If we blame anything or anyone, we blame ourselves, every time. Blame, judgement, love, fear – all of it – is always of ourselves as much as it is of what we perceive in our minds to be separate. Bottom line: unconditional love is the future; and in a world where you are conscious and see ego for what it is, it is also easy and fully understandable.

This is a huge concept, and one for the good of the whole of humanity. It brings unconditional love to the whole world and more specifically to the whole of the universal organism. When as humanity we see the whole, things, ourselves and everyone else for what they are – just a part of this connected sea of consciousness – the only energy possible is love and oneness. Imagine that. In that world there is simply no need for blame and no need for forgiveness. These are old ego- and mind-created ideas. They are simply not the truth or part of the truth and can be lost along with mind identity and ego.

Unity makes everyone and everything equally deserving of love; and while sitting in the seat of consciousness we are well placed to be the change we want to see in the world. It allows us to see egos and to remove blame. It allows us to identify, see and communicate with consciousness or – to use the most beautiful word – souls. It is this soul-to-soul communication that has no race, colour or any form of judgement within it. This has to be the basis for the world that nature intended before the mind took a turn for the unexpected and became a dominant, thought-driven machine, storing the past and overlaying it on to the future to create separateness, comparison and competition.

In this chapter we have now hopefully seen your true purpose: to simply become a conscious point of experience in the universe. To take a different place, in the seat of consciousness; and to purely enjoy the unpredictable and constant stream of experiences, without judgement or preference. To open your heart and let everything go as it happens and to delight in each experience without adding needless labels of good or bad, liked or disliked to be used later in some futile attempt at control. To become the watcher of your thoughts and not to identify with or be controlled by them.

Ultimately this is the next stage of human evolution. It is the change that everyone wants but is mostly too wrapped up in egoic thought to see clearly. Having come so far in this masterclass, you are now on the leading edge of that evolution. But remember: do not make a new ego identity out of that status; it is so easy to do and your ego would love that. Just as you lose the old one, a whole new "conscious", superior ego appears, even more disastrous than the last. There is nothing here to attach to or to judge, just a way of being that will first start to transform your own life for the better and then transform the lives of those around you. This is infectious, and you'll likely (as do we) want to share it with as many people as you have access to. Changes this big don't happen often and this is one really worth shouting about.

ZEN JUNGLE

Step 6: Life as the Watcher

Chapter 16 : Endless experiences

What a ride this is! We have covered so much and quite possibly challenged the basis on which you have been living your whole life. The core principles this masterclass is built upon have been around for thousands of years but have over time unfortunately been distorted and essentially hidden from us. That said, for most of us they are both understandable and strangely familiar, even if they are not what we have been conditioned to understand and believe previously. Exciting, isn't it?

We are now a little more than halfway through the overall masterclass but in terms of content much further than that. This means that in order to make the life changes you want the remainder of the book is as much about embedding the principles we have discussed as it is about adding new ones into the mix. Your aim is to form a whole new set of habits and beliefs. You will notice that doing so requires the unlearning of a great many conditioned behaviours and what have become automated reactions and defences. We have all been learning them for as long as we can remember, almost since birth, so they are deeply embedded and often reinforced by everything and everyone around us.

As we progress through the masterclass, the intention is to continue to introduce new ideas while constantly reinforcing change, with techniques that will make the process easier and easier. Together, we will seamlessly help you to create a whole new way of living and a new state of being.

In Chapter 10 you were introduced to the concept of presence and we discussed in detail what it is and how to achieve it. Presence is a fundamental foundation of this masterclass. It facilitates and accelerates many of the mindset changes that we've discussed and gives you the space from your endless thoughts to become abundantly more conscious. In recent chapters, we further developed our understanding of presence and deep significance was given to conscious awareness. We floated the idea of this as our primary state of being and the essence of life itself. We discussed the fact that it's really our natural state; it is our life energy at work and the conduit of all immediate experience, which I suggested was our fundamental purpose in life. We are the one who experiences and we are simply tasked with having those experiences as deeply as possible, in an endless and perpetual sequence, without judgement, preference, resistance or control. We are literally experiential machines of consciousness and a very fortunate vehicle of and for the universe to experience itself.

I really hope that by now you've begun to see this purpose for yourself and have gained an important new perspective on life, welcoming each and every experience you have in every single moment as the unique and beautiful unpredictable adventures they are. This shift in perspective takes you into an ultimately peaceful and relaxed state of being. Interestingly, this conscious state of being is also at a fundamental level the state of presence itself.

Our aim when practicing presence is to be here, now, in this moment with all of our attention focused on it; to experience the "now" as intensely as we possibly can and to remove the background of thinking that otherwise never stops, in favour of absorbing this rich sequence of experiences and adventures. This endless thinking is the very same thinking that has us living in the future or the past permanently, strongly influencing us to ignore and avoid the present moment altogether. If consciousness is life and we are made to experience the present moment in the richest way possible, it stands to reason that we must remain deeply present in order to be there and do that without being sidetracked by thought.

With that aim, it is now time for us to further develop our understanding of presence and to amplify the intensity of this state of being. It takes commitment and diligence to come this far so presumably you are already practicing presence in as many situations as possible and as often as possible throughout your day. We've already noted that without that practice, success in this masterclass is unlikely. Practice is not an optional activity – you have been warned...

In Chapter 10 we spoke about intense thoughtless awareness and learned how to become present by fixing our view on something and removing all thought activity by focusing on the breath or other sensations that reduce the ability of the mind and voice in the head to comment and think. Hopefully that's working really well for you now and has also become your go-to state when you find yourself challenged or anxious. You'll also recall that it was made clear that those frustrating thoughts that pop into your mind while practicing presence are where you can make real progress towards becoming the watcher of those thoughts and to having a quiet mind. They are your friend, not your enemy, and should be welcomed wholeheartedly and fully accepted. This is important because your aim is to become the watcher and observer, not to do battle with your mind or try to resist it.

Together, the previous few chapters now offer a really exciting development in our understanding of the relationship between presence and consciousness and how they can be developed purposefully as a state of being. Presence is conscious awareness, and conscious awareness is the state in which we can truly be the experiencer. It is the state of being where everything is simply the real-time series of experiences of the now, the experiences that happen in every present moment. It has intensity and vibrancy, and it feels joyful and loving. By altering our conceptual perception of presence very slightly, we can also see it as a state of intense, immediate experience without thought. This subtle shift in perspective will allow us to intensify the feelings of aliveness and vibrancy that we've been experiencing so far and multiply it many times over.

In presence you are the conscious *you*, you are now starting to identify with. Presence is *you* fully experiencing the now through a body that has been designed to do just that. Remember: your body is not simply a thinking machine or a vehicle; it has at least five senses that offer surround sound, vision, feeling, taste and smell too. This means that presence is certainly not a one-dimensional state of experience but rather a rich, deep and emotional state with endless vibrancy and intensity. As we start to move what we have so far considered to be presence towards a multisensory experience of the now, our heightened sensation of it will create some amazing feelings and surprises.

It feels profoundly alive to simply focus on the now with only our vision and to become aware of the body and breathing in order to do so. As we now slowly add sound and silence, smell, taste and feeling, it will become far more obvious that this deep experiential state is indeed our most important default and natural state. If the body is for experience, with the use of our conscious awareness, we can begin to blend rich signals from all of our senses and not just the limited subset we have used so far. Obviously, using all five senses may not always be possible but it turns out that using four out of five almost always is – and believe me it has some beautiful and powerful results.

From this moment forward, presence now essentially means "deeply experiencing the now" in as much detail and resolution as is possible. The more senses we can invoke and the more rich and emotional the feeling of love for the moment will be. As we start to practice this new "multi-channel" state of presence, you will start to find that even the most basic and simple of moments can become intense and will feel rich and beautiful. It is now that we start to see just how much time we spend in our minds, rather than where we actually are. We have all been almost permanently locked into thoughts of the future or the past but the feeling of experiencing the present moment with your whole body and senses is so deep and moving you'll wonder why you've never been there before. And by the way, you really haven't.

The mission for today, should you choose to accept it, is to make the state of presence a whole-body and consciousness experience. An intense aliveness in the now. An all-senses awareness of where you are in this moment, in every minute detail possible. This is about opening up the full range of bodily senses and using your consciousness for its intended purpose: the richest possible experience of the universe. It is worth noting here that while the conventional assumption is that the body has only five senses, presence is certainly not limited to just those. Knowing and intuition, connectivity and emotions themselves are also forms of sensual experience and we are certainly not limited to even those. It is thought that we only scratch the surface of our capabilities and have senses that we cannot even imagine at this moment.

If you're thinking that we can always hear, feel, smell and see everything, present or not, then hold that thought. Here is where we really see the power of taking your conscious attention to those senses and truly being in the moment on an all-senses level. Stay with me on this, but in order for you to experience the true depth of the experience available to you, we need to begin a process of extending slowly forward from our sense of vision. Building up to even five-sense awareness takes a little practice and can be a little overpowering, so my suggestion is that we start by adding one extra sense at a time. This is a complete sensory-awareness field that you will soon find has almost never been used. Later in this chapter we'll arrive at the concept of "listening with the whole body". At that point it will become clearer than ever that the body is simply a vehicle for consciousness to experience deeply. For now, though, we should build up slowly – not least because the process is a really beautiful experience, very similar to rediscovering all of your senses over and again.

If you need to get more familiar with Chapter 10 again to remind yourself of presence, please do so now. We're going to be using essentially the same technique, as an addition to what we've already established, so I'll keep the explanation to a minimum to keep it as simple as it really is. I have found over time that there are multiple benefits to performing this extended practice outside in nature, where there's added stimuli to increase the intensity of experience. However, outdoors anywhere is the main thing initially (for reasons that will soon become clear) so you can even start the process while you're walking your dog or heading to the shop. Later you'll be able to perform the activity anywhere at all. Our final aim will be an intense, thoughtless, involved and all-senses awareness of the present moment. Sound easy and exciting? Let's get to it.

So, assuming you're in your chosen outdoor space, we begin as we did before. Take your awareness and conscious focus to the complete view ahead of you, becoming intensely aware of it. This is not intense staring, just you becoming aware of everything around you in its entirety all at once. As before, there is no need for mind activity or to label, question or narrate the scene. In fact, don't. The aim is simple awareness and not to in any way differentiate what we see. As you will know by now, your consciousness is aware of everything you see instantly and has no requirement for your mind to put a name to everything or anything at all. You can, if it helps, also focus on your breathing, watching the breath go all the way in and all the way out. Done simultaneously with seeing and taking in your whole surroundings, this will take up the majority of your consciousness and leave little or no opportunity for your mind to interrupt with involuntary thinking. So you are now present, as you've likely been many times before. Great.

By default, we enter the state of presence and (oddly) become largely unaware of the senses we're not focusing on. We see the scene and we feel the breath but everything else becomes more muted and hazy. How interesting that the subject of our focus intensifies while what we're not focusing on is de-prioritised...

This focusing out is partly the reason that we enter presence in the way we do. The aim is to saturate our conscious mind with one or more focuses other than the mind and thought activity. These normally and consistently take up almost all of your awareness to the detriment of everything else. It seems we have limited usable conscious energy and it is spread across a multitude of bodily functions, senses and the mind. Intensely focusing on what we see in front of us and the breath reduces the amount of consciousness available for the other senses and the mind too, so they essentially become muted or go almost totally unnoticed.

To make today's practice of presence a far more sensory experience we're going to add sound to the mix. We keep our visual focus and also our focus on the breath for now, which is essentially a focus on awareness of the "now" and on "feeling" the breath all the way in and all the way out. We then add a new intense focus on sound; specifically, on low-level background sounds. Importantly, our focus is more on the silence between any sounds, rather than on sounds that are loud and jump out of that silence. This requires us to really listen very keenly to all of the sounds in the environment around us. Of course we'll hear the louder more contrasting sounds too but the background hum is our focus. Our aim is to feel what we thought before was silence but to now see that it is something else, with details and hidden depth.

Even in an almost silent environment we can now sense sound. Our practice is now to be intensely present and to experience this moment by seeing, feeling the breath and by intensely listening to the environmental sounds, focused on the sound in the background not in the foreground. Again there is no labelling or differentiation of the sounds. You are now truly moving into being experientially present in the scene you see and feeling it at multiple levels. This has the immediate effect of creating far more of an experience from a simple practice. Suddenly we have a much deeper feeling of aliveness and are aware not only of our breathing, where we are and what is around us but also the lowest possible sounds in the environment. It is like an experiential, situational awareness that somehow begins to deeply connect us with both ourselves and the surrounding space.

As you start this practice, you'll quickly notice layers of sound from the lowest background sounds to the slightly louder ones. The contrasting sounds will now have more direction and the whole scene will have a progressively richer feeling of experience. Your listening will uncover sounds that you were totally unaware of before. This is you moving into the seat of alive consciousness and it is the feeling and experience of your raw senses being translated with an aliveness and immediacy, unobstructed by the mind. There is now no mind noise, just multisensory awareness.

This is a state of being that will become quite richly addictive. As you practice, and with time, you will begin to feel that the new level of vibrancy you achieved with your sight in our basic mode of presence is replicated as your hearing becomes super alert too. It's almost like a superpower, making you so much more aware and alert than you ever were before. This is the result of the focus of your consciousness directly on to your senses and of removing that same amount of consciousness from mind activity and the past or future. It is a very different state of being than the one you've become used to, and you'll now start to clearly see how, with more attention focused on each of the senses and removed from the mind, the world immediately becomes a richer, more experiential place.

We have added only one extra sense to our presence at this point and already it will start to become deeply meaningful that the body has been designed primarily as an amazing instrument for sensing the present moment in high definition. Suddenly, this level of presence brings a richness of detail to sight and hearing that most of have never experienced before. I know that for me it was like becoming truly alive for the first time.

Your presence is a habit and also a skill, so repetition of this process – taking your mind back to presence when thoughts come and trying to avoid the temptation to narrate how amazing it all is – becomes very much part of this new multisensory practice, just as it was before. While your senses are beginning to saturate your consciousness and taking all of the attention away from the mind, there's a much stronger element of experience that the mind will be tempted to talk to you about on the way. It can now see, hear and feel things all at once. Again, that really is OK. Just recognise the thoughts, accept them, reset and continue. Keep watching the thoughts without fighting them or trying to stop them.

You are now the observer and as such need not interfere. Your mind is beautiful, so don't fight it, chastise it or resist it. This practice will slowly train it and needs no force or attempts of control. Just persistence. Now is actually a great moment to break from the book and to practice and consolidate, returning here later when you've experienced the fullest possible depth of experience.

You are aiming to extend your presence towards becoming fully experiential because you are now making the conscious choice to identify with your consciousness and not with your mind. This state of presence will soon become your base of experience and your default state, so the richer and more sensory it is, the more you'll enjoy it and the more anchored within it you'll become. This rich and addictive state of being can be with you always. It costs nothing, and brings intense joy once mastered. Every sense can be brought into action and each one can become something like an additional superpower over time.

How are you feeling right now? Have you tried it and achieved it? If not, repeat the exercises here until you experience the richness. If you already have, I am anticipating that you've started to feel a deep sense of peace, wonder and happiness with it too. This state, without past or present, will soon become increasingly intense, bringing a deep happiness or what is in effect joy and love. I call it love because this level of experiential awareness is truly emotional and deeply peaceful. It becomes clear that it is who you actually are and it makes you feel whole and one with the world.

Until this level of consciousness hits you, the only way you ever got this feeling was for a fleeting moment when in love, getting something you had chased, experiencing great excitement or in the various other mechanisms your identity has always sought to make you happy. The difference here is that this is not something external to be chased or waited for. It is not the "high" between the "lows", and it does not depend on where you are, what you have, who you are with or what you are doing. It is available always and everywhere. It is inside you and this is the beginning of a new state of being. You may not be fully there yet, and we have more work to do, but this is a taste of what is to come and the simplicity of what it takes to feel whole and alive from the inside out.

I don't need to hold your hand through the process of adding in every sense, one at a time. By now, you are seeing both the method and the objective. If the aim is the richest possible experience of the present moment, then there are senses to invoke to that end; this is usually a conscious choice in the early stages. As you progress to full consciousness you will use all senses more and more. At this point, adding them slowly and one by one is a great way to allow your mind to learn the necessary habits; to become quieter and for you to observe the thoughts and feelings without becoming them.

Once more finely tuned, these senses and experiences will work for you on a busy street, at work, while driving or commuting, eating, drinking... Any situation really. They are a state of being and as such don't require a given location or conditions. The more that state is used and the more you will become it and feel the amazing and positive effect. Remember that you *are* that consciousness and not the mind activity and thoughts you came to believe.

When you're adding senses consciously, do so in the same way each time. Start with the subtle levels and you will realise the more stark levels sat on top. After hearing add the smells, looking for those subtly in the background rather than the stronger ones on top. If you're in nature you'll sense so much with sight, hearing, feeling and smell. Feeling can be your body and your breath and/or the ground beneath your feet, now experienced in great detail and resolution. These are things most of us have never really done and never do but they are what we're made for and we do it in the most incredibly deep, intense and experiential way. This state of being can be as rich as you want it to be and the more you do it, the deeper and more emotional it becomes. It brings endless waves of deep love and joy.

Clearly, if you next add taste you'll have created a whole new range of deep-presence opportunities, with every meal time and every drink becoming a sensual experience. You can essentially choose the best senses for the situation and focus on them by removing others from the mix. You can close your eyes, tasting, smelling and feeling your food in minute detail in a state of completely new awareness. This is your own personal world of sensory experience and it comes with you everywhere you go; you can use it as you wish and go as deep as is necessary. The rules are: no thought and become the watcher; our practice is to watch and experience and our aim is to become the conscious observer of our inner self and mind.

Importantly, there is no judgement of anything we see, hear, taste, feel or smell. Our previously established rules of non-judgement apply strongly and fundamentally here just as they do everywhere. Observe it, don't label or differentiate it. These will soon become the true golden rules of the whole masterclass.

We're now setting the scene for a new state of being, where we are almost permanently ready, sensing and listening to the "now" with all of our senses to experience the world in a progressively richer way and ultimately be an always-on mechanism for that experience. In terms of perception, this essentially converts the consciousness, body and emotional, heart-energy system into a complete field of sensory experience.

Only yesterday, sitting in the garden on a warm day in the rain, I experienced such an amazing multisensory experience on so many levels. Sitting there, listening and looking, feeling, smelling and making my whole body receptive, I experienced rich multisensory love. The sounds were layered and amazing, the view was complex and vivid, and the smells and feelings of the body made me feel so alive. The rain fell on my bare arms like tiny touches of electricity to be felt individually and specifically.

What other instrument could come close to that as a sensory experience? Nature has created something truly wonderful and incomprehensibly complex.

This state is now you as the conscious awareness that drives your body and mind. You are now moving through the world turned up to the highest levels of awareness and bodily sensitivity. You are a point of universal awareness. Energy and connected universal consciousness living its true purpose and experiencing itself in the richest possible way, without thought and all that comes with it to distract you. If that is not now, it will be soon.

As I repeat the truth of who you are, hopefully the validity and ultimate truth of this explanation is now starting to embed within you. Hopefully it all starts to make deep and even logical sense to you as a fundamental answer to who you are and why you exist. As consciousness, you currently inhabit the body and mind simply as tools of your sensory experience. In time, this masterclass will move your identification away from body and mind to the conscious awareness that you are. It will ultimately lead to you sitting permanently in the seat of consciousness and becoming the watcher of all thought and emotional energy within you and at one with everyone and everything. If you are now aligned with that goal, we are making perfect progress.

Chapter 17 : Conscious communication

To continue the theme of extending presence, it is now time to develop the idea that you will soon progress to becoming present and conscious almost anywhere and doing anything. This extension of presence is clearly designed to encourage a shift away from your previous personal identity that you built as thoughts in the mind. That shift moves us to a new connected identity, seated in conscious awareness and as the experiencer not the thinker.

So far, this masterclass has looked deeply at the cause of ego identity and the principles that need to be employed to remove the prison of imposed lack of peace and happiness that it creates. We have spoken about letting the past go and about removing the future focus; and about allowing previously stored emotions and experiences to be freed as energy, never again to be raised or allowed to continue to ruin your life experiences. This is the future; together with non-judgement, removal of preferences and blame, we have the makings of a complete recipe for peace and happiness. Or are we missing something?

Maybe you haven't noticed or maybe you have: there could well be a fly in the ointment, as the saying goes. While all of the principles we've covered so far go together well and support each other, there are external forces in action that seem to go against us and make some of this stuff really hard to make truly practical. They appear to throw us the unpredictable "adventures" in ways that are really hard not to react to and they make remaining present and without judgement, preference or blame feel almost impossible.

Generally these challenges come from what we perceive as life, society and the circumstances of the illusion that we're all currently living in. They also regularly come from the people we directly interact with and who are up close and personal in our lives. The illusion has us judging and preferring so much. The peer pressure is intense and the expectations are endless. The people are unpredictable; they attract and repel us and they constantly hit our emotions and responses.

These things often appear very emotive and hard to resist in terms of emotional reaction and the impact they may have on our lives. They have incredible impact on the ego identity and can make it respond very strongly; when it comes to love, sex, freedom and status, they can be very, very hard to avoid. Some are wrapped up in symbolism – such as money as some kind of measure of status and self-worth – while others impact self-worth more in terms of wanting to be right, loved, happy and beautiful and a winner not a loser. This is a collective world of ego and in that world we deal with other people on a visible or invisible level all the time.

We have a boss, a government, friends, family, authority figures, teachers, police, people we find attractive, people we attach to and "love", our partners, husbands and wives... In this connected universe and especially in what I will call the "Western version of society", the truth is that everything is either directly or indirectly communicating with mind-created identity or ego, triggering it at every opportunity.

There is a collective identity that has been embedded since we were born, consolidated for sixteen or more years in school and higher education then added to at work and fuelled by media. On top of that, there is our additional home-grown personal ego identity, created from every experience and influence we ever had in our lives and the origin of most of our overthinking. The conscious beings among us are also in a minority, so the lack of role models plays a huge part.

Almost every construct of the modern world is created by those identities and is a function of the fact that we've all been taught a single popular opinion of the truth over time. This means that the ego identity is the underlying entity we deal with in almost every type of communication. It is what drives media and government, friends, family, work colleagues, strangers and lovers. Everyone is in the ego bubble. They all subscribe and they all see the world through the lens of their thoughts, preferences, opinions and judgements. Subjectivity reigns.

They all also try to control the world around them and they all chase happiness, power, status, money and more. No wonder, then, that staying on the outside of all that might seem hard. After all, you may not judge, prefer or blame them; you may not create unhealthy attachments to things, chase and respond in the way they do – but how could you possibly live in this place without getting totally sucked in? The term "That's life" is their motto and they think that means this ball of ego thinking that we're all submerged and embedded into.

This whole masterclass so far has been about a shift in perspective – and once your viewpoint changes in the way intended you will never fall back into the collective vision of the world. In reality, the element of you that is susceptible to being sucked in by popular opinion is only the ego. It is not the conscious awareness. Once seated there you are impregnable to it and will have a growing and often disconcerting awareness of it. It truly is like exiting the matrix. Until then, and as we've already touched upon, it's really important to understand that your interactions will almost always be with ego and not consciousness. This should be seen as a significant challenge of conscious living.

Interacting with others, directly and indirectly, will bring all of the bother and visible characteristics of ego. Presence in ego interactions is pivotal to our sustained success and we must learn to stay present in every interaction whether remote, direct or indirect. This means interactions by letter, email, telephone and video conference, in face-to-face meetings, when watching TV and film and consuming media. Communication and interaction that originates in ego is everywhere and comes from all channels, so it's important that we remain present and as the watcher, no matter how our ego reacts.

Throughout the masterclass, until now, our ability to be present has had little or no external distraction. Nothing has been attacking it or directly influencing it and pushing our proverbial buttons. We've not had the reactions, arguments and uncontrolled emotions of others directly attacking our state of being. This is an important hurdle that we'll need to learn how to jump if we're to remain successful.

.

The aim now is to experience and listen to all universal communication with our whole body, and that includes not only the communication coming into our senses when we're calm and in nature but also what's coming from the human world around us almost twenty-four hours a day. If the unpredictable adventure of life is real and fundamental to existence, it is never more visible than in humanity itself.

Whereas you're here learning how the illusion works, the principles behind your ego identity and how to become present, almost everyone around you is judging, preferring, clinging to things, resisting everything and trying to control things and they're totally oblivious as to why. This is a sea of people and social constructs created from ego and living for ego. To take just one very obvious example: governments basically comprise a small group of people who, on the premise of their democratic election to represent popular or mass opinion, then foist the "judgements" and "preferences" of their own egos on the masses in order to impose control.

The whole structure is designed to increase their power and status and to allow them to "manage" society by imposing ideas and strategies that keep everyone where *they* "think" everyone else should be, doing what *they* "think" everyone else "should" do. This is egoic by definition. Ego drives every war, and the need to be right and attachments of those egos drive almost everything in the world around us. Ego essentially creates the whole framework in which we live.

Does that matter? Yes and no. Our aim here is to progress to a place where we can love life. One aspect of that is to be present and permanently conscious, so at the moment we need not concern ourselves with the bigger picture of how the world works and can stay focused on the smaller picture of how we ourselves will see it more clearly in the future. It starts with remaining conscious in every conversation and in all communication.

As mentioned in Chapter 10, we are all constantly thinking during almost all types of communication. We hear only a few words from the other party and not only start predicting their answers but also preparing our own answer to what we're predicting they're going to say. This means we interrupt and are actually communicating about something very different than we "think" we are. This is ego at work and a fair representation of almost every conversation we have. Most of us even know we are doing it too.

The life change we seek and our move to peace and happiness starts with the clear vision that everyone we meet has three important parts. A consciousness or soul, a body and a mind. This clear, conceptual visual helps us begin to create more conscious communication. It doesn't matter whether we're receiving an email, call, speaking face to face or watching TV; our aim is to remain conscious and to always see the "who" we are speaking to, while staying firmly seated in our own consciousness. It means being totally present exactly as previously described: present while fully taking in the experience and communication. The key is wholly understanding the entity that's communicating with us and replying only from consciousness, rather than from thought or ego.

This consciousness and the lack of parallel thought during the communication will in the first instance give the other party an uncommon space. When you then notice and understand that you're communicating with an ego entity rather than consciousness, as will usually be the case, you will easily see that ego characterised by the judgements, preferences, resistance, attachments, opinion and control; these are things it cannot help but be and exhibit. This slower method of communication, where you listen and wait to formulate responses, will also give you your own time in which to watch and experience your own self and mind, without falling into exhibiting judgement, attachment or resistance yourself.

This type of conscious communication offers a feeling of space and so does not promote your own involuntary ego reactions, which we can now watch without acting upon them. Giving yourself time to become the watcher is everything. We have to be the experiencer and we now know there is no place for judgements, blame or grudges. We also know that there is nothing helpful in applying the past to a present situation or in forecasting or speculating on the future, so with time we can remove these elements too. Time, space and allowing the other person to speak until they stop before we formulate a considered and conscious answer is key.

Conceptually, the huge leap for you – and actually for those around you experiencing your new communications style – is when you realise and see the beautiful conscious awareness in everyone and everything, whether communicating remotely or directly face to face. In most instances, you will not be communicating with an awakened individual who is sitting in a seat of consciousness and giving you the same space. Remember: an ego, created over a lifetime from experiences, judgements, preferences and popular opinion or collective judgement, is the other side of almost every communication we have. They will offer no space, they will interrupt, they will feel the need to be right, they will defend what needs no defence as if it were their own self.

Once awake, you will instantly see and feel the awakeness of someone else. They are simply present and they are now. They are factual and they are not attached to outcomes. They offer space and they do not judge. Be aware, though, that our assessment of people and with whom we are communicating can easily become judgement too. That is not the purpose. The purpose is simply to give space and to manage our own self effectively when confronted by ego. Our style is designed to help us to forgive, to love, to learn and progress towards becoming more conscious. After all, what better teacher than the visible ego traits of others.

Either way, conscious or not, the people with whom you communicate are essentially consciousness at heart. While they may be distracted by their ego and operate from that seat, they are the same as you and in essence are still driven by consciousness. That means that your communication and your vision of them should be directed towards that consciousness; irrespective of the reactions their egos may have, your own responses can be from your own consciousness to theirs. The thirst for experience is still there in them and over time they will begin to respond from their own consciousness, albeit subconsciously.

As I said earlier, this is all about your perspective and what you see and from where you respond to these situations. It is largely irrelevant where the other person or entity in your communication is currently sat. Ego or consciousness, you simply and always converse with consciousness and so remain present throughout.

How do we do that? The first stage is to see who and what you are communicating with in the way described above. The next is to simply treat that communication as another deep and rich experience, allowing the thoughts, judgements and emotions to come in and go out without taking action. Like everything else in your life, communication is now a multisensory experience of present awareness. Open it up and listen with your whole body and see not just the ego in others but the consciousness behind it. More than that, communicate in more than words and use every sense to do so. Open up all the senses and start to feel the other person in so many more ways and see the beauty of their conscious being – a being that you now know is one with you and part of the whole.

Take your time to then listen deeply. Do it with the whole body and be conscious that you're always listening until it is time for you to speak. When you do speak, do so without any intermediate stage of mind thinking in between and importantly do not think and formulate answers in any way until the other person has stopped speaking. This is an amazing experience of space. You'll soon realise that there is literally no need to think or prepare anything until the other person is finished, at which point the words and responses will come all on their own without the need of formulation or thought. Try it; it is special.

This approach also and clearly prohibits blame and judgement, attachment and resistance. It is simply the most pure form of communication possible. It is instinctive and multisensory. It is based on presence and love, a connection and an understanding that we are all just experiencing the universe as one singular organism wanting differing perspectives. Everyone is right and everyone is wrong all at the same time. There are no defences or arguments; there are no fights or battles. The ego is in the back seat and there is no need to be or defend any of the identities or roles it has created for you. You are not your preferences and you are not your opinions. You are you for the first time.

One primary way in which this move to conscious communication creates change is in relation to comparison. As ego we are all constantly challenged with either trying to be superior to others or having a sense of inferiority. This is one of the most destructive elements of ego psychologically and it fuels much of our competitive society. We almost automatically judge or belittle people just as they judge us in many cases. We try to outdo them, out-know them, know things first, be more liked, more beautiful, more intelligent, richer and so on. Ironically, in our own ego seeing the ego of others, we feel inferior in many ways too – seeing them as better-looking, having more, being more confident, more intelligent and so on. This comparison and reaction is true only within ego communication; with the ultimate oneness of consciousness it disappears. I see others as I see myself. We are all simply a conscious point of energy and awareness and we are all part of the truth.

What is truth? That we are on a planet in a galaxy that is one of billions of planets in billions of galaxies. That there is land, there is water and there are animals in and on both. There are millions of species and life exists everywhere in everything. There is an endless cycle of life and we see the forms around us born, grow, live, die and decay everywhere. When life comes, things are alive; when it leaves they die but the underlying life continues eternally. We are only one species of millions of species on the planet. We are only one of the ways in which life becomes aware of itself.

Our bodies are recycling constantly and birth and death are never-ending for us and for every other animal, plant and organism of all kinds. The difference is that at some point as humans we developed mind and ego. We got lost in judgement and preference, resistance and the will to control something that could never be controlled. Life and the universe has been happening for billions of years with or without us and will continue to happen long after we are gone – and in that sense everything we do, think or believe is meaningless and changes nothing at all.

Why do I make this point? Because in some ways it is all you need to know. The separation that we feel from others and the universe is mind-created. Our oneness is a simple truth and it is ultimately based on consciousness, which is the endless life that permeates everything and everyone. Remembering this will change your relationship with almost everything. Remembering it in communication will bring out the watcher and move the ego back. Do it now and see how different that feels.

Chapter 18 : Connecting to the whole

Up to this point, we've discussed presence more as a state of being than as what it truly represents. Learning how to feel and enter this state, deepen it and make it our base has been the ultimate aim. The primary reason for this is that we're aiming to quiet the voice in the head or mind-created identity as well as learning the techniques that will allow us to become the watcher of thoughts rather than being identified with them. Presence is truly powerful and in terms of achieving all of the results promised in this masterclass, our learnings so far will take us close to our end state.

That said, there inevitably remain some gaps in understanding that left unchecked may find us with a slightly confusing relationship with our thinking mind. The fact that we don't want the ego involved in our lives is clear, but a few other things are less so. When and how do we then use the thinking mind? Are we allowed to actually think and what about? Which thoughts specifically are good to have and which are bad to have? And so on.

This is something I personally found difficult early on in my own journey through this process. I found myself confused as to what I should be doing and what I should not be doing. It should be clear that this process is not geared towards leaving you with no thoughts at all; certainly not on a permanent basis anyway. It is merely concerned with a mind running away with itself and thinking involuntary thoughts, and with your own emotional and involuntary reactions to those thoughts. It is also very concerned with how this problem takes away your peace and happiness and with the fact that this applies to nearly everyone.

To answer the question, then, of how we should use the mind... Our end state will allow you to use the mind as a tool to be picked up as needed and placed back in its beautiful semi-soundproof box when not in use. Our minds are the best problem-solvers in the world and they certainly do have their uses. Some problems require practical reasoning and calculation, for which there is no better instrument. Remember that in the diagram we drew in Chapter 9 we brought skills with us to the present for just this reason. What the mind must not be entrusted with is holding on to a ball of random thoughts with which we identify. It will not be tasked with controlling an uncontrollable world based on a list of arbitrary thoughts that we have held on to as preferences, opinions, collective beliefs and so on. Until very recently, precisely this activity has taken up almost all of our mind energy and more importantly our conscious awareness too. Also (and worryingly) the intensity of this activity has accelerated to such an extent throughout our lives that these judgements and attachments, resistance and control have become the primary use for mind and awareness. It has taken our peace and taken our happiness. If that hasn't already stopped then it stops today. From now on, the mind will be a simple tool for reasoning, used for that purpose as necessary.

Creativity and decision-making, knowing what's right and plotting our life journey is certainly not a job for the mind. If we use it to these ends we'll quickly arrive back where we started: with the endless and stressful debates of the voice in our head. We will immediately lose our peace and we will not be sleeping too well either. The mind identity and illusory self simply do not have the level of insight and knowing required to carry out this directional intuitive purpose. In previous chapters I have several times mentioned flow state in reference to my writing for the purpose of demonstrating that the flow of knowing and creativity emanates from well behind or above the mind and requires little or no thought or reasoning. This is connected consciousness and the source of ultimate intelligence.

This leads us nicely on to the concept of conscious connection to infinite intelligence. In addition to the countless benefits of the practice of presence we've discussed so far, presence also affords a clear state of connection to a bigger intelligence. The strength of this connection varies in different states of presence, but for most people presence creates a flow of knowing and intelligence that's simply not available when thinking or seated within the ego. Placing yourself in the here and now, with no prior plan or thought save for a direction, allows you to tap into energy and intelligence from an unlimited and unknown source. I am present and choose to write about a subject and the words appear on the page. The words I write are as much a mystery to me as they may well be to you right now. This flow is available to us in all activities and spaces. It manifests as synchronicities, information flow, often supernatural abilities and more, but it is intelligence that none of us even know we have when it appears.

This isn't some technique or ability reserved for the special few; it is available to all of us who simply decide to be present and take the leap, choosing only to visualise our goal and to expect inspiration to appear. It always does and will never cease to amaze you. This is a connection to the infinite intelligence of the universe. Transmission through our consciousness, through all things and pooled to manifest exactly what you require, when you require it. By learning presence in all situations, places and in communication, we bring this intelligence into everything we do.

We are now many chapters into the book and it is here and in reference to connection to the whole that we're going to discuss true meditation. Meditation is a form of presence and connection that is actioned far more specifically and with more specific intent. It has many added and useful benefits over and above the techniques for presence we've already discussed, but they are in many ways one and the same. Our techniques so far have been a living, moving, always-available form of meditation and if our aim is to arrive in permanent presence these must take first priority. Meditation has all of the same benefits but affords space and time to focus more on connection to the whole, and with it will come the release of trapped energy, body healing, transcendence and more. It is also another effective and additional method to help the move of identity from the ego to the conscious awareness. Our new "I am".

As a practice it requires set times; usually 20–30 minutes in the morning and the same at night is recommended. Consequently it can be seen as either more intrusive to life or quite conversely as you allocating much needed personal time each and every day to help your mind to go quieter and to become the watcher of your thoughts. However you choose to see it, and even for the most present and awakened among us, meditation has some important mind and body benefits and is a great choice of daily practice in addition to what we have been doing already.

The practice of yoga, though often misunderstood as a form of physical exercise, is really a practice aimed at connection to infinite intelligence and the systematic freeing and balance of the energy systems of the body. While there are many forms of yoga to choose from, both kriya and kundalini yoga will closely complement this masterclass. They will improve connection to oneness and creativity, will clear the mind and free the trapped energies of the body – the kundalini flow – and will help to release the remnants of past emotions, pains and attachments from your body.

There are many more books that teach meditation and yoga better than I ever could, so that's not the aim here. As a start, though, choose a place where you can be quiet, sit on a cushion cross-legged or on a chair with your spine straight upright and simply close your eyes and watch your breathing; this is the simple way to begin the process of meditation. This process is perfect to create a new and peaceful way to find presence. With your eyes closed, look through the spot between your eyes and while watching your breathing, and with practice, you will fall into the sea of consciousness around you. By passively watching your thoughts and keeping the focus as we have already done in presence, this practice can be peaceful and filled with bliss and love too.

Meditation provides a great place to focus your conscious energy progressively through all parts of your body in a type of body scan or scan of the energy centres. This is an easy form of focused awareness but by centring on almost any and all parts of your body for periods of 20–30 seconds you can bring healing and health to them through the power of direct consciousness. With intent to heal and a belief in the healing the power of consciousness will become visible to you. There are many guided meditations that will help this focus.

In both kriya and kundalini yoga you will focus on deep connection, the energy centres and breathing techniques in certain positions in order to free your trapped energy and help the flow of it through the energy centres up the spine. This is a way to whole body health but much more relevant here is the nature of the deeper and deeper connection that it brings to universal consciousness. This consciousness is experiential and it strengthens the awakening process, removing fear and uncertainty too.

To complete these chapters on living life as the watcher, it is important to say that presence and meditation constitute a way of life and both promote the very state of being that we wish to deeply identify with. Once realised and more permanent, that state is both addictive and enlightening. It is who we really are and these practices will all progressively connect us to it. As we move forward, the state of presence will slowly cease to be a practice, becoming where we feel ultimately comfortable, peaceful and above all, feel like who we truly are. In that state and in the deeper and slightly more connected state of meditation, we gain control and we gain freedom and peace. In this state, the mind identity becomes progressively unable to overtake and disrupt our lives.

What started as a practice and brought an amazing vibrancy and beauty to what we experience, has now become the state in which we live. As we connect to the whole within that state, we bring further and profound knowing and intuition too. As we lose the mind identity or ego, we gain this beautiful and deeply connected awareness. Every moment now becomes a richer and richer experience.

ZEN JUNGLE

Step 7: Becoming Nobody

Chapter 19: Truth and illusion

To the ego or mind identity this step header, "Becoming Nobody", is truly emotive. It quotes the 1960s spiritual speaker Ram Dass and evokes a truly challenging thought process that tends to create a level of resistance and challenge bordering on violent. "Why on earth would I want to be a nobody?" is a normal and common response. It is interesting just how strong the will to be "somebody" exists in almost all of us and as a concept of the ego – an ego which could be described simply as a means for being and building a "somebody". The ego is of course the thought-creating mind identity and voice in the head that most of us identify with more than any other part of us. Bearing that in mind, it's really no wonder that most of us spend our whole lives trying to be a "somebody" in one way or another. In fact being a "somebody" would seem to end up at the heart of how we try to find purpose.

Hold on to your hats because – for the reasons outlined above – the next chapters may be the most challenging. As a collective we're almost all aligned on the idea of individuality, unique personality and the will to be great and stand out in some way. We have spent our lives becoming more and more unique, in many ways, in the hope of becoming that special somebody who achieves a form of greatness through being an exceptional "individual". What follows is an interesting and thought-provoking look at what that process is and how it got there. Try to stay as open as you can; it may change your life.

It will help now to recap on the nature of truth and to compare it to what is not truth. This sits at the heart of our discussion and will offer what can sometimes be a slightly scary perspective on the world we've come to know and think we understand. The idea of what we know to be true, versus what is opinion and more subjective, is core to who we really are and, just as importantly, who we *think* we are.

The masterclass so far has included lots of discussion about the ego and mind identity and in the earlier chapters deeply explained how it is made up and how busy we've been creating this ball of thoughts. Hopefully we have now progressed, but this was the identity that we came to "think" was who we were. We've shown that this identity is in fact just a very subjective set of thoughts; and, while it becomes a filter through which we see the world, it is really quite arbitrary and very different in all of us. That said, it actually holds no true or real "right" or "wrong", just opinions of what is right or wrong, good or bad, liked and disliked and so on. The key point being that these opinions are all *subjective*. This is important to consider as we progress here.

So truth, then, is true, and everything else is subjective. Subjective means that something is only true when seen from a particular viewpoint and is not factual beyond question. You'll recall that we discussed good and bad in these terms, for instance: both are truly subjective because you may believe something to be good and have judged it so at some point, while I may have judged the very same thing to be bad. For each of us this judgement now appears to be *true*. Strange that opposite "facts" – or, more accurately, opinions – can be true for both of us. Obviously, though, and as we have already discussed at length, that is the nature of judgement and preferences.

We're now going to recap on what "truth" means. Importantly, you don't need granular detail of truth because the general picture is enough to understand almost everything. I could drill this explanation down endlessly but that would serve only to make it too complex and bog you down with details you really don't need at this moment. Essentially what follows will show that the universe is true and that all thought is subjective. Before we begin, it is useful to note that both the words and the conclusions drawn are actually also thought constructs used to signpost and describe the reality that exists. The words themselves are not the truth; they simply label it and point to it. Remember that words and language were devised by humans to aid our description and communication of things we can see in our environment. This includes not only words but maths and many of the sciences – which, like language, are also thought frameworks invented by humans.

So, what we "know" to be true... We are on a spherical planet in a galaxy within the universe; a universe beyond which we have no awareness. That galaxy, named the Milky Way, is reportedly one of billions of galaxies and the planet Earth is one of billions of planets. This is all true. Our planet has water and it has land, broadly speaking. Living both on the land and in the water are millions of species, of which humans are just one. So what is true so far is that we are one species of millions, on one planet in billions, in one galaxy of billions, as part of a universe beyond which we have no understanding. Like many of the other species of plants and animals on this planet, the human population is several billion – over 7 billion as we speak. This means that there are a huge number, many billions, of living organisms on this planet and that you are just one of them. This is all true so far.

Interestingly, in addition to this, we are all made of the same base stuff, which in previous chapters we have called intelligent light or consciousness but even that bit may be more subjective as we don't yet (and may never have) all the verifiable answers. What is true is that the base material for everything in the universe is the same. The universe and that base material has then organised everything in an unimaginably complex way that culminates in everything being self-perpetuating and interrelated in incomprehensible ways. Every organism is linked to other organisms in such a way that to define an organism as a single thing is simply not the truth.

For instance, bees and flowers are not two organisms but one, because one cannot exist without the other. As you widen your view, you see that the sunshine, the rain and the soil are also other interrelated parts of that same organism, as are the oxygen and other gases and the space itself around the flower, in which the bees fly. It goes on, endlessly, spreading out until the whole universe becomes involved in flowers and bees. This is a tiny example of the connections but shows how complex and interrelated this all really is.

Continuing with the description of truth, next is that humans did not make any of this. It just "happens" and actually, more than that, we are simply a small part of that "happening". In fact everything is a "happening" and is taking shape and changing moment to moment with no two moments being the same and is independent of and including humans. This is true. We do not actually understand any of it or why it "happens" and we have no control of it at all, although some would argue that we do because we have analysed small parts and can use them to our advantage. We don't, though, and we don't know how it was created or by what or who. It is simply life and it is the mystery we will probably never solve. This is all true.

On top of this, we can visibly see birth and death happening around us everywhere. The distinction I make here in saying birth and death rather than life and death is important because life is continuous but forms are born, grow, die and decay eternally. The forest is a great place to see this, in that the forest floor is an ever-changing mass of plants and flowers that sprout from nowhere, grow, flower and then die off. They carry life for a while, then they decay and support new forms of life as they compost and become the earth, only to recycle and be born again later, doing the same thing all over again unceasingly if left alone. This cycling is visible in every species and every form on the planet. Even manmade forms are transient. Nothing that is manifested as a form lasts forever; all are born and die, endlessly. I include even buildings and cities in this. This is all true.

Life, on the other hand, never stops. It continues to "happen" and is at the heart of everything in the universe, which together makes a single organism. It is all interdependent in the most complex ways on a micro and a macro level. It is literally mindboggling in terms of how beautifully it all just works and how unimaginable the complexity is that drives it but it is all true. It happens and it is there. In truth there is also only ever the present moment, too, which is perpetual; an unending moment where things are and exist without past or future except in our memory or imagination as thought. This is also true.

Truth is simple and truth means that we are part of an amazing organism that we did not create and don't understand. Truth means that as one species on a planet with millions of species, in a galaxy of millions of planets, in a universe of billions of galaxies, humans are totally insignificant as a species. As individuals, if you were to believe that is what we are, we are totally meaningless and nothing at all that we do matters at all or makes a difference. This is all true and can't be denied or argued. In fact, on a universal scale and as a statistical reality, humans don't even really exist materially. A single human could not even be represented as a percentage we could write down or perceive of the overall universe, let alone as having an influence on it.

What is also true is that we don't make babies and the reproduction of every species on the planet is an urge and a process that happens *to* us, not *by* us. What I mean by that is, as mentioned in previous chapters, that we do not have any understanding of how babies are made and we know nothing about building a human being. We have sex and later some magical process happens where cells and things get together in very specific, very intelligent ways and they build a baby inside another body. We play no part in that and when the baby is ready to come out, it just does. These cells make a heart and lungs, skin and bones, hair and eyeballs, blood and so on. For what we know about how that happens, we should simply call it magic; but is it truth? Yes it is. It's amazing and incomprehensible like all the other truth on the list.

Have you ever thought about what and who you really are in this context? Certainly we're used to being confined to existing as a set of labels – a girl or a boy, a human, a mother, an electrician or police officer – and maybe we're happier like that because it's way less to think about and consider. Are those labels the truth, though?

It's all a bit sobering, isn't it? But not as sobering as what comes next. Let's now move on to what is illusion. To do that, allow me to discuss your life so far. This will make it personal and also hit what is left of that ego as hard as it has ever been hit. We can do this just for fun and as a great opportunity to practice "watching" your feelings and thoughts. It may hurt a little and challenge a few beliefs and opinions that are quite close to you. In fact they may be everything that you've come to know and understand, so you may be very tempted to attach to them, defend them or deny the concepts that follow. So be ready. Watch that energy rising and let it go. Just listen with your whole body and soak up the whole explanation.

In our aim to look at what "becoming nobody" really means, we're now going to consider where needing to be somebody may have come from – and the answer might not be what you thought. I don't know how old you are but currently I am forty-seven years old. I reached this age without seeing the perspective on life I'm about to share now. It is a perspective that once seen is very hard to un-see. It gave me a whole new way to look at things and the world around me and if the saying "the truth will set you free" was meant to mean anything specific then I suspect that this is it.

So how did we all find the need to become "somebody"? Is that truth, is it natural and is it what nature intended? The answer to this is found firmly in humanity and firmly in subjective thought, which we've just established is the opposite of truth. None of the following should be read as political or attached to an agenda; it isn't. I will try not to delve deep into the history and to keep with the facts.

Since humanity began there has been a prevalence of judgement and thoughts, preferences and resistance, expectations and a will to control. That is visible in the present because we can see clearly how societies have evolved and we can see the level of egoic behaviours that have been an enduring characteristic of the history of our species. Conflicts, wars and the need for power and hierarchy have driven almost everything; and these are of course, at their heart, ego concepts being played out on a global scale.

The ego wants to be right. It wants to impose views and beliefs and it wants to control the world and ultimately to have power. As we've mentioned before, every war has been fought essentially in order to impose the views of a few on to the many and to spread a singular way of thinking, based on a singular set of thoughts. This is ego making judgements, deciding on preferences and then trying to control the population of the whole world. How does it affect you and me in our lives today? Well. You and I both were probably born in the Western world. We probably had a very similar pattern of existence and it was probably a series of experiences that we could compare and contrast to find a very similar format. The question is where did the format come from?

The pattern for most people on the planet is now the same and we have come to believe it as the "right' pattern. (Which is of course another subjective opinion.) We are born into the world and enter as a baby. We then move into a life that has been fully defined for us and enter a four-stage process of human existence. These stages are: baby, at school, at work and finally retirement. Which part of the truth detailed above is this? And who or what decided on that "idea" of a format? Looking more closely, we are all taught a set of beliefs that are broadly the same, no matter what school we attend. In addition to our practical skills of language and maths, we also learn a set of very specific beliefs and norms that our society wants to impose on us.

We learn a version of religion and we learn a version of the life sciences that suit our culture. What we learn is defined as what "someone" thinks we should learn and it is *true* only because they say it is – although interestingly we specifically don't learn the subjects in this masterclass and how to relate to and manage our minds. This is curious when you consider that this content has been true for thousands of years. We also learn that we will always be "told what to do" and we learn that we should have a place in supporting the framework of the society. The framework is already there and was "thought up" long before we arrived and it is not instantly clear by whom. In the "truth" as previously outlined, we are all part of a free species on a planet orbiting a sun; but in the illusion of humanity we're born into, we find ourselves amid a very rigid "thought" framework that we literally have implanted and are conditioned to believe in almost from birth.

This framework is taught from the first day of school and is accepted as truth and real, but in reality it is the views of others being systematically imposed on us. We simply accept that even though we are a free animal, born on to a planet that humans do not own, we must do as we are told – because that is the way it is. We are immediately under the control of someone and a system. There is authority at school and there will be authority at work. We will have a short time as a baby, followed by sixteen or more years in "education" that is not of our choosing, or even that of our parents – or conditioning, as I like to think of it – during which we will be learning what someone else "thinks" we should learn in order to be useful within *their* system.

It will be primarily opinion and we can't even be sure that it is popular opinion because we've never been asked to contribute to it. (After all, it could be the thoughts of a small group who sought and gained control at some point in the past. They could have even written the history books on which we rely for the truth.) We will then go to work for around fifty years, again being told what to do. We will all be chasing a future where we will be happy and to that end we'll focus on our retirement, when we can relax and "find some peace". This sixty-six-year chapter of school and work will lead to a final ten to twenty years of possible "freedom" in retirement that we have worked hard for, saved and planned for. That's the format we have been given.

The world will give us key lessons to learn. It will embed comparison and competition, a work ethic and the need to work for an employer. Money will be a concept that has been created long before we came and is the norm. There will be people who own a lot and people who own very little. There will be politics and economics, thought constructs that are teaching us the control hierarchy –that some people make decisions for us but that we get to choose who they are every few years.

There will be the media reinforcing this message and there will be repetition of the key concepts again and again almost everywhere we go. We will endlessly be shown things that scare us; threats of conflict, virus and war. We will be shown things that we need to buy and shown people who have risen to elevated levels in the innumerable pyramids of power in corporations and governments. Money will become central and status will become massively important. Those who have, have; and those who have not, don't. It's well thought out and we're told that it is what has been decided is best over time in some democratic way.

Interestingly, there will be a never-ending series of wars, even though we know nobody who wants wars. There will be visible conflicts and there will be police and control mechanisms to make sure we all comply. Comply with what? The opinions and rules that someone decided were "right" or "wrong" at some point long ago, for reasons we will never know. We will have laws and religions that detail our rules of engagement. We will be told that we must succeed at all costs and will be constantly reminded that death is final and to be the fundamental fear of all of us.

This finality will create fear and urgency and we will need to achieve at pace, stay busy, stay at work and make hay while the sun shines or before we die, whichever is the sooner. Doing so will take away our time to consider and prevent us from challenging, or even to see anything of how it works and why, because we are too busy and need to live and make money for our families and can't risk things going wrong.

There will be whole structures of ego and parts to play within them. When we disagree, we will have a legal system that will have lawyers and "judges". We will have many roles and many functions and we will have norms to comply with and we will be expected to maintain them. Since nature created the "truth", this human-created world is now a very different place. It is wrapped in ideas and opinion; it has leaders and sets endless expectations. It creates fear and a need to be protected and governed. In fact, it manifests every concept that we've been aiming to remove from our being during the masterclass so far. This illusion is the characteristics of ego incarnate and it embeds and reinforces them endlessly from birth.

It also systematically creates structures that have the many working for the few, with the wealth flowing upwards in a pyramid that represents both freedom and power. It creates what is almost a vacuum for the ones at the bottom so they want to move upwards and work so hard in order to do so. It promotes more and more expectations on ourselves and on others and it drives judgement and preferences, wants and needs, likes and dislikes in the most effective way possible. It does this systematically through blanket communication and media and it does it through school and through work, through peer pressure and collective popular opinion. By showing disease, conflict and war in an overly dramatic and perpetual cycle, it drives a need to be protected and anxiety about safety.

This is the illusion of human life. The phrase "that's life" did not come about in any way by accident. It has been developed over time and it both purposefully and aggressively creates every unhelpful mind pattern that we've discussed so far. It is the "life" that we have all come to accept and it is why 7 billion people can be controlled by just a few.

These mind patterns lock us into ourselves and to endless overthinking and they give us little room to consider or even see what is happening around us. We are busy becoming "somebody", busy conforming and believing in a system created to build and fuel frantic egoic behaviour. It is hypnotic and all-consuming and it is taking up almost all of our consciousness all of our time. We are hamsters in the wheel of this illusion, diligently running as fast as we can, buying its goods, believing its rules, conforming to its norms, embedding in subjective opinions, being scared and feeling unsafe and fighting to meet its growing expectations and the growing number of roles that we need to play.

The questions of why this illusion exists and who designed and maintains it are for another book entirely; for our purpose moving forward on this transformational journey we're more concerned with the effect of it all. But as we discuss the effect it's certainly worth considering why it has been created this way and who and how many might benefit from it.

So what is the effect? Everyone needs to work hard to be someone before death, which is said to be the end and final. Born on to a planet as a natural "happening" by nature, we are thrust into a hierarchical world of control structures. We are given rules and things to do and achieve. We must earn money and we must comply with a thought framework of someone else's making. We are simply sheep in a field with shepherds; and for the shepherd to retain control we must have fear, need protection, be too busy to revolt and embed ourselves in these ego patterns so that we worry and think endlessly and have no time for wider consideration. It all works so well.

This masterclass is all about overthinking and we've been looking at its causes and effects; here we can see both played out on the grandest of scales, almost all of us are so busy thinking, worrying and attaching that we cannot even see outside the human illusion. Humanity has lost sight of the "truth", and we have forgotten who we are in favour of getting totally wrapped up in a manmade subjective, thought driven system. It is an illusion of life with no visible edges or exit routes.

So then off we go. We build our identity, our "somebody", our individualism – because that is exactly what we need to operate in this illusion. We must judge and be judged, compete and compare. We must endlessly create our wants and likes and we must get busy resisting what we don't like or want, chasing the future and dwelling on the past. Even if it just is and can't be changed. We see control everywhere and so we want our own control and progress.

We think we really are this thought identity and collectively buy into the idea that we are not life and that death is final. This creates our proverbial and fundamental "deadline", a time by which we need to have completed our successes and stamped out our individualism. We need to have worked upwards in the pyramid and reached new and higher levels. We need to have met all the norms and been and done whatever the world and this illusion says we must.

Wow. What a ball of ego thoughts we have been born into. What a methodical structure it is. Does it compare to truth? No. Does it promote the creation of ego and everything that comes with it? It is an ego-making engine! It is everywhere, being systematically and constantly reinforced with drama and fear. So is this will to be "somebody" part of nature and truth? Maybe, and maybe this illusion simply contributes to it. That's for you to decide. The point is, though, do you need to buy into it all? No. Not at all.

Spending your life overthinking and creating endless, unrealistic expectations of yourself is what this system provokes you to do. It is why you have no peace, why you have a constant feeling of fear and why you have no time. Our ego identities are, to some degree at least, a scary product of this thing. Are we a victim and should we blame it? No, because that does not serve us. Although it is interesting to wonder what the world would be like if the whole thing didn't exist. What if this illusion simply disappeared and left the whole planet free to become the conscious beings that this masterclass intends to create? Would there still be wars? Would we simply love each other? Would we simply share the resources of the planet equally, instead of the top ten humans by wealth, having more than 50 per cent of the money by world population? These are important questions. I also wonder whether we'd all have this ego identity, this ball of thoughts that is fighting to be individual, competing, comparing, fighting to be right, setting expectations, being scared, anxious and creating endless mind activity as a result.

Either way, I have personally decided that I don't need it and don't want it. It doesn't serve me and if there is someone I want to be, it certainly isn't the ego me and all that comes with it. This whole book is essentially about that entity, its impact on your life and the endless pain it causes. It's about moving away from it and seeing that you are the watcher and not the thinking mind. You are simply not the thought ball created in part by this illusion; in realising that, you are free and there is no need to comply.

Once you see this illusion for what it is, you can never go back and you can never un-see that the ego you have is likely a product of it, and is systematically implanted, programmed and fuelled by it, whether by accident or design. It's time to consider that we may all be on a ride that we never bought a ticket for. We may also have been taken for that ride deliberately, to serve someone else's purpose. If that is even a possibility that is now in your knowing, maybe it's time to truly become the consciousness and to drop the ego identity totally.

Chapter 20: No more separation

It is really interesting to see and understand truth and illusion in this way. Removing the illusion brings clarity to the world and a feeling of who we really are. We are all so wrapped up in the framework that humanity has built that we generally fail to see our own nature in context with the universe. In fact, it is quite amazing that we can be sat as a singular species within this unique planetary and universal organism and have life and nature all around us and still lose our context. On any given day, we simply get embedded in the human illusory world and fail to appreciate our place in the universe; it's as if we're wearing some sort of blinkers. We forget how special we and the universe are and how so little of what we do or think matters at all to it just happening around us.

We are so lucky to be here as consciousness. To have this amazing body and mind and to be able to have these unique and rich moment-to-moment experiences. Until now, and like the rest of humanity, we have been so submerged in the illusion that we've failed to see the vibrancy of life itself. Until we become conscious and present, we are simply and endlessly thinking about concepts in that human-created reality rather than in the actual reality happening inside and outside us. It's amazing just how vacuous this false framework that we've inherited and accidentally accepted is, and odd that we have not seen it or been allowed a say in whether to accept or to conform to it.

Everything we've learned in this masterclass so far is about the move of identity away from the false and thought-driven version of ourselves that we've basically been forced to build in order to fit in. This programmed need to judge, to prefer, to resist and to endlessly try to control is the way that humanity has currently chosen for us to live. The aim is to make us all want strongly to be somebody, to become increasingly individual, to be special, to stand out and to want to rise up the ladder of status, wealth and power. It is not concerned either with peace and or happiness. Being "somebody" is the process of moving from being like everyone else to becoming unique and alone, with a specific set of special abilities that are better and different than everyone else's.

Our aim here is of course exactly the opposite: to remove all judgement and comparison, resistance and preference and become more centred and without blame. To transform our behaviour away from judgement and more towards non-attachment and neutrality. To prefer less and accept more and to understand deeply that it is these ego concepts that prevent us from having a life of peace, joy and ultimately freedom and love.

Our objective is to move to the seat of consciousness, from which we will see clearly that we are all connected and all essentially the same – that we are one. To remove the blame and to forgive fully and to see that as a single universal organism we are all very much part of a singularity. As we move forwards we should continue to reflect on the fact of the entire universe being made of the same basic stuff, vibrating at different frequencies but with no edges. It, we, and everything else, are all one and are just manifestations of life itself.

When we consider this alongside the truth as outlined in the previous chapter, we can start to see that in reality we are one and we are connected. There is a single consciousness, one mind that we all share, and we make up a single organism – the universe – made up of sub-organisms in much the same way as the human body has organs, systems and cells that comprise one entity. Everything works together to make the whole thing "happen" in the way that life "happens"; just like the bees and the flowers, one thing does not exist without the others.

This beauty, oneness and the interconnected nature of everything demonstrates why the framework built over time from thought, by a small group of humans, is truly at odds with creation. It stands out as separate. It promotes separateness and it leaves us competing, comparing and conflicting with each other. The fuelling of individualism and the sub-groups of belief-oriented egos that want to be separate and want to create conflict simply to impose their own beliefs is a sign that something went wrong.

This is a singular organism at war with itself, organised into hierarchy and made purposefully separate by every one of the ego concepts. We have been taught to judge everything and everybody. To fight for control and to win at all costs. To see our beliefs as part of our being and identify with them so strongly that we should even go to war to defend them. We have made weapons on that basis and humans have killed more than 100 million other humans in the twentieth century alone. Not only that, but in most cases we were never asked if we wanted war; after all, who would have said yes? We were told it was right, while behind the scenes scientists made discoveries that could help the whole of humanity and instead used them to create atomic bombs and countless other weapons for the ego to use for attack on a global scale.

This illusion has been designed in such a way that it creates separation and that we have never had a choice as to whether to join. It is wholly and starkly unlike the "truth" and it defies everything else we see in nature. I wonder what will happen when we realise we are all connected, that we're all one? Who would have power? Who would be wealthy? Would we share and be happy and could we live as this masterclass suggests, seated in consciousness and with no judgement, preferences, blame or guilt and unconditional forgiveness? Would quality of life for all and every species on the planet then be our aim? The answer is that it is certainly possible. Consciousness brings more than anything; it brings love, the very fabric of the universe.

Why am I making this point so deeply and strongly? Because this transformational journey is about loving life and that starts right here with the reason we don't already. We are spending all of our waking moments thinking. We are walking ego identities, trying to be somebody in a framework that is designed to keep us running on the hamster wheel and wanting to be special. As I stated before, "the truth will set you free" – and it really will. The truth is that we are one, we are life and we are part of the universal organism. As soon as we realise the nature of ourselves, we are then free to stop chasing separation; and the sooner we become one, the sooner we realise the true power and peace of nature as a unity.

Nature is not focused on separation and comparison; it is a singularity, one consciousness experiencing itself. We are all a point of awareness in that consciousness and we are all exactly the same life energy. There is only love between us and without ego that will shine through as our natural state. This human reality was made by a few humans, not created by nature, and it's time to exit it and to stop playing by those rules in favour of the truth and the shared unity of consciousness. Together we can find love, peace, happiness and fulfilment.

All this requires is the shift of identity from ego or mind-created identity over to our conscious awareness of the now. By following the masterclass and creating your own peace, you will automatically exit the illusion around you. This process starts with the removal of judgement, preferences, resistance and the attempt to control, and results in a seismic shift in your state of being. It is who you really are and not who you have been conditioned to believe you are. As soon as we stop attachment – to positions, to subjective beliefs, to our roles in humanity, the norms and the arbitrary concepts of right and wrong, good and bad – we will finally see ourselves as the experiencer and the watcher, not as the thinker.

Being "somebody" is wrapped up in this ego, in this judgement, in this falsely constructed world that humanity has created. You are you as the consciousness; you have a unique perspective and a unique awareness and in that you are individual. Other than that you are one with everything and everyone else. The whole universe. You are not separate; you are joined. Part of the same organism on a micro and macro level and as soon as you realise it the love in you will flow. The peace will come and the blocked energy will be freed.

Start by becoming the observer and the watcher of thoughts and feelings. Let them come and go, removing all judgement. Remove all blame and guilt and replace them with clarity. Clarity to see the world as it is: part of you; a singularity and a single organism that can work together for the good of the whole. That organism needs no division or separation and can only benefit from the shared state of being that nature intended.

This is the end of separation and it is the beginning of the end of the ego too. As soon as we collectively move our identification, ego can no longer exist. This is us dropping the need to be separate in favour of being one; dropping the need to be special in favour of the realisation that we are all special and the same. The "somebody" that we have been trying to be has been primarily the product of our environment and quite probably a mind game. That mind game, if real, has been orchestrated by the few to essentially enslave the many. It is a prison of the ego where there is no time and constant overthinking. Either way, it is time to lose that identity for good, to move to consciousness and, for the purposes of this false illusory framework at least, become the "nobody" that will bring you ultimate peace, love and happiness.

As "nobody" there is no judgement, no preference, no resistance and no attempt to control. There is no need for constant defence of ideas that you're attached to and no conflict or fighting. There is no endless mind activity and no need to attach to anything or these thoughts or positions. In the end, this is the next stage of evolution. It is simply us all as a point of consciousness, united and happy as one. We are not the body and we are not the mind. We are the universal intelligence and as such have no need for fear, protection, unique opinion, status, power or money. We know that we don't own the world on which we were born and we don't claim its land. We don't pollute and destroy it for money and we respect both its support and the fact that it is part of us. We simply become part of it "happening" and we know we can't control it and that it will "do" whatever it "does". We can willingly accept "what is" and be unaffected by anything that is not part of the truth and the love that comes with it.

The illusion is here for now; we can't immediately change that but as we disregard it and become conscious it loses its power. Really, it is just a few humans trying to control billions of conscious beings. Beings who have no fear and are the observers and watchers of their thoughts and feelings. These beings are centred and don't react and without fear they cannot be controlled. In an ironic twist of logic, being "nobody" is the biggest "somebody" we can ever be. Why? Because at that point there is no possibility of control and the illusion ends for good. It really is that simple.

Hopefully by now you're seeing that this masterclass is bigger than a simple aim to "love life". By following the steps here you will certainly reach that outcome but more than that, together we will remove separation, create peace and be the change that we want to see in the world. It's as simple as that shift in identity away from ego. When the ego dies, we will all get our first true taste of freedom.

ZEN JUNGLE

Step 8 : The Real You, Found

Chapter 21 : A compulsive misuse of the mind

So is the masterclass nearly over? Have we reached nirvana, become peaceful and seen the back of all of the overthinking that we came here to lose? Probably not just yet. If you're right now breathing that sigh of relief that comes when you've been worried you missed something important along the way, that's OK. The good and bad news is that most people will still be getting lost in thought quite often, even if they've been working hard to understand why and practice avoiding it.

Consciousness and you are one in the same. So why is it so difficult to make a simple transition away from being in the mind to the place where you can permanently know who you are and have the beautiful state of being that comes with it? We have been interchanging words like awareness, consciousness and presence readily throughout the course and hopefully by now, having experienced the feeling of conscious awareness, you are totally bought in to the truth that it is who you really are. When you are present and aware of all your senses, it is by far the most alive that you have ever felt. You have also experienced the rich flow of energy or love that comes with it by now and you want more and more of it. So what is the problem? Why is the transition so hard?

Interestingly, another great truth is that the only problems that exist are in the mind and for this one that is doubly so. Nothing is ever a problem until the mind makes it so. Problems come from non-acceptance of what is and a mind perspective that dwells on not wanting something to be true, rather than simple acceptance of what is and working with it to move forward. So what is the current problem? You keep getting sucked into your thoughts and even though you are working hard to avoid it you're still getting taken by them and lost in them sometimes or even quite regularly. Am I right? It is literally like you're walking down the street, totally present and aware, and somebody suddenly drugs and blindfolds you simultaneously. The next thing you know, the blindfold comes off and you realise that it wasn't some nasty kidnappers wanting to steal your bodily organs; rather, your own mind had taken you off to some secret location – that location being a deep rabbit hole of meaningless thoughts. And the first you knew about going there was when the blindfold was lifted as you came around from the drugs that made you lose consciousness. Wow, the mind is sneaky isn't it?

As we have mentioned many times throughout the masterclass so far, there are two kinds of thought. Those that you choose and can order your mind to do at will; and those that are involuntary, over which you seem to have no control at all. Our techniques of presence are incredibly effective but at the moment, when the mind really wants your attention, it can still have it without you even realising fast enough to put up a fight. More accurately, you don't get the chance to watch it and become a participant rather than a spectator. After all, our aim has been simply to watch the thoughts – but in these moments of becoming lost we seem not to get the opportunity to even see thoughts coming.

This essentially leaves us with two kinds of involuntary thoughts. Those we can see and watch as they happen and pass us by as the observer and those that we cannot see happening at all until they've run their course and are complete. When we get sucked in, we can also be sucked in for some time, even days; so, yes, these rabbit holes can certainly be deep and are often quite dark too.

You might have just breathed a second sigh of deep relief because this description of what's been happening reassured you that you're not as bonkers as you thought and haven't "failed" somehow; you're just like everyone else. This is a great example of the nature of our mind conditioning in action. Here we have the fear of failure, the peer pressure that we feel to be normal and our deep need to compare ourselves with other people we don't even know (in this instance other people doing this masterclass)... What's ultimately going on here is something learned over many years. In past chapters we've looked at how we're taken from our parents, go to school for many years, then go to work and are nearly always interacting with an ego-based world. A world almost entirely based on the idea of separation and being "someone" individually, on competition, preferences, comparison and all the fears and expectations it brings. This is actually all we know and is the strongest habit we have.

Every thought and reaction we have is part of this conditioning – and the need for the mind to go off on kidnapping missions, making us think about the past, creating ways to get what we want and building intricate strategies to avoid what we don't want has all now become the norm, an instinct. However old you are, in almost every moment that you've been alive so far you've been told, taught and encouraged to have this behaviour. Every mildly significant experience, judgement or opinion you have has been stored just for this purpose; stored to use later, to hatch all the plans and strategies that your beautiful and creative mind essentially appears to live for. They say that a habit can be created in twenty-one days. What kind of habit can you create in twenty, thirty, or forty years?

What does this mean? Your mind has been effectively trying to control your outside environment for almost all of your life and it isn't going to give that up easily. Don't get me started on the fact that these attempts at control have never worked so far, or that the universe and all people, places and things are unpredictable – because we've been there before and hopefully we don't need to go over it again. The universe is unpredictable and uncontrollable, that's it. That said, whether we know and believe it or not, here we are endlessly spending our time in this ball of thoughts. We continue to make those plans and trying to control the world, knowing inside that it will never, ever work and ends only in disappointment. The good news is, it is just a habit and habits can be broken just as fast as they can be made, in twenty-one days or less, so we don't have to live here forever is the great news.

You now have the most amazing toolkit. It has been built during the masterclass in order to retrain this habit and is there for you to become both aware and present, ultimately becoming the watcher of your thoughts. It works and will take some time to implement but "succeed you will" as Master Yoda of *Star Wars* fame would say. Our aim is to inhabit the state of presence both permanently and as we relax into it, to know that it is actually who we are. We are the consciousness and we are the one who experiences. We can now feel it at will and we also "know" it deep within.

By becoming aware of the feeling of conscious presence, we are essentially focusing our awareness or consciousness on itself. If we are the awareness, and being present is our natural and self-realised state of being, then by realising it and feeling that state we allow the consciousness to become aware of what it feels like to be conscious. It's like one of those mirrors set at just the right angle so your reflection repeats itself and goes off in the distance to eternity. Consciousness is actually very similar to that because once it's been found, it opens everything up into an infinite space to be realised within you.

Once we truly realise who we are, and start to become and identify with that conscious awareness, it demonstrates our dysfunctional relationship with thought and shows what is needed for change. As we have already discussed, this use of mind for the process of trying to control your outer world is both futile and meaningless. The use of mind for worry, regret and many other involuntary actions will soon become totally redundant. Soon, we will use our mind only for the correct and specific purposes for which it was designed, such as calculations and differentiation.

A change is coming, where we free the mind from strategy and debate and where we consciously take over all decision-making and start to be the one who can set the mind into action whenever it is needed. This means that, today, we have a bridge to cross in order to reach that state. We must move from where we currently are, having involuntary mind storms and being taken down rabbit holes, to a place where the mind becomes our tool, to do with as we please.

Chapter 22 : The anatomy of uncontrolled thoughts

Kidnappings are rarely random and as any good kidnap and ransom detective will tell you (I'm making this bit up, by the way), there are always some signs and a trail of clues that point to the abduction plan before it's even carried out. The great news is that these "mind-nappings" and adventures down the rabbit hole of thought are very similar. They also have a trail and clues. Not only is it possible to see the mind start working before a thought comes, but we can also see the motive and often remove both that and the thought at source too. What I am saying here, in case it's gotten lost in analogy, is that we're not totally defenceless in preventing the moments where we get lost in thought. There are ways that we can see them early enough and not only watch them but cut them off at source too. Have I got your attention? Would that be a good thing to learn?

By being totally present 100 percent of the time, our aim is clearly to both richly experience life and become the very conscious watcher of a much quieter mind. The more present we become, the more we can watch the thoughts; and, interestingly, the more we watch rather than taking part, the fewer thoughts we eventually get. Why? Because, as they say, an ignored guest will soon leave and the mind is no different – the less attention it gets, the more it loses interest in working hard to think simply to be ignored. The first and key challenge for us at this time, then, is to find a way to avoid being taken against our will. We need a way to stay as the watcher without unwittingly becoming a participant. We need to stop getting sucked into the thoughts.

Something that we haven't discussed up until now is what watching a thought actually feels and looks like in action. A key take-out from my own journey of self-discovery and self-realisation has been the feeling of understanding what I'm supposed to do but having no idea how to do it. This is one of the main reasons that we created the masterclass and wrote this book: we wanted something understandable, that could be actioned and was easy to follow. Becoming the witness or watcher of your thought is one of the most pivotal elements in finding peace and happiness but for some it is also one of the more mysterious ideas. Even if you find it simple to grasp the concept, it is unclear from most teachings what it really feels like and how to know that you're doing it correctly.

Watching thoughts is a process and essentially a skill that develops over time. It comes as you increase your practice of presence and develop an increasingly strong ability to become more consciously aware. In my experience, the more you practice presence in any and all situations, the faster you'll progress to actually seeing thoughts as and during the time that they "happen". This, however, is where the challenge may start. So, are you seeing the thoughts before, during or after they happen? Are you inside of them or are they there in front of you? Are you the consciousness behind them and watching them actually form and pass by or not? It is certainly worth considering these things now, if you haven't already done so.

Progress normally follows a specific pattern. At first, as you learn the practice of presence, you'll find that you start to see thoughts just after they've happened. You will be happily doing something – and may well be working on your ability to be present at the time – and then you'll suddenly awake to find that there has been a mini-kidnapping of your consciousness by your mind. You realise the thoughts you had, reset and are now back present. You have been aware and have seen the thoughts for what they were, even if it was a little late. That is a great step forward. If you've been following the advice in this masterclass intently, you'll also have instantly forgiven the mind for this indiscretion and will quite probably have smiled to yourself, seeing that you have once again been taken down a very small rabbit hole. How cute it all is.

The key point here is that your awareness and ability to see the thought is behind the thought. You are aware and watching the thought but *after* the event, and can only realise that you had it and what it was just after it happened. Clearly you are only just becoming the watcher at this point in the process. So what would it feel like if you were able to truly watch it? Would you be aware enough to see it form and grow in front of your conscious awareness and would you then simply watch the whole thing happen and let it go? Maybe learning what the end state is will help you to create it? In the interests of understanding it often helps to describe the process in detail, so that's what we'll do.

This end "watcher" state very much requires a deeper understanding of the thoughts themselves. With the aim of making this part of the masterclass truly meaningful, and to help you become truly and permanently present, we should discuss several further dimensions of the thoughts themselves. We'll deal mainly with only one of them here, but we'll go on to discuss thought fully later because your understanding of them will be crucial to your final outcome.

The first of the two dimensions is that each thought has a lifecycle. It starts somewhere, it grows and it ends. The second dimension – and the one we're going to primarily cover just now – is that *all* of these thoughts are totally meaningless. When I say all I mean all of them without exception. We'll deepen this understanding as we go but if you can simply accept it for now that will really help. Essentially, there is a really good reason that you don't consciously choose to have the involuntary thoughts that you're having at random all day every day. It is because you really don't need them and they do not progress any situation you have in your life, for the better or in any way. They are simply the mind spewing out random thoughts based on previously stored meaningless information that has been accumulated over time.

The nature of these thoughts is quite diverse but the structure of most of them is now very familiar to us. They have been a core part of the masterclass so far. Interestingly, they are predominantly incarnations of all of the patterns that we have decided to remove from our lives for good. Most are also a result of that very same long-term conditioning, received from the world around you, that we've detailed in previous chapters. This is a vicious circle of habits that create thoughts and thoughts that create habits. It is all compounded by and interrelated with our conditioned understanding of what is "normal" and "expected" of us in the world. These thoughts are actually one in the same. They create habits and habits create them.

So how do these habits actually take place? They basically comprise a fountain of totally random and meaningless thoughts. Many are needless debate and differentiation, a single voice in your head arguing with itself about what the "right" option is to take. Often this is also based on a choice of two "bad" options, where neither should be chosen anyway. Most are also an act of judgement. They happen as you judge anything and everything and they take place based on things you saw or heard earlier, or things happening right now in real time that hit something inside you to which your mind reacts. "She was rude to me; I don't need to put up with that." "I really like him; I wonder if he likes me?" "Why did he say that about my hair? What was he getting at?" "The meal wasn't as good as last time; I'm not going there again..." And so the list goes on, triggered by anything or nothing at all. Meaningless.

They are simply the reactive "follow up" to any experience. They are often, and importantly, also the seeds from which we build all of our preference and/or opinions. They will have you attaching meaning to something that has none so it can later be identified with, or (my personal favourite) they represent the process of you building a strategy based on all of the above, to essentially try to control people, places and things in the world around you. These are the thoughts that suck you in and they are constantly happening.

In addition to being a form of control, they are the anxiety, they are the worry, they are the fear and they are the regret. They are what happens when you've stored information that you should have let go of – needlessly and randomly over time. Don't worry about that too much at this point, though, because we've all done it. All that information and emotionally charged energy is constantly being stirred by something happening now or recently, only to be brought back in the form of overthinking. Sometimes it's obvious and you know why your mind has been triggered; sometimes it isn't and you don't. Either way, you're now thinking thoughts that you didn't ask for or want to think. Again, though, the key take-out here is that they are all totally meaningless. Have I made that point strongly enough?

All this emphasis on the fact that these thoughts are meaningless is because we want to know what it feels like to reach the point of being a proficient watcher. Before we get to what we'll see and feel from these thoughts, though, there's something else to consider. You're far enough into this transformational journey to truly know the nature of these thoughts, of course, but bear with me because all this reiteration is important to deeper understanding. These thoughts are actually much more than meaningless. On analysis, we can see that they're also the very patterns that this whole masterclass is focused on removing.

They are judgements, blame, the birth of preferences; they are resistance to what is and complaints; they are the very creation of expectations and they are the visible process of building control strategies. You know, the ones that really don't work. As I said, these involuntary thoughts are so much more than meaningless. Not only is their content meaningless, but every one of them is the heart of a pattern that we have clear need to fully remove from our lives in order to bring peace, freedom and happiness.

This reality brings a stark realisation. Rather than looking to watch the birth, growth and death of these involuntary thoughts, it is now in your best interests to find the gentle move towards seeing where and how they begin and totally disregarding them before they ever completely form and before you even find out what they are about. Why? Because they have nothing at all to offer you; to use my earlier analogy, if you see the kidnappers on their way over, you should simply get up and move somewhere else – somewhere they can't find you. Why wait for them to arrive and try to sell you some wonderful story about why they're not the kidnapper you *know* they are?

Becoming the watcher is a process that evolves over time. We start by waking up to find that we have been lost in thought after the event, and we progress our practice and move towards a state where we can start to see the thoughts coming in the distance. Then, knowing they are all meaningless, and by total disregard, we do not give them any attention or interest. Essentially we do not give them time to take our consciousness away at all. By doing this we also stop them growing into a fully formed thought. We remove our conscious energy and we give them no reason or fuel to form.

Every thought should be considered similar to the planting of a seed. These thought seeds grow blindingly fast but they are all part of a similar pattern and cycle that needs to be understood. There is the seed of internal or external stimulus, there are older, retained thoughts, blocked energies and sensitivities that are like the nutrients in the soil, needed for them to grow and without which they would starve, and there is a catalyst like water that then enables and helps them to grow. That catalyst or water is your conscious attention. The more conscious attention they get and the more they combine with the old thoughts and grow. These thoughts fast become a forest. Faster than any other thing you've seen or heard of. If you feed them with your attention just that little bit too much, they become totally uncontrollable and you'll be immediately sucked in and become overgrown and immersed in them. Conversely, if you see the seed and remove the water, they simply die off and disappear. In order to remove all attention effectively, we only need to understand two things: first, how to recognise the arrival of a seed; and second, that all seeds are meaningless.

Chapter 23 : A disturbance in the force

We are making so much progress in this masterclass so far. We have learned and understand that what we now want is to feel the richest possible experiences in the present, permanently and with all senses firing. We also know lots more than we did before. We know that it is incredibly difficult to become the watcher of thought in a truly effective way. And we know that we are being ambushed and taken down rabbit holes of the mind on a regular and very rude basis. We also know that these rabbit holes are pointless and meaningless, and we know that the most common thoughts are the very patterns that we need and want to remove from our lives completely. Wow, this seems to be a circle that is truly coming together. We are making personal progress in learning to get closer and closer to becoming the watcher of the thoughts, and that is giving us more and more peace. That said, most of us will still find it difficult to recognise the thoughts ahead of their creation or growth.

How great would it be to see the whole lifecycle of a thought? Oh, to see the very beginning, the middle and the end of every thought and to be at a sufficient level of abstraction away from it, in order to simply be a watcher of it. At this moment, though, we're often actually within the thought itself and on many occasions the thought is still becoming who we actually are. By the time we're aware of being taken by thought, we can be in a spiral that feels like it has no exits until it's complete. This prohibits us from seeing it and behaving more rationally until it is all over.

However, we've now seen that we are the experiencer and at almost any given moment can become present and know ourselves and the consciousness that we are. This knowing means it is only a matter of time before we become the watcher we want to become more permanently, and start to realise and identify with our true conscious self. The question we would love to answer is, how do we start to see these random thoughts earlier and how do we gain an ability to head them off before they can do us any harm or damage? After all, past experience tells us that harm and damage is likely and very possible. Once you are in the spiral and off down the rabbit hole, you have to resurface before you can become yourself again.

This is the second dimension of thought, mentioned in the previous chapter. We know that there is a lifecycle and we know that in order to effectively watch these thoughts we need to both see the seed and remove the conscious awareness from it at just the right moment. So how is that done and how do we make further progress with the circle of permanent presence? This is where Master Yoda might return, because finding a "disturbance in the force" is critical to this process. Watching the force rather than the mind and thoughts now becomes the critical part of finding the seeds. So where is the force and how do we watch it?

Before we discuss that, it's worth us having a quick detour into the generally negative nature of thought. Our experience of overthinking tends to have a negative flavour; even when thoughts or experiences are positive there's usually what seems to be an underlying negativity. Understanding this will help us to understand how to better watch the "force" and see the seeds of involuntary thoughts. At the heart of most thoughts and emotions are judgements and preferences. As we have already discussed, these are the beginning of overthinking and are the fuel for our predisposition to resist what is and to attempt to control our world. This overthinking is all about what we want and what we don't want. More accurately – and as per the reason we're constantly trying to control everything – it is all about trying to make sure that we do get what we want and don't get what we don't want.

These two objectives are what keeps our minds endlessly busy and are why we're basically judging everything, building preferences and then, via control strategies, trying to make the outside world meet those preferences. So why is there an underlying feeling of negativity around the good stuff as well as the bad stuff? The bad stuff feeling negative is understandable but it's hard to see why the good stuff doesn't cancel the negativity out; the feeling always seems to be more negative than positive. And even though we go through life storing preferences of the things we "like" as well as the things we don't, on the whole it's feelings of un-fulfilment and emptiness that drive the need to control and our underlying fear. Really, you'd expect good and bad experiences and likes and dislikes to simply balance and become a more neutral feeling, wouldn't you?

The reason for this is simple. As we experience things we like and things we don't like, and store them off for use later in controlling the world, they then manifest in very similar, ultimately negative ways. Once we have a preference and like something, rather than it simply becoming something we want that's nice when we get it, it becomes something that we want more of and then start to worry about not having again. What strange creatures we are. Equally, when we have a negative experience we are making plans to avoid it and worrying about not having it again. This means that we think about the good things and worry about not having them again or wanting more of them, and we think about the "bad' things and worry about them happening.

In this beautiful twist of life and the mind, the good things then turn into worries and become bad and the bad things are worrying and bad anyway. Wonderful isn't it? Within that, the balance that could theoretically happen were we happy or relieved when we don't experience the bad simply goes unnoticed. It doesn't happen at all. This not only makes most things more thought-provoking but also makes them way more negative than they need to be. The positives simply end up disregarded, which is why gratefulness is promoted in many self-help teachings.

This matters because it is a really interesting quirk of the human mind (as if we needed more of them) but also, more than that, because it's this pattern that helps to create a more recognisable disturbance in the force. Of course, the force I mean here is your inner energy: the energy flow in and around your mind and body, which we've discussed in earlier chapters. We are essentially a field of energy, which when free-flowing gives us the feeling of wholeness and love. When blocked and obstructed by the samskaras we've also discussed previously, however, it creates disturbances. As already noted, these blockages are the subject of our practices to let go and to free those energies. These blockages essentially happen around anything we attach to.

For the purposes of this "disturbance in the force" conversation, what we attach to means anything at all that we give meaning and can trigger us and anything that something can attach to create a stimulus for the mind to think in order to gain control. That means anything from a simple judgement or opinion right up to blame, deep dislikes, loves, hates, expectations or disappointments. In fact these disturbances happen almost all the time in the most inert of circumstances and they are almost always the seed of thought.

We are constantly being triggered in this disturbed energy flow; and all of the experiences and even ideas that we have previously stored can be triggered at any time at all and start the pattern of overthinking. We can trigger ourselves internally and externally and so can simply and spontaneously have a shift in the energy that leads to a new stream of thought. This means that until we free this energy and release it all, we are prickly and can be triggered (a bit like a porcupine) to think meaningless thoughts at any and every moment, as a reactive instinct. We are not in control and will be triggered often and for even the smallest reasons.

The great news is that all this is your new best friend. The seed of each thought that has yet to receive the water of your conscious awareness is contained within this disturbance of energy. The porcupine that you are has a beautiful and smooth energy flow when you're completely unblocked but at this point is being repeatedly triggered because of those inner energy blockages. The cycle is effectively endless. But this now gives us something more to work with, in terms of finding more permanent presence and becoming the watcher. First, we can make an elevated attempt to both notice and remove the blockages as they are triggered; we must be vigilant and let them go. Second, we can start to see and feel the disturbances that those blockages and triggers make; to feel the energy change as it happens and well before it actually is born into and becomes a thought. There is always a change in the energy just before and as a thought is conceived. While you may not yet have directly noticed it, you will have subconsciously come to know it's there.

There is a series of events that happens before we act on a thought. It always starts with an energy shift, followed by thought and or emotion and then often by an action or response. This energy shift is the same for thought as it is for emotion; it's just slightly different depending on what we've come to know as the feeling of each one. Love feels one way and anger feels another; hate or fear feel another way and empathy or sympathy have a different effect still. They are all simply different energy movements and patterns. The energy moves from still and calm to erupting and you feel different energies and emotions around your field of consciousness, in your heart centre, your gut or elsewhere. As we become increasingly aware of our energy throughout the body, we can see smaller and smaller changes in it and start to understand the origin of the different outcomes.

For most of us the truth is that at the moment our energy is rarely calm and free-flowing. It is moving erratically and blocked to one level or another in quite a few places. This means that watching that energy is like driving over a bumpy road. At first, all we can look for are the slightly bigger bumps. As we free the blockages, which I know you have already been doing, we gain a calmer base from which to see smaller and smaller ripples. Every thought is a ripple in the energy somewhere across your energy centres. It could be in the head or the heart, the gut or elsewhere. As we become more still and present, and as we feel and unblock the blockages by letting them go, we increase our sensitivity and early visibility. But starting with the big things and moving on to the smaller and smaller is the natural process and finding and releasing those blockages and past stored samskaras involves essentially the same process.

We have already added the awareness of all senses to our practice of presence. In order to become more permanently present and to reduce the number of "mind-nappings" that we experience, we must now add a deep awareness of the whole body and the energies within it. In the final state of being you want to achieve, you will be present and will sense a thought very early, by a change in energy somewhere. You will then take consciousness away from it, relaxing and letting go before it ever forms. There will be no interest in what it is or what it has to say. There will be no moment of focus on it and nothing given to feed it. You will simply relax with disregard, and you'll do so from the immediate moment that the energy is felt. This will give you a slow path towards hugely reducing the frequency with which you're taken by thought and rudely interrupted from your presence.

This may seem like a technique and a process but it is not. It is a new state of being within your presence and a new and additional awareness for you. We've added energy awareness to the all-senses awareness we've reached so far. We've added this later in the masterclass, after your ability to be present has built to become stronger and stronger. As with all presence and meditation, this will require regular and frequent practice. To feel more and more of the whole inner body and the energy centres will take time; and while it may be useful to follow meditations on and around your energy centres, to find and release blockages, this practice is the whole body and watches your energy as a complete system. If you can conceptually understand it, then you can watch the energy from the base of your spine to the top of your head. Feeling the specific intermediate centres at levels just below your navel, your solar plexus, your heart, neck, internal to your head at the back and the top of your crown. By feeling and focusing on these areas from bottom to top and consciously squeezing the energy upwards, you will learn to feel and to move the flow.

Your permanent presence is now close to complete and you have everything you need to reach a state of conscious, thoughtless awareness. The more you practice, the more this state will simply come to you and be available whenever you need it. Your aim is now to actually become that awareness, to be it. There is no mind-created end point; there is just a moment that comes when you simply are the experience. You are the consciousness that is aware of the inside and of outside. You are aware of all senses and aware of the energy and thought disturbances. You can see the kidnappers coming and you can move to safe ground and disregard them.

As the stronger energy disturbances come, you can also make it your practice to let go of them without curiosity or needing to know why they are there. This watching and releasing is crucial because these are your samskaras and they will remove a blockage every time you release them, often never to be seen again.

The circle is almost complete here. The thoughts are created by the judgements and preferences and the energy is disturbed too. You now have a full system and ability to drop the judgements at source by watching the energy; and as the energy blockages are slowly reduced and let go, you will feel more and more present, have an increasingly quiet mind and stop collecting the new judgements and blockages. At some point in the near future you will be free. The effect will not be instant and takes lots of practice to achieve. It should be your state of being now in any and all situations and in dedicated meditations too. It works and it is life-changing. Presence will bring a fountain of permanent love and bliss that cannot be matched by anything external. The calmer and more pure the energy inside you, the fewer blockages you'll have and the more powerful it gets.

Chapter 24 : The senses of the heart

Your movement into complete consciousness is not over just yet. The thrill of permanent presence still has some stages of beautiful rocket fuel to experience and there's a new and richer experience to bring to you now. As we now know, presence is our deep experiential, true state of being. It is the state that reveals who we really are and it is an all-senses awareness of the present moment. We have dealt with the residual and intrusive thought ambushes that some of you will still be experiencing and we can now move on to developing a deeper and more experiential state of presence. This state of presence is likely to be such a rich sensory experience that you'll consequently notice further reduction in your passing thoughts; but more than that, we now start an even deeper connection to nature that can be deeply felt and experienced.

The truth is that our awareness is much more than the sensory awareness that we have been describing so far. In earlier chapters we've discussed the five senses and have been focused on the all-senses awareness that brings a deeper and richer experience of the world. Hopefully you are now regularly practicing being present in this all-senses way and are doing it in more and more situations and locations. After all, our aim here is that over time you realise that this state really is you. It is the you before thought and the you that is simply the experiencer, your ultimate purpose. It is also the you that is directly connected to the intelligent energy around you and the you that can directly interact with this sea of consciousness that essentially makes up the whole universe.

This is an important concept because we can now start to develop the idea of your full field of consciousness and the way in which you can feel the intense love and connection to the whole in a deeper and far more tangible way. When you fully discover your true self, you will find that while it is very much associated with your senses it is a field that pervades your whole body. It is really useful at this point to dispense with the notion of you only having five senses and start to understand that your whole energy field both in and around your body is capable of many more. In this step we've been focused on watching the disturbances in the energy field, which has heightened your awareness of it, but there is so much more to be done here.

It's time for us to start to widen our senses further and to stretch ourselves well beyond the all-senses awareness and presence that we've arrived at via previous chapters. It's exciting and profound and there are some really simple steps to getting there.

We're now going to bring in the heart centre of the body to our all-senses presence. This is not the heart organ of the body but rather the energy centres of the whole body, focused around the heart area. Our objective now is to transform your presence to something so much richer. If we begin by becoming all-senses present. For this, at least initially, it would be great if you are not driving or operating dangerous machinery. This practice has a deeper impact and will create a more blissful feeling than you may have sensed before. Hopefully by now you've begun to base yourself in an all-senses present state, aware and thoughtless for the main and with all of your senses elevated and alive. Until now, the centre point for that feeling has probably been up around your head and around your ears and eyes. It's time to move that centre.

While conscious, very simply and gently, without force or too much effort, move your hub of awareness down your body to rest in a wide area around the chest and heart. At this point we are not targeting how you feel emotionally, so this is a wide field of awareness in and all around the heart centre. All the while you are keeping your visual awareness and that of the eyes, ears, nose and taste if it is in play. We are simply looking to broaden the scope of awareness to the heart centre and base our centre of awareness there.

This is a feeling of awareness of the energy in that area. It is almost like we're creating a foundation of awareness in the heart space and we should start to feel a gentle warmth and presence in it. You may feel this quite strongly and immediately, or you may need to work at bringing the awareness down and focusing it on the wider area of the chest and heart. Essentially, we are using the heart as a base for the whole energy system but we are staying primarily in and around the chest. It may help to also breathe deeply and to have awareness of that breath. Over time, you should feel an expanding and energetic growth and warmth of energy in the chest. Don't worry, this is normal.

I am sure that you've already started to notice some marked changes in your level of awareness and consciousness. The senses have begun not only to emanate from a quiet and peaceful centre around the heart, but also to have a very different feel to them. You will notice that what you are looking at and hearing takes on a deeper and richer depth too, and that there is an emotional nature and feeling of deep love for everything you see. You are likely to be feeling a very positive state that will often make you smile across your whole body.

As this exercise is not aimed at opening your heart or looking at blocked energy, it's important to keep the awareness on the chest wide and it is good to feel the whole-body energy too. What will deepen your experience hugely and really increase the nature of the feelings you're experiencing is to truly feel love for that heart centre and energy at the same time. The act of feeling gratitude and love for your heart should deepen this state and bring a wave of wonderful, blissful feelings from almost anything you see and hear. It is such a beautiful state and represents your first true energy-connected experience in the masterclass so far.

As you practice, which you should do as often as possible, you will feel more and more grounded in the heart energy as the conscious awareness. This process isn't taking you back into the body, because that energy field transcends the body; instead it is giving you a more complete base for your awareness. There are transcendent states that do not use the heart as a base, but this state will bring a unique and beautiful aspect to your consciousness. Be aware that as you practice, your senses will appear to be routed back to your heart centre and they will seem to be coming from the quiet space in the centre of that energy.

As a driver for you to extend your presence more permanently, this state will bring a deep and engaging reason to be present. Do it when in the company of others and start to consider how your thoughts of others and awareness of them changes in this state. This is the first step into truly seeing the beauty and oneness of what is all around you. It brings that sense of deep love that you've perhaps not experienced so deeply before now. I would fully expect you to lose yourself in this state as much as possible and that's exactly what you should do. Our path to permanent presence can feel so good that soon there's no reason to ever leave it.

Chapter 25 : Moment to moment without thought

Has anyone ever told you to live in the moment? That they don't worry about anything and they take life as it comes? Have you ever considered what that really means or ever met someone you're sure is doing it? After all, what would living in every moment really mean? Is it even possible? There are so many things that we need to think about and to get done in our "real lives", aren't there.

This masterclass is something of a magical mystery tour of new wisdom and techniques that are clearly true and right. You can feel it by now and it cannot be questioned. The book so far has been clear in what you need to do more of, less of and differently; and underlying everything has been the aim of moving you into a new state of being, taking you from being embedded in the mind to the rich experiences of the conscious awareness and all that comes with it. This is who you now are – and as this conscious, aware entity you are to truly be and live at the leading edge of life. Your challenge is simply to experience the world before thought and to take it all in, in the richest and deepest way possible.

You are now heading towards a place where you're essentially here as a point of pure awareness. Taking the mind out of the picture for a second, you will also no longer be misusing your personal past in order to falsely make the world into what you have previously come to believe it is. Everything now changes. Without this lens of the past, you will simply see the true and present world. The universe, all the people, places and things, even yourself, will be experienced only as they are in this very moment. And the next, and the next... There will be no judgement, no blame and no guilt. It will simply be rich and deep experience and that experience will no longer have a mind endlessly working to apply past experiences, opinions, preferences, control and expectations, or creating a rigid, planned future. This will be the end of constant internal debate and impossible decisions; it will require you to have a new and ultimate trust that it will all simply turn out OK, so you can dispense with all the worry. The question is, can that even work?

When people say they live in the moment, is all this what they really mean? Are they actually in this world of becoming their own conscious awareness, connected to the whole, looked after by the universe and always on the right track? Are they without worry and having only the richest, deepest experiences from moment to moment. Does anyone actually get to live that life – and if they do, what does it actually and really look like? What happens if you do simply live in a totally non-conflicted, serendipitous way, trusting the universe to guide all of your choices without debate; what happens then and why? You've probably thought about this at least to some degree but if you haven't already, right now is a good time to start. For me it raises the further question of whether most of us have been conditioned too much. Realistically, can and will we ever let go enough to achieve the desired degree of freedom, happiness, peace and trust?

In answering this question for ourselves – and ultimately taking a totally non-conflicted step in the proposed direction – this becomes the moment when we discover that we really can totally trust that nature is going to take us exactly where we want to go. Not only that, but she'll do it faster and more efficiently than we have been doing and could ever have done for ourselves. It may not be perfect or without some pain and learning, but it has to be better than how we got here and the mess we've already made and experienced.

Our record up until now is that we have nervously and endlessly collected experiences, created judgements about literally everything and decided on a really strong set of preferences that are driving our lives and limiting our happiness. We have spent all of our time and energy resisting what we don't "want" and in order to chase the things we decided arbitrarily to like. We have even complained and resisted things that have already happened, that we can't change and that warrant no further part in our lives.

We have essentially also spent almost every moment of this brief time we have in this body, between birth and death, in between chased futures that are supposedly where our happiness will be found. We've been forever in the gap between external sources of happiness, leapfrogging from one to another after they each fail to deliver and just bring new disappointment, and consequently have been spending our lives generally suffering in one way or another. Further, we've made an institution of all this and it has become the norm. The iconic song "Somewhere Over the Rainbow" from *The Wizard of Oz* provides a beautiful metaphor for this endless and repetitive search for peace, love or happiness.

As our consciousness now takes the controls of our mind and body for the first time, however, we now realise that every moment can be rich and amazing. We see that we have been given an unknown, fixed number of those moments in which to become fulfilled, to be at peace and to be truly happy and feel love. We realise we don't know how many moments we'll get, and that we have little idea at all when it will end, but now that we really know how to live them we understand that no moment should be wasted.

It also dawns on us that we previously got it so wrong. Having moved from one thing to another, focusing constantly on what we believed would tick the happiness box, we now notice that almost all of us make the same mistakes. We all follow the exact same futile pattern. We want new things, partners, careers, bigger things, houses, bigger houses, friends, new friends, cars, better cars, holidays, new partners, children... The list goes on and on. We live in a mess of fear and expectation and we compete and compare. What is even more scary and obvious is all that time wasted in the long gaps between happiness events, characterised by waiting, wanting, complaining, resistance, fear, overthinking and disappointment; not to mention that this is time spent missing the now and living in a future or past made by the mind.

When taking this obvious leap of faith, it really is worth reminding ourselves that much of this pattern isn't even of our own choosing and the fact that we all follow the same one really is of no surprise. The conditioning we discussed earlier really does have lots to answer for. During the Industrial Revolution, children were used for labour from a very early age, first in factories and then for manual and hard labour by the industrialists of that time. Slowly, as needs changed, they were put in schools to prepare them for the new and more sophisticated roles that societies deemed necessary.

This still happens today: most children spend much of their early lives being programmed with what society wants them to know, not what interests them or what equips them for the best future. We have now also accepted that we finish school and immediately enter into "real life". A "real" life where we start work, we need to earn money and are expected to serve and play a part in a world we didn't create or ask for and in someone else's idea of a socially helpful and acceptable way.

That's up to seventy years of our lives spent in a structure that gets chosen for us, during which time we are all simply chasing those happiness-oriented patterns mentioned above – the ones that never end and bring only repeated disappointment. Why does this matter? Because the reality is that we place our trust in this over nature and we do so through conditioning. We buy into it and we opt for it instead of nature's guidance and intuitive serendipity. We spend the precious moments we have thinking about how to have precious moments, missing the whole point of why we are here and who we actually are and being without the connection to what matters.

Living in the seat of consciousness, undertaken in a non-conflicted way and without judgements, preference and the need to control, brings permanent happiness in the "real world" and in fact wherever you are and whatever you are doing. The removal of endless thought, far from becoming a problem, brings with it freedom and realisation that demonstrate so clearly that the thoughts were actually doing nothing at all for you anyway.

The richness of experience is now and it is in every moment. Without endless, intrusive thought, people are just as you find them in this moment, and this one, and this one... Without preference and blame, you *cannot* be offended by anything at all and you need to seek and chase nothing at all. You have the ability to find happiness and peace in every new moment, even when in sorrow and even when sad. You can also feel real freedom for the very first time because the only real freedom is the freedom from your own mind and thoughts and having the choice to choose them. Until we have that, we can never be free at all.

The state of presence and of connected consciousness means that we place our trust in nature instead of in the system we're submerged in. We now have a newfound superpower that allows us to be present and to simply "know" what to do, without thinking or debate. We can become non-conflicted and clear for the first time and can use intelligence that is so much greater than our own mind possesses, whenever and wherever we need it.

That intelligence is the intelligence of nature itself and just look at what nature has created. Can you really compare that in any way to humanity? While nature built everything as a symbiotic organism based on deep co-operation and interrelated benefit, humanity went and built a society based on division, chasing happiness and created ego full of endless anxiety and suffering.

Nature is everywhere and we now have the choice to truly trust her. Those who do will find that she has their back. Those who are not conflicted and choose to identify with their consciousness and to be ever present will find that they not only enjoy every single moment but are also at peace and no longer need to chase and overthink. This is an important pillar of this masterclass and that's why I'm making the point strongly: if you trust and commit fully, you will start to see the benefits in stronger ways than you ever thought possible.

The downside is that it is all or nothing. You must remove your inner conflict, be present and simply know and do, rather than thinking and worrying. This is a part of the transformational journey that requires a quantum leap and your will must be stronger than your sense of fear.

Permanent presence is the perfect description of living moment to moment. There is no future and there is no past. You can have a vision of your future and you can make a plan in the present, but you must be flexible and without attachment, letting nature guide you in every way. Focus on how you want to feel and release what you "think" will make you feel that way. Moment to moment, with no judgement, blame, fear or resistance is a place that you have never been. That is scary in itself but the reward is deep and permanent love. No more preferences and no more pressure to control your life. The last step to permanent presence is your 100 percent non-conflicted commitment and practice. After that it is yours.

ZEN JUNGLE

Step 9 : It's Life and Death, Fear and Pain

Chapter 26 : But what about the fear?

It's always good to take a rollercoaster ride once in a while. For some it is terrifying and for others like a walk in the park but it can really make you feel truly alive. Why? Because as the speed builds and the ups and downs flow your fear and survival instincts kick in, in just the right amounts. It's a little like this masterclass: we have taken a journey of ups and downs and have found new wisdom, identified lifelong mistakes and discovered a totally new and beautiful state of being. You are now becoming the conscious experiencer of both the inner and outer worlds, choosing how you respond and how you react, more and more often. You are slowly becoming the being that experiences, before the thoughts and feelings kick in and spoil all the fun. We are removing the mind-created ego identity and are starting the process of reliably watching thoughts and feelings without participating or reacting to them.

Since I began writing this book and masterclass, I have been looking forward to this step more than any other. Even the step title is so emotive – from experience, I know that any step of a book, event or even a conversation that mentions "death" and puts it up for consideration is divisive to say the very least. This step has it all. Fear, pain and death. The perfect subject matter to create unnatural fear before we go any deeper than the words themselves. Because although we have progressed beyond susceptibility to the ego mind and the way it gives false context to our thoughts and feelings, there are still occasions when some specifically sensitive concepts make it through. Our deep conditioning and our life so far have together taught us to treat fear, pain and death as things to be naturally – or perhaps unnaturally – avoided.

How could we ever leave you in a place where you truly love life without helping you to overcome this trifecta of challenging labels. Labels, incidentally, that you may have very unique and subjective ideas about, built over many years in the ego mind. What's more, there is also a high likelihood that these ideas are actually more subconscious than conscious, meaning that we avoid them so much we're not even conscious of the avoidance.

What if this step could remove almost all of your fears, helping you to see and feel pain differently and gain a totally new perspective on death? Would that make the slight or more than slight discomfort you feel about challenging those concepts worth the adventure? After all, our aim is for you to treat life as a beautiful adventure. A beautiful adventure where thoughts and feelings come and go without taking your mind down involuntary rabbit holes of doom and getting you unconsciously lost in the process – which is a process that you often fail to see you're in until you awaken from it and are conscious once again.

The truth is, however, that when it comes to fear, pain and death, many of us have that involuntary reaction strongly kicking in very early and very intensely. As already said, this reaction is often subconscious as well as conscious, meaning that we suppress and react to the fear as if we are not scared at all. That is just another ego reaction at work. On the mere mention of these things, we immediately feel what we may believe to be a survival mode or a natural reaction in which we seem to play little or no part and exercise little choice. It happens and we react. The great news is that this fundamentally does not need to be the case and is learned behaviour not a natural one.

This step, which comprises the next six chapters, will progressively discuss the reasons for those reactions, how it all happens and how we have been conditioned to have the reactions, either by accident or intentionally. Above all, it will provide lots of food for open-minded consideration. It might be condescending for me to say "be brave" in working your way through this content, but it is incredibly important that you apply your newfound presence and conscious skill set in order to absorb and consider the content deeply, feel the "truth" in it, and then apply the techniques with intent and effectively. The reward in completing this part of the masterclass is huge and may well be one of the most wonderful gifts that you can give to yourself. It is where we embark on the removal of almost all fear, a new and more positive relationship with pain and way more special personal transformation around death. All of these changes and more may well be just around the corner. Are you ready for a rollercoaster ride? Then let's go.

The bottom line is that fear, pain and death overlap as concepts and have a sweet spot in that we almost all certainly fear a painful death. That said, not all fear and pain result in death and not all death is painful or frightening. Fear is also present and can be totally debilitating, whether there is the threat of pain and/or death or no real threat at all. In fact, fear can take control of our lives very deeply and rule what we do and how we live almost completely. In order to complete this part of the transformational journey, we will need to break apart all three subjects individually and conceptually then bring them back together later to have them work as a group in their especially scary way. Although really this experience will be more enlightening and liberating than scary. It will certainly not be painful. And, if I do my job well, death will in all likelihood take on a whole new meaning.

In order to get started on fear, it is interesting to look at the question: "Where does dislike end and fear begin?" Over the course of the lessons so far, we have seen the birth and nature of "preferences" at the deepest possible level. We have seen that all preferences essentially start as a judgement made by the mind at the point of a conscious experience. We endlessly decide if things we see and feel, hear and experience are to be liked or disliked, loved or hated. It has become super clear that these judgements then move on to become preferences and limit our enjoyment of the world. In fact, throughout the book we have deliberately noted many times that the more judgements we make and the more preferences we have, the less happy we will be. Consequently we have made a conscious decision to remove both judgement and preference from our lives.

This matters here in relation to fear because there are certainly at least two kinds of fear. One is deep and a survival instinct, "supposedly" programmed at a genetic level through generations to protect us from immediate and potentially life-threatening danger. (We'll address the matter of why "supposedly" appears in quotes very soon.) In fact, it is partly this pattern of "deeper" fear that creates our natural predisposition to judge. As a human in the wild, and in some locations on earth such as war zones and where there are predators, it is incredibly important to quickly judge everything you see, hear, smell and experience. We can then deem it as safe or unsafe, life-threatening or not. This allows us to quickly decide whether to stay, fight or run away.

This is the fear response and with that response comes what is basically a judgement followed by immediate action. One aspect of this particular innate judgement worth noting is that it's often applied to situations or things it's never previously encountered yet accurately decides whether they're safe or dangerous. Sadly, however, over time and generations, this has given rise to what appears to be judgement of almost everything in our immediate field of awareness, life-threatening or not.

Today, our judgments and perceptions, opinions and thoughts create a list of preferences and drive us to place things in the box of "like" or "dislike". But of course there are things we like and dislike to varying degrees; not everything is liked or disliked equally. To deeply consider fear and the modern nature of it, we must look at these relative likes and dislikes some more, with a focus on the dislikes. The objective here is to understand at what point a strong dislike becomes what we now lovingly call fear.

We must also deeply consider if what we call fear in modern terms is actually true fear or a product of thought, preference and a pattern driven by the ego and what we have stored in our mind. If we can fear something that is not life-threatening, a thought or concept and not actually reality, then that fear is essentially subjective and originates in a choice or judgement from some point in the past. Should we then consider it true fear or simply a preference? While these "fears" may be a strong preference, are they simply a preference nevertheless?

In the judgement, preference, resistance and control loop that we're familiar with by now, we judge and give birth to preferences that we later resist and aim to control in the world around us. This is the basic, life-sapping principle of avoiding what we don't want and craving what we do. A dislike is obviously something that we don't want and needs to be avoided; a strong dislike is something we really don't like and try to control out of existence in the world around us in order to avoid it. This is true in exactly the same way of many fears.

We strongly avoid what we fear and we aim to control our outside world in order not to encounter the things we fear most. This means that strong dislikes have for some become a substitute for real fears. They can be a fear of something, a situation or someone but what they have in common is that they are not life-threatening and have been created by the exact same method as a preference: the process of subjective judgement. As such, and for the purposes of this masterclass, such fears really are simply preferences. They may be stronger than normal dislikes but they are simple preferences nonetheless.

Any preference that has become a fear has done so through ego attachment. There has been what's effectively a choice made and thus, by removing and releasing these patterns as we're doing throughout this masterclass, these fears should be reclassified as the strong preferences they are. This classification will be very helpful to you moving forward because conceptually speaking dropping a strong preference is much easier than releasing a fear, which we will discuss further very soon.

A great sign of just such a "strong preference" is when a fear is wholly subjective; where if you were to ask 100 people whether they were scared or fearful of a particular thing you'd get broadly mixed answers. This indicates that the ego has created a personal thought construct and that fearing that thing is a personal choice made in judgement. As we re-identify with the conscious being within and take that seat of consciousness, such fears will be managed by the techniques found earlier in the book. Only deeply irrational fears of this nature will make it through our processes; and as we start to find our balance and centre, through permanent presence and being on energy watch, these will surface as slightly faster, involuntary responses. They may also be the ones we find sucking us into the thought world before we become aware of the energy shift or thought and purposefully release it.

In reality, with practice, our newly embraced techniques and state of being will be ultimately effective against subjective and personal judgement-based fears. With time we will see the energy shift and catch the pattern at the root, relaxing and releasing, without even seeing the fear emerge as a reaction or thought this time or (eventually) ever again. These ego-based fears have no place in our lives moving forward because fear of our own irrational, simple thought constructs certainly does not serve us. These constructs include the basic fears of the ego, the fear of being nobody, the fear of failure, the fear of foods and things, phobias and many other preference-based learned fears. When fear is simply a strong preference or dislike, it is not really fear at all. You can safely relax and release it.

Fear becomes much more tangible or real as we move towards things that may cause pain and or death. When an experience puts your survival into question, the answer is often involuntary and results in fear or not. This is more instinctive or possibly what some would call a genetically programmed fear. Over generations and collectively, our genetics seem to be encoded in order to make us react in a certain way to life-threatening situations, people and things. This is because we have an instinct to live and experience, which ultimately requires our survival. The question of genetic programming and instinctual fear will be answered later in some surprising ways.

We also learn over time that we don't "like" the sensation of pain. So part of our fear is the avoidance of pain and the avoidance of what we perceive will be painful, but more on that later. As a guiding principle, true fear tends to be true for most participants in a species. So for humanity and for our purposes here, "real fear" is fear of common, generally survival-threatening things that almost everyone shares fear of. This fear is far more instinctive and far more rapid in invoking reaction and response. Our techniques can inhibit and manage deep preference and dislike, but it is our consciousness that signals true fear and as such the response is harder if not impossible to inhibit. Does that mean that you now have these fears permanently? Please read on.

As already indicated, the reason that this step covers fear, pain and death is that this allows me to nicely relate the three and communicate the fact that "deep" fear is almost always related to survival and/or the prevention of pain and death. In this, we can now see how dependent we are on pain and death to define fear – because only by including pain and death can we explain what is and is not a fear we should decide to keep. Subjective fears, meanwhile, should be effectively dispensed with using the techniques we've learned. After all, if our aim is to love life, it stands to reason that removing all fear would be a really helpful change in our state of being. What a great step forward it would be if that were possible.

What follows in the next chapter will become a step change in your understanding of life in its entirety, but most importantly it will offer the purpose and context that most of us have been searching for since birth. What appears to be madness in the fact that we all have an ego that seems to be our undoing will be shown to be the most beautiful and natural system of nature working as a process. This is the system that is at the core of the whole universe. It is here that we slightly change our model of how things really work and start to see an alternative answer and possibility to consider. Our masterclass, based on wisdom that works, relies on your consciousness simply "knowing" the truth; it just does not serve our purpose here to become distracted chasing down rabbit holes for evidence of the facts. Please trust your knowing because this wisdom is highly effective. We very much hope that "knowing" it changes your life as it has done ours.

We'll return to fear later, after the detour ahead. Having differentiated between the strong preference or dislike that many of us call fear (the subjective and choice-driven version) and fear on a deeper level (related to pain and mortality), it is important that we look at how false fears have emerged and the role that humanity has played in creating them. This is best done with the following new model of understanding to help gain a deeper and actionable knowing and comprehension. With that in place, we will see how we and the whole universe are likely to be really working.

We will follow that by deeply reviewing many of the collective ego fears impacting almost all of humanity, such as the fear of failure or not being "somebody" before you die. Clearly this is an important and conditioned fear, created in order to drive societal control and, quite probably, greater production. In fact we're going to find an interesting coincidence. All of the preference-based shallow fears also drive the ability for control and the underlying fear required for the construct of the subjective society that is currently in place. Of course, this is the same fear that drives the conflict, comparison, competition and consumerism within it. All are part of the ego; well, in our current understanding anyway.

It is the relationship between conditioning and what creates true fear and fear of mortality that makes this part of the masterclass so deeply interesting and gives us lots of food for deep thought. We now have so many artificial, preference-based fears that it is difficult for any of us to really understand what fear is and how we can mitigate it – or if that's even possible at all. It is clear that what we now consider to be our true fears include false fears made of simple ideas and thoughts. More alarming, however, is how those constructs now also play into the only two real fears: those of pain and death. We will rip the plaster off pain and death after this interlude...

Chapter 27 : The universe is simpler than you "think"

Hopefully you can start this chapter in a quiet room and at peace. In it we will develop something potentially life-changing, if you allow yourself to understand and receive it. Consider it deeply and the implications will offer you a chance to find meaning and coherence in almost everything, if not absolutely everything. Now is that an offer you can't refuse, or what? What we cover in this chapter is not found in any science books and has been arrived at in flow and connection with broader universal consciousness. It is for you to determine as truth or not truth but the model we put forward here really works and has given us profound results, so it fits our deepest aim: to provide you with real wisdom that works and help you to "truly love life".

Before we go further, let's detail the stages we will go through so you can understand things deeply and in full. This will give you a clear picture of the beginning, middle and end of the following learning process, which will be useful because in rollercoaster terms this one is likely the highest and tallest you've encountered so far. You do have to be open and willing to release any and all resistance, although resistance is uncommon at this stage.

From here on in, we're going on a journey that elaborates on, yet also simplifies the suggestion that the whole universe is made of consciousness and that consciousness is actually the fabric of life itself. There will be a journey of understanding into that consciousness and you'll understand both vibration and attraction deeply in this step, though there are some more learnings in later chapters. We're going to see simply what consciousness as life craves and how manifestation actually works. We'll see the true relationship of it all to you and also what really fuels what you currently call your ego or mind identity. This fresh perspective will shed a whole new light on the voice in your head and the involuntary nature of thought. We're going to look at fear and deeper fear at the base level, too, exposing the origins and the fundamentals of truth and instinct.

It is incredibly important that by the time you've finished the masterclass you are able to truly understand the nature of the mind and the voice in your head. Why is it there and why would nature do such a thing? What can and can't be achieved by training it, and how and what it is constantly trying to do while often appearing to be chaotic and slightly mad? We will soon discover that there's absolutely nothing unnatural about the ego mind and that what it is doing is totally coherent and useful; it is just unexpected as a process. Understanding it at a deep level, however, is totally necessary in order to fully utilise it. The fact is, if you understand the following model of the universe and feel the truth within it, you'll soon see that your personal mind or ego is very much part of the whole. It is simply doing what the whole does, which is actually the fundamental underlying process of life.

We have illustrations online (in the free members area) to accompany the content that follows and they can be really helpful in terms of gaining deeper context. Here, we'll paint a beautiful picture in your mind and make this as simple and coherent as it is in reality. In a sense you need to allow the following content to gracefully replace what you've already learned, without comparison or resistance. If it seems to contend or conflict with anything you've taken from the masterclass so far, that's definitely OK. Simply accept the differences. This is a step-by-step learning process towards changing your state of being and each lesson works to pave the way to the next.

We're going to pick up where a previous discussion left off: with the idea that the universe is made of consciousness and consciousness is life itself. As already indicated, quantum physics now broadly agrees with the yogic traditions that arrived at these conclusions hundreds if not thousands of years before the science caught up and proved it – these are certainly well-explored ideas. In any case, the "life is consciousness" model is a really useful starting point for us now. The following is a conceptual model, which we're using to help us imagine and conceptualise things effectively. As will be very obvious, it necessarily hugely simplifies the underlying truths; it will nonetheless serve your ability to understand and use the core wisdom perfectly – in fact, that's its job.

In previous chapters we described a sea of consciousness that connects us all. It's everything. The things, the space, the gases, the planets, the source material of literally everything... You get it. But what does that really look like and what does it mean? Our model relies on you seeing this consciousness as the smallest base units of anything that exists in the universe. The smallest possible building block, of which literally everything else, including you, is made. Remember the god particle? I like to think of them as dots of intelligent energy, though "dots" is not quite the word because they have no fixed shape. Imagine that these *smallest possible* entities, much smaller than an atom or molecule, smaller than an electron, neutron, a quark or a lepton, are infinitesimally small plasma or jelly-like spots of intelligent energy. (Quarks and leptons may not be your thing but for the purposes here: they are unimaginably small elements of the universe that have already been discovered, these energies that we are describing are way smaller than even them.)

As already discussed, these little intelligent energy guys are the base units of consciousness itself and as we said, everything else is made from them. Not only are they energetic but they have energy too, which means that they also have a frequency and a vibration. They are clearly also intelligent but we'll develop what that means a little later. For now, it will help us greatly to give them a name that we all agree means these little energy guys; so, moving forward, we will affectionately refer to them as our conceptual micro-magicians. Micro because they are small; and magicians because, as we discover their nature and possibilities, we will see that by understanding them nothing at all is impossible.

Having established their new and affectionate name, we should now refer back to an earlier, very important concept in the book: that of our bodies being a simple vehicle for consciousness. We previously concluded that our likely purpose in life and of life itself is simply for the universe to experience itself. As a field of consciousness we *are* the universe and the universe, including our bodies, is made of consciousness. So anything experienced is always the universe experiencing itself. We summarised that we are a field of consciousness, using a body – which is also essentially a field of consciousness – as a simple vehicle for experience. When we understand that the aim is to experience the universe in the deepest and richest way, we can see that the body was created as the perfect vehicle to do that.

The conclusion to be drawn here is that this universe is actually all about experience. The consciousness thrives on it and there exists fields upon fields of consciousness, almost magically coming together and finding ways to make a broad range of vehicles to experience itself. We are here simply for that experience and for the universe to experience itself. This all seems great and how uncomplicated – but can it really be the case and if so, why and how?

Let's now move back to those beautifully named micro-magicians. The smallest possible unit of energy and intelligence, holding that energy in a unique vibration. Maybe the relationship with energy is that the higher the vibration, the more energy they have. To best describe this universal sea of them means to explain that they are literally everything and everywhere: they make up the solids, the liquids, the gases, even the atoms, electrons, protons and neutrons – in fact everything. Who knows, there may even be millions or billions or even an infinite number of these micro-magicians in a single electron but we really don't need the science to creep in so let's forget that for now. Because by the way – and before the mental resistance arrives – the concept matters but the science really doesn't. For our purposes here and what will serve us in life, we need only to consider this as an idea, not to prove it with equations, so I'll be keeping this as simple as possible. It's just something for you to visualise.

So here's the hugely important part: these "micro-magicians" have a thirst for and crave experience, and as they experience they change their vibration. Experience can be anything at all that they encounter but crucially they can have both direct and perceived experience – which is simply exposure to a thought, concept or visualisation. To make this easy, all experiences of thought or in reality are the same and each carries a vibration; because at this quantum level, thoughts are also things and are also made of the micro-magicians. And *that* is because, as we know, thoughts really are things. They exist somewhere and in a universe completely made of micro-magicians, this makes them also a field of micro-magicians. Are we following OK? It's really quite simple: these micro-magicians are the building blocks of life, thought and the whole universe and they LOVE to experience themselves in as many ways as possible.

"Experience themselves..." you may say. Yes, because there is no such thing as space; there is only a sea of micro-magicians whose only differentiation is (as previously discussed) in fields of similar and different vibration. Put simply, because they have a vibration, they influence and offer experience to other micro-magicians near them, each impacting the others and influencing or changing the vibration of every other micro-magician. This stuff really matters, so to recap: they create fields of micro-magicians and each field has a vibration. When that vibration comes close or influences another field, it will change the vibration of both fields just because they are next to each other.

So we now have this universal sea of micro-magicians, differentiated only by their vibrational frequency. Some are the air, some are the table, some are the floor – but importantly they are all the same thing with no edges and no end or beginning. They make up every molecule and subatomic particle, every substance and all of life. They get together in fields, where they vibrate similarly and together, and they love and are fuelled by and thrive on any and all experience. Even thought experience. This soup of them is and makes consciousness. They experience and vibrate and that is the essence of how consciousness actually works. They are intelligent because they have intent, seek experience and vibrate at specific rates based on that experience. That is something truly intelligent.

All of this is really important because these little guys are what make you, me and everything in the whole universe. In addition to the above, it's fun to consider that when they get super excited they divide and make more micro-magicians because they literally burst with excitement. When you wave your arms, think, breath, eat, dream, imagine or just *live*, they have experience. It's the same for all objects, animate and inanimate; they are all technically part of the sea of these micro-magicians, intelligent and conscious.

In this context a chemical reaction could simply be two fields of micro-magicians meeting each other, affecting the vibration of each other and finding a new vibration together. That would be them making a new substance. They really love other micro-magicians and fields of micro-magicians that have the same vibration as they do;

consequently there's an incredible force of attraction between them and they move together. Importantly, though, while our conceptual model is bound by time and space, they are not; so they attract each other over vast distances – universal distances, in fact, and possibly beyond the dimensions of time and space itself. The universe is ultimately made of fields within fields within fields of these little guys and when a field has an overall vibration it attracts the same or very similar vibrations across the whole universe.

I watched an airplane moving across a clear sky yesterday and on seeing the jet trails considered the micro-magicians at work, having wonderful little experiences. As the fields of them that made up the jet passed through the fields of them that make up the sky, they gave each other an experience. As the jet pushed through the huge field of micro-magicians that is the sky, the experience changed the vibrations of both the sky and the jet and the ones in the sky become a jet trail of visible water vapour. We may have learned this in school, but this was at the next layer of abstraction and looked more at the effect, the gases and the reactions, not the lowest level *cause,* which is of course the micro-magicians. At the cause we see consciousness (micro-magicians) have an experience and change vibration, the *effect* being that the sky turns to water vapour as the jet passes through. It's the same outcome as we learned in science, just viewed before the chemical reaction itself, which leads to the final state and vapour.

We can explore this model more later but the important thing to realise is that these guys change vibration on experience. They are what everything is made up of and they are why the universe as a macro entity is craving experience of itself. This is happening at all levels from micro (or much smaller) to macro and even universal. The same thing happens for a single energy as happens for a field, no matter how large. They have experiences and they vibrate. For those familiar with micro and macro levels, they are being used here for the purpose of example and not as a guide to specific size.

Clearly, every experience has a frequency and depending on what the starting vibration of these entities is, the experience will change their vibration a little or a lot. It's like a series of smaller waves in the sea in synchronisation that will grow into a bigger wave when they get together. Waves that are out of sync, on the other hand, will be destructive and reduce the collective vibration; likewise a huge wave can immediately make a small wave huge, which represents a dramatic shift from the starting vibration. This is the simple principle at work. If a field of these micro-magicians encounters a field with a hugely different vibration, both fields are changed to a new vibration that will be significantly different to their previous vibration. Yet if two fields have very similar vibration, there will be almost no change to either field. The level of change is directly proportional to the vibration of the experience itself and the differential of the experience from the starting vibration of the field.

Don't worry if this seems a lot to take in. The basics will come through for you over time. At this point it's the picture in your mind that matters, and the basic philosophy of "energy guys have experience and change their vibration". The rest is simply making the point that they are everywhere and there are fields within fields within fields of them.

Now back to you. On the basis we've established here, you are made up of fields within fields within fields of micro-magicians. Each field has a broad frequency and there are a huge number of systems and subsystems (also fields) that make you as an overall field. Some fields make up the physical body and systems within; some the overall field of consciousness around it. All are vibrating as a result of the combination of the inner and outer fields and systems. Consequently you have an overall vibration and many sub-vibrations and you are simply a field of consciousness within the field of consciousness that is the universe, with more fields inside you as a field making you work as you do.

What matters specifically in terms of the whole model is attraction between fields of similar vibration. When two fields have the same vibration and are aligned, they attract each other – very strongly and over great distances. The fun bit here is that these fields and subfields make up everything in the universe, including thoughts, which means that like thoughts attract and opposite thoughts may repel. It also means that even the complete field of consciousness that is you will attract other fields of consciousness that have the same vibration and alignment. No, this is not the simple attraction between people although that does play a huge part in it. That's for another chapter, though.

So there is our model of the universe. Hold it in your mind for a short while because we're going to give you an amazing way to make great use of it.

Chapter 28 : Help! I need context – give me answers fast

After that diversion we now have another (smaller) one that should bring a conceptual realisation that, together with the last, finally brings understanding and the life change we want. This chapter title is fun because it's something nobody ever said. Context, what the hell is context? And why would I crave it so much?

To explain this, we are coming back to the ego and back to the idea of how we build up a set of experiences, beliefs, opinions and more to make up the mind-created identity. The very same identity that we now know effectively ambushes us in what we think and perceive about the world around us. In order to more deeply understand it, we need to visit our childhood or our experience as parents and find out what context is and why it matters.

When we are born, we start in the world as a hybrid of two separate things. We have a body (or vehicle) that has "inherited" certain characteristics or genetic programming. From our conceptual model, you may recognise that genetics and programming are merely certain vibrations in certain fields of consciousness, but for now and for ease let's stick with the idea of genetics being genetics. We have a newly born physical body that has a profile (genetic or vibrational fields, whatever you see best), that's inhabited as a vehicle by consciousness. This means that collectively we start as the sum of two vibrations and have a new combination of baby body and consciousness that enter the world together. As such, it is all immediately looking for experience and has some pre-programmed fears and reactions inherited from the parental origin of the body itself.

What matters here is that the personal mind or ego is largely unpopulated and has no points of reference and the consciousness is more pure, untainted by a life of experience and as such, is largely still in the driving seat. This baby is not suffering from the voice in the head; it has no personal identity and is simply exploring and experiencing as per the micro-magicians it is essentially comprised of. In this state there is no baggage and there is a pure form of experiential adventure, thirsty for any and all experience in the new physical world.

So imagine for a second that the baby is now exploring and experiencing. Imagine it's a toddler running along happily but then it falls pretty hard (or indeed not so hard) on the floor. We have all seen the following process in action, so most of us will immediately recognise it. The toddler falls and then lifts its head and there is a moment of silence or hesitation. The baby looks around to find a point of reference – or "context" – and on finding its mother or father, whom it recognises and trusts, looks to them for the answers and context for this experience. Their reaction dictates everything. Was this experience good and thus should be ignored and/or stored in the "fun" bank, or was this experience bad, and one to be stored in the scary bank of fear?

The bottom line here is that if the mum responds with a smile and the implied "ignore it" message, which may be a smile and a gesture to get on with life, the toddler gets up, brushes itself off and continues its exploration. If, on the other hand, mum is terrified and shows it with urgency and obvious worry, the toddler instantly sees and senses that and starts to cry and panic. Not only do they cry and panic, but the micro-magicians behind the scenes are also diligently storing the trauma in the form of their vibrations. Because it was scary, the vibrational shift from the norm at which they started is large. This is now a samskara (which we've talked about in previous chapters) and something to be recalled from memory in similar future situations.

For all of us, this process is repeated over time: the accidents, falling and reactions of those we trust in the outside world – which provide the required context – happen again and again in all different ways as we get older. We become a sponge for context in any and every situation. There is a period in early childhood when all we're doing is storing off the vibrations as samskaras. We do this with both good and bad events and in the process become filled with information, mainly from the outside world – a bit like a computer hard drive.

The key thought to consider. Why is there a period when we have this almost new computer and literally fill it from the outer world, without using any of what we have already stored inside as a resource to find our own context? The answer is that we do use it but it requires a critical mass of information in order to offer a valid and valuable range of context. Until then we must find almost all our context in the outside world, from what we see, hear and are told and from what others around us do in reaction to the situations we encounter.

It is important to understand, though, that the order of seeking context, has not changed to being in the outside world first. As can be seen when we grow older, we clearly go to the mind first to gain context and only if we fail to find it there, do we then seek it in the outer world and elsewhere. So the order is: experience; need context; check the mind; check the outside world. There's then also a final stage that results in a "dig deeper" approach and will become ultimately significant as we develop a deeper understanding of this process and how amazing it is.

This is all really exciting and creates part of the new understanding that we need in order to make more sense of both the ego and the process we're working to change and to some degree control within this masterclass. What is clear (and deeply related to fear, by the way) is that as a small child or more purely conscious being we do not have the information stored in our minds in order to decide on the context of any given experience. This means that from birth and for many years we are incredibly dependent on the outer world and what we're told as we develop and populate our own "context generator", also known as the ego. We fill it with lots of personal experience but that personal experience is, interestingly, punctuated by the responses and behaviours of those outside at the time who responded and reacted in ways that gave us more *complete* context.

So: a child who has fallen repeatedly and whose mother was scared and fearful of an injury, reacting with fear and grabbing the child to see if they are OK and so on, will soon learn that falling is traumatic. A child whose parents or those in close proximity respond without severity and with a simple "pick yourself up and get on with it" message, will learn to have little fear of falling and will always get themselves up without crying. We don't need to delve deeper into how this can become a metaphor for lots of things in life and applies to much more than falling down. It is often and essentially the birth of fear.

The reason this matters is that this early-life period is one of formative "conditioning". It is a conditioning opportunity in which, in the absence of context *inside*, the child will seek context *outside* and will embed that context for later use. The pattern of "experience it; contextualise it; store what is significant" is the key take-out from this and the sequence and nature of the context is clearly "mind; outer world; seek broader context only where needed". The experiences can be very, very small or very large; the process is always the same. As entities we need both experience and context because without context or meaning an experience may as well never have happened. If our purpose is fundamentally to experience, which we say it is, how could this possibly work without the essential need to understand the experiences and catalogue their context? This is essentially the universe creating a record of the experiences that matter and giving them meaning. It's quite possibly the whole point of existence.

We will discuss fear in relation to pain and death later, but for now it is useful for us to consider what happens when we seek the context for death in the same way as above – especially in close family and those close to us and around us. This context will become incredibly important in this step but for now let's just consider how death was contextualised for you early in life by your family. To be clear, I mean the context given the first time you encountered death in relation to your immediate family. Imagine the baby running and falling and directly apply this context to your life as a child, experiencing death for the first time. The similarities will usually be significant.

Imagine the moment that someone dies and as a young child you hear it and metaphorically look up to get context. What do you see? You see your family, strong people, maybe your father or mother, distraught and crying. This might well be the first time in your life you've ever seen that response from them. It's likely that many people around you are unable to control themselves. Importantly, your age is irrelevant because on the first occasion it happens you by definition have simply no context at all in your mind to draw on. You go to the mind first, asking, "What does this mean?" You find nothing at all inside and you then look out and up to those you trust for answers or context. What you then immediately learn is that death is terrifying, awful and something to be avoided at all costs. Witnessing your parents like this is a trauma in itself. You have now had your first taste of death and the reaction to it is way worse than it's been to any trip or fall.

Now just for a moment consider where your parents and their parents got *their* context for the reaction that they now have to death. Same experience? You get the picture... While this does not explain the nature of the fear of death, it does answer the question of how we end up conditioned to believe that death is terrifying and awful, sad and scary. We see it in our search for context in our first few experiences with it. Or rather most of us do. Because a key part of the fear of death is not in the early conditioning and context but in the conceptualisation of death itself – that is, what we think death actually is. There are many concepts of death, which we can discuss a little later; but the nature of the conditioning and contextualisation as shown above happens only where the concept of death is specifically a very negative one. Unfortunately that sad and scary concept is the one held true by almost all of us in the Western world, and there is very much a reason for that.

However, for now we're not seeking to resolve the fear of death or contemplating what death is – there's much more fun stuff to cover before we do that. To that end, we need to bring back our micro-magicians and look at their part in our search for context – this is amazing, beautiful in a way that you never thought possible. As we know, these micro-magicians are the base element of everything and they are simply beautiful little vehicles of experience. They make up all things, people, thoughts and everything else in the whole universe and they are literally all there is. There is no space between them; there is only them and they are intelligent and have deep intent to have experiences.

These micro-magicians change their vibration due to experience – and because their purpose is experience, this means that the purpose of everything, including you and me, is essentially also experience. Therefore even, say, a virus is made of them – so a virus is micro-magicians chasing and having experiences; likewise a disease and a wooden fence post. Wave your arms in the air and you are giving an infinite number of them an experience. Think about something and the same applies. How wonderful that you can provide so many experiences and have so many experiences! As you wave (or think or read or anything) the collective fields of micro-magicians are all having the experience and consequently changing their vibration. This is how everything works in our model. None is individual because everything is fields happening inside other fields. So the universe is the big field and has every other field and experience within it. It is all one and all connected and directly related to each other.

In relation to our discussion of context, two things about this matter most. First, matching vibrations very strongly attract each other and over great distances. Second, as these fields and vibrations can be thoughts as well as things, there can be information essentially stored in their vibrations. I really hope that you're ready for what's coming because the elegance and simplicity is mind-blowing.

If experiences – which can be thoughts, physical events, feelings and so on – are all essentially a field of consciousness with a vibration, this makes the mind or ego simply a larger field of consciousness (micro-magicians) storing all of the information of your experiences in vibrations. This means that as soon as we have an experience, that experience instantly attracts any matching experiences in your mind. It is like an incredibly sophisticated version of Google. As you have an experience, everything that matches that experience is automatically and instantly returned from your mind as a field of consciousness too; essentially trying to give you immediate context using what you have already stored.

To put it another way: we have this near field of consciousness, the first port of call that we use to find context. We call it our self, the mind or ego but it obviously includes the body too. It is a field of micro-magicians (aka consciousness) and it is what makes us up as a single conscious point of awareness. When we have an experience as an overall field of consciousness, the "ego" field within simply returns every subfield that matches or even resembles the vibration of the experience we're currently having, in order for us to see it. It does this instantly and automatically and simply because the vibrations of the current and stored experiences broadly match.

This means that the nature of the voice in your head and thought is very different than you have come to think it is. Rather than being an uncontrolled involuntary voice, this is simply your near field of consciousness returning results that match the thoughts and vibrations of your current experience. In essence, the natural process of attraction simply raises stored thoughts or fields of consciousness to front of mind when they match the vibration of the experience you're currently having. Remember that these experiences can be super subtle or super significant but they all get the best matching results no matter what.

To understand why this is so important here we must dig a little deeper into the process of gaining context. Please stay with me and imagine for a moment that you as the conscious self are a broad and overall field of consciousness, with many subfields of consciousness. The subfields may make up your body, systems, mind, thoughts and more, but please, if you will, treat the body as fields vibrating as solids and the rest vibrating as invisible unmanifested entities.

Thoughts are a great example of what's meant by an "unmanifested entity", which is not a solid thing we can feel or touch and not an entity we normally consider to have a form. What we do know is that they are made of consciousness, or held there at least, just like everything else. Overall this whole field is you, yet it is also a subfield within the bigger fields of the immediate outer world, the wider world and the universe too. You have a field of direct awareness that is around you and that reaches to a limit where you become unaware, then there is everything else you can't see or currently perceive. So there's you, what you are aware of and what is further away, which you're unaware of.

You'll recall that we outlined the sequence in which we search for context. Putting that in terms of our fields of consciousness: we check in the near field (personal mind or ego); we then go to the outer field (mum, dad and the outer world that we can see, feel, smell and hear); and if we can't find context there we go to the far field (the rest of the whole universe). So near field is the information stored within our own direct consciousness and outer field is what's outside that we are directly aware of. This gives us access as a waterfall of search and access to every single field of universal consciousness. Importantly, it also follows the path of least resistance from near to far – if I get the context from near field, I need look no further; if not, I may search in the outer and far fields in succession. It's complicated but also really simple, and very elegant and logical.

It goes without saying that our model is simplified, but it plays a huge part in understanding the nature of the mind-created identity. By viewing the mind identity as a search engine that uses the attraction of like vibrations, we can clearly see that there's little or no choice in what it returns and when. Mind noise is simply a process and is driven by prevailing experience, not will. It is a product of what has been stored and it is fundamentally created by the purposeful and not so purposeful conditioning that we have undergone by filling the near field with experiential vibrations. The model also shows, I hope relatively clearly, that the quality of results from the near field, if any, will be dictated by what's stored and (importantly) what's released when it's of no further use. As discussed previously, the suppression of this process in order to stop the thoughts is certainly not a possibility. Relaxing and releasing what's already stored when we recognise the energy shifts certainly is. If we release this stored energy – or vibration – then we will reduce the information available for return from the near field and, over time, create more useful results based on truth not opinion. But more about that later.

We are coming to the conclusion of this early description of the context generator (search engine of consciousness) and the experience-matching search algorithm it naturally has, all driven by our little friends the micro-magicians, having now fully established that they are our intelligent energy substrate of the whole universe. It is, however, very important that we further understand the third layer of this waterfall of search for context, the far field. As explained, our consciousness logically begins in the near-field storage and if that yields no results we go to the immediate outer field. But it's when we find no results in the outer field either that things start heating up a little.

This is like getting no results on Google and then asking your immediate friends or experts and looking all around you and still finding no results or answers. What happens now? At this point the universe itself hears your question. At this point the whole field of consciousness is brought to bear on answering your experience. The important thing here is that this is not the immediate and stored local information. There is no limit to the distance and the origin of the answers that you will return when your frequency of experience reaches the entire (far) field; you will simply get the best answers possible.

The nature of the results is what matters – and I like to consider this as a pretty fundamental rule in life and for everything. I should note at this point that our whole team have learned to trust this process unconditionally and the more trust and surrender we place into it, the more perfect, trusted results we appear to get back. Much of the content in this chapter has its origins in the third layer of this context search. We are learning to deeply experience the questions and to then attract the third-layer, far-field answers. This means that it is important that our summary and understanding of the nature of these different layers or fields is fully understood.

We see that responses from layer one, the near field of the mind and ego, are at best opinions and almost always meaningless. They are by nature subjective and are driven by collecting many, many things from the immediate outer field – stuff like our parents' reactions to us falling, or to a death in the family. What we conclude is that they are generally very subjective and can almost never be described as truth.

Responses from layer two, the outer field, are what we get when we can't get results from the near field. Interestingly, they are often broader and potentially more reliable as they may encompass multiple external perspectives. They are, however, also generally very subjective and could hardly ever be described as the truth either. After all, how much more subjective can you get than the response of a mother to a child falling or the response of a family member to a death in the immediate family? Consider again how our family members gain the context that informs their own reactions. This response and context gained from the outer field is dependent on the perceptions of the family members we see around us when we experience death and is either cultural or generational but almost always subjective.

By way of example, had I been born into an Indian or Buddhist family, I'd likely believe that when I die my soul will move to a new and better state of being. Importantly, that state will be one of ultimate unity and love, making me both peaceful and joyful in the face of death; it is a celebration and something to be congratulated. If my family have the prevalent Western perspective, however, they will have a very different and fearful response. They will have ultimately been conditioned to believe that death is final and must be avoided at all costs.

This subjectivity in the outer field is geographic, cultural, political and educational and is unfortunately the core and most basic and impactful programming we receive as children. It is learned while we are essentially populating the context generator for the first time, as is most of our education. It happens in the years up until the point when our "context generator" can finally answer most experiences from the near field. The results accumulated however, can be literally anything taken from the outer field on the way, combined to create the meaningless responses we are getting today. That endlessly noisy voice in your head. Early outer-field responses are literally its origin.

Layer three in this model is the only layer that really matters. This layer goes to the wider universe for context and it usually returns – wait for it! – the truth. This process is about experiences and vibration, attracting experiences and vibration, so of course is not as simple as asking a question and getting an answer in words or simple signals from "the universe" – though instinct or intuition may be a close match for what happens. The confusing part about layer three is that we access it as a last resort and only when layers one and two, the near field and the outer field, don't return any context for an experience. This brings an important opportunity to make use of it, that we'll discuss later and has been the subject of many teachings and seekers for centuries. As you will see when we discuss it further, this model may well unlock the truth behind that teaching and until now, mystical process.

This discussion on context is in some ways a revision of the whole masterclass. It unlocks the deepest conceptual understanding of the mind and ego and shows what's going on behind the scenes; by doing so it allows you to change your relationship with life in some foundational ways. It changes none of the processes in the masterclass so far but it does conceptually change some of the fundamentals behind them and how they work.

Take for example the nature of the voice in your head. The reason for its existence should now be clearer than ever. You'll understand by now that suppressing it and the noise it makes is neither desirable nor possible, so that's no longer what you hope to do. And so that leaves you with a "watch it and ignore it" strategy – the one we've already suggested as the right approach. Clearly the big take-out here is to remove (or release as we have called it earlier in the masterclass) and replace the things that are stored in your ego mind (the near field) and then begin to choose what you store much more carefully. After all, in order to generate good search results you need sound and factual truth only and not subjective opinion.

Another big take-out concerns the semantics of context. Here's the bombshell: context is a form of judgement. We gain context as a matter of necessity and without it cannot reconcile the experiences we have, which is clearly a need if you are to catalogue and understand all experiences, as is the purpose of the universe. Right at this moment, it sounds like I am a fan of judgement and we all know that will never be true, so what am I saying? I am saying that we now have a really clear picture of the world, the universe and importantly our own nature as part of the universe. It answers every question in psychology and it gives us some clear rules, with real reasons to live by. Nothing has changed and judgement still creates preference, resistance and the will to control. Hopefully this will still be obvious but the key thing here is that we now need to develop and learn the process of passing our experiences to the far field for context and as such, ask for truth not opinion.

There is no judgement in truth; there is nothing to resist and nothing to control. Truth is content, what is and what matters. Everything else is simply noise, like the voice in your head. By learning to watch the mind, understanding that it is busy with meaningless and subjective stored opinion and gaining a deep understanding of the outer field, with which it was primed, we can learn that the only source of context that really matters is the far field. The universal field of consciousness. We have said before that when you get the truth you "know" it. This should resonate in this chapter.

When the truth comes, you should recognise it and store it. Use it for quick access later, trust it and don't expect to find any resistance. Why? Because there is only peace in the truth.

Talking of peace, we now need to return to fear, pain and death, but armed with the new knowledge and truth from this chapter. As we will find out, this has a profound impact on all of them.

Chapter 29 : You can trust the far field for fear and death

Well, hopefully we've just created a brand-new relationship with our mind and the near field of consciousness. Since we were young, we have been taking information from the outer field of awareness and populating the near field with what is by and large arbitrary and subjective information. Why is most of it arbitrary? As we take a look at the information that we've stored and realise where it came from and why we stored it, we see a long chain of the same pattern through generation after generation.

The outer field of awareness is mainly one of direct experience and the opinion and influence of others, as theirs was for them. This pattern simply creates a chain of bad information being passed from generation to generation, from peer group to peer group and held within any given culture and geography. In early childhood we accumulate sufficient "bad information" to build the context for almost every experience that we subsequently have, but prior to that we simply take it from direct experience and the reactions and things we are shown and told by others.

To take the example of death: if we are born in the West and we have a very negative perception of death, we will in all likelihood experience a very negative first encounter with death. This will be due to the perceptions around death that have built over time, meaning that those in our family will likely fear it, feel it is sad and see it as a final end. They will also very unconsciously but selfishly mourn for themselves and the close family, as they have been conditioned to do, rather than contemplating what death really is or thinking of those who have died. The body will be whisked away quickly and there will not be much direct experience of the fact that life has left it. Thus as young children our experience will often be limited to seeing our parents react in a way that we've simply never seen before and is likely to be utterly terrifying. Our context will be clear but it will also be fundamentally subjective and fundamentally flawed. It will also have the effect of reducing the likelihood that we will, over time, consider death more deeply and will therefore begin our participation in a cultural pattern of avoidance of the whole concept.

This is what happens when generation after generation of children experience the same method of learning. Direct experience is tainted by the influence of others in the outer field. The child who fell as a baby would clearly be fine and stand right back up, but the terrified reaction of the mother – which is seen when it searches for context – makes falling much more scary for them. As a prelude to fundamental fear, or at least to preference-based fear, the child who falls and repeatedly has the same experience will later have a fundamental fear not only of falling but also of so many more things in life that got the same reaction from others when the vital context was needed. This means that fear is created not by their direct experience but by the outer-field responses that punctuated it, turning an experience that would otherwise have been brushed off or ignored into something ultimately scary. This pattern creates a basic and judgement-based, essentially subjective and in all probability irrational fear. It's where the fundamental flaw lies in our outer-field learned conditioning.

We have a near-field consciousness, previously called our ego, that's there for the purposes of context. It is driven by an infinite number of our micro-magicians, who all crave experience and store it as a vibration from the moment they have it. The context found in the near, outer or far field then decides if the magicians keep the vibration or not. This context is the "meaning" that relates to attachment. It may result in joy, happiness, fear, trauma, pain, anger or any other reaction at all but it's the context that determines whether or not the experience is stored. Context means meaning – and without meaning the experience is not worth storing. If it is not to be stored our micro-magicians simply release it and return to their resonant or near-field frequency, as if it never happened, like when you see something you've seen a thousand times and pay it no interest.

Once a field is vibrating, it keeps that vibration until a bigger event significantly changes the vibration or until the energy within it is released purposefully by consciousness and the process of "relax and release". Reliving it or digging deeper is pointless; release is the only effective method. Why? Because it's only a field of vibration and really *means* nothing. The meaning is given by subjective context that was and is always flawed at its heart. Yes, it really is that simple – because to complicate it is to keep it and we don't want that.

This is what this whole masterclass has been heading towards. This conceptual model demonstrates not only the nature of consciousness but also the simple nature of the ego mind, and the reactions and patterns that it causes. The choice to store or not to store experiences has been at the core of our techniques and principles so far. To accept or judge, to blame or forgive; these are the direct actions that relate to the storing or not storing of these experiential vibrations, and the choices we have. It really is that simple. And when we release the energy of a previously stored samskara, we are simply letting the energy of a stored field of vibration go. This is the key, underlying model, on which every other thing hangs; it drives not just our own happiness and peace but the inner workings of the whole universe too. It also fully explains the underlying search engine that is the ego mind, and the voice in the head that is the barrage of endless results it returns.

Equipped with this model of the ego mind, we can more easily consider the two things that matter. The first being what we choose to store in the near field and why; the second being how we release the things that we now realise are there but that serve no purpose? These are the experiences that will be returned again and again if we leave them there, needlessly creating the voice in our head and taking our peace. While we can deal with pain more fully later, it is the population of the search engine that will first take our focus, specifically in relation to fear and death.

Clearly, the outer field is responsible for the majority of our conditioning. We start as unconditioned children with little or nothing in this search engine; and as we seek context from the outside world for the experiences we have, we populate it. This is how the outside world conditions us – this isn't conditioning in the societal or intentional sense we have previously used; more that we start the whole process of creating the ego mind and become what we store. If we have fears, including our responses around death itself, they clearly came from the outer field at some point, as did our basic perception of death. As an aside, it may also not have gone unnoticed that the very concept of the universe being made of consciousness (micro-magicians) also has a direct relevance to what we should perceive as death too but let's get to that later.

We have already seen how unreliable the outer field can be when we are creating the fears that may stay with us for a whole lifetime. In our example of the young child falling, where context was gained from a trusted adult, we saw how the subjective nature of a mother's reaction could essentially create a fear or simply encourage the child to get up and move on. This is a great demonstration of how arbitrary and subjective the context can be. By considering different cultures, we have also seen variations in the outer-field context around our first encounter with death as a child. Fear for a child of Western culture; celebration for an Indian child following the yogic traditions. Both of these examples show the outer field giving a conditioned and tainted context to experiences. What is relevant here is that none of the context gained is *truth*; all of it is simply subjective opinion. The result: most of us are programmed subjectively and arbitrarily for both falling and death, and in very similar ways.

The outer field is almost all subjective for the purposes of our reality. It offers context to almost everything we do, all day every day. It is sometimes stark and sometimes subtle but rarely ever truth. Every argument, every belief, every meeting, every bill to pay, every learning, every experience, however small, is usually first contextualised by something or someone in this subjective outer field. This is how we attain the identity of the ego mind; usually from someone else who themselves relied on their own outer-field context in the same way, for the same thing. A great example being that when as children we fall, the way our mother reacts is probably a result of some context *she* gained, also in the outer field. If she fears falling, she reacts with fear; if not, she doesn't. The contexts are contagious.

Experiences that evoke fear are either placed in context by the outer field, or where we have previous experience, by the near field. Importantly, this means that the far field – and *truth* – rarely get involved. Subjectivity reigns as we build that identity. In relation to fear, these near- and outer-field responses tend to be the judgement- and preference-based fears that we discussed and discounted in Chapter 26. That's because they are mostly not "real fear", just strong dislikes. Your contexts for existential threats and fears, will normally be the truth; and while truth does exist in the near field, responses will often be instinctive and directly from the far field.

In fact, the rule of thumb here is that fears given context from the near field of consciousness, or ego, are almost all judgement- and preference-based fears; fears given context in the outer field are someone else's judgement- or preference-based fears and are thus equally subjective; and fears given context by the far field are real fears. Those fears are the truth and will involve survival or avoidance of pain. Why is that so? Because universal consciousness protects the whole organism's ability to have experiences. The far field has no interest in contextualising meaningless experiences that can be contextualised closer to home. To put this another way: you have personal or inherited context right up to the moment you existentially threaten your own ability to experience; then the far field becomes loud and visible, it interrupts, gives instinctual support and is helpful in responding with absolute truth as context. Then you react to preserve your safety, and fast.

What does this look like in the real world? In a life-or-death situation, far-field consciousness will be the one to step in, provide context and elicit an immediate reaction that works. Often people who've been in a car accident will say that the world slowed down and what they needed to do came to them – that they felt they had time to do the best thing they could for survival in the circumstances. This is clearly not near- or outer-field support; it is clarity and truth driven by the far field. Similarly, we are all instinctively aware of the nature of a deadly animal. We usually react immediately when faced with something life-threatening, even if we've never come across that animal or situation before: the far field steps in and offers deep context and we react accordingly. This is instinct in action; coming from the far field.

The layers of the fields and context are what we have discussed throughout the book and the simple take-out is that you can trust the far field for guidance when truth and or real fear is needed. The rest is meaningless and can be accepted, forgiven or dropped as subjective. Once stored, subjective experiences can also be dropped with relax and release, including subjective fears. Be conscious, don't judge or blame, watch the energy then relax and release.

That's about it regarding fear. However, as we progress, we will deepen the understanding of how we can artificially invoke the far-field response by disregarding the near-and outer-field contexts, and also consider what those responses feel and look like. The important part is that when there's literally no context available in the near and outer fields of consciousness – or none that we trust – we invoke a direct connection to the far field. This is a very valuable and important skill. This is actually also the part of the process of spiritual awakening that we've previously discussed and or enlightenment. It is what we mean by "connected to oneness" and is the root method to create a more connected consciousness. For many of those lucky enough to awaken by accident or randomly, this rule was at work during a crisis of no context being available.

In times of deep crisis or disillusion, we often lose the ability to gain context from the near and outer fields. We no longer trust what we know or what we are told and see. This creates a void to be progressively filled by the far-field consciousness. Essentially, when you cease to be able to trust the near and outer fields of consciousness, you are simply mimicking the idea of getting no results back from the experiential search engine in those two fields. This means that the far field happily provides the results and importantly the truth.

Part of the process we are invoking in this transformational journey by becoming the watcher is the ability to disregard both near- and outer-field results. The watcher does not store further new meaningless experiences as they happen, through acceptance, and watches and releases those already stored through the "relax and release" technique. Our non-reaction to the prevailing energy of an experience is the disregard of near and outer-field context, which will often then go on to produce an answer or response of knowing from the far-field; this will often be at some later point in time. Clearly this is not the introduction of a new technique but gives a better understanding of the power of what we have already been learning throughout. It also leaves us with a further ability and opportunity; if we can receive the answers from the far field, we can seek universal truth both intentionally and systematically, something that we will explore in depth later.

Getting back to the important *death* stuff, let's now properly explore death and our perceptions of it and do a deep dive into the fact that most of them originated in the subjective outer field – which in this case usually means a direct experience, deeply tainted by other people's collective and cultural opinion, or simply what we have been told and conditioned to believe over time. The following chapter looks at the outer-field impact on death and the one immediately after that discusses the truth and the far-field information on death.

The key here is that we'll demonstrate the nature of the collective, flawed context on death that most of us have been *given*. We will cover the sources and the nature of the messaging too, so that we can all firmly see the resulting conscious or subconscious and ultimately irrational fear of or aversion to death. I can't tell you how excited I am for you to reach this stage. The truth of death is a point of true liberation for most, the end of a life-long conscious or subconscious belief. Transformative!

Chapter 30 : The outer field and death

So, hopefully we are by now becoming fully comfortable with this sea of micro-magicians that make up literally everything. From the smallest atom to the universe itself, it's all made of them. They are intelligent, they are light, they are energy, they are vibration, they are consciousness itself and they are aware in order to experience. They totally love and crave experience! It's their purpose and as a result it is yours too; it is the whole reason that anything and everything exists at all. In the end it really is that simple and that beautiful.

We've also now introduced what we've seen as the three fields of consciousness that matter. The near field, which is you and everything you are, including the consciousness, the mind, the body and the subsystems of it all. The outer field, which is everything that you are consciously aware of, so what you see, hear, are told, smell, touch or feel and taste; this is everything that directly influences you and your immediate experiences too. Then we have the far field, the universe itself and everything in it – which also includes you. In addition, we have created the very simple model that everything vibrates and every experience causes a change in the vibration of a field of micro-magicians. These fields then attract or repel based on the similarity and phase shift of their vibrations. If they are in sync and have similar vibrations in frequency and magnitude, then they attract over unlimited distances; if they are opposites they will repel and there are degrees of both for everything in between.

Why does this matter and why does it bear repeating? Because it means that in having experiences and requiring context we have a perfect system whereby the experience has a vibration and attracts the stored thought fields of experiences with similar vibration. It does this firstly from the near field, then from the outer field, and then the far field, on a simple "path of least resistance" basis. It's basically the perfect search engine but it's also the reason that we're constantly seeing what seem like random thoughts coming up in the mind. It fuels the voice in our head, which is essentially a search-engine response to the experiences we are currently having in either perception or reality.

The system is perfect and beautiful but only if you know how to use it to your advantage. If the near field is filled with stored subjective opinion and noise, you will see noise constantly as a response to experience. If you release the noise and replace it with truth, you will see more and more truth and the veil that is essentially over most humans in the world will be lifted. What do I mean by "veil"? Well. The reason I recapped the process of attraction and the search engine of consciousness was to reinforce the reality of what you are experiencing all the time. You experience anything and everything, big or small, thought, perception or "real world" experience and the search engine is constantly at work bringing back past experiences and trying to make sense of lots of results. It's both a foreground and a background process, so some thoughts trigger the voice in your head, and some don't; but there is a huge amount of action around every experience big, small and even tiny and lots of needless noise.

This noise, mainly from what you have stored in the near field – which at the moment is nearly all subjective judgement and not truth – acts as a veil or a filter on your perception of the world. Every experience you have, everything you see, hear, touch, taste and smell is experienced not directly but through this veil of noise that is happily trying to contextualise everything as it happens. The huge problem being that the near field is generally full of subjective nonsense that you have thought, judged and experienced in the past. This means that the key word for this process and phenomenon is actually perspective and distortion of it.

Your perspective on everything is coloured by this very limited and very subjective context being drawn from an incredibly unreliable source. As we know, the near field is full mainly of a combination of your direct experiences and judgements, tainted by the opinions and subjective thoughts of others either told to you or implied by people and things in the outer field of your immediate awareness. I have previously said that it is all meaningless, but maybe a more important and easy-to-accept thought is that most of it is not the truth. Sure, there is truth in there in tiny quantities, but it is largely drowned out and overpowered by subjective judgement – and if you want reliable, objective context for your experiences, only the truth will provide it. This thing I'm calling the near field, really does need restocking with the truth.

"OK, OK," I hear you say. "You've made your point but what has this got to do with death?" My reply is, "A lot." Having already described your first "experience" of death and the context you are likely to have drawn from it, it's worth detailing that example as a context. When death is even mentioned or considered, this is one of the key results that will be brought back, even now, so many years later. That context is something like: grandma died, everyone was distraught, I have never seen my dad so sad, it's the first time I saw him cry, there was nothing I could say to him, he didn't really speak to any of us for a few weeks, after that he was really stressed and touchy, the funeral was awful and so on. This is a single close experience of death and some examples of the context that a search engine of consciousness would possibly bring back when death is mentioned today. This can be conscious or subconscious, so to be clear, we are not saying you would perceive all that as a result. If that was your results, would it make you fearful of death? If so, why? For now, hold that thought.

What is interesting about the outer field is that it is not simply the source of experience alone. It is the source of lots of context too. Learning is a great example of this; it is experience followed by the immediate delivery of context. Almost everything in the outer field of awareness carries both experience for the micro-magicians and some form of follow-up context. Think of the media or films. We often get a perceived experience on screen and then the contextual explanation too – that's context that we can add to the direct experience and store as a full and complete perceived experience, complete with meaning, in our near field.

Interestingly, when these outer-field context-packaged experiences happen, we search for context at first in the near field, just as usual. Subsequently we then take further meaning or context from the outer field or as in the example above, from the same source as the experience itself. Any context we get then simply supports the context we already got back from the near field and adds to it. So now we have whatever our near-field consciousness or mind context was, plus the outer-field context all happening and blending in some sort of experience-context loop and synthesis.

This means that context seems to start as a seed, and then grows as the experience or thought continues or is repeated. We take source experience from the outer field in the form of events, experience, messages and what we are told, together with the inferred or underlying messages in those experiences – as context - then raise and add similar vibrational contexts using results from the search engine of the near field. A point to note here is that when perceived experiences attract further stored vibrational experiences as context, these results are often only approximate in nature; in other words, results returned from the search engine for any given experience, may only be a loose match to that experience, not always being the *best* or even valid context (or meaning) for it. Equally, it may be that the returned experience was also originally stored as a hybrid of near- and outer-field context, as in this example, which would give rise to an even more mixed reference of only broad and loose relevance; meaning you then associate an experience with a broad, largely unrelated context which is of course not great if it is needed to be relied upon later.

Back to that thought you were holding on to: if you are fearful of death it can be better explained and considered now with the last paragraph in mind. Even though the personal reactions of those close to someone who has died, seen in the outer-field, are totally unrelated to death itself, they somehow and erroneously send a message or context to you that defines the underlying concept of death to take forward with you in life. Rather than simply associating those reactions to the loss people are feeling, you now relate them to the very idea of death as a primary concept. In reality, there is nothing in this first or any subsequent experience of death that actually tells you anything about the underlying concept of death; it is simply an experience in and of outer-field *reactions* to death.

The underlying message taken away, however, implies that death as the primary concept is bad and that it should be avoided because it has now been associated with this awful experience and given that context. This first experience also governs how you should respond to the next death you encounter and establishes a protocol of sadness, distress, fear, lack of words to comfort and so on. It should be noted however, that on the deeper meaning and concept of death, this experience taught you nothing tangible at all. Death was never defined or truly contextualised in any way.

While you didn't explicitly learn anything about death itself or if it is good or bad, you certainly did learn by demonstration, how to behave in its presence. Through that behavioural influence, many of us also learn by association either a conscious or subconscious context for, and ultimately a fear of, death. This happens irrespective of if there is actually any direct relevance or relationship to death in the reactions of those we see experiencing it. After all, death as a concept was never described or explained by what you saw while observing the reactions of others.

The truth is, though, that this is the tip of the iceberg when it comes to both direct and indirect messaging around death in the outer field. Remember I said that it is all subjective and meaningless? Well, hold on to your hat again because it's time to take a closer look at what that really means. Let's return to another aspect of what we've already discussed: the body of somebody who died being immediately and purposefully whisked away, only to be returned and then revealed with make-up, packing and more, to make it look essentially *alive* in a coffin at the funeral. This will then in all likelihood be experienced for no more than a few moments too. As we grow up, this also sends a further clear message and added context about death. It is clearly horrible to see and to be avoided by convention and in all forms.

Let us now move on to the many religions that have a broad concept of heaven and hell – something of a dogma purposefully added, by the way, to religions such as Christianity. This is certainly not part of the teachings associated with Jesus, and was added later as a way to establish a form of behavioural control of the "god-fearing" masses. That added dogma sets up a list of subjective "rights" and "wrongs", rules or commandments; establishing alternate destinations at the point of death dependent on your behaviour, which is subjectively defined as "good" or "bad".

The point to be made here is what message does this send about death? Could it be further fear, maybe because you are never really sure that you won't go to hell? You may say, "I don't believe in all that," but when it comes to the near field gaining context on death this is, for most of us, a slightly worrying result. Are we ever sure that we've been "good" enough? I could also cover further structures added to many religions that bring further fear and further control, adding to this contextual recipe for added fear of death, but there are cool things to discuss beyond the religious.

Next and one of my personal favourites is the medical industry. Pharmaceuticals, hospitals, care homes and everything in between. In our outer field these have become huge institutions with essentially one goal: to delay or avoid death and or pain. While pain is a subject for later and an "experience" we can debate, there is a simple message around death to be easily taken from the whole medical industry: "Avoid or delay it at all costs." The message is not subtle but it is certainly and ironically based on only a particular thought and specific concept of death.

That concept can't be good because this whole industry has been made to delay it or to avoid it. What's more, it even delays or avoids it against your will. You will be kept alive no matter what, like it or not, want it or not. Every measure possible will be used and drugs will be administered in order to delay or cheat death, often with zero interest in your quality of life. This applies to really old people who can't function for themselves in care homes, people who are "brain dead", people in crippling pain and people who are not even conscious and in a coma. Drugs must be administered, care must be given and death must be avoided and/or delayed at all costs.

The message sent by this whole establishment is to deeply fear death, even if living is currently a horrendous and painful experience. It suggests that you should experience that suffering in favour of death because death must be worse. On what basis? What concept of death are they having you avoid? It must be a concept because they don't know, and in nature birth and death is a simple renewal cycle. This means the precedent to fear it must be a human-invented one and obviously based on a thought not experience. What actually is that thought? In yogic traditions death is a beautiful concept, a concept of the consciousness changing state and re-finding the love and unity that we were in before we were born. After all, isn't the logic that we simply go back to where we were before we were born pretty sound? Why not choose that one as an idea?

So as we start to see more of the subjectivity and thought-driven nature of the outer field, we can see less truth in it too. The ego and thought-created mind or near field of consciousness that we're now speaking of is a collection of those thoughts. It is driven by greed, comparison, status, control, competition, money and so on. It's everywhere you look in the outer field. As we lift the veil I referred to, ego in action is starkly visible and literally everywhere around us. If you are interested, do research religion in depth to see the control layers and the nature of the experiences and context that has been force fed over time in the aim to control.

Fear as a control mechanism is second to none and the fear of death beats them all. As previously discussed, a certain type of this fear makes our perception of life that it is a limited-time thing where you need to become *somebody* before you die. It means you work hard, comply with the rules and try to achieve something as a legacy of ego or as something for your short and very indefinite retirement, while missing the moment you are in and treating it as a means to an end. It's hard to miss the irony, too, that later you may be kept alive against your will, dribbling in a care home until you finally "move on". On the more pleasant side, amusingly you will be avoiding a death that you have no real concept of, have likely never even thought about the reality of but that nonetheless you will fear irrationally, just like everyone else around you.

Death and fear are quite central to the messages in the broader outer field and just for fun, given that we can see ego everywhere running the world and systems, it's amusing to consider who actually benefits from the message that death should be avoided, or from keeping you alive against your will while medicating you and caring for you when you can no longer care for yourself. Who benefits from your "healthy" fear of death and the message that "death is bad" and should be feared? Is anyone selling anything as a result of this? Is anyone building wealth or power while you fear death, work hard to be *somebody* before you die and are delaying and avoiding your final moments as much as possible? Who made that collective concept of death? Where did the concept come from? The one that we are working so hard not to even think about and that must be avoided more than anything else in the whole of humanity?

Fun isn't it? And we haven't even started on the messages of the media and the creation of both experience and context, all happening in the direct outer field right at this moment. Have you noticed a disproportionate sell on fear and security, conflict and health and disease? Has the news been starting to become more visible to you as a medium to evoke an experience of fear and to reinforce death too?

We are "lucky" to be writing this book at a key moment in history, a moment when the outer field is currently in baseless, subjective overdrive. Coronavirus (COVID-19) is currently in circulation and our world is under siege. A society, previously uninterested in its older generations is in a blanket lockdown and financial crisis because we are trying to "protect" a small proportion, generally the older people and those with pre-existing and severe medical conditions, from a virus that may add to what they have and kill them in combination. Based on this, we face a societal meltdown. A meltdown that is essentially based on this concept and the fear of death itself. The concept of death literally has the world population on the verge of reset and systematic disaster, and all in the name of saving what is in reality only a tiny fraction of a percent of the people.

What a beautiful vehicle and message or experience of fear. Fear of death too. The world population is locking down to protect a minority from death. In order to manage this, we must be controlled, tracked and have the message that we could die reinforced heavily. In the end the suggestion is that we will be given health passports and tracked in the name of safety, which is also the avoidance of death; we may also have forced vaccination, bought from people who have not fully tested them and be injected to "regain our freedom". This is all in the name of cheating death, which is again being conceptually sold as the worst thing that could possibly happen to any of us. So bad, in fact, that the whole world population must unite under disproportionate control and fear it together. This is making death our single enemy, leaving us oblivious to the fact of who benefits or what is true in terms of the concept of death and what is there to actually be feared.

Truth. It's probably a great time to talk about truth, because in contrast to what has been said so far, the truth does in fact exist in the outer field. If only we look up long enough to notice it and who we are. The truth is in nature. An endless cycle of forms taking birth and death, renewing themselves and becoming temporary vehicles for the consciousness that is the substance of the universe to experience itself. It's literally everywhere around us. Consciousness and the little – in fact *very* little – micro-magicians are all there really is. They are in field upon field of vibrations. They are intelligent and looking for new forms of experience.

In doing so, they have created so many forms, animals, plants, substances, gases, space and planets, galaxies and stars and they have done so in order to act as vehicles to deepen that experience. It is all to gain unique perspectives on the universe and themselves and they have, in creating humanity, excelled themselves. A conscious being with senses that can consider, and use the process of attraction we've described, in order to seek out new experience and experience more deeply and in more dimensions than anything else we know of, certainly on earth anyway. When you consider it, the creation of humans is a natural answer and gives a whole other perspective on experience that is deeper and richer than anything created before or since. Magical.

So, what is the problem? We are mistaking the vehicle of consciousness for the consciousness itself. For who we are. The field of consciousness does not live and die with the physical body. The body is simply a vehicle on which our micro-magicians catch a ride. Our ego identification with it has happened naturally and has been driven by us seeking context in opinion, creating thoughts as if they are truth and pretending that those subjective opinions are who we actually are. What better example than the idea of you being a body and the narrative we are sold that death is bad and death is final. Who says and why?

Why, because ego is at work and things are getting sold. People are working hard to become somebody before they die, and somebody invented a clever control structure that they want to perpetuate. That structure says that you are born, and you go to school for conditioning and to have your near field filled with their opinions. You emerge believing what they want you to believe, shackled in fear, having learned to do as you are told, and to compare and compete, and being readied for fifty years of hard labour while buying the things they sell and fearing for your security and health.

You then buy into the fear of death because it is implied, explicit and reinforced everywhere. You fail to see the truth of nature, even though it is everywhere and all around you, and you comply by avoiding the spectre of their version of death like the plague (pardon the pun). So much so that you may even fail to consider its reality at all or seek any real and true context for it. Finally, you find yourself trapped in your own ego or the near-field conditioned contexts that our micro-magicians have diligently stored from bad subjective information. That ego gains all the wrong contexts and can't connect with the truth, so it taints every perspective with collective opinion and subjectivity.

At its core, your thought of death becomes, "Everyone is scared and avoiding it, so I should too." And as soon as that happens you immediately lose sight of the renewal of forms that is everywhere in nature and the exciting new adventure of life that follows after the death of this form and after this body you're hitching a ride on willingly dies to be renewed.

What a missed opportunity. This is a whole of life structure built on a false perception. It is so far from truth that it doesn't even resemble it. Imagine the sadness and pain that you've had and the wasted time in life. The endless work and the chasing of becoming *somebody* in such a limited time, it all meaning nothing and all hanging on your unconscious fear of and avoidance of death. If death is merely a continuance, what then? How would you live life differently? How would it change your perception of life? Because it is time to start that process now and immediately.

Without fear of death and with the healthy excitement of knowing that energy is never created or destroyed and just changes form, you know inside that your magicians can never, ever die and that your experiences are and will be eternal. That means in this life and the next, and the next, and the next. Death is simply a shift and a step to either rebirth or another state. It simply cannot be any other way because that is the law of the universe and the conscious energy that you are. You are life and one thing we can see and experience is that life is truly eternal, so you are too.

I know that this chapter may have been a rollercoaster and sometimes complex, sometimes challenging. It may be that you need to recap it or to give it some time to settle in, but its importance is huge so take that time if necessary. We have touched on some really deeply held concepts and beliefs, so I am asking you to take in a lot in one sitting – but the rest of your life and your ability to love it really do rest on you embracing this chapter.

If it feels true, then it probably is true; if you think too much it becomes subjective. Ultimately, at this point and in the entirety of this transformational journey, we are not here to deal with proof or science but instead to communicate wisdom that really works and that serves you in your ultimate quest to love life. This really is the wisdom that works; it's a model of the universe that will immediately become visible in everything you are, see and do. It stacks up under all practical testing and will serve you far better than any fear of a conceptually uncomfortable or bad outcome in death. Not only that – and we'll see this in the chapters to come – but this model of the universe will create a direct connection to the whole. It will give you deep access to the truth and it will allow you to make the process of life itself really work for you moving forward. My advice is to trust it, because as someone who does I can only say that the benefits are amazing and so far-reaching.

If I have done my job, you are now either about to lose your fear of death or you have already done so. Certainly on a conceptual level anyway. If not, you may need time to absorb what you've just read. Either way, keep going. Today can be the beginning of the rest of your life and will be the same for others with whom you share this book. While the temptation may be to communicate some of the contents of this chapter in order to change opinion, our suggestion would be to deeply respect the process you have been through and understand that this content will not change a deeply held opinion without the foundations you experienced in earlier chapters. If you want to share anything, please share the whole book because with it we can all change lives for the better. Until then, read on and we can add a better understanding of pain into the mix.

Chapter 31 : It hurts and I don't want any more

Wow, what just happened? Hopefully we had some fun in overturning the commonly held subjective thought construct of death – one that is in all likelihood the product of deep (and probably purposeful) conditioning. It is really interesting how the conscious or subconscious fear of death can totally change how we live our lives. Even without fear, death acts as a stark deadline for the ego to latch on to, giving a very limited time in which to "achieve" something and to become somebody. Being somebody, by the way, can simply mean achieving your previously perceived life purpose or some conscious or subconscious level that the ego "thought" you needed to attain. In any event, it keeps us in the control system and helps us to comply with a societal structure that we had no part in creating.

The previous chapters challenge more than the fear of death, though. They challenge the nature of death and the ultimate perspective that we should or should not have on it. Should we welcome it, want it or fear it and avoid it? All are really interesting take-outs from the structural model that we, as humans, have created. And for those still in the "but you don't actually know what happens when you die" camp, maybe that thought plays into our new suggested concept of death better than the one most of us have been living. Our version of life and the way the universe works is super simple: we are made of these little energy guys that crave experience and vibrate when they get it. The whole universe is only that stuff, essentially experiencing itself. While this strongly aligns with science and nature, it is a model you should experience for yourself to check its validity. In this universal model there can literally be no death, only a state change with life continuing and us *experiencing* eternally.

Strangely, and even though it conflicts with the science, the model we are sold through conditioning seems to heavily suggest that we are the body and when the body dies, so do we. We are then, presumably, back to where we were before we were born or are we simply nowhere at all? We simply don't exist; and as we don't seem to remember where we were before birth, that could easily be true of where we were then too. If we do go to where we were before birth, then surely our return to here is entirely possible and likely – after all, we did it this time, so why not again? If we are nowhere forever, then we won't know or be aware of that, so not much to fear there is there? Or am I missing something?

So how have we got all this fear and the perspective of some big deadline? Surely, when you rationalise it all, there is little or nothing to fear at all. And by the way, if we dreamed up something to fear, it would only be a concept or an idea; because we clearly have no way to directly experience death or interview someone who's been to it. That said, there are many yogis who would love to offer direct, experiential reviews of death and who on face value at any rate could comment on the conclusions in our model. That's if we were interested enough to ask them and could handle the lack of absolute proof. Proof that will incidentally in all likelihood never be available on this subject.

So how and what is allowing us to gain this irrational fear of death or dying? We can see that everyone is avoiding it and we also have lots stored in our near field of consciousness that suggests we should fear it, but there are some other issues that confuse it too. One question that we need to look at is how pain impacts our perception of death and whether we really differentiate the two. How many of those people with a fear of death are really scared of the pain of dying more than of death itself? There is an interesting issue in that pain and death seem to go together, even though not every death is painful and many are actually quiet and peaceful transitions.

This masterclass would not be complete without looking at pain itself and our relationship to it. Not just in relation to death but in general too. Pain certainly impacts our perception of death dramatically, not least of all because we often create it. "What?" I hear you say. Or at least I'm going to imagine you did because it serves my purpose. I say this because the concept is relevant to everything we are discussing. When somebody wants you to perceive or think a certain way, it's usually because it suits their purpose. Think about death and the last chapter. We create pain by extending life and keeping people alive against their will. This brings the key question that we can deal with here: "What is pain?" If a person has no physical pain, does that mean that they are not suffering? Is suffering a form of pain? The answer to this is found in a simple definition. Pain is a sensation of deep discomfort. By that definition, is a person who is being kept alive against their will, with no quality of life, in pain? The answer to that seems like a "yes" to me.

Interestingly, in what I may contentiously say is an aim to give death an even worse rep, it seems plausible that we avoid and delay death systematically in order to purposefully extend suffering. This allows us to present that suffering as if it is strongly related to death, simply by association. Of course, this is only for those taking their context from what they see in the outer field. We have almost all seen people who are being kept alive against their will, wanting to die but instead suffering because prolonging life is the belief that our society holds to.

A great example of this is someone having the will to commit suicide. Someone suffering so much that they are looking for an exit is not free enough as a human to be able to take their own life. It is seen as unacceptable and has deep stigma. If they succeed, then clearly, they won't be chastised, but if they don't, they may be locked up on mental health grounds; ironically compounding the suffering that they're obviously undergoing. Wonderful, and again who benefits? What does it do for the perception of death? It's another signpost that death is bad and suits all the same purposes, as the entire media and medical system tells you.

The real issue here is our perception of pain. What is pain to one person is not to another. I know this well, because after having a few tattoos when I was younger, I have a clear perception of my limits and pain threshold. It kicks in for me at around three and a half hours of being scribed by a needle on the skin. For others, however, that threshold is much longer, and some people actually enjoy it. This clearly demonstrates that there's subjectivity to pain. There are also many nuanced forms of pain, some physical, some neurological and others, as I described earlier, termed as simple suffering. All fit the description of a sensation of deep discomfort, however.

One thing that's generally true is that not many of us seek out pain. We tend to naturally avoid it. Or do we? Some people do actively seek out pain and do so in an aggressive way. In the sadomasochism fraternity, and without going into any detail, pain is something very close to pleasure. It's a turn on and people really like it.

Sometimes it is an amazing level of pain that they crave too. Why is that? And therein lies our answer to pain as part of this transformational journey. We are back to the sea of consciousness and we are back to experiences causing vibration and the responses of the micro-magicians to experience. Pain is so obviously subjective and is of course simply a signal that the body, our precious vehicle of consciousness, is under some sort of threat. Persistent pain clearly signals a problem and that some action must be taken in order to protect the body, either from itself or from an external source.

The kind of pain – whether psychological or physical – is almost irrelevant. It's actually all about the experience that the micro-magicians are having and the resulting vibration. That vibration returns a context of discomfort – deep discomfort – and that's kind of it. So, going back to earlier steps of the masterclass, our whole process is about learning to watch thoughts and emotions without reacting to them. Seeing them for what they are and creating the ability to re-contextualise them as clearly not you. They are just a process that's happening, which we now know is experience driving the little energy-consciousness guys in our inner field to vibrate and seek context. How we respond is a decision of consciousness and ultimately the whole masterclass has been about a change of context for those thoughts and feelings, to allow them to be ignored and a choice of reaction to prevail.

Underlying absolutely everything is the consciousness, in the form of micro-magicians having experiences, expressing them as a change of vibration and automatically searching for context. That context is a stored context in the near field, a context from the outer field or a context from the far field. Interestingly, in the example of the child falling and looking for context from the outer field, we see that two outcomes are possible. One is to ignore the pain and get right back up; the other is to fear the fall or pain and dwell in that fear. This beautifully demonstrates that the context is incredibly important and defines and describes what is often a wholly subjective reaction.

Mental pain is clearly already covered in the masterclass. Mental pain is a dysfunctional relationship between your consciousness and ego mind – or, more accurately and brought up to date, it is a near field filled with things that are uncomfortably triggered by too many experiences. What matters there? Two things. One, that we empty and replace the things stored in the near field; and two, that we gain the ability not to react by re-contextualising the thoughts as meaningless and become able to both watch and ignore them. It is the re-contextualising that can help us to combat physical pain in a similar way.

If pain is a deeply uncomfortable sensation, then who branded that sensation that way? After all, we are a field of consciousness, chasing any and all experiences, so isn't pain simply another experience that can have any context you wish to give it and elicit any reaction you choose to want from it? The answer to this is actually and surprisingly, yes.

Pain hurts because your context for, and reaction to it is discomfort. Discomfort is a proportional tool to help recognise a threat to the body or mind, but the "*sensation*" of pain is only deeply uncomfortable because of the *context* that you give to it. This context is in the near field and although it is not initially easy to replace, you can certainly become the watcher of it in the exact same way as thought, and you can re-contextualise it as a more pleasurable feeling. Remember the sadomasochists? This is a simple difference in the context given to certain forms of pain. Each form of pain has its own experience and vibration and so its own context; but, as you can try to do with a simple headache, by contextualising the pain as an experience first and as pleasurable second, you will soon learn to have a very different relationship to the pain or more accurately the *sensation* of pain itself.

One fun way to consider pain is by going back to the analogy of the body as a vehicle and extending it a little. Think of pain as a car alarm on that body vehicle. The alarm is sounded when the vehicle is under threat; the sound of the alarm is initially unpleasant but, interestingly, once we've been alerted to the issue of threat, we can decide to enjoy the sound of the alarm. Clearly pain can be a very important alert, but the sensation is only extreme discomfort because that's the context you have given it. It is quite possible and fun to look at how to change that context.

This is the same process as not acting on thoughts and is born out of the context that is being returned; but to allay your fears, pain will always and forever be generally painful or uncomfortable at its outset. Once the signal is established, and without the need for drugs, you can re-contextualise it and remove any associated suffering. Pain is certainly an important part of the experience we have in life, and it's an important alert or signpost too, but it is very much linked to the same systems and techniques that this masterclass teaches for watching, ignoring and releasing the sensations, thoughts and feelings. It will demonstrate the amazing power of the method too.

As for the psychological pain or suffering of most mental-health conditions, clearly, they are core to the whole masterclass – and if you are progressing as expected, you will by now have started to master a new state of being and have freedom from those rogue thoughts and that voice in your head.

While pain itself cannot be totally removed, there is certainly nothing to fear within it and the conscious dissociation of it from death will bring freedom from almost all of the associated fear of death related to pain. Every day we learn, we take a huge step forward into freedom and into the deep love of life that this transformational journey is so focused on. This step ends having made some profound shifts in perception that are sure to be life-changing if practiced. We have our new model of the universe and the ability to use consciousness and the little guys who love experience so much to our advantage; so now, starting at the next step, we're going to hand over the keys to the universe. Everything else is simply the icing on this amazing cake of adventure and experience.

The bottom line here is that you may well be able to remove almost all of your fears, especially that of death. More than that, changing your basic concept of death means that life changes instantly. Your whole world of experience opens up – because, after all, what is the worst that can happen? As we begin to see that every moment is an experience, and that we can enjoy them all equally with absolutely no fear, we find that life becomes richer, deeper and more fulfilling and certainly not about a purpose devised as part of a human illusion that would have us all believe we need to perform before we die. This could not be further from the truth.

The ultimate *true* "reality" is simply that experience is at the centre of our existence and purpose. There is a new and amazing way to live life and that is to seek out any and every new experience that you can. Even better, and as the masterclass has taught all along, there is an experience to be had in every moment and a love and beauty at the heart of life and the universe. Until now, ego has been systematically taking that away – and now is the time to get your life back.

The beauty of a universe that exists only to experience itself and that has deep love at its centre is now coming into view. The more you test the logic, the more you will experience the changes. If this step has been a real challenge – which it will have been for most – you owe it to yourself to have a second read. See you in the next step.

ZEN JUNGLE

Step 10 : A Reset for Your Dream Life

Chapter 32 : And then everything became super simple

How are you feeling after all that? Good? Are you still with me? If you have understood and taken in even a fraction of what we've covered in the past chapters, then this is where the world, and your own personal transformation, becomes more simple than you would have ever thought possible. If you're making progress but need to join a few more dots together before it all clicks, then this is where that happens. This is where what has likely been a hard learning process suddenly becomes simple and clear enough to be deeply understood – and, most importantly, put into action.

This has been an immersive learning experience; we've taken a longer journey in order to aid both reception and acceptance and to allow you to practice and embed the process. The purpose of this step is to both consolidate and distil the whole masterclass so far, revealing the truth and simplicity behind everything that underlies it and showing you how to bring the whole thing into your "real life" and experience transformation in every area as a result. This is where loving life becomes uncomplicated.

Let's begin at the beginning. We have learned that, up until now, there are and have been essentially two "you"s. There is the mind-created identity that you've created over time, which we have called the ego or mind identity, and the true self – the one we have found and are slowly becoming by practicing presence. The true self can be characterised simply as pure awareness, the consciousness before thought or, as has been our aim throughout, the conscious watcher and experiencer.

As we have progressed through the masterclass so far we have found that the ego, far from being your actual identity or who you are, is really just a simple process. More accurately, it is a process and storage medium for cataloguing experiences as vibrations. When we are having new prevailing experiences as the present consciousness, the ego then uses the vibrations of those experiences to return similar vibrations that were stored in the past. It does this for reference and context – meaning that it would ideally help us to make sense of the experiences we are having, based on the experiences of the past. We have likened this to the ego being like

Google, bringing back endless amounts of stored similar results based on the vibrations of our current experience and, importantly, our perceived experience too.

Direct experience and perceived experience are in fact broadly similar because we never have an experience without these results combining and converging with it, meaning that every experience is based on our personal perception. All direct experiences are tainted and coloured by a mass of "ego" or mind results that merge with them, hopefully but not often as it turns out, adding further context.

The reason this happens is simple, or sort of simple anyway. Everything that exists in the universe is made of intelligent energy fields. These fields vibrate based on the experience they represent and include thoughts, things, substances, places, situations, emotions and the space in between them. Everything, without exception, is actually a field of these vibrating energies. The ego as a search engine works by looking at the vibration of a perceived experience that you're currently having and returning stored perceived experiences with similar vibrations. Both are fields of intelligent energy. We have established that this process is not limited to the near field of consciousness (or ego), and that the process also reaches to both the outer and far fields too.

As a search engine the ego is very powerful. It returns lots of results, endlessly and broadly matching our experiences and perceived experiences. When it finds stored experiences that match it brings them back to us, causing what we lovingly know as the voice in our head. While many of the results returned create subconscious responses too, many cause the voice in our head to chatter, narrate and create constant mental dialogue. The key thing here being that everything is technically experience; everything includes feelings, thoughts, influences and all the other things that we experience through our direct awareness. This means we are constantly experiencing and returning results.

We can go back to the step on presence for a great example to illustrate this process in action. When we observe a view in nature, for instance, as the conscious watcher, we see and identify the whole thing without the need to narrate it. If it's allowed to, though, and if focus is narrowed, narration of it begins. This is the results being returned from the ego mind based on the experience of the constituent parts of that direct experience of looking at the view. So, I look into the countryside and, after the direct awareness becomes aware of and experiences the whole view, the ego search engine if left unattended will start to bring back results such as tree, grass, squirrel and so on. The process is ongoing and triggered by sight, sound, smell, taste, touch and more. It may seem to be an involuntary act but in reality, it is a completely natural process of similar vibrations attracting one another.

The ego has no personality and has no intent at all; it is not the enemy and it is not trying to make noise or take away your peace. Importantly, though, it cannot be fought either – and while it has no intent, it is nonetheless extremely clever. It is not clever because it is scheming against you, however; it is clever because the underlying process of vibrations is the fundamental law of the universe itself.

Experience and the perception of experience endlessly trigger this search process. When we see, hear, think, smell, consider, visualise, perceive, feel and so on, we are sending out a search request by changing our vibration and immediately get a torrent of answers simply because they have similar vibrations and are attracted by the experience. These answers are coming from near and far; the fastest come from the near field and the ones we have called "truth" in previous chapters may take longer, as they invariably come from the far field.

We'll discuss this in more detail later. What matters here is that this search engine of our consciousness is literally reaching into our own near field and then to the whole universe for results and bringing back answers in all forms. The ego or mind-created identity is simply the storage that is closest to us and returns results fastest – hence all the mind noise and the voice in our head. This noise is directly proportional to the nature and meaning given to what has been previously stored.

What you may or may not have already realised is that we, as consciousness, choose in real time what to store in the near field and what to ignore or release. Previously in the masterclass we've referred to this specifically as the process of judgement, attachment and blame. Our early chapters detailed the case against all of them but here we now start to learn the basic mechanics of why. The noise, the voice in our head and the nature and volume of the results that bombard us are directly proportional to the primarily subjective things we have chosen to judge, attach to and store.

That attachment process is primarily judgement and blame. The more we judge, the more we store and the more noise we get in the results later and the louder and more chaotic the voice in our head will be. The choice not to store an experience as a future result is that of acceptance, forgiveness, love and joy. These are the simple methods by which we essentially release prevailing experiences and make them less likely to be brought back later as results. Essentially, what we accept and forgive, love and enjoy is not stored in a way that will be returned chaotically.

At this point it's probably really useful to have a reminder that judgement is an opinion and a polarity. It can be like or dislike, wrong or right, happy or sad, love or hate. The act of judging is happening in almost every moment of every day, and the storage mechanism and search engine to which we relate here is impacted by the strength and not the polarity of those judgements. Fears and dislikes are the same as likes and loves. They all result in equal attachment and are equally likely to produce the noise. We will then get results on an ongoing basis that will taint our perceptions and see us avoiding or craving things to varying degrees depending on the polarity with which we stored them. Importantly, it is all simply needless, avoidable noise.

Our ego, then, is just a process; a simple product of what we store and returns endless results in real time based on that process. For most of us it is this process that takes our peace and creates the endless and annoying voice in our head. This pivotally refines the view of ego built in early chapters and also clears up a few outstanding complications. Firstly, it is not out to get you. Secondly, you cannot suppress or fight it. As you experience or perceive experience, it will make searches and return stored results. That is what it does and you definitely cannot stop it. You can, of course, choose whether to simply watch or to participate in the results – this thread runs throughout the masterclass. The bottom line is that as long as you have the results stored, the process remains ongoing. Stopping it by force is simply not an option.

What certainly *is* a real option, however, is cleaning up the results, setting them free and changing their nature from subjectivity to truth. Noise in, creates noise out. The moment that you stop storing the noise and release it is the moment you'll have fewer results to return and the quieter that voice in your head will become. Replace the noise with fact or truth and suddenly the voice in your head becomes your new best friend, which is an idea we'll be developing later. The simple antidote to the ego, overthinking and almost all patterns labelled as "mental illness" is rooted in cleansing these results while learning to ignore them rather than participate in them. This secondary process is that of becoming the conscious watcher, which is also a recurring theme throughout the masterclass and only possible after the self-realisation process of presence.

That nicely leads me on to the "other you" or the real you. This ego process that you've been fooled into thinking defines you and is your identity, is blatantly not who you are. The fact that almost everything you've stored is a subjective opinion, and has in reality been some sort of failed attempt at you becoming unique, does not mean that this process is a real identity or who you are. Most of us have purposefully, albeit unconsciously, stored huge amounts of subjective nonsense in the hope it will all combine to make us an individual or a "somebody". Irrespective, it simply doesn't make anything even closely related to who you really are. It's all a red herring, simply a background process that can be anything you want it to be, depending on what you store within it and how you deal with the results when they arrive. Importantly, embedded here is the true concept of you.

You are the one who decides and directly experiences. The masterclass has slowly embedded the practice of presence and developed it progressively. Hopefully by now it has become far more permanent and will act as the foundation of change. Why? Because it is in this state that you become aware of who you really are. This is the state of direct awareness before we create the searches, before we get results and at the leading edge of the experiences we have in every moment of every day. In this state we are the one who sees, hears, feels, tastes, touches, and intuitively knows.

We also, incidentally, synthesise the search results into that awareness to form a combined perspective or perception. These attributes are the ingredients of experience, in addition to which there is intent, which allows us to actually create and visualise perceived experiences from consciousness too. Intent and visualisation mean that we can literally have experiences just because we intend to do so and visualise and feel them – but more on that later.

Most importantly, we have already seen that this self is the one that is sat in the midst of the ego process and the one that is essentially both making the searches and getting the results. It actually is the one getting bombarded by the results and the one that unsurprisingly became confused to such a degree that it misconceived the results for who it really was. Poor thing. Both the awakening process that we are going through in this masterclass and the truth itself show us that we simply are not the voice in our head.

The ego self is a process; the conscious self or watcher is the truth of who we are. Our natural state is presence, and the noise is ego. The conscious self sits in front of the ego process and it has complete awareness. It also has the ultimate choice of how to use and interpret the ego. What we have learned so far, though, is that there is much to unlearn in order to take back and exercise that control and choice. Our learning and conditioning since birth has embedded heavily and distorted our natural state, making transformation harder as we get older. The great news being that for children this process is much easier to embed.

In truth, our consciousness was born with free will and is a small part of the core of intelligent energy. As the experiencer and watcher, it acts as a few things, some that are relevant here and some that we need not consider too deeply. In previous chapters, we have seen that intelligent energy or micro-magicians make up everything and that they are the consciousness that makes everything in the universe and that *is* the universe. We are simply a part of that field of energy; there are no boundaries and there's no space in between. There are only fields that vibrate differently, at different frequencies, amplitudes and wavelengths. These fields then have other fields around them, within them and next to them.

We're touching on this here only because it helps us to remember that the physical body is simply a vehicle of experience for our near field of consciousness. It is certainly not who we are. As the vehicle of experience, the body brings mobility and a plethora of senses. We can largely ignore control of the physical body as a function of consciousness because it's like speaking of the car in relation to a destination or journey. Save to say that one function of consciousness is to drive and protect the body and it does it beautifully, without need of our interference, as long as our vibrations stay within the spectrum of health. More on that later but essentially a part of our consciousness is a trusty chauffeur; as it's very reliable and a great driver, though, we don't need to get involved in that part of the process.

Now to address the two main features of consciousness. These are actually two dimensions of the same thing, having experiences. Consciousness has outer-field experiences, and it has near-field experiences – outer field being all the senses and our intuitive knowing when considered as a sense, and near field being the *experience* of dealing with returned local search results. Intuition though considered like a sense of the outer-field, is a different form of search results, it is *the truth* coming from the far field.

This helps the world to become very simple. As your true, conscious and present self you have these two areas of focus, the near and outer fields. Near field is simply to decide what to do with the endless near-field search results. There are facts, knowledge and subjective opinions but the noise comes only from the subjective results. Facts are recalled on demand and will not create noise. Subjective opinion is noise and debate, guilt and blame. This is what we call ego results and what we have been focused on throughout.

You always have two ways of dealing with the subjective, personal-ego results. You can ignore them, disbelieve them and disregard them, or you can participate in them and react and respond to them as if they are real. This is a simple choice. Our masterclass so far has detailed the subjective nature of most of these results and shown that the voice in your head is mostly the return of previous subjective judgements, blame and influences. It is not a whole lot of truth and can be mainly ignored. I would go further in saying that these results and the noise they create are all meaningless. This means that we react and respond to these noisy results at our peril. The choice is always our own, made by our true self, but in order to have choice we must become the "watcher" and firmly take the seat of consciousness. This takes practice but hopefully, after the first nine steps of the masterclass, is becoming your new-found state of being.

As we learn to watch and ignore, disregard and disbelieve the results, this is where the real magic of the near-field functions of consciousness takes place. We release the subjective stored vibrations and they then lose their energy; and it begins the process of emptying the ego, creating a path toward having clean and reduced results and noise in the future. The more we see the meaningless subjective nature of the results as the watcher, and the easier it becomes to ignore them, creating a virtuous circle of clearing. As this process quickens with fewer and fewer results stored, peace quickly starts to prevail. With fewer results to return, the peaceful gaps between them are extended from moment to moment. How magical then that we have learned to watch and release these vibrations throughout the masterclass, without realising that we were freeing ourselves from a subjective, opinionated search engine that we had no chance of stopping.

The primary function of consciousness is actually aligned with your own fundamental purpose in life. As we have suggested many times, this is simply to have experience in the richest and deepest way possible. Of course, really it is not only your purpose but also the purpose of the whole universe. This means that we are having a universal experience that matters; we are playing a part in the whole, experiencing itself in the broadest possible sense and greatest number of ways. Obviously, this also means that it certainly could never have been intended to be full of regurgitated, repetitive experiences born of endlessly storing and reliving the search results of the ego. Why would that make any sense in such an otherwise perfect system?

Rich experience is based on a focus on the new, on adventures to be had by our direct awareness focused on the outer field. Our outer field of senses and awareness is rich and endlessly seeking something to excite and of interest. Again what's important is that we were also given ultimate free will and can choose the interpretation. We can experience, interpret and choose to store experiences or not; we can choose to store what matters and what serves us, or naively choose to store the unnecessary and the repetitive.

This is the basis of the second function of consciousness. Just like the near-field awareness and related choices, it is truly simple: to experience and then decide if we store or release those experiences in real time as they happen. The experience is the experience and what is, just is. How and if we decide to retain it has no bearing on the past and, importantly, no bearing on the future either. These are all perceptions of experience and as such have nothing to do with truth, so it comes down to a simple choice between storing or not storing. Judging them or accepting them.

Whether to store or release the experience is the core of what we are here for and has no bearing on knowledge or recall of fact; it is personal perception and is simply used in the search engine of the ego for local, near-field results. If we judge an experience, we will store it giving it meaning, forming attachment, resistance and at some point later, a will to control the world. If we release it, we will simply accept it as what is, moving on without attachment or the creation of needless stored results to be brought back later as noise and to fuel the voice in our head. Really simple to understand now isn't it?

Storage is all a form of judgment. Blame is a judgement; attachment is judgement and preference, resistance and control are the products of judgement. Our masterclass so far has been all about showing you that judgement brings you noise and lost peace. Now you know the real reason why. Judgement makes a search result that you don't need and acceptance basically doesn't. That's it. Acceptance is your choice to accept, forgive, love and enjoy, which leads to release. Beautiful, isn't it? Judgement is your choice to judge, blame, resist and control, which causes noise and needless, meaningless search results.

Your experiential self is like a sentry on duty to protect your mind and peace – a sentry who both protects the storage of your search engine and releases the wrongly imprisoned experiences that were inappropriately judged and stored. Watch and be free; accept and be free. The combination of preventing subjective storage and watching without participation is the perfect recipe for a new state of being. We now have all of the techniques and processes to make this happen and support your peace. Today we have learned what is going on behind the scenes and why. This is the epitome of wisdom that works.

Before we conclude this part of our explanation, it is important to mention where knowledge and memory sits in all of this. Knowledge and memory are not exactly the same as judged and subjective experience; they are nuanced and different. The vibration of the experience is influenced by many things. The content – what actually happened – and the emotion, meaning and feeling attached to the content in total make experience, combining to create a vibration for the event or experience. Knowledge and memory are simply the content; the rest is the way it made you feel.

An important distinction to make is that by ignoring and releasing the experiences you are not forgetting them; instead you're changing their context and making the resulting vibration inert or friendly. Letting go of the past does not mean forgetting everything. Facts or content and experience are explicitly separate and different. This is not about challenging you to forget; it's about changing these results to simply become inert content that will no longer be triggered by prevailing experiences. Content is memory and knowledge and will not relate to experiences as their vibrations are very different.

Knowledge really is an interesting dimension here too, and worth mentioning specifically. Much like anything else, knowledge can be truth or opinion. Interestingly, though, most knowledge is actually opinion and is subjective. Schooling is a form of conditioning and religion, science and philosophy all represent current opinion and change over time. They are fundamentally subjective and do not represent truth, so at best they can be a working model for our time.

Why does this matter? Because as a rule of thumb they should be treated as if they were purely subjective opinion and the content stored without judgement and with zero attachment. It will and may change, so attaching to it will cause conflict and disappointment at some point. Languages and mathematics are true because they are languages not opinions. They are systems of communication and not truth or subjective. This matters because they too are content and need no judgment or attachment – but, importantly, they are unlikely to ever change. They are, however, limited by vocabulary and may not be suitable to describe all things for all time. The point is that knowledge is content. Treat it all as subjective and you cannot go far wrong. Be willing to see it change, do not attach and use it as a working model or theory.

If there was any inference in the preceding content that there is a full-time process, where you need to watch for judgement and consciously decide whether to store or not store, that is simply not the case. Judgement is always subjective and will always result in storage and the act of simply accepting *what is* will not. So your simple rule of thumb: if it is not the truth, simply accept it and be willing for it to change at any time. Don't form an opinion or attach to a viewpoint, as you will later resist and defend, prefer and or try to control the world as a result. Let it all go and enjoy it all. Let it go and find peace, or judge it and create needless noise. It couldn't be any simpler at all.

Underlying all of the above learnings is the idea of acceptance creating release and of judgement creating results for future searches to return, usually inappropriately. Without judgement, only content is returned; and as the vibration of content is not personal it will not be returned endlessly and inappropriately. Anything we don't judge or attach to can simply be recalled by choice and on demand but will not become a reaction to experience and as such needless noise. This works alongside the ability to accept *what is* to reduce the impact on our imagined future.

It is a combination of these results that can cause anxiety when combined with an imagined future. We literally create imagined futures, by synthesising them from ego search results. We combine them creatively with *what is* and we create many scenarios, many of them scary. With fewer results to draw on, and a more watchful self, we create only the desired future. We become free of the subjective fear that is always embedded in those near-field, subjective ego judgements and results. This fear can, if allowed, change our perspective of the whole world and limit us to a thought construct instead of the conscious self that we really are. Protect your near field and protect your perception. Removing the perceptual veil reveals a very different, less scary and friendlier world.

At this point it will be useful to summarise both this chapter and a huge proportion of the work we have done so far. Here are the simplified highlights:

We have found the "true you"

As we have now seen, our practices of presence have given the space for us to become ultimately aware that we are the experiencer and watcher. We are the raw and intense awareness that receives information from all the senses and that hears the voice in your head. Importantly, we have seen that we are not the voice in our head. This is an uncomplicated ongoing process that is simply vibrations attracting like vibrations in the form of experiences. It is a single input to our true self, the experiencer, the watcher. Also importantly, we have learned to allow our true self to become the watcher of that voice. So, in summary: we are the true self and the direct experiencer before thought and before any other process is added.

Our true self has two points of choice

We have seen that the true self has free will and is the seat of intention and intuition, and that we have a choice in how we process the world. Importantly, we have seen that we are processing the internal world or voice in the head, and the external world or direct experience. We have also seen that we are blending the direct experiences we have with the voice in the head – or, more accurately, the results from the ego search engine – to create our perceptions of the world. It is around these internal experiences of the search result and the external direct experiences and synthesised perceptions that we have important choices to make. They are as follows:

1.   On direct experiences in the outer-field

We have found that we are living a continuous set of moments in what is an uncontrollable, unpredictable adventure. In finding this, we have also seen that we are in the habit of essentially judging everything as it happens, giving it meaning, having an opinion and subsequently identifying with those judgements. We have seen that this creates both resistance and the will to control the outside world.

The choices that we have are simple, then. We have found that if we simply live the adventure as that unpredictable, uncontrollable thing that it is and we accept everything *that is*, rather than judging it, this will simply allow us to let it all go. It will not be stored in the ego search engine and it will not come back later as the voice in our head. Importantly, this will also mean that we have no need of resistance and no need to defend it as an opinion or part of who we think we are. We've concluded that although this habit of judgement is difficult to unlearn, it *is* a habit and *can* be unlearned with practice. By unlearning this habit, we are preparing ourselves for a clear ego search engine that will offer us peace as we move forward accepting the world and every person, place, situation and event as it is, even enjoying the adventure and unpredictability of it all.

Clearly, the only alternative at this point of choice is to continue as we have learned to do so far, subjectively judging almost everything, storing it and setting ourselves up for a more limited world of preference, resistance and control. We have shown that preference effectively reduces what we can enjoy in the world, each time we place something in the subjective and arbitrary box of things we "don't like". This raises the question: "How well does it serve me to decide to like or dislike almost everything I experience?"

This masterclass is about finding what serves you and arriving at a point where you can truly love life, so the choice here is simply non-judgement and non-resistance to *what is*. That is what works. Now that we realise we are the experiencer and have a choice, we can easily see that this is a choice we can make of our own free will, and make it simply because it is what serves us.

2. On the experience of the voice in the head or search results of ego

The second choice for our "true self" or consciousness to make is how to handle and respond to the voice in the head, involuntary thoughts otherwise known as the search results that are being constantly generated by the ego mind from the things we have judged and stored.

What's very important here is how these results were stored. Referring back to point 1, we can see that almost everything in this "search engine" ego is voluntarily stored as a subjective judgement. This means that all of the results retrieved from it are opinion and subjective; this makes them non-truth and essentially meaningless. The idea of it all being meaningless sometimes causes resistance, but in reality, the choice here is whether to resist, identify or react to subjective opinion in our daily lives, or re-route our loyalty to only the truth. The bottom line is that by moving to truth we can bring peace, fulfilment and joy to our lives.

What does this mean for our conscious choices? It means we either choose to listen to and participate in the search results or the voice in our head, or we choose to disregard it totally, learning to release it at its root as described in previous chapters. The latter allows us to remain at peace but also releases the search results slowly until we are left with only fact and truth, rather than subjective nonsense.

Throughout the masterclass we have gained a deep understanding of how this all works, and we have hopefully made these choices very easy to make. Ignoring and releasing these search results has a profound impact on our lives. The peace we have now found in presence, and the ability to watch these thoughts rather than participate, has now become central. It shows the silence that can and will be achieved as we essentially empty the search engine of its results.

This nicely summarises a huge part of our journey so far. We have found who we are, we have become the watcher and dis-identified from the voice in our head. We have also clearly seen that the world is an unpredictable adventure and should be viewed as just that, accepting everything as it is as we go without judgement or attachment. In becoming the watcher, we have also gained the ability to ignore the voice in the head and to systematically release its noise at source. The simple reason we have learned to do this is that it works and brings the life you've always wanted. Simple.

As can be seen on the "system of the self" infographic (online in the members area), in making changes at both points of choice as detailed above, we have started the beginning of the end of the ego as the destructive loop entity it is. The ego search engine takes judgements, stores them and then blends them into the direct awareness of everything we experience, essentially creating a veil of false perception. If allowed, this destructive loop then cycles until what we see and feel has no bearing on the truth or the real experience we are having. In the end, ego disappears, and acceptance is all we need.

The infographic shows that this destructive loop has now been broken by means of our key choices. We accept everything as it happens, as simply part of our adventure; and we ignore the noise from the voice in our head until it simply reduces and goes away. Once the noise has gone, and by living in total acceptance, we are able to remove all traces of the ego, which leaves us with non-subjective facts. This allows us to operate in neutrality and without identification with a position or attachment. It allows us to focus on the moment and to do anything we want to or believe in for the journey and not because we are attached to the result.

It has become clear that life is purely about the journey. The outcomes are created futures and the past has gone. The journey happens in this moment, not yesterday and not tomorrow. This means that to perpetually accept without attachment allows us to then bring our own joy to each and every moment. To enjoy life deeply and without a need for resistance. Love and joy is always within you; once judgement is lost, you can apply them to any and all things, even those that were previously judged as bad or sad. Without judgment, there is no longer a need for this learned subjectivity and even those experiences can be enjoyed for the beauty of the experience they are, not governed by the polarity we arbitrarily attached to them.

We have learned a lot so far and this summary reflects only part of it. It is great to see how simple life can really be and the underlying beauty of how to live it. We have lived so long under the veil of ego but by now we can see the light at the end of that tunnel; there really is another way. This chapter helps to consolidate and clarify the details of "what" you need to do and "why", so that you can make the final leaps forward. What follows in the coming chapters will add incredible strength and power to all of this. Hopefully you're now enjoying the ride and feeling the positive effects?

Chapter 33 : The truth is always available

This amazing search engine of consciousness is far more special than it may at first appear. So far we have spoken a lot about the ability of our experience and perceived experiences to return results. We have rightly and largely dwelled on the subjective noise that comes from our near field because it's the fuel for the voice in your head – the things we have judged subjectively and chosen to store. The great news is, these search results can also be far more exciting and useful than these egoic responses. The connected nature of everything, and the fact that the base element of the whole universe is consciousness itself, means that there's an innate ability to use this search engine purposefully to receive real truth rather than the subjective noise we're all so accustomed to.

Until now, we have discussed a simplistic idea that as we have or perceive experiences, we get results on a "path of least resistance" basis. This means we get them firstly from our personal near field, which is our direct conscious self, internal and external, including the body and what's immediately around it. Then we gain results from the outer field, which is everything we perceive in our direct field of awareness, what we can see, hear, touch, smell, feel, taste and are told, etc. Then we reach the far field, which for our purposes here is everything else in the whole universe. We have also discussed a pattern seen in our team, by direct experience, showing that both the near field and the outer field are predominantly subjective and suggested that the far field brings something far more special and useful. More often than not, universal truth.

This distinction between truth and subjective opinion is really important in taking your life forward. Truth is a very limited, very specific thing and essentially is defined as that which tracks back to the laws of the universe and is always, well, *true*. Subjective opinion is almost everything else and simply a form of creative thought. It is the product of judgement – yours or more often someone else's – and it is broadly and importantly unwise to attach to it or rely on it. Things that are true are true in all instances, for everyone and everything. Things that are subjective are not. Of course, perception plays a great part in this; the fact that every human on the planet perceives a thing to be true does not mean it would be true from another viewpoint based on a different set of senses. We perceive because of our senses, so what we see as truth is true because we can all experience it and see, smell, hear, touch, taste or know it in the same way. For another species or things in the universe there *may* be totally different truths.

All that said, the basic principle here is that information and guidance becomes more useful and reliable as it becomes less subjective. It becomes less subjective when we look outside of our own near field and outside the outer field too, which as we know is also essentially filled with opinion. We can do this in favour of trusting information from the far field. Why? Because the near and outer fields are simply full of judgement and subjectivity and it is incredibly difficult to see past the illusion that we as humans have created, been conditioned into and often fail to identify as a false reality. Meaning we now blindly believe what we see and are told because it looks very real on many levels; and more to the point, almost everyone else believes it too.

This matters greatly for another concept that we have covered deeply in the book – one that will definitely become a valuable tool in moving forward. This is around the inner workings of the process of surrender. In previous chapters we floated the idea – though not very strongly, I have to say – that the universe would have your back and that you should trust it for guidance. This is the suggestion that if you follow the signs and your destiny, things will turn out well or at least better. This was covered in Step 2, so may now be a distant memory; in any case you may or may not have noticed that we left this a little open-ended, we will firmly resolve that here.

It's time to bring that back to life and make it real and tangible, so that you can use it to your advantage. Why? Because the process of bringing back answers from the near, outer and far fields, together with the idea of truth, actually depends on surrender. There is some in-depth demonstration within what follows, which should explain something that *may* have been playing on your mind when it comes to actually practicing some of the previous content in the masterclass. Namely, how do we actually differentiate and identify a far-field response and what does it look like?

Don't worry, we won't leave you searching for answers, but we may have unintentionally set up a notion that far-field answers just appear as a vision or voice that follows on from answers or results from the near and outer fields. This is obviously not the case. Interestingly, the reality is closely related to why surrender is valid as a process and what that process really looks like. Surrender in a nutshell being, "Trust the guidance of the universe and go with it."

Far-field answers can be trusted and are less subjective or are essentially the truth, which means it's really important to realise how to ask for them and how to recognise them when they arrive. So, we now know well the basic premise of experience creating vibration and like vibrations (experiences) attracting each other. At its base level our micro-magicians thrive on experience and they change vibrations based on that experience. They then attract similar vibrations over great distances, based on that new vibration. This starts with a single one of these little energy guys and multiplies up until they are in field, upon field, upon field of themselves.

Everything, including thoughts and ideas, dreams and perceptions, are essentially experiences characterised by a vibration. They vibrate and attract similar vibrations, driving our amazing little consciousness search engine. In doing so, they reach out into the whole universe. As we will cover later, it is not as simple as thoughts attracting similar thoughts. Things, places, feelings and circumstances can all have similar vibrations to an experience and so be attracted to it. The vibration is not related to the thing it represents; it is simply a vibration that characterises an experience and will attract similar vibrations, which in turn are essentially similar to the experience.

All of this is worth repeating because it shows us how a search request is formed on both an intentional and involuntary level. Whatever experience we have or create in our perception has a vibration and attracts similar vibrations. This is a request that could be anything from a question, a perception, a fear, a desire and consideration, an obsession and more. They are all search requests and will all reach the near, outer and far fields as a matter of course in order to bring answers. Once these search requests are formed, the return of answers is an ongoing process.

With a clear mind, a state of presence and focused, singular, perceived experiences, you are essentially curating and making clear the requests or searches. Alternatively, with a busy and unclear mind, you are making so many chaotic requests that you'd be unlikely to see any answers returned amid the noise of other answers. This masterclass has prepared you for clearance and removal of those noisy, chaotic requests in finding a clearer and quieter mind. As described in the previous chapter, this allows us to replace the near-field noise, by learning to watch rather than participate in results, which is essentially a way to release them.

This is where clarity and peace begin to prevail. As we progress further, we can begin to form focused and intentional search queries by creating more singular, less chaotic experiences in perception. What does this mean? Let's use writing this book as an example: as my focus becomes singular and fixed only on clear consideration of the points needed for the book, when I have little or no other thought noise to distract me, I make clearer and clearer requests for information and truth from the far field. In the absence of all the thought noise, I also become better able to see results when they arrive. Let me explain this some more.

As you start to realise and experience far-field results, you will see that they arrive in many weird and wonderful forms. They are not often an idea or "knowing" that simply pops into your head; they come by way of some atypical, unexpected *happening*. This is often an event or thing that arises and has a hidden or sometimes obvious meaning – what we can essentially consider *a sign*. Of course, these signs or meanings are visible only if you choose to see them.

This time Isaac Newton provides a simple example. While pondering gravitational theory for many years and refining his research (interestingly, during a period of isolating in a pandemic), Newton became very prolific in providing answers to many complex questions. At home, considering these problems without the noise of a busy and interrupted life, he was basically creating very focused search queries within his conscious perception. The most famous answer he got was perfectly characteristic of a far-field response. This was when an apple fell from a tree, quite possibly (if the stories are correct) directly on to his head. That apple falling gave birth to modern gravitational theory and demonstrated the truth of the matter to Newton. On seeing the apple fall, he knew that there was a message in that experience; he saw that answer because he then looked for it.

Our experiences in writing the book and creating the masterclass as a team have often been characterised similarly. The experiences are then seen as answers simply by questioning what an atypical or unexpected event is telling us. In other words: we question any unexpected or atypical event and look for the message in it.

This is not reserved for special cases or geniuses discovering truths about gravitation. It ripples out to most of us, constantly, in everyday life. Unexpected events are almost always a message or returned results. They are also often seen as something to be judged and/or attached to, but that is simply not the case. Surprises, shocks and things that seem out of the ordinary or unexpected are usually both an experience and an answer to something we have been deeply considering. Of course, this is only true when we choose to ask the correct question and then find and see the answer provided for what it actually is.

Why does this matter? Because in your own life so far, you have had so many of these "surprises" or unexpected events, often without knowing that they are really simply messages and importantly have no other significance. They can be big events or small but are characterised as falling outside of what was expected. On observation, they are then found to hold a meaning, an answer or *guidance* – but only of course if you care to look. The traumatic ones are generally the best and most visible examples to quote here as they will often be at the front of your memory.

Things happen unexpectedly and many of us judge and attach rather than asking the right questions and taking the correct next action. We then get further repeated messages until the answers are finally seen and heard, or until the result becomes catastrophic. This happens in health, relationships, work life, problem-solving and more and is simply because subconsciously we're accidentally making search requests and the results are coming from the far field in an unexpected format. That format matches the vibration we sent out, but is not always obviously similar to the question or experience; rather, it is simply related to it by having a similar vibration. We consider something, or often "know" something, and then get the results to give us answers. Many are really obvious or develop their nature to become more so with time. Frequently we only see them when looking back, after the event is long gone. This is happening all of the time and we can usually see a series of those answers before the final event or answer comes – the one that starkly and finally shows the nature of truth.

A simple search request and being open to the signs (by recognising the atypical events and asking the right question) can save us so much time and pain and allow us to see the world very differently and with much less resistance and friction. Surrender is at the heart of this process. Surrender is not the divine intervention of the universe on some mystical level – or at least is unlikely to be. Surrender is more the simple recognition and observation of an answer to a question, found in an event or experience, that then allows you to take the best next action. This is where we "trust the universe", "see the signs" or truth and take our next action based on pure trust and not subjective opinion.

How many times have we all ignored these signs or answers? How many times were there multiple signs that repeatedly gave the same message again and again around a certain perception, consideration or situational experience? It is hard to find anyone who cannot relate to this as a pattern; but without a deep understanding of what we are seeing, very few of us recognise it and can harness its power. This is the micro-magicians doing their finest work.

As a matter of normality, we live in a predominantly or even totally subjective world. We rely on our inner and outer fields for almost all of our answers and information. We have been conditioned to do so and depend mainly on what we've been taught, told and "think" subjectively. Consequently, we generally don't see or recognise guidance or truth from the far field, even though it is all around us. This is because we are not educated to understand our own consciousness and our deeply connected relationship to a universe that is constantly giving us the truthful answers we seek. Importantly, those answers are also simply part of a process and unlikely to be coming to us with any benevolent intent, although of course that's a possibility for consideration.

Every situation, idea, response and sign is far more likely to be somehow related to the vibrations in our perception than it is to be the work of any magical or mystical, alternate divine personality with our best interests at heart. Why? Because things are normally incredibly simple and complicated things rarely work well. This means that vibrational attraction as a simple and basic law that governs everything is a really likely answer. This simple law, underpinned by our experience-thirsty micro-magicians that simply change their vibration based on their experience, can actually answer almost everything, if not everything, in this amazing universe. It really is likely to be that uncomplicated.

This means that we are all essentially geniuses! We can all form perceived experiences that are basically questions or search queries and we can seek and see the answers. That is, of course, if we are willing to learn to recognise them when they come and to ask the right questions. Genius is certainly unlikely to be some physiological brain characteristic. The brain is merely a symptom of consciousness and not the cause; it changes based on perception and is not likely to be the cause of perception. The brain is just more of those conscious little energy guys having experiences and changing their vibration as a result.

The inner field of consciousness is simply our own, local point of experience and that is the same for all of us. Our close-range slice of universal consciousness and the universal mind. This means that ultimately our true self and the intent contained within can access the universal truth about anything on which we want to ponder or focus our perception. It can deliver the results of genius, if only we choose to see past the subjective results of the near and outer fields. There simply is no barrier to you or me finding the same genius as Newton, Einstein, Chikowsky or anyone else for that matter; we are all just as connected and part of the same sea of the same thing. All we need to do is experience and perceive whatever questions of whatever size we want – even huge questions like theirs.

This makes clear the process of surrender. This is the process of formulating clear questions in your perception, clearing your mind of noise and then of taking the time to recognise the answers. On seeing an event that's likely to represent an answer, it is then all about asking the right questions of that event, reading the answer and gaining a "knowing" that allows you to take the right actions. It is about seeing each stage of this process clearly, at which point you can fully trust the responses as being the truth. As we have already discussed in previous chapters, our ability to "know" the truth is also fundamental.

This book is a transformational journey, and has been created in large part through our own transformational journey that more than anything featured trust in and reliance on this method. Much research and consideration then gave way to a torrent of far-field answers. Ironically, seeing this and progressively recognising the process has also allowed us to deeply detail the process itself. This is how all of the greatest discoveries of humanity were made and it is available to you, me and everyone else on the planet, without limit or distinction. It is a fundamental understanding that we can now use in moving our lives forward and in hatching the plan or vision for the life we want. Off we go to use it to do something truly special. The more you experience it, the more your trust will build. You will remove resistance and find that acceptance and surrender are fundamental to your success.

As a final note on acceptance and surrender, this process has a profound impact on the friction in your life and on your ability to simply accept and move on. As you formulate better search queries and become increasingly clear, you will see firstly that the traumatic answers become fewer in number and frequency. Why? Because you will see the answer before it becomes traumatic. You will know the question you are asking, and you will see the early responses from the far field. This allows you to become fluid, to adapt the direction of your life without attachment and to create perpetual forward motion, without resistance or friction. Just imagine if the signs that you now know you should have seen much earlier in your past were never again necessary. If you could unconditionally accept change, knowing its truth, without resisting or holding on until the universal-messaging sledgehammer hits you in the face. From now on we can see it in all of its beauty and surrender to it willingly.

Chapter 34 : A vision for life and forward-only movement

We have covered so much, and this has been such a journey. In recent chapters the process has become far clearer and hopefully far more actionable as a result. We have learned some very strongly punctuated realities. The number one for me is that life is much more about how you live it than it is about how it will feel at any imagined destination. It's also now obvious that it is all about what is happening on the inside and very little about what happens on the outside. After all, we have learned beyond a doubt that we cannot control the outside, and that it simply takes away our peace when we try to and repeatedly fail.

Over the second part of the masterclass, we have removed almost all reference to things on the outside because that's not where the life you want can be found. Little or no attention has been given to material things and we have focused very tightly on the relationship between your true self and your ego self – or the search-engine process that we now know the ego to be. That dialogue between the real you and the voice in your head is what really matters now.

For almost all of us, this represents a truly fundamental change to our perception of what life is all about. More importantly, this change in perspective gives us real clarity about how life really works and how we fit into it. It has shown us our true and natural purpose – to simply and deeply experience – and at the most basic level it has shown us that experience is the fundamental fuel of the universe. As we experience, vibrations change to create more and different experiences. Literally everything we experience in our reality is also the product of experience; experiences even vibrate with the experience and attract like experiences.

We took this simple idea of experiences changing vibrations and creating further experiences and attraction, and applied it to things we learned about the mind-created identity in the first steps of the book. In doing so we learned that this same idea can be applied to every concept, big and small, that we encounter in our lives. As a result, and importantly, we realised a stark reality: until now, our attention within our lives has been focused completely in the wrong places. Like almost everyone on the planet, we have been living life primarily focused on the outside, on the result and not the cause. Our peace and happiness has so far been conditional on things, people, circumstances and places, being what we want, prefer, like and feel is right.

What we've now learned is that what we've always wanted was waiting within us all the time, had we only known how to unlock it and free ourselves from the prison of the ego mind. The fact that outer things don't bring the happiness we seek is newly and deeply understood. We have been repeatedly reminded that, for most of us, getting what we think will make us feel good in the outside world tends to do so only momentarily if at all. It can even be the source of our ongoing lack of fulfilment.

The great news is that we've now moved on and we never need to look back again, ever. There is a new dawn of focus. Focus on the inside and not the outside. This brings new clarity to how we're made, what matters and what we need to do to make the changes. It shows us a simple recipe that we've never seen before on how to live the life we want – which is a life that delivers the happiness we've always wanted. Realising our true self and taking control of the ego process is a fundamental aim here; as is removing the fear or idea of death and understanding that we are in control of literally everything we perceive, including our happiness, love, fulfilment and purpose.

Enjoying life, however it may be, is now firmly within our power. The only remaining question is: "What does this look like in the real world we live in?" In other words, how do we integrate this new state of being and have it work seamlessly in our existing life and with who we were before we began this transformational journey? The success of this masterclass is fully dependent on that integration, so we're now going to bring everything together to create symbiosis between the inner and outer life. This will be a relationship to exceed your wildest dreams.

We're now going to apply everything we've learned to the creation of a deeply peaceful, free and fulfilled life plan. This will be your own personal life plan, and will deliver the aim of the masterclass in a personalised way and in full. You will now move towards the fundamental goal of taking your current life and transforming it, almost immediately, into a life that you can truly love. We'll move forward in several stages, covering each one in order, so that we're offering the most practical and actionable route.

Those stages are as follows:

1. Creating a present-moment status report
2. Creating your life vision
3. Creating and taking steps towards your vision

Before we begin on this part of the journey, though, there's an important point to address. The three stages above may appear to suggest a need for preferences, likes, dislikes, wants and control of the outside world, which we now know is impossible to achieve. It is crucial to realise that for most of us our vision of the future is, underlying everything, simply a state of being. It's not about the outer, material things, although we're likely to have been confused about that in the past.

There is no destination, there's just the journey – and it's fundamentally important to keep that in mind as we move through the following stages. We will not be setting the scene for your arrival at a future destination, at which point you'll achieve your vision. On the contrary, you will set a plan to reach your vision now in this moment and stay within that vision throughout the rest of your life. There is no thought of, "Tomorrow I will be at peace and happy"; there is only this moment, now. This is important because without this understanding we can get lost in our *destination* as the vehicle or object of happiness, rather than focusing on the fulfilment that can be found permanently in and on the journey itself. Let's move on to the first stage knowing that this is certainly not about judgement, preferences, likes, dislikes and wants that need to be manifested in the outside world.

Creating a present-moment status report

Present-moment awareness is of course a fundamental aspect of the masterclass and this activity-based process will challenge and test everything you've learned so far. Your status report is going to reflect where you are right now, so your progress will become clear – and so will the reality that your transformational journey has really only just begun.

The fun way to begin is for me to simply throw it out there: where are you in this present moment? A perfect way to do this would be for you to immediately get a pen and paper and then detail what you understand by that question. What is your status right now in the present moment? Write it down, using bullet points, itemised status statements and/or a fully detailed picture to express where you are in your life right here and now. Every plan or strategy must have an origin and if we're to make tangible progress towards a vision or goal we must know where we are today, in this moment. It is best to write it as you feel it, setting down what matters to you about where you are right now.

My strong suggestion is to immediately stop reading and write it down now. Create the heading "Where is my life in this moment?" or "What is my status report?" and beneath it complete the details as best you can but please don't write more than a single page. Be brave: stop reading now and go do it! We should meet back here when you're happy it's done. It might be tempting to read on without indulging me here, but your growth will come from doing it and doing it now with full commitment – so I'll see you when you get back. Do it, do it, do it...

So, how did that go? Did you find it easy or difficult? At this moment, I would truly love to be able to sit down with you and review your document together. Your status tells us everything we need to know about how far you've come and, more importantly, what you need to do next. Just remember that there is no success or failure in this exercise – you're simply where you are – so please don't judge yourself in any way on the findings. They're not graded and don't carry a pass or fail either.

Before we continue it would be useful to discuss your status in relation to the masterclass so far. What would the "perfect" page of results or answers look like here? Your status would simply be a picture or description of your internal state at this moment, based on a target state that you wanted to achieve. It would have no references to anything in the past, because the past has gone. It would have no references to anything in the future, because the future is only in your imagination; it is a creation and may have many versions and alternatives. Nor would it have any reference to your life situation, what you have, who you're with, your labels and roles, your opinions and beliefs, ideal "perfect world" scenarios or anything else that would require you to have strict control of the world.

In fact, to make this simpler and to reference concepts that we're now really familiar with, your status would not reference anything at all that would exist or feature in your ego identity. This content is all judgement-based and subjective and as such has no place here anyway; but importantly it should be disregarded because all of it was stored in the past and produces a distorted perspective and a need for control, whether it's applied to now or the future. This ego content may well be still present, albeit to a diminishing degree; but it is in the past nevertheless and should play no part in your current status.

Your state is essentially a measure of what matters right now and with no past at all involved. It comes with a total acceptance of what is and no attachment to any previously judged like or dislike, opinion, want or belief. There should also be zero resistance. This means that today your only concern is how closely the way you feel resembles the way you want to feel for the rest of your life. What would life feel like if you were to actually "love life" and how close to that are you in this moment?

This revelation might make the fact that you were asked to perform the exercise feel like a sort of trick question. Of course, that wasn't the intention. We just needed to see how you would like your life to be on some or all levels before we could possibly isolate your current status. After all, status is measured on a scale of zero to at-destination. The usefulness (and trick) in the question is the realisation that without that pre-guidance almost everyone gives answers that are littered with the past, the present, material things, people, partners and ultimately their feelings, in a disparate and largely directionless clutter.

Status is extremely important in deciding the next steps of your transformational journey and also in showing that without a real goal or vision of your life you cannot assess where you currently are at all. This is something that most of us fail to notice. We move through life without a clear goal or destination and are essentially taking a journey to nowhere at all, without directions or a map – and if we do have a destination or goal in mind it is often material or external.

Progress through the masterclass helps to move the focus away from external goals, but they are almost always present when we ask for a status. This doesn't mean you or anyone else is fundamentally confused; it simply demonstrates how quickly and easily the ego results can take over and end up defining who we actually are. After all, a status is a description of *who* we are as much as it is of *where* we are. Clearly it should now be recognised that these external goals and ego descriptions will play no part in delivering the results we want from this transformational journey. They can therefore be immediately dispensed with. It is easy to feel a little lost at this point but as we move on it will become obvious that this was simply a key learning, needed in order for the next step to be taken. We will return to the status report after creating a vision or destination, so let's now get started on that.

Creating a life vision

Don't worry: this doesn't involve another trick question. We're going to consider and work on this bit together, in order to generate something more actionable and to ensure that we all deeply understand the basics of what it means and how it becomes truly tangible. Importantly, the vision of your life is not what you want at some point in the future; it is the vision of what your perfect life would and should be right now in this moment. This presents an interesting and fun challenge. A vision is slightly different from a goal and we're using the word specifically, because this exercise is about *imagining* how the perfect life would be and feel. Adding the idea of the present moment will help to drive a better outcome in terms of actioning the process without ending up down a dead end or rabbit hole. Let me explain.

Even after taking the time to complete this masterclass, your idea of a vision is likely to still be in essence a future goal. Why? Because you have likely been conditioned to believe that goals and visions are the same and that they are future-facing concepts. Most of us when asked for a life vision would begin to speak of material things in our outer world or life situation. This would usually include people to love, activities to do, places to visit, freedoms of varying kinds, things to own and have, money, houses, cars and so on. It might also include feelings that we want to have and forms of security and stability, which are often represented by money and status.

How else would you describe your life vision and the life you want to have? As has been deeply embedded in the masterclass so far, external things cannot successfully deliver the life we want. Though we repeatedly chase them, we almost never find them in any sustainable way in the life we really want. They may bring short periods of satisfaction but they almost always disappoint in the end. This is because when we choose the things that will make us happy or think will create the life we want, we're usually not asking the correct questions.

Those questions have been covered in earlier chapters but really they can be phrased as one bigger question: "Why?" If we were to create that outer-based vision of the life we want, we would need to list all of the things and characteristics we want it to include and then deeply focus on *why* we want each one. The question of "Why?" would then reveal our deeper truths – what we are really seeking – but only when asked over and over again around each item we "think" we want, until the lowest-level answer is found.

So, take for example, "I want a beautiful, perfect family." We would take this idea on a journey through the whys and past some ego concepts in order to arrive at the underlying thing we are seeking, which in this instance would loosely equate to a desire to feel love. The journey past ego is mentioned because external goals tend to include an element relating to appearances, fitting in and comparison within them – why say "beautiful" or "perfect"? The words give important exposure to the underlying want but must be analysed in order to do so. In this example, then, we can see that fitting in, comparing and the family itself are a search for love in multiple dimensions. It would therefore have been more accurate to simply say, "I want to feel love and loved."

When we create our life vision, it should not be related to a future goal or to material, outer things either. If we start with the outside, we have to ask, "Why?", "Why?", "Why?" in order to find the root desire or want. Our vision of life must therefore be entirely internal in the first place. It must also be available in its entirety *right now*. Not only is this exciting, because it places our true goals within reach, but it also makes our effort and journey far shorter and simpler. By the way, you may be pleased to note that doing things this way certainly doesn't preclude a side effect of material gains and in fact usually results in far more external success – it just becomes a spinoff of the perfect journey and not the goal or future destination.

Interestingly, our collective life visions don't vary too much at all. Once we've got past the questions of *why*, they tend to converge and (as those chasing them in the outer world will testify) have little to do with things, people, places and circumstances. What we all seek is a state of mind and rarely is it too different for any of us.

So, what is that life vision and state that most of us want? It is defined by a set of the same simple characteristics, which may be more or less important to each of us individually but, in their totality and without exception, seem to reflect what most humans seek. I wonder why that would be? In a universe characterised by extensions of a single consciousness with a single purpose and governed by only a few rules, it hardly seems surprising that we have a common vision of the perfect life. We can understand that more deeply by looking closely at the common characteristics themselves.

Our vision of life is generally defined by seven characteristics:

- Freedom
- Peace
- Love
- Joy or happiness
- Adventure or experience
- Purpose, fulfilment, to feel whole
- Life, health and security

It is good to become deeply aware that some of these properties are a product of the society in which we live rather than naturally-occurring facets of being. This is as a result of the ego-mind-related human illusion that has been created around us. For instance, life, health and security are all based on an idea of death that is born of conditioning and is ultimately the fear of losing something, rather than indicating a forward-facing goal or state of being. This is because in the human illusion the threat of loss can feel very real; thus retaining things that we perceive can be lost becomes part of our vision of the perfect life or state of being.

Take for example health, which as a direct result and product of a health consciousness is not something that we can lose unless our thinking falls into an unhealthy state. In this illusion, where the ego process has taken over and where judgements and fear are the norm, we are conditioned to believe that health is something that we could somehow lose at any moment. In reality, poor health is simply a warning of the dysfunctional thinking that results from our submergence in ego. After all, consciousness is the essence of body and mind, meaning that healthy consciousness cannot fail to create a healthy body.

Security, similarly concerns the fear of loss and/or violence and stems from a societal framework rather than being naturally present. These things are no less real, and are valid perceptions; but they are products of the conditioning of our near field and the results we bring back from it, which make us both nervous for our safety and to whatever degree feel a lack of safety and security. Importantly, they relate deeply to ego and ultimately the fear of death. Something that the human illusion loves to reinforce through media, conflicts and wars. This transformational journey is about the neutralisation of both, so as their impact diminishes or disappears altogether these false visions will begin to fall away.

In the absence or neutralisation of ego the characteristics of our ultimate life vision will start to closely align with those listed above. Ego brings the externalities – such as power, status, comparison, competition and preferences, or the need for things, people and more – as simple metaphors for them. Hopefully none of these externalities are among our present needs or wants as we make the transition into knowing what brings true peace, fulfilment or purpose. Instead, we are left with a menu of feelings and internally accessible states that we basically want in their entirety and without reference to degrees. To clarify: this means that our collective and common vision of the perfect life and perfect state of being would include all of them in totality and without exception.

This nicely brings us back to the present moment and to the status report in the previous exercise. The vision we now have of our perfect life or desired state of being provides us with something tangible that our present-moment status can be defined by and measure against. In other words: now we have the end state, we can decide how close we are to it right now. Our status report defined.

To help you understand how to do this it will be useful to have a real-world picture of what the process looks like in action. To that end I'm going to explain it in relation to the steps I took myself with my own vision and status report; so I'll outline some of my personal considerations and status measures and demonstrate how the process impacted both my state of being in the present and (as a side effect) the state of the outer world around me. For me, the internal vision and status report were the drivers for the creation of this masterclass – importantly, not the other way around. This was the realisation of my own inner vision and a set of steps that enriched my experiences and feeling of fulfilment specifically in the present moment and through the journey to completion, and in doing so brought me immediate and permanent fulfilment and peace.

The key question for me had been around how I could have these feelings in every moment and how they would relate to my actions in the outer world. Ultimately the journey of creating the masterclass answered this as I was writing and consuming the content itself; not only did it bring me the profound result of the vision but also (because the masterclass centres on reaching as many people as possible) it created the side effect of further fulfilment and positive impact on the outer world. This was a win-win situation originated internally.

The extent to which we all feel love, freedom, peace, purpose, fulfilment, adventure and joy is clearly central to the masterclass, and as it happens my own has come from creating it and helping others to make the internal choices necessary to take the same fulfilling journey. The core challenge and measure of success on this transformational journey is finding that vision within, without any dependency or reference to the world outside. It worked for me personally and I've assured success for others in the outside world too – even though neither of these things were actually ever part of or necessary for my vision or goal.

There are some truths that are common to all of us in achieving our personal vision and the methods here address them and help to guarantee success. After all, it will be absolutely clear by now that the ego process simply takes away our peace, freedom, love, fulfilment, joy and more, and it does so for nearly all of us in very similar ways. Ironically, of course, these are the very ingredients of our common vision and the state of being that most of us seek and truly want underneath the external metaphors. The noise created by the ego process can be resolved but only internally, by following our steps in this masterclass. Those steps begin with self-realisation and finding who you really are as the conscious experiencer of life itself; importantly, done by removing identification with that noisy voice in your head because it's not really who you are at all.

Once you realise this, you can become a passive watcher of the endless search results ego creates, learning to ignore them and release them, rendering them never to be seen again. Based on your direct all-senses experience, you must then choose to unconditionally accept and forgive *everything* as it happens, living moment to moment with no retention of the past – unconditionally, and no matter the circumstance or nature of the experience. You do this knowing that it is simply what serves you best: you retain your power and you let go of the ego urge to believe that acceptance or forgiveness would make you weaker or somehow diminish who you are. It won't. These steps are, in my own direct experience, the only ones that matter in life. Progress toward the vision, moment to moment, depends simply on choosing when to watch and when to accept, with all judgment and blame removed. I measure my own progress each and every day on the results I achieve in this.

If you follow the simple rules we have uncovered in the masterclass, there are simply no boundaries to having all seven of the beautiful characteristics of the vision, immediately and in every single moment. Clearly progress is ongoing, but the state of being can be accessed as above in this very moment and every moment following. Soon it becomes an unconscious habit, not a conscious decision needing to be made and remade.

Creating the steps and taking them

This whole transformational journey is about the steps towards this common vision of the "perfect" life. Making them second nature has become the most important thing in my own life. It means you have taken control and can own and deliver for yourself. Doing what serves you, simply because it does, and by influence serving everyone around you too. Externalities are gone and there is no dependency on anyone or anything outside of your own self to achieve your inner goals.

My own status report at this moment is that I have "almost" reached every one of the seven characteristics of the vision, almost. Why almost? Because the complete picture for me personally does include some of these conditioned societal aims, such as security, life and health – as I'm sure it will for you. Though these elements are simply "what is" and must be accepted, they can and do also form part of the steps towards that life vision, albeit as side effects. The outside can be impacted by my own inner steps and become a by-product of my own journey. It is certainly acceptable to be aware of and seek change in these externalities, especially if your inner state will ultimately impact upon them.

Our moment-to moment-state of being is an internal step, but with a wider focus there can also be a deeply related external vision as a by-product. In my own case, I see in the outer world that both the effect of ego and the fear of death are driving fear of loss and lack of security; my internal steps, if replicated for others, can effectively have an impact in changing the world. This is not something on which my personal state of being and vision depends, but it is an active choice and plays into the internal steps I am taking. External realisation will remain a side effect, but my outer world can and will fundamentally change as a result of the changes made to my inner world.

This means that I can represent the vision now and in every moment of every day and I am not at all dependent on any outer changes. I have peace, freedom, love, joy, adventure, purpose and health while on my journey; but I also have an ultimate destination to help others and change the world with the very same process I am following. By taking action to maintain that state, further progress is constantly being made; and by sharing the method with others, impact on the outer vision results. This demonstrates how maintaining my own state and delivering my own experiential purpose, with moment-to-moment internal steps, is possible through the clarity I now have to focus on enjoying the moment-to-moment adventures of life, however unpredictable they may be.

Embracing that unpredictability, and recognising and interpreting the far-field messages, allows life to follow a perfect and dynamic course, which is seamlessly and dynamically adjusted as it goes. The vision is realised in this acceptance and surrender, and in the journey; not by attaching to and waiting to reach a constantly varying, perpetually extending list of destinations. On realising this method for yourself and the beautiful freedom and non-resistance of surrender, you will enable your own vision to instantly appear. You can make that choice and reach that state in this very moment, without any need to wait.

Removing that which does not serve you

The successful realisation of this vision process requires you to additionally allow for the removal of anything that does not support you in your journey, or interferes with reaching the state of peace, love, freedom and fulfilment. A simple test for this is asking of each experience, "Does this serve me and does it take me closer or further away from my vision?" which will easily reveal what can stay and what must go. This applies to all internal and external situations, patterns and experiences. In order to reach our personal vision of freedom, love, peace and fulfilment, we will all need to change many internal patterns and some external circumstances that will, if retained, prevent us reaching this state. These are things that we now recognise, fundamentally do not serve us. We may then, if necessary, replace them with things that do.

What matters here is choosing the wisdom that works. Once we have a clear understanding of the destination or state we desire, it is relatively simple to refocus on only that which takes us forward towards it. Consequently, we must test everything we are, do and experience with intuitive "knowing". This is not about subjective judgement; it is the deeper knowing that tells us the truth, and does so without deliberation and internal dialogue with the voice in your head. This is not a case *for* or *against*, running around your mind. It is a deep-seated knowing that is always underlying. In order to access this knowing, it is important that we become more permanently conscious and present. In the silence that presence creates, we can see that knowing more clearly and we can more easily allow ourselves to trust it.

With a quieter mind and the ability to watch our thoughts, the knowing gets louder and louder. It is the guide that will allow you to instantly and unemotionally remove that which you know is not matched to your ultimate journey. Decisions that previously seemed difficult and debateable will now become clear and can be made practically and with ultimate trust that they are right. At first this process requires a leap of faith, but as we practice it, we find that the choices made are always the ones that serve us – and, importantly, are not made by listening to the results of a search engine that simply brings back random information and ultimately no truth. Incidentally, following any decision of "knowing", there will often be the ego noise of debate and uncertainty. The "Have I done the wrong thing?" moment. Be the watcher and let it pass.

Clearly, this process combines instinctual, conscious "knowing" and the signs and results that come from the far field. The cool thing is that when we "know", we inadvertently ask the universal search engine for an answer too – and the great news is that it never fails to give the signs and answers that contain the truth, when properly interpreted. Surrender and follow them. Don't use subjectivity and debate, only "knowing" and the truth from the far field. Most situations and patterns we need to exit are actually full of the signs that tell us so. Surrender and follow them without resistance and with perfect trust. They will always tell you what to keep in your life and what to leave behind. The difference now is that you know the destination and characteristics of the vision you want to live. You know that state of being and you know you want it right now, which means that you can purposefully submit the right perceived experience, express the resulting vibrations and glean your perfect answers from this magical universal search engine.

The beauty of the process is that when it goes wrong, it is actually always going right. What I mean by that is that you can take what may well be the "wrong" path and make "wrong" choices but they will always provide a learning experience, which will then show the right way and get you back on track. As you start to express clear vibrations and to look for the messages returned, life simply becomes a series of steps, messages and trusting surrender to the flow. There are no mistakes, just learnings and adjustments; and as soon as you see that, you can accept anything and everything that happens. It is just a moment-to-moment, unpredictable adventure to be enjoyed unconditionally as just that. An adventure.

Once awake and aware, you will always arrive where you want to be and much more efficiently and directly than you did previously. It is fundamentally impossible to experience anything else. The basis of accepting "what is" is knowing that it will always self-correct and that you are always on the right path and where you are supposed to be. Balance will always return and everything is a sign, learning and an experience to be joyful that you can have. See the signs, read the messages and adjust the steering, that's all there is to it. Nothing is significant and nothing really matters, because your state of being is internal and there really is no prospect of controlling the outside anyway. Let the outside move as it will, while internally you attach to nothing. Expect the unexpected and surrender as you go, and suddenly all that resistance and friction you have been feeling, probably for your whole life, will immediately fall away. It really is far easier than you have been making it for all this time.

The takeaway point, the rule of existence, is that this is a dynamic, transient journey. It changes and varies constantly, and that is fine. In fact it's great, because it makes life a beautiful unpredictable adventure, where literally nothing can go wrong as long as you always accept and never judge, blame and attach. Your lifelong conditioning is the reason you can't relax and that you endlessly worry, but that is based on an ego process that simply has you reacting, craving control and ultimately seeing life as an assault course that you just have to get through and won't get a second chance. Not the case; relax, set the steps and watch the signs.

There is simply no chance of failure now that you know who you are and have your vision. Your purpose is and always has been to have the deepest, richest experience. That means that every experience, whether good, bad or neutral by "judgement", is a valid part of your *current* adventure and will serve your ultimate, universal purpose. Love all of them just because you can have them. Feel privileged to be able to experience everything so richly and deeply. There is no risk and there is no downside; there aren't even any wrong turns, disasters or mistakes. "What is" just is and doesn't need to be labelled, judged or reacted to. Adventure is good, as are rollercoasters, but only when you're free of your ego search results, which bring fear, sadness and worry and dramatically alter your perception of this beautiful and simple universe. Go and have fun with it and focus on your state of being and the vision, because when you accept it all it simply can't go wrong.

There can only ever be forward motion; fear and avoidance are not a destination
Ultimately, your state of being is your only and immediate goal. That means that it is for now in this moment and for later too, in every single moment of your life. That means it's not "coming soon" or "in the end" and it is not only to be experienced at some future destination. We have been there chasing rainbows and we know it just doesn't work. That state is right here and now.

That said, it is important to understand that our vision of life and your state of being is also a forward-moving picture. There is no past involved. Why? Because the past has zero impact on now or the future. We really can forget and remove attachment to what has gone before today. Other than our vision, there is also no future to be worried about, so it is essential that we now disregard that too. Our aim is to ensure that in this moment we are only progressing towards our vision of the perfect internal state of being. It means that every step we create and take must take us only forward and towards that vision. More freedom, more peace, more love, more purpose, more joy, more experience, more health and so on. How will you feel it today? This is more,

more, more and more in every single moment. It is the conscious choice you make, to constantly add all of these characteristics to each and every experience you have.

This raises an incredibly important point. Your vision and life goals cannot be achieved with any fear and avoidance at all. Fear and avoidance have no associated forward motion and are fundamentally not a destination at all. The problem is that for many of us they can manifest as some sort of weird quasi goal. We can literally be confused into believing that life can be about avoiding your fears, rather than travelling toward a vision, goal or destination. To put this into perspective, this is as if you could get into your car and drive towards avoiding something. To give a great example, many of us are simply avoiding being poor or avoiding losing money. We do not have a monetary goal, a destination with steps that will ensure our financial security builds; we simply continue on a path where the *only* objective is not to run out of cash.

Avoidance as a quasi destination is more common than you would think. We may avoid being ill or death, losing our spouses or partners – in fact we avoid any and all kinds of loss. It is also common around feelings; we often try to avoid feeling sad, feeling pain, feeling scared and more, failing to realise that avoiding fear is actually the same as experiencing fear. It is essentially the fear of fear. Avoiding loss is loss and avoiding pain is a form of discomfort or pain. What you avoid, you immediately experience – and the experience of avoidance brings the experience of the very thing you are avoiding.

It really is that simple. As soon as focus shifts to avoidance, we take focus away from the forward-facing goal. When we avoid losing money, we are less focused on making it. When we worry about or try to avoid losing a partner, we become less of the person our partner was attracted to and are more worried and insecure than loving. Avoidance and loss and fear and worry really do deliver whatever their subject is. To avoid fear or loss effectively, we must simply move *towards* love, joy and abundance. These are goals, whereas avoiding fear or loss is not a tangible direction at all.

You can't travel towards avoiding loss and you simply cannot create steps in a particular direction that represent avoidance. Take health and death as great examples. You can move towards a particular level of health and have a health goal but you cannot have a goal of avoiding bad health or try to avoid death. This can be confused also by people who avoid death or risk by essentially avoiding living life. This is what avoidance does: it removes your forward motion and gets in the way of your true purpose, which is of course experience. There can only be positive forward movement – and to move forward it must be towards a specific destination. In outer goals, those who become fixed on the avoidance of losing what they have, soon start to realise that they are moving backwards and doing just that – losing what they have. Why? Because they no longer have positive forward motion or goal. Loss always comes in the absence of forward motion.

The same is true in our own internal vision of success. We cannot fend off overthinking by trying not to. We cannot avoid the problems we have by trying not to have them. We cannot stop feeling sad by trying not to feel sad. Why? Because none of these things are a destination. We must always aim to feel love, joy, peace, fulfilment, adventure and we should implement steps that take us on an ever-moving, forward-facing journey toward them. Our goals in this masterclass are simple. They all have forward traction and they can be measured. Remember: any step taken towards avoidance will be a step towards the thing we are trying to avoid. This is a simple truth. Avoid your fears and you will fear them more.

The key point is that if our vision is peace, freedom, love, fulfilment, adventure, health and joy, then the aim is to follow the steps to feel them now. We must add more into our lives that will build the rich state of being that includes those characteristics, and we must remove anything that does not serve us in that goal. The right things enter our lives tangibly and immediately by our acceptance of *what is*, and adding enjoyment to our moment-to-moment steps until we realise the ultimate vision.

Chapter 35 : Using the ultimate search engine of life

Something very special and quite unexpected (for me at least) has now occurred. In our transformational journey towards living life in a different state of being, and the many lessons of the masterclass so far, some deep and diverse concepts have been covered in order to arrive at some relatively clear and simple conclusions. The ego has been exposed as the process, so we now understand how to effectively neutralise it with a few simple rules of engagement. We have also found who we really are, and it is not quite as we'd previously thought – certainly and fundamentally we are now clear that we are *not* the mind or the body, and especially not the voice in our head.

By practicing presence on an ongoing basis, there has been a progressive realisation that we are one small part or field within of a sea of universal consciousness; and while that may be the driver of our mind and body, it is certainly not limited to or defined by them. We are the experiencer and are essentially the near-field of consciousness, one that is local to us but also directly part of and connected to everything else that *is* the whole universe. Meaning *we are* the universe. Amazing, isn't it?

Before we discuss something even more fundamental, it is worth reflecting on the fact that we have all been a product of deep human conditioning. We were born into a world whose clear systems and methodologies were in place well before we ever arrived here. These structures have been created over time, but they all essentially represent a subjective version (and someone's idea) of the way we humans should live. The system has been designed for a particular effect and it has specific structural patterns working to that end: ultimately, whether purposefully or inadvertently, it promotes a great deal of subjectivity and conflicting opinion. This in turn creates much of the ego process, which is the very process we are taking deep and intense effort to unlearn.

It's hardly surprising that this involves such work, given that we've been subject to this conditioning since the moment we were born. From our school days right through to our working lives and retirement, a set pattern of behaviour and expectations is placed upon us. This is specifically relevant in terms of our expectations, because it means that almost all of them have been predetermined. Everything we know – from school to work, the things we're told to do and believe, our political, economic and religious or cultural understanding – stems from the inherent subjectivity and the expectations in the system.

Several effects of this conditioning are worthy of note. It has made our real purpose in life generally unclear and has instilled many beliefs that are counter-productive to that purpose, it means the process of unlearning this conditioning requires a huge transformation of thinking – essentially the purpose of this masterclass. We have also seen how key fundamentals such as our perception or idea of death were decided well before we were born, when Western society chose ultimately to hide from and fear death, to create a negative perception of it and avoid it at all costs. The obvious alternative would have been self-realisation, and would have seen us relaxed and excited about an end of human-life transition in our state of being.

If, as this masterclass suggests, we are simply a point of consciousness in a huge, universal sea of consciousness, and we are neither our body nor our mind, there would appear to be little to fear in death at all. Of course, the underlying point here isn't limited to death; it is more that we have been somehow submerged in an almost completely subjective version of *life itself* and it doesn't always serve us well – add to that it was made by someone else long before we arrived and you may feel that it has been more than our bodies that were *taken for a ride*.

So engulfed have we been, by this essentially subjective reality that we now find it incredibly hard to take a step back and see the real, magical, natural universe around us. We find ourselves completely wrapped up in the illusions of money, competition, comparison and endless, conflicting, subjective opinions; all getting us nowhere. Well actually, the great news is that it did get you here. You clearly asked the right questions, wanted something more and you're now finding lots of new and interesting wisdom that sits well outside of the subjective illusion.

Many of the more complex subjects we've covered here in this masterclass have been resolved relatively simply thanks to a deeper understanding of the ego – which was, ironically, assisted by a more complex concept. The idea of a sea of consciousness chasing experience and then changing vibration to represent that experience was no doubt at first both complicated and may have been hard to accept. However, with the simple understanding that these fields of consciousness (or micro-magicians) attract other such fields that are vibrating at the same vibration, and over great distances, it did explain the nature and working of the ego as a simple search engine or process. This knowledge and principle has been fundamental in helping us to dis-identify with the ego for good. It also brings realisation that the voice in our head is absolutely not who we are. As we will soon find out, this understanding also brings so much more, something that we're not yet aware of.

Underlying our explanations of consciousness, and this simple model in which the universe is actually a huge sea of consciousness, is one of the most fundamental laws of the universe. Held within our model is also the key that unlocks its beneficial use. The idea or model shows that similar or like experiences attract each other; it's why and how the ego works as a search engine. It uses vibrational attraction to endlessly bring back stored experiences, similar in vibration to the prevailing experience that we are either having or perceiving in this very moment. This process of vibrations attracting really matters. Many books have been written on this subject, but our Zen Jungle masterclass has actually arrived here quite by accident. In our aim to remedy your dysfunctional relationship with your ego mind, the voice in your head and your true self, we have inadvertently created some gold dust for you to use with huge personal benefit as you move forward.

As you make this transformational journey and undertake the masterclass practices, your mind should be becoming clearer and clearer. Your mind noise is now reducing, and you are able to watch and accept both your thoughts and, importantly, your experiences on an increasingly tangible level. This means that you have become more and more aware of what you are thinking and have found a huge amount of extra peace as your learning has grown. This is life-changing but in fact only the tip of the iceberg in terms of the gifts this transformational journey will bring. We have now created the perfect conditions for you to take another huge leap forward, and this one is super exciting and powerful.

The search engine that can bring ANYTHING back

So, what do we now know that can be used to our advantage? Experiences create vibration and vibrations attract similar or identical vibrations. Hold this thought in mind and start to consider that this universe does not limit the vibrations to a simple thought. As we have seen, when we perceive (or directly have) an experience, we then express it as a vibration and consequently bring other similar vibrations from the near, outer and far fields towards us.

When we previously discussed the fact that "the truth is always available", we saw that the far field brings us the truth in some very weird and wonderful ways, with atypical events and what are essentially answers to our vibration in the form of signs. We showed that this process is ongoing, and it happens whether we want it to or not. Simply put, if we are experiencing a certain thing or circumstance in our lives, we will bring back experiences that match or are similar or related to that thing. We also learned that this will then become something that, if we are ready to recognise it, can provide answers and direction for how our lives will go and the direction we must take to move forward to best effect.

At this point, and for the first time, it is probably worth discussing the possibility that this all sounds like magic or a kind of mystical fairy tale – it probably does to some at least. The reality could not be further from the truth. Consider for a moment everything you see in nature and that can be observed in the whole natural universe. Everything is a product of this one simple law and effect. On the smallest level to the greatest, the universe is experiencing itself, changing vibration and simply attracting like vibrations. Is it magic, sort of, but only because we don't understand any part of the true mechanics of how it works. Regardless, everywhere in nature and in life, this law is hard at work.

Consciousness is, everywhere and always, vibrating and attracting more of the same or similar consciousness, usually in fields. As it does so, it is creating chain reactions that change the form of that consciousness and blend it through experience to become form, with new vibrations. In turn it becomes newly manifested forms. As a tree grows, or as leaves fall off trees in winter, as flowers bloom and as animals are born and die, this single law is working hard at the heart and sustains all processes. Consciousness is having experiences by meeting other consciousness at different frequencies, then changing vibration and attracting more of the same or similar consciousness, then manifesting into new forms. It is literally how everything works and it is the root cause, not a secondary effect, especially for the purposes of our slightly simplified model.

Why is this important? The amazing thing about humans is that we can think up and perceive experiences without ever actually having them. This seems to be a generally unique and advanced capability of the human species (there is some evidence of similar among certain other species but is not directly verifiable or comparable) and appears to give us some unique abilities. That is, of course, if we learn how to actually use it. We have already seen how it can work in our favour when finding the truth. We have also seen it work against us when we're bombarded with involuntary ego results. Most importantly, we have seen that most of it until now has been involuntary and that it brings back attracted results in some very quirky and unexpected ways.

That is because vibration is not yet well understood. While there are many books written on attraction, we do not fully understand the mechanics of this natural process except that experiences attract experiences with similar and identical vibrations. This means that we are constantly attracting similar vibrations and experiences via the search engine and that we vibrate with any and all of the frequencies of the experiences we are currently having. We have been likened to a transmitter with a search reach that extends to the very extremes of the universe, as can be evidenced in us finding truth. More importantly, it brings back a diverse set of results that vibrate very similarly but are experiential – which means that they can be situations, people, things and more; they are not limited to a single form.

How this works is not something we can or need to deeply explain or understand. What matters is that this happens and it is a real phenomenon, written about over centuries. What also matters is that it can be used directly to your advantage. It's also worth noting that without a deeper knowledge of it, we may inadvertently find it working against us, and without us even knowing it.

What you experience, you will experience

This section heading explains things in the most succinct way I've ever seen. It also helpfully relies on our model of consciousness and the micro-magicians, which is also the simplest explanation of the Law of Attraction that we have ever seen as a team. It should help make all this a very actionable learning. "What you experience, you will experience" gives a broad understanding of the Law of Attraction and while it might sound like a paradox, or at least a vicious circle, it is nowhere near as complex as it sounds. Here comes the magic...

Firstly, we should define what is meant by "experience", to ensure that we all have the same understanding of it. As a being of consciousness, everything you are aware of is actually an experience. When we developed the all-senses presence in earlier chapters, the discussion rotated around the idea of your consciousness being shared across all of your bodily senses and your intuition. We later developed that idea further and now have a beautiful infographic available online that allows us to see that this includes other inputs too: of intuition and of the ego results or voice in your head. This is important because your experiences are *not ever* direct experiences. They are perceived by synthesising all of your bodily senses, with ego results, thought and intuition.

This means that what you experience is rarely experienced without a filter or veil of thoughts and ego results; as such, very few of your experiences are simple, direct experiences without ego and thought involvement. This matters greatly in the construction of the "idea" of what experience actually is, and especially in specific regard to the Law of Attraction. This normal pattern of synthesis of the real, direct experience, thoughts and ego search results, means that we almost never vibrate and attract based on only direct and simple sensory, experience. We are vibrating, and so attracting, using a blend of the real, direct inputs from the senses, *what is*, and thought in the form of ego results layered in on top. Our experience is partially thought or search results, and partially direct, through the senses.

This fact has huge consequences. It means we have innate ability to both artificially create *true* experience and to change our vibration to represent whatever experience we wish it to. In turn, changing your vibration at will, and specifically, gives you ultimate control of the kinds of experiences you will then attract. As all experience is a synthesis of thought and direct experiences; this shows us that the universe, consciousness and attraction does not differentiate between what we imagine or create in the mind as experience, and what we directly experience through our senses. As a result, if you can create and perceive a realistic experience in your mind, it stands to reason that you will change your vibration to that of the imagined experience. Basically, you can take control of the process and change your vibration to any experience you can imagine. This gives you a superpower: the power to attract any experiences you want, rather than those you don't want. Stay with me because this really works and it is easy to prove for yourself.

What we must deeply understand is that when we vibrate with strong vibrations of a perceived experience, we will then attract similar experiences from the far-field in a very similar way to when we set out to attract the truth from the far-field in previous chapters. Related experiences with similar vibrations will then arrive, represented like we saw in the truth chapter examples, in the form of atypical events to be recognised, surrendered to and followed. Importantly, what is attracted will not be in the form of magic materialisations where things simply appear from nowhere.

This is simple utilisation of the Law of Attraction to bring you experiences that you want, those similar to the ones that you created in imagination and so perceived. Of course, it all follows the same patterns as attracting the truth from the far field. Why? Because that's essentially what it is. It is you falsely experiencing something, changing your vibration, in order to attract like vibrations in whatever unpredictable form they come.

The process we are describing is simply a slightly more directed and controlled version and can be done at will. Clearly the process requires the same ability to recognise and surrender to those returned experiences as we have seen before when seeking and later recognising the truth in the returned results. In this however, attracted experiences will likely be in a more similar form to the imagined and perceived experience. While they may lead to something resembling your imagined experience, they will rarely be a direct manifestation of it – although we are not commenting here on that innate possibility.

The skills required to perform this process are important and many books detail methods to achieve an experience that your consciousness will believe is real; all of them represent the basic premise that "what you experience, you will experience". Cleary, in order to make this whole thing actionable you must be able to truly and realistically perceive any experience that you wish to attract – so what does that actually look like?

The answer lies in what we've learned about the synthesis of the senses, thoughts and ego results that make up almost all of your perceived experiences. On seeing what most experiences comprise, you can see what might be required in order to create one that will be deeply perceived as real by your consciousness. In normal circumstances, an experience will be a synthesis of what you see, hear, touch, taste, small, feel, intuit and think – "think" being the ego results or conscious, creative thought. This means that the perfect imagined and strongly perceived experiences will include as many of those elements as possible.

Interestingly, the power of thought and of our imagination is capable of recreating almost all senses, vision, feelings and thoughts as if they are totally real, so this is the skill that is to be purposefully developed. In practice this means: first, think up and visualise the thing or experience to be attracted; and second, add to that the senses of smell, touch, sound, taste, feeling or emotion and so on while deeply believing in its presence in thought. This will create a deeply held perception of that experience; this perception will in turn change your vibration and will then attract similar experiences as per the law. It's easy, you just need to spend the time building that alternate reality in your mind.

These are complete and full experiences, not simply things you want or objects of desire. In order to experience tangible attraction we must fully experience, not simply want something. Want will not create any perceived experience at all and, crucially, will not, change your vibration or attract more of the same vibration.

We positioned this process toward the end of the masterclass for a very specific reason. We have of course devoted much time to proving that externalities do not bring any of the core ingredients of our vision, which are peace, freedom, joy, fulfilment, adventure or experience and love. We know that aiming for the external metaphors that may have previously represented these is largely a waste of our time, and that they do not bring any lasting happiness. This is something we must truly understand to move forward using only wisdom that works. It means that Law of Attraction is best placed where and when you are ready to use it to enhance your transformational journey, rather than become a distraction or destructive to your understanding and progress.

The aim of the entire masterclass has been to create equanimity on the deepest level, which allows us to remain centred and neutral no matter what the internal or external experience. We can then bring the qualities of our vision to those experiences, enriching each and every one of them with the deepest love and joy. Then, we no longer need to chase or cling to future external experiences or wants, because we know that they do not bring the ultimate fulfilment we desire. Having all of this now embedded puts you in a very unique position in relation to the power of the Law of Attraction.

The currently created conditions support a super clear and quiet mind and give us the ability to control thought, response and reaction. This in turn controls our perceived experiences and the reactions to them that usually follow. These reactions can be broadly seen as our resulting change in vibration, after having the experience. This means that we have already learned control of the change in vibration delivered by experience and are consequently now controlling many more of the experiences that we attract without ever knowing. As we apply love and joy to almost all our experiences, we are now constantly attracting more loving and joyful experiences to us.

In learning the techniques in the steps up until this point, you have inadvertently – or as a side effect – reduced the vibrations relating to any negative experience you have. As you have also reduced the mind noise and have the ability to stay centred and calm, you have as a result prevented or reduced the vibrations that would bring further destructive experiences into your life. As you move forward, becoming more aware and practicing the techniques, you will see huge inherent changes in what you experience on the outside. This was never and could never have been the objective of the masterclass; but as you near the end it of course will be a very welcome side effect.

It means that you, as the aerial of vibration, are now bringing back happier and more neutral experiential results on an ongoing basis – without you even being aware of it or trying to do so. This will be a great start on the journey towards learning to use the Law of Attraction in a more focused way.

Importantly, you must retain your understanding that everything you want is found on the inside and not on the outside. As we've already discussed, once the inside is filled with peace, love, joy, fulfilment, adventure and so on, then the outside will take care of itself. The Law of Attraction will be working on your behalf in order to make it so. If you are feeling an experience of inner love, you will attract love. If you are feeling an experience of inner joy, you will vibrate with joy and attract joy. This is fundamental. As you experience your inner vision, you vibrate with its vibration and therefore realise everything that is inside that vision. You have no need of metaphors or chasing outer wants, because your vision is there to guide you on the inside. The Law of Attraction is about understanding that the metaphors come automatically, when you vibrate with the feelings that they will ultimately bring before you ever have them.

Success with this masterclass means that every external effect will be a welcome but unintentional side effect. Why? Because our foundation is to create a robust state of being, where you love life no matter what the external circumstances. You now have no need of trying to fake experiences because your state of being is a super attractor of all the right things. Your experience and your perceived experience are now aligned and you will attract beautiful things and circumstances like a beacon, travelling to the ends of the universe.

A word of warning, though: this law is unbending. It has no principle other than itself. It doesn't care about you or have compassion; it is not benevolent and doesn't understand what you want or the language you use to ask for it. It simply brings experiences to you that match the experience of your current vibration. This matters because it also explains why avoidance does not work and why it brings the very thing you are avoiding most.

During avoidance and fear, you are simply experiencing and thus vibrating with the frequency of the thing that you really don't want or fear most. This means you are simplistically and inadvertently attracting it to you. You will experience it and there is no reference to what you like or do not like; the universe has no interest in that because that is not the law. This law does not speak in your chosen language and was never taught a vocabulary. It deals only with your prevailing and perceived experience, which it understands by the signature vibration. The point being, it is essential that you're fully aware – and that you beware of what you experience or perceive as experience because you will get more of it, whether you want it or not.

Focus on the characteristics of the vision; focus on love and joy and the techniques of this masterclass. Take control of the ego and find a way to forgive and accept all prevailing experiences, because the alternative is to attract more of the experience you are currently having, like it or not. The only experience you want and need is love, peace, adventure, fulfilment, joy, abundance and at their heart they are all love, love, love. Experience only love and love will be your predominant experience – and if that isn't a simple rule to live by, I really don't know what is.

ZEN JUNGLE

Step 11 : Relationships reimagined

Chapter 36 : The tuning fork of life

This final step of the journey brings it all together with a focus on human relationships, and will likely help you to understand many of the events that have shaped and impacted on your life so far. It covers our seemingly insatiable will to "couple" and to find life partners and companions, and explains the diverse difficulties that many of us face in doing so. We often hear that humans are social animals, with the implicit suggestion of a lot of the commentary being that we naturally seek to find a mate and companion and cannot be "complete" until we do so. Anyone who has found their "soulmate" for life will no doubt happily agree with that message, though it may be less thrilling to those who have repeatedly experienced failure and disaster in love.

Perspective is everything. Indeed, for some people the act of taking this transformational journey will fundamentally impact on their current relationship situation, for either the better or the worse and whether they realise it or not. Step 11 will make sense of the process – and of life itself – to help us determine how to have the perfect relationship and manage the changes that may already be happening in your existing partnership.

Throughout the masterclass so far, we have been deeply focused on our inner selves and the struggle around the various ways in which we try to change or control our unpredictable and uncontrollable outer world. We have created steps and a process, practices and conceptualisations that have had us look within for the things that will deeply fulfil us. In Step 10 we created a life vision, which we recognise as fundamentally internal; certainly it does not rely on external metaphors, such as people or things, to deliver the deeply fulfilled feelings that we crave, which can come only from the inside. We have established that underlying all external wants are desires for feelings that already exist inside us, in abundance and always, if only we tap into them.

It is up to us to release these feelings – and none more so than the feeling of love. Love is an internal fountain that can be brought to any and all situations providing our primary state of being is one of balance and equanimity. We have discussed the fact that relationships in their early stages simply serve as a release for love and are not the cause of it, although for some this may well remain a contentious view. We have seen that when we're in a state of presence we can feel deep joy and love in any abstract situation and that we can deliver that feeling at will. Love is our base state; it runs through us and its release is not dependent on any external entity or other person.

The reality we're going to be describing here may not suit everyone, and might cause resistance for some; but it's important to note that it doesn't represent a terminal nail in the coffin for companionship or romance. We're talking about it because the truth is that humans are fundamentally quite self-sufficient and do not actually need other humans as close companions in order to become fulfilled. The reason for the confusion may be that they *do* need them for reproduction, something that may distort the role companionship plays. This is a fact and not conjecture.

Really, this book is a guide to only the state of inner fulfilment. Think about what we have essentially learned: humans are not dependent on anything or anyone outside of them for their fulfilment and feelings. Very importantly, humans are however *all* connected as a single consciousness and there is deep love and oneness at the heart of that. It simply means that all human relationships are special, not just the *more special* ones. Maybe that is something to take away before you read on.

Our modern idea of companionship, most starkly described by marriage, was created and conditioned as a construct by society long ago in the past. Over time, the church and other institutions have been instrumental in promoting and normalising the idea of this coupling and the lifelong bonds and dependency that it can bring. This includes its place as the basis for procreation and parenthood too. Deep conditioning and centuries of implementation have seen the conversion of a species with a will to mate and find companionship, to one for whom lifelong partnership is the acceptable and (more to the point) *expected* norm. The question of whether this is natural is totally redundant here, because irrespective of the answer, we have it and it works well for many and not so well for quite a number too. However, it bears no relation to the self-sufficiency of humans, as individuals, to feel love and fulfilment – although, it must be said, it has come to substitute that self-sufficiency and often promotes an inherent dependency and need of another person.

The alumni of this masterclass will have experienced a mixture of success and failure in their relationships. There'll be many who are or have been in successful lifelong relationships, and quite probably more who have had a more difficult time trying to find a companion. Some will have been married and divorced and others will not yet have found the "right" one. Some will feel that in this respect they are failing *at life* in some way; others that they are unlovable or fundamentally flawed, simply because they can't find or stay with a single person they meet. This is of course simple ego conditioning and can be put down to the subjective view and societal norms found in the outer field. The great news is that it's all basically meaningless and there is no significance in being alone or in a couple, succeeding in relationships or not. Well, except of course the significance we choose to attach to and give to it – but that was us before this masterclass and definitely isn't us now as we have dispensed with attaching all that pointless meaning.

This journey is focused on making the inside centred and healthy while releasing any preoccupation with the outside, which of course we cannot control. The eleven steps here will be hugely beneficial in bringing acceptance into many relationships; it will almost certainly offer a deeper understanding of our partners and companions, while bringing more "knowing" for some and likely *suggesting* actions to take for others. The key point being, of course, that it all starts with you and the inside and only then you can look at your external relationship.

The processes found in this book will cement stability in relationships for some and create a tipping point in others. Your inner stability, increased independence and reduced need for control of the outside world will give your partner, if you have one, some much-needed space and freedom that until now they may never have had. Remember: you have learned to unconditionally accept and can now ignore that voice in your head; your internal world will be calmer and less combative in the absence of the vicious circle of ego results fuelling intensified ego results.

This will make life far easier and will drive different and new relationship dynamics. Some will be deeper and more loving, and others will unfortunately be the opposite. It may be that the space you can now give your partner is welcomed and refreshing, or it may be that your failure to respond and react in the ways you did previously, somehow increases any existing conflict. Either way – even if it hasn't yet happened – there will be fundamental relationship changes ahead. Whether these prove advantageous or terminal, it's important to note that your path will be the right one and should be welcomed not avoided.

We're going to begin by discussing where you have been and where you are right now with reference to some familiar concepts. If you're currently in a relationship, this will help you to truly understand the potential changes ahead; and if you're not, it will benefit your personal transformation. No matter what your situation, you have in all likelihood lived your life so far without equilibrium. How can I be sure? Well, the very fact that you have taken this journey in the hope of transformation suggests that you have experienced swings in different directions that have led you to question *why* on a fundamental level. This is totally normal; and having got this far you'll realise that this is the rule and not the exception. Almost everyone is out of equilibrium, and that fault line starts with the creation of the ego.

Why does equilibrium matter and what do we mean by it? If you have followed the masterclass closely, carried out the practices and worked hard to understand it conceptually too, you'll already know the answer to this. Until you find the ability to dis-identify with the ego and exit the cycle of subjective opinion in which you have a compulsive need to be "somebody", you are swinging up and down trying to find peace and purpose and full of opinion. That's the bottom line. As discussed in Step 10, this ultimately defines both your experience and your vibration – and, crucially, your prevailing vibration attracts similar vibrations, so therein lies the pattern.

You are probably realising where this is going. All your life you have had an inconsistent and destructive vibration. You have swung to different levels, having differing experiences; you have chased the highs and felt the lows. You've attached to things, people and situations and you have been incredibly variable in your overall experience. As your mind and ego played in, so the pattern became magnified – and with the noise from the voice in your head, you have had little or no peace, freedom or purpose at all. On top of all that, love has been felt in waves, with high peaks and low absences. It has been driven predominantly by relationships as the stimulus, because until recently you thought that love was a product of another person and not a fountain of light energy emanating from inside of you. And why wouldn't you think that? That's the story we have all been sold. In any case your resulting vibration has been erratic to say the least and consistency has been hard to find and sustain.

It is important here that we distil all of this down to two things, both of which we discussed at length in the previous chapters. Experience and vibration: your experiences have been erratic and so your vibrations have been very erratic too. The ego method of living your life creates huge peaks and troughs of experience and so vibration. If we consider the ingredients of our common vision, which almost always include freedom, peace, love, joy, fulfilment or purpose, adventure and abundance, then your life so far has been a mixed bag of them all. Clearly this will have created a very mixed and inconsistent overall vibration – the very same vibration that represents your experiences and attracts similar vibrations to it.

The whole point of this transformational journey is for you to become something like a tuning fork. To neutralise the ego, remove the fear, learn to become the watcher and to ultimately self-realise as the consciousness that you actually are. This process gives you equanimity and progressively allows you to add love and joy to every situation, no matter if previously it would have been judged as "good" or "bad", "liked" or "disliked". This then brings a consistency and a purity of vibration, which in turn attracts with a deep and new-found consistency. So what does that all mean for relationships?

Chapter 37 : The perfect partner

Before we move on to the new situation that we've been creating here – and the new attractions it will bring – we should look at your previous situation where your vibrations have been inconsistent and constantly swinging from high to low. When it comes to companions, these vibrations attract similar vibrations at any given moment – just like they do with everything else. They are the driver of that "star-crossed lovers" feeling and they are responsible for you seeing the perfect person very differently depending on the nature of your current swing in vibration. When you are up you bring someone with high vibration; when down you attract the same. What matters here is the underlying inconsistency, which essentially gives very mixed signals to the universe.

To compound this thought, let's consider that the vast majority of people who are out there in the big wide world are similarly unbalanced in their vibrations. They too are fluctuating up and down, in an oscillation that flows with both their ego loop and their circumstances at any given time. The only thing that's true at any given moment is that they and you are attracting far and wide at the vibration you are currently at, at this moment. Let's say you're on the way up in your vibration and someone you meet is on the way down; for a fleeting moment you may well have the same vibration and look like a perfect vibrational match. Of course, shortly thereafter you will be higher and they will go lower, which essentially means there's a real chance this relationship won't end well at all.

This is what our path through life and relationships often looks like and it applies to the vast majority of us. Even when our vibrations are pretty stable and we find a good match at one point, we often change vibration as the cycle of our life progresses. This sometimes means divergence, so what began as a good match then potentially becomes a bad one. Or sometimes vibrations blend and mingle to a compromise, often related to how centred one or both partners is – but we will cover that later.

In most cases of unmatched vibrations, two vibrations that separate on their paths will become ultimately destructive and this means that any relationship based on them will soon also become destructive and fail. It is important to note, however, that sometimes people with two opposite or opposing vibrations do manage to force their vibrations together for the long term. They somehow resolve to a compromised vibration, which is a blend of the two, and they may work hard to stay that way. This might be because they each have a vibration of lower amplitude that consequently blend more easily; so they start off not too similar and end up more aligned. This can be successful or not so in the very long term, but it can work – and is worth noting as an outcome before we move on to more ideal cases and situations.

To go back to the idea of you as a tuning fork... This principle is based on the premise that it is best to find equanimity within yourself and reach a point where you are adding joy to anything and everything in your life, so that you know you are at the right vibration for an attraction. Ideally, this would be done without a partner in tow. Why? Because this is your *own personal* journey towards a stable and ultimately healthy vibration – a vibration that has you essentially in tune with the base vibration of the universe and the natural vibration of humanity itself.

This version of you is not overtaken by ego and opinion; you do not identify with the ego construct and as such you give lots of space to those around you, including any partner. This is also known as being spiritually awakened. This stable vibration, forgetting the vibration itself, makes you an easy person to be around; it is not noisy and means that you don't easily react or defend subjectivity as if it were somehow who you actually are. This makes *you* consistent and stable, what we affectionately call a tuning fork.

Once you become a tuning fork with a universal vibration you'll experience some stark new realities. The first and most obvious of these is that you will most strongly attract other tuning forks with the same or similar vibrations. This is a recipe for true relationship success. Certainly, it will not result in partnerships characterised by erratic peaks and troughs; and more than that, the dynamics of any relationships formed on this basis will be unlike those of any relationships you've had before. There will be very little conflict and, importantly, the relationship will not be rooted in your inherent need of the other person nor indeed theirs for you. It will instead be a form of symbiotic companionship, and will offer ultimate freedom for both parties. You will be independent and will not rely on them for the characteristics of your vision of life and state of being. In turn, they will not be dependent on you for theirs.

This means the relationship will be flexible and if at some point it comes to an end, you'll both be fully accepting of that. There is no ownership or attachment in this kind of relationship. Neither person needs or depends on the other to feel whole; they are simply true companions and feel deep love for each other. Very importantly, they each feel that same deep love for everyone else in the universe too. As tuning forks, we are quite literally one with the universe and feel totally connected to, and a deep love for, everything and everyone in it. No relationships are fundamentally more important than others – although our companion will of course be our choice and the one we wish to spend time with.

As we change and develop throughout this transformational journey, our existing relationships will likely do so too. You may see a positive change in your partner, or you may notice the appearance of some destructive cracks. Being in a relationship as you begin the process slightly alters the tuning-fork method but it will still work to your best advantage and outcome. As you reach your target vibration, this has the profound effect of changing your response to your partner. It reduces the ego reactions and interactions, and it creates a space between you that will usually reduce any conflict, even in circumstances where your partner has previously been combative. In fact, it will often have the effect of making that conflict all but disappear. This is the tuning-fork effect. As one party vibrates and resonates at a stable frequency, this usually has the effect of bringing their partner towards a similar single frequency. This is essentially the "awakened" principle. Your awakening and full equanimity will in all likelihood greatly affect your partner, who will start to mirror that behaviour and feel calmer in your presence.

There are two clear pitfalls for relationships that predate the transformation you have gone through during this masterclass. As you exit the process, you can become profoundly different than you were before. Many partners find this very hard to deal with and see it as an unwelcome change or a threat. That's not necessarily something you can change, and it may be that your relationship ends and you amicably go your separate ways. This is OK, and as the centred person you are now becoming it will be acceptable to you; you'll see it as the right way forward even if it is difficult. There are, however, other less favourable outcomes, usually resulting from more one-sided or inherently problematic relationships. Your new-found calm and ability to withhold response and reaction may incite your partner and frustrate them. This is for you to "know" and understand, while possibly allowing time for adjustment. Clearly, if it continues it will be a sign that the relationship is no longer serving you, at which point you can exit.

This process is one of profound change for you and will be one of profound change for any current partner. Your freedom, joy, love and purpose depends on you and is certainly not dependent on an externality of a relationship, no matter how well established. In most cases, relationships deepen in their companionship and acceptance, and new relationships that are based on tuning-fork attraction are likely to bring profound peace and joy.

Overall, though, and very importantly, this transformational journey has prepared you for a life of total independence. A life where having or not having a relationship or companion is of no concern to you. You are now self-sufficient and internal in your sources of fulfilment. So, whether you have a relationship, wanted a relationship or have lived life feeling that you "should" have a relationship, please know that from this moment forward, a relationship is certainly not a dependent need. It is essentially an ego-driven societal norm and something that you can choose to participate in or not. Having fun and enjoying the adventure is the only rule to live by.

Final words and a recommendation

Wow, you did it. Hopefully the masterclass has been a truly valuable and life-changing experience. You have covered diverse and deep subject matter that has included some very challenging ideas. Much of this content goes directly against a lifetime of conditioning, so be really proud of yourself if you have accepted all or at least most of it. You are now equipped to live and love your life knowing what truly serves you.

Wisdom that works – that's the point of the masterclass. This means wisdom you can either accept at face value or extract the logic from and allow the underlying concepts to be true for you or not. What matters here is that you decide on what personally serves you and use it. In some ways this book represents a selfish means to enhance your quality of life, followed by an unselfish positive impact that you will then have on the lives of others. Selfish is great at first, and then you realise that any consequences on others of your growth must only be good.

My final recommendation is one born of personal experience. If you feel that this book has the potential to totally change your life but hasn't just yet, then stay with it. Read it again. When we're trying to find answers and purpose, it's easy to end up focused on the knowledge and neglect to practice what we learn or take the time to embed it. At first read, this book may be in some ways overwhelming; concepts closer to the front may have become clear only through reading the whole book, so true understanding may not have been found until the end. I suspect that to be deeply true here – and I'm sure that many who've got this far will agree. With that in mind, I respectfully suggest that you read it at least two more times, taking time to do the practices and embed the information, because each read will reveal more that you didn't see at first. This may be the last self-help book you ever need to read, so if it feels like that could be true then spend the time on it, don't dilute it with other content that may conflict.

As you read this, the Zen Jungle online masterclass and or supporting materials may also be available; the work there will deepen and help fully embed what you've learned and found useful in this book.

We would love to hear your reviews. Please also share this book with as many people as you feel will benefit from it. Our purpose in creating it was to change the world, one person at a time. Your help in doing that would be much appreciated.

Good luck and enjoy your re-read. Enjoy your onward journey and thank you for your obvious commitment to yourself and this content.

Printed in Great Britain
by Amazon

60913114R00190

doubt methods of scoring will be experimented with (for example, limiting the number of shots in a rally) before the most exciting formula is achieved.

As new concepts are introduced to squash, the players' approach to the game needs to be further developed. These new scoring systems are no longer going to suit the 'hound dog retriever' type player who relies on opponent's mistakes over a long period of time. Aspects such as technique, the execution of strokes and strategy, will need to be soundly developed. Whether you are a top competitive player possibly having to adapt to different scoring systems, or a club or social player enjoying the traditional scoring system, exciting rallies and the playing of skilful shots make the game more interesting to watch and give more enjoyment and satisfaction to you as a player. Furthermore, the players' approach to the preparation for matches will have to be effectively channelled to produce peak performance.

The future, and the quality of performance in the future, is assured by the numbers of young players entering the game. This is Sarah Spacey who represented England at Under-16 level just a few days after her twelfth birthday.

Squash – A New Approach has been written in an attempt to keep the development of the playing of the game in line with the other innovations. Although it is pointed out that the need for good basic technique can never be challenged, it is vital to reassess ways of learning and achieving that technique. Furthermore, the application of the technique must be reconsidered in constructing new ways to winning squash.

In the first chapter stroke technique and court movement will be described in step-by-step detail to give you the armoury to achieve the objective of the game. Once the individual has mastered the basic grounding in stroke play and court movement, the understanding of the strategy of the basic game and match play is the next stage in making the fresh and improved squash player.

The book moves on to the physical preparation necessary to make him a confident competitor and to complement sound stroke technique. Many people still believe road running is the answer. However, as scientific research into physical training shows, this is not the case. By following a physical training programme designed for the specific movements and demands of the game of squash, the physical performance of players can be greatly improved. Hence, a scientific approach to training and nutrition, as advocated in this book, will greatly enhance preparation for match play, and especially for that vital fifth game.

Most squash books describe the tangible aspects of sports performance such as stroke technique and physical training, but ignore one of the most vital aspects in the preparation and performance of match play – the psychological, or mental, preparation. Many players report that they can perform all the basic squash skills accurately and successfully but not when they need to most; namely when playing those crucial match points. Thus, there is a chapter to assist the player in developing mental fitness: the vital ingredient for performing at peak level.

Lastly, the book examines some injury problems common to the game of squash, considering their possible prevention and cure. It offers guidance on how best to treat an injury problem properly and successfully, setting the player on a quick road to full recovery.

It is hoped that this book gives you, 'Tomorrow's Squash Player', an improved approach and attitude to the game.

PLAYING SQUASH FOR THE FIRST TIME OR AFTER A PROLONGED REST FROM THE GAME

1 It is advisable to have a medical check-up prior to taking up the game of squash. This is important irrespective of age, especially if you have had any serious illness, if you are overweight or if you have not been involved in any form of strenuous exercise.

2 If you are just starting to play squash, begin gently and gradually: get used to the physical demands of the game.

3 Squash is not a dangerous game if played properly. Make sure you are acquainted with both the rules and etiquette that relate to court safety before playing a game; ensure that your opponent is similarly informed.

1 PLAY BETTER SQUASH

The overall aim of playing squash is to play the ball out of an opponent's reach, usually into one of the four corners of the court. This requires *accuracy* and *control*. To achieve accuracy and control when playing a stroke, quick movement to and from the ball is essential and requires correct footwork and body positioning to enable the ball to be hit in the desired direction.

Squash technique can be divided into two parts which complement each other. The first is *stroke production* and the second is *movement around the court* between strokes.

STROKE PRODUCTION

To play successful squash the player must be able to hit the ball precisely where he wants it to go with controlled accuracy and speed. Correct stroke play should become 'second nature'. This will further benefit the player in that he will execute shots using the minimum energy and hence will be able to play effective shots for longer.

The best way for an individual to understand and learn what makes a squash stroke successful is to learn what the individual components which make up a basic stroke are. However, it must be remembered that in practice these components must be executed together as one continuous action.

The basic principles of stroke play can best be described in terms of 14 components. These components should be applied in every squash stroke, both forehand and backhand. Although each stroke in squash has its own particular characteristics which combine to give it a different purpose in a game situation to the other shots, the basic principles of the swing, body position and footwork are the same.

Fundamental components of stroke production and classic technique

1 Grip – same for forehand and backhand strokes

2 Cocked wrist

3 Raised racket head

4 Side-on stance

5 Early backswing

6 Body rotation – movement initiated from the hips

7 Balance

8 Weight transference

9 Knee flexion

10 Elbow lead – the swing

11 Body stillness

12 Impact

13 Sraight follow-through

14 Rhythm – a 'grooved' stroke action

Knowledge of the above components will enable you not only to improve your stroke production and play but also to analyse the technical strengths and weaknesses of your opponents. These listed components will also provide a useful checklist to the coach in assessing his pupil's technical strengths and weaknesses, from which practices or coaching points can be set.

1 THE GRIP

The correct grip is illustrated in the following photographs.

The fingers are spread up the grip. Notice that the forefinger is nearer the racket head than the thumb. The thumb is above the middle fingers.

The 'V' formed by the forefinger and thumb lies a little to the left of the centre of the racket handle so that, when the wrist is cocked, the racket will be in a near-vertical position.

The fingers are comfortably spread with the forefinger bent around the handle well up the shaft. The 'feel' of the racket is in the fingers not in the palm of the hand.

This grip should be used for *both* forehand and backhand strokes. It must *not* be changed and is used to play all the strokes from any area of the court.

There should be no feeling of tension in the racket hand. The grip should be firm but not vice-like. An important objective is to have a sense of touch or 'feel' when playing a shot and to be in control of the racket head at all times. This will not be achieved if the fingers are held too close together or when the racket is held like a vice. Spread the fingers comfortably and firmly but not too tightly around the racket. The recommended position for the hand on the racket is such that the end of the shaft presses onto the heel of the hand. However, if this does not feel comfortable to you, choose a position on the racket handle which is.

To check whether you have the correct grip, cock your wrist (that is lift your hand upwards from the wrist). If the racket is not vertical when you extend your arm into a horizontal position, adjust your grip until it is. This grip should be adopted by both right-handed and left-handed players.

There are no hard and fast rules about the size and shape of the racket handle: it doesn't matter as long as it feels comfortable.

A handy hint: keep a check on the condition of the material of the racket grip. Towelling in particular wears quickly and needs regular replacement. When frightened of having the racket slip out of the hand during stroke execution because of a worn grip, players often hold the racket too tightly, the consequence being tension in the fingers and forearm muscles leading to impairment of stroke effectiveness and early fatigue.

2 COCKED WRIST

Cocking the wrist simply means that you should always keep the racket head raised above the level of your wrist. The wrist must be cocked at all times, from the start of the backswing and throughout the whole stroke. Occasionally, you may have to uncock your wrist in order to strike the ball in an awkward situation, for example, when the ball has come closer to your body than you anticipated. However, in general you should strive always to keep your wrist cocked to give you accuracy and control.

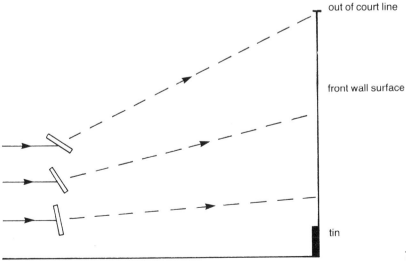

out of court line

front wall surface

tin

floor level

The trajectory of the ball hit with the racket face open. (see over)

The correct grip and cocked wrist also play an important contributory part in conjunction with the forearm to striking the ball with an open racket face. By twisting the forearm gently, the required angle of the racket face can be achieved to execute a stroke. For example, in order to execute an effective lob, the racket face will have to be opened by rotating the forearm outwards to a greater extent than when executing a drive.

When the wrist is cocked during the whole stroke the racket head travels in a uniform arc, allowing for constant control in every stroke, but if the wrist is dropped, the arc of every swing will vary, leading to a loss of consistent racket control.

3 RAISED RACKET HEAD

Many players have the tendency to leave their racket trailing by their knees between strokes. It is essential to lift the racket head with the wrist cocked immediately after completing your previous stroke. If you leave the racket trailing, your stroke preparation takes longer because you have to lift your racket up before beginning your stroke. By having your racket head raised you have time to assess your possible stroke options and are far more likely to be able to deceive your opponent.

Another advantage of a raised racket is that you will be able to retrieve more shots. Even if the ball hits the nick (where the side wall meets the floor) and bounces very low to the floor, it will be possible to play the ball provided your racket is raised and ready to play the shot immediately. Many players lose rallies when the ball shoots out of the nick because their rackets are trailing by their knees and they are, therefore, not prepared to play the ball immediately. By the time they have raised their rackets to play a shot, the ball has bounced two or three times!

4 SIDE-ON STANCE

The position of the feet and body in executing a stroke is very important. Ideally, *every* stroke in squash should be played with a *side-on stance.*

Before and at impact of racket and ball, the body should be facing the side wall or side-on to the direction in which the ball is to be struck. *This is especially important for backhand strokes.* If you stand facing the front wall to hit a shot on your backhand you will find it extremely difficult because of a limited backswing which will restrict your control of the ball. Side-on stance can be achieved consistently in the backhand strokes if you turn your right shoulder around in the backswing so that your back *nearly* faces the front wall. On the forehand side you will turn your left shoulder around in a similar manner. This enables you to swing freely and hit through the ball without the fear of your shoulders and body twisting around to the front wall, at and after impact with the ball.

With such a side-on stance, a *back* foot and a *front* foot can be clearly distinguished. The footwork for all strokes is always the same. If you are in a side-on stance to hit a ball level with or just in front of your body, the front foot should be closer to the side wall you are facing than the back foot. The best way to address the ball is to lead into the shot with your weight moving forward on to your front foot in a side-on stance. This enables you to hit the ball with power and accuracy to any part of the court.

Forehand   *Backhand*

The classic side-on stance

Note that in both the forehand and backhand, the player leads into the shot on her front foot in the side-on stance. The knees are bent and the body is balanced. The wrist is cocked with the racket head raised above the wrist.

If you lead into the shot with the back foot, you will adopt an open stance with the shoulders and body facing or partly facing the front wall thereby limiting power and accuracy. This is because your backswing will be restricted, and you will also have difficulty in transferring the weight of your body onto the leading foot. The most common example of faulty footwork is on the forehand when many players move to the front of the court and lead into the shot with their back foot. Not only is the side-on stance not adopted and the swing restricted but the choice of shots is limited. The most difficult shot to play in this open front-on stance is a straight drive, so a cross-court drive is nearly always opted for.

You must also ensure that you are a comfortable distance away from the ball. Being too close to the ball will result in inaccurate stroking of the ball. The consequent cramped action causes a dropped wrist and the turning of the body towards the front wall resulting in loose shots and unnecessary errors.

The side-on stance is a prerequisite for the effective execution of the other components of stroke play, such as an early backswing, weight transference and a straight follow-through.

5 EARLY BACKSWING

An early backswing is essential in order to generate racket head speed for the power in the stroke. Remember to keep the wrist cocked and bend the elbow at approximately 90°. In the backswing, the racket is drawn upwards vertically in a circular movement until the wrist is level with or above the top of your head. The racket should be behind the head and well laid-back. The backswing is initiated by the body being balanced and then pivoting or rotating from the hips towards the back wall of the court.

6 BODY ROTATION – MOVEMENT INITIATED FROM THE HIPS

The first movement in the execution of a stroke is initiated from the hips. As the hips are turned, the racket is drawn back and upwards in a circular movement in the backswing. Your body weight at this stage is on your back foot. The racket and forearm remain approximately at right angles to each other throughout this movement since the wrist is cocked. The turning of the hips, followed by the trunk and shoulders so that your back partly faces the front wall, enables you to swing freely and consequently to strike the ball with maximum power if so desired. This whole movement and the backswing build-up is like the coiling of a spring which is ready to unwind powerfully into producing a stroke.

The turning of the upper body – hips and shoulders, then initiates the forward movement of the swing. Apart from this role at the beginning of the stroke, they should not be actively involved in the swing. Rather they should be kept out of the movement and simply brought passively around to face the side wall by the movement of the forearm in the swing. Racket-head pace is obtained through the movement of the arm, with the shoulder acting only as the fulcrum of the swing. The main movement in the swing revolves around the elbow and forearm with the body remaining relatively still.

7 BALANCE

While the hips initiate the stroke movement, the knees should be bent and the body evenly balanced to enable you to hit the ball with total control and accuracy in any direction which you desire. Your feet and body must be in the classic position. You must not be running or rushing into a stroke, but rather be completely still and perfectly balanced when striking the ball. Balance can be the overriding factor for success in playing a squash stroke.

8/9 WEIGHT TRANSFERENCE AND KNEE FLEXION

For simplicity these two components are described together. After reaching the top of the backswing, the player drives down and through the ball with the racket, transferring weight onto the leading front foot. As the player transfers weight from the back foot onto the front foot, the knee must bend (knee flexion). This aids the transferring of weight onto the front foot and also enables the player to remain perfectly balanced. Hence, at impact, it is very important that you transfer your weight onto your front foot with bent knees to remain in a balanced position.

A common fault of many players is that they lead into the shot with their back foot. This results in only a slight transfer of weight onto the leading foot, and in some cases players move away from the shot before actual impact. This leads to a loss of accuracy, power and control.

If you bend your knees you are able to get your body down to the level of the flight path of the ball and so keep the racket head above the wrist and forearm which is important for accurate stroking. If you do not bend your knees sufficiently, you will drop your wrist and racket head to reach the ball, often playing inaccurate and loose shots. Further, playing a stroke in an upright or straight stance by not bending the knees often results in bad balance and bad shots.

By bending your knees you can watch the ball at the level at which it is travelling and thus judge angles or the placement of shots better. Obviously if you are executing a volley from a high shot you will not bend your knees to any great extent. Finally, it is easier to return to the 'T' quickly after completing a shot from a bent knee position.

10/11 ELBOW LEAD – THE SWING AND BODY STILLNESS

The generation and build-up of power in a stroke is initiated by the vertical backswing. This gives the player maximum distance in the swing to build up velocity before impact. From this high position the racket moves back and behind the upper body to commence its large arc and build-up of speed. The racket is then driven downwards rapidly into the horizontal plane of the swing. The elbow leads the early forward swing phase with the arm descending from shoulder height. Remember the elbow should be bent at an approximate right angle and the wrist should remain cocked so that the racket face is open. In the horizontal forward movement the elbow, forearm and wrist are responsible for bringing the racket head to meet the ball with pace.

As the elbow, which still leads the racket swing well forward of the wrist and hand, moves forward the forearm begins to rotate inwards along its long axis. This inward rotation of the forearm generates most of the power associated with the drive and will occur naturally if, when swinging forward with the racket in the horizontal plane, you lead with the elbow and lay the racket back so it is nearly at right angles to the forearm by cocking the wrist. Before impact this inward rotation is completed and you gradually straighten your elbow so that the forearm has caught up with it.

The wrist, hand and racket head will, in fact, be almost in line at impact, but the racket head moves quickly ahead immediately after impact. You must ensure you are a comfortable distance away from the ball during the execution of the whole stroke. If you get too close to the ball, there will not be a horizontal swing to meet the ball but the wrist will be dropped to enable the racket head to meet the ball at impact. This often results with a follow-through across and around the body which leads to a loss of control and inaccuracy. The racket follow-through must be in a straight line following in the direction of the ball after impact.

The Swing and Body Position in Forehand and Backhand Strokes

Forehand

1 The elbow leads the forearm and racket as the racket is brought downwards into a horizontal swing in both forehand and backhand strokes.

2 The elbow still leads the racket head. The wrist is cocked and the racket face open. Weight is fully on the front foot and knees are bent.

3 Speed on the swing is generated by gradually straightening the elbow. The forearm turns slightly inwards and the racket head is brought forward so that it is almost in line with the wrist and hand. The body is kept still and out of the stroke action. Rotation of the forearm is not as evident in the backhand stroke.

Backhand

12 IMPACT

As has been mentioned, the racket head should not be dropped below the wrist at impact. This allows the player to hit the ball with greater accuracy and an open-faced racket.

For younger players or players not yet totally confident in their stroke play, the ball should be hit when it is falling towards its second bounce at about the same height as the top of the tin or at knee height, since it is easier to judge the flight of the ball at this time. However, once the player gains confidence in the timing and execution of strokes, he must decide whether in certain situations it would be of more benefit hitting the ball on its fall or hitting it when it is rising from its first bounce so as to hit the ball as early and quickly as possible keeping an opponent under pressure. Playing the ball early and quickly after it has bounced should, of course, only be done if the player can execute the shot accurately.

To gain maximum pace from the ball, it should be hit in front of the leading front foot with your weight predominantly on that foot and your body well-balanced. In executing a backhand stroke, the ball is hit further forward of the leading front foot than in the forehand stroke. This is due to the fact that the front shoulder acts as the fulcrum of the swing in the backhand stroke, whilst the back shoulder is involved in the forehand stroke.

By playing the ball early as it is rising after its first bounce, not only will your opponent be kept moving under pressure but also, when hitting the ball with pace, it is easier to make the ball stay low and not bounce off the back wall. Hitting the ball in front of the leading foot also makes it easier to hit an accurate cross-court drive, using the same swing to meet the ball as in the straight drive.

13 STRAIGHT FOLLOW-THROUGH

The player must follow-through with the racket after impact. Keeping the body still during the execution of the forward swing allows for an unrestrained follow-through. The player's racket hand should follow straight after the ball, then swing upwards with the elbow bending and the racket head finishing in a near-vertical position to the left (forehand) or right (backhand) of his head.

The follow-through is both essential and natural in that it allows the player to attain optimal racket pace at impact. The follow-through of the stroke also helps the player to avoid muscle and joint injury of the shoulder and arm because the racket comes to a gradual stop, rather than suddenly being checked. Some players tend to pull their rackets away from the ball immediately after impact, thus checking their swing which not only causes a loss in accuracy and control but also a loss in velocity of the racket before impact.

Throughout the stroke your left arm should be held away from the body to aid in maintaining good balance. When the stroke is completed with a full follow-through the body is balanced ready to return to a central court position with the weight once more evenly distributed, poised for the opponent's return shot.

Gawain Briars versus Stuart Davenport in the 1984 World Masters. Briars is adopting the classic position to play a forehand drive.

14 RHYTHM – A 'GROOVED' STROKE ACTION

The full swing and positioning of the body should be linked to form one continuous smooth and co-ordinated movement. You should concentrate on watching the ball intently at all times during a match, but it is even more important to watch the ball carefully during the execution of the stroke to ensure the ball is hit in the sweet spot of the racket with control and accuracy.

You must *practise* until the swing and body positioning becomes second nature. The playing of the stroke must be one continuous and smooth movement which is automatic, accurate and powerful (if so desired) rather than a jerky, unsure movement.

The grooved stroke action is illustrated by the photographs on the next three pages of the forehand and backhand straight drive, since these are the foundation strokes in the game of squash.

Forehand drive

1 Early backswing
The racket is drawn upwards behind the head. The wrist is cocked and the elbow bent at 90°, ready to unleash the power in the shot. The hips, trunk and shoulders have pivoted ready to initiate the forward swing. The player leads with the front foot.

2 Downswing
The elbow leads the stroke well ahead of the forearm and racket head as the racket is brought downwards behind the body into the horizontal swing. Note the player's side-on stance.

Backhand drive

It is even more important in the backhand strokes to pivot the hips, trunk and shoulders so that the body is facing the side wall during the horizontal swing and at impact. Many players struggle with this stroke, allowing the ball to pass too close to the body. This can be prevented by turning the shoulders right around in the backswing so that the back partly faces the front wall.

3 Horizontal swing

The elbow still leads the forearm and racket. The wrist is cocked and the racket face open. Weight is transferred on to the front foot and the knees are bent. The body and shoulders are kept out of the stroke.

4 Prior to impact

Racket head speed is generated by inwardly turning the forearm slightly and gradually straightening the elbow. The racket head is brought forward and has almost caught up with the wrist. Weight is fully on the front foot, and the body balanced. Eyes are watching the ball. Turning of the forearm is not as evident in the backhand drive.

5 Impact

The racket head is virtually in line with the wrist at impact. Contact with the ball is slightly ahead of the front foot. The racket head does not drop below the wrist. Weight is fully on the front foot and the body balanced. The left arm is held away from the body to aid balance. In the backhand, the impact takes place further ahead of the front foot than in the forehand.

6 Follow-through
The racket head follows-through after the ball. It is important to follow-through straight behind the ball rather than letting the wrist drop with the racket following-through across the body. Pay particular attention to firmness of the wrist when playing the backhand stroke. The weight is still on the front foot.

7 Return to 'T'
The elbow bends and the racket swings up to finish in a near-vertical position over the left shoulder. Eyes are still watching the ball. Weight is still partially on the front foot to ensure that the player does not pull away from the shot at impact. The player is now able to push off with the front foot to return to the 'T'.

2 DEVELOPING SKILLS

IMPROVISATION

The ability to *improvise* well in playing shots is an essential skill in squash. For example, the ball may shoot out of the nick unexpectedly resulting in the player being too close to the ball to achieve the classic side-on body position when striking the ball. He will therefore have to improvise in attempting to play a straight drive. Improvisation of strokes can only be achieved if the player has sound stroke technique.

If you have to improvise, always try to hit the ball in a manner and position such that as many as possible of the *14 fundamental components* of stroke production are obeyed.

Sometimes you will be forced to execute drives and other shots off your back foot because you will not have time to move into the correct position because of the fast approach of the ball or the limited time you have when under pressure to move towards the ball. You may only have enough time to step sideways with the right foot on the forehand or the left foot on the backhand. You must, however, still attempt to turn your hips and shoulders as much as you can and transfer weight on to the leading foot. You should hit the ball with as near the correct swing as possible keeping the body still and balanced. The backswing, however, will be somewhat restricted because you cannot turn the hips, trunk and shoulders to the same extent as you can when leading with the front foot. Usually at top level, because correct stroke production has become second nature to most players, they are able to improvise and play a forehand or backhand drive off the back foot with accuracy but *not* with the same power. This was found not to be true of club level players whose drives were mostly inaccurate when played off the back foot. Playing a drive leading off the back foot will save you time in not adopting the classic side-on stance, but beware, there are the following disadvantages of executing the shot in this manner.

1 You cannot drive the ball with the same power or accuracy as you can when you drive off the front foot.

2 Many players hit the ball back too closely to themselves because their shoulders are facing the front wall at impact. This is particularly dangerous when you are at the front of the court, because if your opponent is in a ready position at the 'T', he will be able to play a quick counter-attacking shot, for example, a

volley, before you have time to recover back to the centre of the court. You will either be placed under further pressure or even lose the rally because you cannot reach the next shot.

3 A further consequence is that, since your shoulders are facing the front wall as a result of your open stance when leading off the back foot, you cannot watch the ball very easily when playing a drive to the back of the court. In this open stance most players move backwards to the 'T' position watching the ball by turning their head and looking over their shoulder. Thus, they cannot watch the ball or their opponent effectively and so are often caught flat-footed. In the classic side-on stance you are ideally positioned to watch both the ball and your opponent with ease.

So the advice is: unless you are forced to improvise by playing a shot off your back foot, always try to get into the classic side-on stance to execute a stroke. However, make sure you are proficient and confident in the correct stroke technique so that, if you are forced to improvise, you can play the stroke with as many of the *14 components* of stroke production as possible.

THE IMPORTANCE OF PRACTICE

It cannot be stressed enough how important it is to develop effective stroke technique early in your career. The only way to achieve this is through *practice.*

If you decide to make a fundamental change in technique, especially if you have been playing for a long time and your own particular style is well-established, you must be prepared to *practise* and, in this case more importantly, be prepared to work at the classic stroke production for at least two to three months. For those of you trying to change your stroke technique, be prepared for a period during which the standard of your game will drop. After this period your game and stroke production will improve – so do not feel disheartened. Stick with your goal of learning the correct stroke production. A coach can be particularly supportive during this phase in maintaining the player's motivation and confidence. If you are a serious league player and are going to change your technique you must plan carefully the period in which you are going to do it. During the summer months or in the out-of-season period is usually the best time to concentrate solely on learning the correct technique which will ultimately improve your squash. You will become a new force to be reckoned with in the coming season!

Practice routines shall be suggested for each stroke. You can devise your own variations in practices. The suggested routines are designed to develop all aspects of the correct stroke play as long as you, the player, concentrate on executing the strokes in practice in the correct manner. *Sloppily performed practices are of no benefit to the player whatsoever.*

Further practices should be simple to start with to develop rhythm and a 'grooved' stroke action, moving on to practices which simulate game-like situations in which you can learn to cope with playing shots under pressure.

Jahangir Khan: action shot of the champion volleying off the wrong foot. He shows good racket control and good improvisation.

THE DRIVE

When driving the ball straight you should aim to:

1 keep the ball close to the sidewalls to prevent an opponent from volleying the ball

2 hit the ball with enough pace to ensure that it bounces behind the service box to force an opponent into the back corners of the court. This is known as a *length* shot.

The point at which to aim on the front wall to achieve good length depends not only on the pace at which the ball is hit, but where the ball is aimed on the front wall. If you are hitting a drive from the front court you can hit the ball with a lot of pace aiming the ball so it hits the wall 10 – 30 centimetres above the tin. If you aim the ball too high on the front wall it will not bounce before hitting the back wall, making it easy for your opponent to retrieve. When hitting a drive from the back court it is generally essential to aim sufficiently high on the front wall to be certain that the ball will bounce behind the service box.

There are no hard and fast rules on where to aim the ball on to the front wall or how much pace you should generate in a drive, but instead you should, in practice, experiment in playing drives from all parts of the court to decide where to aim the ball on the front wall and how hard to hit the ball to achieve effective length shots.

The execution of the drive has been dealt with in the previous chapter under the description of a grooved swing action (pp.00 – 00). This is the fundamental shot of the game and this deserves its treatment under the section dedicated to the *14 components* of stroke production.

● PRACTICES ●

Solo

1 Play consecutive drives to land behind the service box.

Pairs

2 Player 'A' feeds a short shot from behind the service box, player 'B' must hit forehand straight drives from the 'T' into the back corner using the classic stroke technique. Repeat on the backhand stroke.

3 Player 'A' feeds alternate forehand and backhand boasts, from behind the service box, player 'B' on the 'T' must hit alternate forehand and backhand straight drives accurately to a good length. Pay particular attention to correct court movement to adopt classic side-on stance when addressing the ball.

4 A further progression is for player 'A' to feed any type of short shot, such as a boast, a straight or cross-court drop shot or reverse angle boast from the back court. Player 'B' plays straight drives only accurately to a good length. This places player 'B' under more pressure who again should pay attention to points suggested in practice 3.

Jahangir Khan playing Chris Dittmar, in the World Masters tournament, 1984. Khan is about to unleash a powerful backhand drive while Dittmar is ideally placed, watching both the ball and opponent.

CROSS-COURT DRIVE

The preparation and swing of the cross-court drive is the same as in the straight drive. However, at impact the ball is hit well forward of the front foot and the racket followed-through across the body in the direction in which the ball is hit, finishing in a near-vertical position as in the straight drive. Because the ball is struck in front of the leading foot, the racket head will naturally be brought closer to the feet as it is swung forward to meet the ball.

Forehand cross-court drive

Backhand cross-court drive

The preparation and downswing of the cross-court drive is similar to that of a straight drive. Contact is made between the racket head and ball ahead of the front foot. The arm swings close to the body and the

racket follows-through across the body in the direction of the shot. In the backhand the contact between the racket and ball is made further forward of the front foot.

The cross-court drive should be played to hit the side wall at the back of the service box near the nick area. This is an effective shot because the ball stays low and forces an opponent into the back corner of the court, limiting the choice of return shot. When an opponent is well-placed in the centre of the court to intercept any loose shots, it is a good idea to angle the cross-court drive higher on to the side wall out of his reach. He will not be able to volley the ball accurately or effectively and so will again be forced into the back corner of the court.

THE DRIVE KILL

The drive kill is hit when the ball is at the peak of its bounce and well in front of the body with the player's weight forward on the front foot. It is hit down just above the tin so that the ball stays very low.

The ball may be aimed either to hit the nick or across the court when an opponent is out of position. The safest drive kill is one that is hit along the side wall so there is no chance of it coming out into the middle of the court. Another advantage is that if it is hit further back in the court than originally intended, it will still be close to the side wall and therefore difficult for an opponent to attack.

● PRACTICES ●

Solo

1 Set up a high bouncing shot and try to hit it powerfully down into the nick, across the court or straight.

Pairs

2 Player 'A' feeds a high short shot, player 'B' tries to kill the ball straight, either across the court or into the nick. Player 'A' must attempt to keep the rally going.

THE VOLLEY

The volley is played with the same body, forearm and racket head action as in the drive. As you prepare for the shot, take your racket upwards to a near-vertical position whilst pivoting at the hips. The body should face the side wall when the hips pivot whilst the racket is drawn upwards and backwards until the hand is level with the left shoulder from where the forward swing is initiated. You should be in the classic side-on stance where weight is transferred on to the front foot as the forward swing commences. It is very important to keep the wrist cocked with the racket head above it throughout the stroke to ensure good control of the ball. The volley must be played precisely as it is more difficult to control the ball than in the drive. A floppy or dropped wrist will almost certainly result in an error. The ball should be struck with a firm hitting action and preferably at a point slightly ahead of the front foot on the forehand and even further forward on the backhand. You must hit through the ball with the racket, trying not to place excessive slice on the ball, but hitting it hard and flat to ensure that it goes to the back of the court. The left arm should be held away from the body to aid balance as in the drive shot.

You must be well-balanced throughout the stroke and careful not to pull away from the ball just before or at impact. Some players find it helpful in timing the stroke if they actually stamp their foot on the floor as they play the volley.

The racket follows-through in a near-horizontal plane before being brought to finish over the left shoulder. The follow-through in the volley may not be as exaggerated as in the drive since often the player does not have time to take a full backswing because of the speed at which the ball may approach. This shows the importance of keeping the racket raised between strokes.

The volley is an essential shot to keep your opponent moving, allowing him as little time as possible to recover or prepare for his shot. In most volleys the ball is directed to the back of the court.

Forehand volley

1 *Hips, trunk and shoulders pivoted ready to initiate forward swing with a good, vertical backswing. The player is in the classic side-on stance, leading with the front foot.*

2 *The body is well-balanced and body weight transferred onto the front foot. The wrist is still cocked and the swing the same action as in the drive. The elbow straightens as the racket swings through to meet the ball ahead of the front foot. Impact with the ball should be at shoulder height when volleying to the back of the court.*

3 *The follow-through is straight in the direction of the ball, but may not be as exaggerated as in the drive. This is especially true when playing a drop volley.*

Backhand volley

Backview: *The wrist is cocked and the elbow is bent at 90°. The elbow leads well ahead of the racket in the forward swing. The left arm should be held away from the body to aid good balance.*

Once you can volley the ball to the back of the court confidently you will have developed good control of the racket head with a firm wrist. This will give you the option of playing a drop volley.

The drop volley is played with little or no backswing and the racket face open so that slice is imparted to the shot. With good timing and the right amount of slice, it is possible to take the speed off the ball to make it drop after hitting the front wall. This shot should only be played if the player is well-balanced and not hurried when playing the shot.

Another effective volley is the volley kill, when the ball hits the front wall hard and just above the tin so that the ball stays low. This shot is often executed from an opponent's weak lob.

You may not have time to achieve the side-on stance or full backswing so you will have to improvise in a similar manner as in the drive. Hopefully you will have your racket already raised! You may only have time to step sideways leading with your back foot rather than your front foot. You must, however, turn your hips so that your body partly faces the side wall. It is still important that you transfer your weight on to your leading foot maintaining good balance. You should strike the ball as early as possible, ensuring the racket head is firmly held above the wrist, and follow-through after impact in a similar manner to the classic volley.

● PRACTICES ●

Because the volley is such a precise stroke and often a winning shot, practice of this stroke is essential.

Solo

1 Volley rally: start close to the front wall, volley 10 or more consecutive forehand straight volleys. Move two paces further back, repeat the volley. Keep moving back until you are behind the service box. Repeat on the backhand side.

Pairs

2 Player 'A' feeds straight shots from behind the service box. From the 'T' player 'B' volleys the ball straight aiming to keep the ball tight to the side wall and hitting it into the back corner. After player 'A' has developed good timing in volleying to a length, he can then attempt volley drops or volley kills.

3 Player 'A' feeds a high cross-court and then a high straight drive alternately from behind. From the 'T', player 'B' plays only straight volleys to the back of the court. He will therefore, play two forehand volleys and two backhand volleys. This is a good exercise for improving your ability to turn on court and then volley accurately to the back of the court.

4 The final progression is for player 'A' to play either straight or cross-court feeds at random whilst player 'B' must play only straight volleys or, straight or cross-court volleys into the back corners of the court from the 'T'. This practice simulates game conditions as closely as possible and is, therefore, a good exercise not only in improving your volleying ability but also improving your court movement in order to execute a volley under pressure.

Alex Cowie, 1985 British Open Champion in the over-35's bracket, playing a technically perfect drop volley. She is well balanced, has played with minimum backswing and with good timing and, with some slice, the speed will be taken from the ball. Pondering the problem of how to retrieve the shot is Barbara Diggens.

THE SERVICE

Far too often this shot is neglected, hurried or played without care, viewed simply as a means of starting a rally. Try to serve the ball accurately in such a way that your opponent is forced to make a hurried or defensive return from the back corner of the court, whilst you can move quickly into a balanced position in the centre of the court. Remember to watch the ball as it goes into the back of the court.

Two types of service will be described but you will discover variations to keep your opponent under pressure and guessing.

The lob serve

This is executed from a balanced position, using an open racket face. The racket is brought up under the ball aiming it to strike high up on the front wall. At impact the body should be facing the front wall. The ball should strike the opposite side wall high up and behind the service box so that it drops off the side wall and bounces close to the back wall. Remember to move towards the centre of the court after serving and watch the ball and your opponent behind you. Most players prefer to serve with a forehand action whether it is from the left or right service box. To gain consistency and accuracy in serving, each time you serve always position yourself carefully in the same place and in the same manner.

1 The player steps forward to play the lob serve. Wrist is cocked as racket is brought forward to meet the ball.

2 At impact, shoulders are facing the front wall to enable the player to angle the ball cross-court. Contact with the ball is well in front of the the body with racket face open. Left arm is held away from the body to aid balance.

3 The racket follows-through into a high, vertical position. The player watches the ball intently after impact and is ready to move quickly to the 'T' position.

Lob serve from right service box

1 *Position of the feet is different when serving from the left. Eyes watch the ball intently.*

2 *Contact with the ball is not as far in front of the body as in the serve from the right. The body adopts more of a side-on stance. The wrist is cocked and the racket face open. Contact with the ball is higher.*

Lob serve from left service box

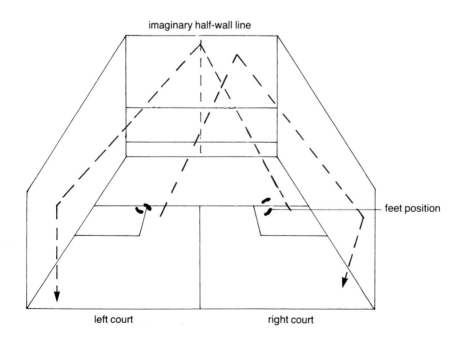

imaginary half-wall line

feet position

left court   right court

Lob serve: where to aim the ball

For a right-handed player it is often easier to serve from the right service box than from the left service box. This is because the player will be facing the side wall and can hit the ball at a greater angle on to the front wall. The ball should be aimed high up in the middle of the front wall, or just left of centre. When serving from the left service box, the angle is narrowed because the body faces towards the centre of the court. The ball, therefore, has to be aimed to hit the centre of the furthest half of the front wall to achieve the most effective angle in serving. This is illustrated in the diagram below. It also means that the position of the feet and body is different when serving from each side.

The hard, flatter service

This service should be driven hard across the court via the front wall and is aimed to hit the opposite side wall and force your opponent into the back of the court. Be careful that it does not rebound out too far from the side or back walls towards the centre of the court preventing you from moving into the centre of the court because you have to give your opponent a fair view of the front wall.

The positioning of the feet and body will remain much the same as for the lob service since the angle of service will not have changed. Strike the ball hard so that it hits the front wall just above the fault line. This means that the face of your racket should be only fractionally open. If the serve is hit hard and accurately, your opponent will not be able to move in to hit the ball early and take the initiative.

A variation of this serve is to drive the ball (via the front wall) straight at your opponent's body. This often catches your opponent unawares and leaves him undecided which way to move his body or whether to play a forehand or backhand shot.

● PRACTICES ●

Again, the saying 'practice makes perfect', and you should attempt to obtain a 'grooved' consistent service. Always concentrate on practising your service in friendly games and matches.

Pairs

Player 'A' serves from the right service box in such a manner as to prevent player 'B' from volleying the return of service. Hence accuracy is the order of the day. Repeat from the left service box.

imaginary half-wall line

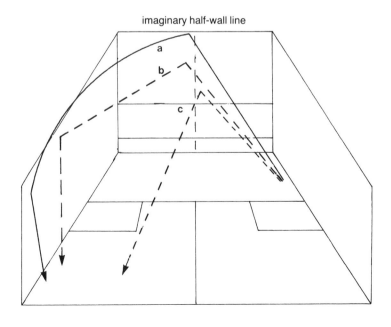

Variations of service
a) Lob serve
b) Hard, flat serve
c) Ball driven to opponent's body

RECEIVING SERVICE

The aim of returning service is to play the ball in such a way that you can get yourself out of the back court and move your opponent away from the 'T' position. The safest and best reply is a volley or drive straight and close to the side wall into the back corner of the court. A cross-court drive or volley may also be played for variety, as long as good width and depth is achieved. Similarly, a drop shot or boast should be mastered to be used off a loose or weak serve.

Your reply will be to some extent dictated by the accuracy and speed of your opponent's serve. The position on the court you should adopt to receive your service will be the same no matter what kind of service your opponent uses.

How many times have you been able to return a service only by volleying cross-court? Many players learn how to volley a return of service across the court only because they are badly positioned and have no choice. Particular attention should be paid to the positioning and stance of the body in receiving service.

1 Give yourself space to swing. Do not get cramped deep in the corner. The best stance is just behind the service box and near to the half-court line. Stand with your feet apart, knees slightly bent and the body in the side-on stance and well-balanced. It is absolutely essential when you return the ball, that you turn your

Service reception

Forehand

Notice the player's stance behind the service box and near the half-court line. The player is not cramped in the corner or near the side wall. The feet are apart and knees slightly bent with the body well-balanced, ready to adopt the side-on stance. The racket head is raised with the wrist cocked. The player is watching the server and the ball intently. The dotted lines show the path of the ball.

shoulders around to partly face the back wall from where you will begin your forward swing. This will enable you to volley the ball straight down the side wall. Many players do not do this which results in the shoulders turning to face the front wall (an open stance) at impact so that the player can play a cross-court shot only. You must be prepared to move your feet and adjust your position, depending where the service is hit, so as to adopt this classic stance. Remember, the return of serve straight down the side wall is the most effective shot.

2 Keep your racket head raised and watch the server *and* the ball.

3 Be prepared to volley the ball early, moving forward to the 'T' position after returning serve in preparation for your next stroke. Remember to keep watching the ball *and* your opponent.

4 Do not let the server rush you by serving before you are ready and balanced.

● **PRACTICES** ●

Pairs

Player 'A' serves whilst player 'B' must attempt to return the serve, preferably by volleying, accurately either straight down the wall into the back court or across the court with good width and depth.

Backhand

In the photograph of backhand service reception the player has moved from the perfect starting position to play a backhand volley return.

THE DROP SHOT

A successful drop shot has its origin in stillness. Correct body position will facilitate vast potential for spotless accuracy and ensure natural development of disguise and deception. This correct body alignment can only be achieved if the correct pathway to the ball has been chosen.

The drop shot requires real bending of the knees. Slightly kicking away the rear leg will assist. A cocked wrist allows the ball to be cut. The swing of the racket must be easy and controlled with a full swing being favoured to assist in disguise. It is highly desirable to *stroke* the ball when it is slightly below the tin. Obviously the follow-through is much shorter than in a drive as the shot requires touch and feel to give additional control and back spin.

An immediate return to the 'T' position usually causes a collision with the opponent. Inevitably, the person at fault is the person playing the straight drop. Therefore, after completing the stroke, to ensure your opponent has a clear path to the ball, you should move obliquely towards the furthest side wall before moving backwards to the 'T' position.

The drop shot is looked upon as a 'natural' shot (that is you can either play the shot or you can't). Further, many players are loath to play it because they are obsessed with playing the ball to the back of the court. However, the drop shot is basically a 'dummy drive' and until you can successfully execute it you will never truly be able to test your opponent's stamina reserves. A mixture of delicately placed drops, with drives and lobs to the back of the court will cause your opponent to run faster and most importantly breathe faster. Even Mr Khan would eventually use all the energy stored in his muscles if you constantly made him run the diagonal!

No power is needed for this shot. Just remember to practise getting down to the ball and stroking it on to the front wall with a very short follow-through. Be wary of playing cross-court drops unless you find yourself in a cramped position.

Forehand drop shot

1 The preparation for the drop shot is similar to that for a straight drive to assist in disguising the shot. Weight is well forward and the knees bent. The player is watching the ball intently.

Backhand drop shot

● PRACTICES ●

Solo

1 Set a ball up in mid-court and play a drop shot. Repeat for the backhand stroke.

Pairs

2 Player 'A' plays an angle or a boast from the back of the court and player 'B' plays the drop shot.

3 Player 'A' plays a boast, player 'B' plays a drop shot. Player 'A' plays a straight lob, player 'B' plays the boast.

2 The elbow leads at impact. The ball is stroked with the racket held firmly.

3 The head is well down and weight forward. Note the bending of the knees.

4 Follow-through is much shorter than in the drive as the shot requires touch and feel to give additional control and backspin.

THE CROSS-COURT LOB

Most squash players have a flat 'two-dimensional' view of space and are oblivious to all the room 'up there' on the squash court. The tendency is to play the lob stroke only when they are in trouble. However, there is a lot of offensive space up there. As a squash player you are in the '*Risk Business*' and as such should look upon the lob shot as an attacking option. It must be another scoring threat in your armoury of strokes.

Once again, the classic side-on stance keeps your opponent guessing. It also ensures you are in the best position to get under the ball, to stroke it high onto the front wall and into the back corners. The stroke (under and upwards) is very similar to the lob service described on p. 37. A successful cross-court lob should be too high for your opponent to volley and it should be struck with just enough pace to hit the side wall high behind the service box and then come to rest in the back corner.

Tactically, the cross-court lob has many uses. Veteran squash players with ailing aerobic capacities fully utilise this stroke. Not only does this ploy give them the breathing space they need, but it also enables the ball to land in the back corner. A lob gives variation.

The lob is both an attacking and defensive shot which adds disciplined variety to your game. Remember, you don't have to 'bludgeon' the ball through the front wall every time!

Forehand cross-court lob

1 Eyes watch the ball intently. Early racket preparation. The weight is forward.

Backhand cross-court lob

● PRACTICES ●

Solo

1 Set a ball up in the front forehand court and play a cross-court lob. Repeat on the backhand stroke.

Pairs

2 Player 'A' sets a ball up in the front of the court. Player 'B' plays a cross-court lob. Player 'A' repeats his stroke while player 'B' returns to the 'T' position before playing his next stroke. Change places.

2 *Feet are correctly positioned with the weight firmly on the front foot and the racket face is open.*

3 *Racket face opened more to 'lift' the ball high onto the front wall.*

4 *Ball hit with less pace than a drive. Player returns quickly to base.*

BOASTS

We have spent a lot of time in this book explaining the importance of stroke technique because with good technique you can fully explore the back corners. By getting the ball into the back corners you are trying to make your opponent play a defensive boast. A defensive boast is played only when you can't play the ball directly to the front wall. A defensive boast is a 'set up' for your opponent, giving him many options at the front of the court. The defensive boast is an angle shot hit to the nearest side wall and springing back on to the front wall and then coming to rest at the nick at the opposite side wall.

Defensive forehand boast

1 Player is facing the back wall. Note the early racket preparation, and eyes watching the ball intently.

2 The body is well-balanced and body weight transferred onto the front foot. The wrist is still cocked and the swing the same action as in the drive. The elbow straightens as the racket swings through to meet the ball ahead of the front foot.

3 Straight follow-through behind the ball.

Defensive backhand boast

However, a boast can also be a very useful attacking stroke. As your opponent waits pensively at the 'T' position, if you delay your stroke he will have to overcome inertia to reach the ball at the front, making it difficult for him to adopt the side-on stance and play a powerful shot.

Attacking forehand boast

1 Note early racket preparation and side-on stance. Eyes watch the ball intently.

2 Weight is transferred through the shot. Ball is hit hard on to side wall. Remember to hit through the ball.

3 Follow-through then return to base.

Attacking backhand boast

Two further types of shot may be included in this category:

Reverse angle

This stroke is played across court to the farthest away side wall, on to the front wall and returned to the other side wall. The stroke allows the player plenty of room to mask the ball. Used sparingly, it may bewilder an opponent, but an alert opponent quick to the 'T' position will smother any inaccuracies.

Trickle boast

This stroke is an angle played onto the side wall rebounding off the front wall and into the side wall nick. It is imperative that the ball dies near the farthest side wall because if it comes back into the middle of the court, the point will be lost. It is very much a touch shot played nearer the front of the court than the traditional boast.

COURT MOVEMENT

The learning of stroke play is very important in the game of squash but the strokes cannot be used to their full potential without the correct court movement. Knowledge of the best way to move around the court enables the player to approach and address the ball in a manner which will have his feet and body naturally in the classic position to execute a stroke with ease. *The importance of movement around the court cannot be overstressed.*

Many players have the ability to execute strokes in the classic manner but because of their bad or incorrect movement, find themselves continually addressing the ball with the feet and body in the wrong position. A common example is when a player moves forward to the front court to hit a stroke off a boast or drop shot. The player charges straight towards the ball, getting too close to it with his body facing the front wall and leading into the shot with his back foot instead of being in the classic side-on stance. The result is often a loose or weak shot which an opponent can pounce on, taking full advantage of his bad positioning to keep him under pressure.

Successful stroke play will result if the following important aspects of court movement and body positioning are considered.

BODY POSITIONING WHEN YOUR OPPONENT IS PLAYING A SHOT

A player's best position when his opponent is hitting the ball should normally be in the centre of the court about half a metre behind the 'T' position (unless the opponent is incapable of playing a hard, accurate length shot – in this case he can move forward towards the 'T' or just in front of the 'T' position).

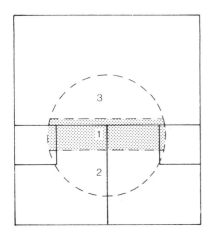

The 'T' area

1 The 'T' area where you should be positioned watching the opponent and the ball.

2 You could position yourself in this area if you are certain your opponent is going to return the shot to the back of the court. However, it is not always advisable to anticipate where your opponent will play the return as you may be wrong-footed.

3 You could move forward into this area if you are certain your opponent can only boast defensively out of the back court or that your opponent's shot is going to bounce in the front court.

Jahangir Kahn versus Qamar Zaman in the British Open, 1984. In the battle of the great Pakistan players both intense concentration and sound positioning are exhibited.

When you are positioned in the 'T' area, do not watch the front wall or half-watch the ball and your opponent over your shoulder. When you hit a shot which moves your opponent to the back of the court you must turn and watch both the ball and the action of your opponent as he is hitting the ball. His foot placement and the manner of his swing often give you a clue as to where he is going to hit the ball. Make sure that you actually watch your opponent's racket head hit through the ball and the resultant flight of the ball. If you stand with your back to your opponent watching the front wall you will have no idea where he is going to hit the ball. It is absolutely vital that you position yourself in such a way that you can watch the ball and your opponent with ease. You should be well-balanced with your feet apart and your knees bent ready to move quickly after your opponent has hit the ball. Make sure that you are on your toes or the balls of your feet, as it will then be easier to turn and move forwards or backwards. Standing on your heels makes it almost impossible to move forward quickly. Be prepared, with your racket raised ready to play any shot.

Do not try to anticipate or guess where your opponent is going to play the ball by moving from the 'T' before he has actually hit the ball. This will often result in you being wrong-footed or stranded out of position. Only make a preliminary move if you can confidently assess

Stance in the 'T' area

Backhand side: position yourself just left of the centre of the half-court line ready to cover any loose shots down the side wall. Note the player's position – her feet and body are at an angle to the front wall, knees bent, body balanced, and her racket raised. She is watching the ball and the opponent behind her.

Forehand side: position yourself just right of centre of the half-court line ready to cover any loose shots down the wall.

where your opponent is going to play the ball or if his choice of shot is limited, for example, when he is digging the ball out of the back corners.

The position of your body when you are in the 'T' position, waiting for an opponent to strike the ball, will depend on where he is. Only when he is in front of you will you position your body and feet so that they are facing the front wall, with knees bent, good balance and racket raised. When your opponent is behind you or alongside of you, your feet and body should be positioned as illustrated in the photographs on p. 50, with your feet and body at an angle to the front wall of approximately 45°. On the backhand side of the court, your left foot should be nearest the back wall and on the forehand side of the court, your right foot should be nearest the back wall. Hence, if your opponent hits the ball from the back of the court, position your feet at an approximate 45° angle to the front wall so that your body does not face the front wall. This makes it easier for you to turn your head and shoulders so that you can watch your opponent playing his stroke and the path of the ball both before and after it is struck. Positioning yourself in this way also facilitates quick movement to the corners of the court. The most difficult movement being to turn and move towards a shot hit across the court into the back corner behind you. The importance, therefore, of watching the ball and your opponent carefully to enable you to move quickly to a possible cross-court shot cannot be stressed enough. It is advisable always to initiate your movement leading with the front foot first and turning your hips, which will automatically turn your body without any extra effort.

MOVEMENT TOWARDS THE BALL

Correct movement to the ball enables you to address the ball correctly and play the stroke effectively. When your opponent has struck the ball you must immediately assess where the ball is going to bounce and where you will position yourself to play the stroke in the correct manner. You must then move from the centre of the court in the following way so that you can position your body and feet:

1 Never run straight towards the ball. Most players tend to do this which results in bad positioning. Moving straight towards the ball to play a shot often results in the player getting too close to the ball with his body facing the front wall. This causes a cramped and incorrect stroke action from which an inaccurate and weak shot is often played.

2 You should move so that your last step with your front foot is towards the side wall on either the forehand or backhand side. You will then automatically adopt the classic side-on stance. Make sure that you are a comfortable distance away from the ball so that you can keep your shot options open and strike the ball with a grooved stroke action. If this movement is obeyed it is often easy to use deception using the classic racket preparation. Running straight

towards the ball limits the player's choice of shot in that he can often only play the ball across the court. The following diagrams illustrate the path of movement which you should take in your game of squash:

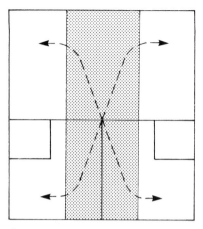

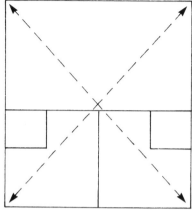

Correct court movement

In moving up and down the court, keep in this central channel until you move to take up your side-on stance.

These are the ideal movement paths from the 'T' position to the ball. Your last step should take you to a side-on stance at a comfortable distance from the ball. Be careful not to step too close to the ball.

Incorrect court movement

Take care not to run straight towards the ball or to the corners of the court. This bad-positioning results in a cramped and incorrect stroke action leading to an inaccurate, weak shot.

The correct movement to the ball also enables you to make a split-second adjustment to your body and feet position if the ball bounces in an unexpected manner. This is not possible if you run straight towards the ball.

Do not overrun the ball in eagerness to strike it, or position your feet prematurely until you are sure of the place and bounce of the ball. Many players, in their enthusiasm or over-eagerness to get to the ball, overrun the ball because they have misjudged its bounce. Conversely, some players plant their feet firmly in position with a lot of time to spare only to find the ball bounces further away from them or closer to them than expected which again results in an improvised stroke! You must be able to make a final, split-second adjustment if needed. You should have completed your backswing by the time you have firmly positioned your front foot ready to execute a stroke.

The size of the steps the player uses in court movement will depend on the individual. Many players find that they can reach most shots in two or three steps. If you cannot you may have to use short, fast steps. You must, however, practise this movement to ensure the last step you take to address the ball is with your front foot towards the side wall.

When you are striking the ball you must be motionless and perfectly balanced in the classic side-on stance so that you can play the ball in whatever manner and direction you desire. This means that you must not be running in or rushing away from the stroke when you are actually striking the ball. You should, therefore, position yourself at the point where you wish to strike the ball with sufficient time to allow for any necessary adjustment. Remember you must be able to strike the ball in front of or level with the front foot.

It is important that you are motionless and well-balanced at impact with the ball so that you can move quickly back to the 'T' position after hitting it. If you are moving forward at contact with the ball you will not be able to move back to the 'T' position immediately or chase your opponent's shot if he volleys it. Do not, however, make the mistake of moving away from the ball before you have finished hitting it in an attempt to recover to the 'T' position quickly. Stand with your weight forward on the front foot and your body balanced and motionless until your racket has hit through the ball so as not to lose power and accuracy. However, do not wait until you have completed your follow-through before moving towards the 'T' position. Just stand still long enough to ensure that your racket has hit through the ball.

MOVEMENT AFTER HITTING THE BALL

Your footwork and court movement after hitting the ball is also very important and must not be neglected. After playing a shot you must watch the ball. This means that you will, therefore, have to turn your head and shoulders to watch the ball if you play it behind you into the back corners of the court. The easiest and best way to do this is to turn your hips and feet towards the side of the court to which you have hit the ball and then move backwards to the 'T' position whilst watching the ball. This ensures that after playing a shot from the front court you can turn and move towards the 'T' area with a good view of the ball and your opponent. You must remain well-balanced with your knees bent so that you can quickly change direction if necessary or chase your opponent's return shot. The movement back to the 'T' area ensures that you do not retreat backwards with your body facing the front wall giving you no or limited sight of the ball or opponent. Many players make such an awkward movement back to the centre of the court that they are often badly-balanced when doing so. From such an awkward movement it is difficult to change direction or turn because they have not been watching the ball and opponent behind them.

The coach has an important role to play in helping the player learn and achieve the correct and best court movement. The coach should play with the pupil often and stop the game when the player does not watch the ball properly or moves incorrectly and should direct his attention to the correct aspect of court movement.

● PRACTICES ●

Practising the correct court movement is essential in order that it becomes automatic and smooth. Hence, 'shadow ghosting' (simulating movements) during a game is recommended. The following exercise is designed to achieve this. You should practise it regularly. Not only will it improve your movement around the court but also your stamina.

It is played by the coach and player. The coach calls the instructions of play and the player moves correctly and at full speed, plays an imaginary shot and then recovers quickly to the 'T' position ready for the next direction. The instructor nominates the corner which the player must move to by pointing to it and the shot which the player must shadow. Correct footwork, movement, pace and balance must be used throughout this exercise and the player must simulate the nominated stroke correctly.

The coach has an important role to play in ensuring that the player moves around the court correctly in the curved pathways as illustrated on p.52 and not straight into the corners. The player should keep his racket head raised between strokes. *Remember, sloppily-performed practices are of no benefit at all to the player but just form bad habits.*

THE ROLE OF THE COACH

The modern squash coach needs to realise that skill practices ought to predominate. He must be able to motivate the players to persevere when things are not going well. Ideally, the coach needs a sports science background or access to sports medicine and sports training principles.

Since the technique chapter in this book is based on research an *orthodox model* of play evolves. However, today the coach must realise that an *individually-tailored model* is needed. Previous coaching books make scant allowance for individual differences. Although you still need an orthodox model of play the coach can now tailor the training to suit the individual. Squash players are heterogeneous. They all react differently to setbacks in their careers. More will be said about the role of the coach in both physical and mental training later, but in coaching for the improvement of skills, the instructor has a vital role to play.

It is the coach who has the advantage of watching stroke production from the outside. The player will know if a shot instinctively feels right – and this message should not be ignored – but the coach has the opportunity of seeing objectively whether a shot is being played correctly. It may be that, with guidance, the player can improve upon his or her style and still retain that instinctively correct feel. In this business of shot observation video recordings can be a very useful tool. They enable slow motion analysis and a unique opportunity for a player to watch himself in action – doing things both correctly and incorrectly. Of course video analysis will show up the strengths and weaknesses of both the player in question and the opponent, and watching others play is, of course, an important part of the learning process.

The chart pictured opposite is one way in which the coach can monitor improvement, or areas that need attention. Obviously the simple model shown can be modified to suit individual needs.

On a more specialised front a coach can utilise a chart like the one shown for skill development where setting limited goals is the key. The coach and player can identify an area of play or a particular shot and score it during a match. The method recommended is to note the number of times in a rally, game or match (whichever is appropriate to the frequency of the technique) that a particular shot or skill is performed. The coach can note the number of times the play is executed correctly. A percentage score of a certain level, to be advanced throughout the season, is the target. Careful monitoring on record charts will provide a tangible record of improvement. Psychologically this type of assessment can be advantageous. A 'no hope' match against a vastly superior opponent can still yield success if the goal is limited to, say, playing two drop volley winners or two winning service returns in the match.

TECHNIQUE	GOOD	WEAK	POINTERS
forehand drive			
grip			
backswing			
vertical swing			
racket position impact			
follow through			
footwork			
balance			
body position			

SHOT EXECUTION

FOREHAND DRIVE – LENGTH	GOOD	WEAK
depth		
height on front wall		
back corners		
tight to wall		

3 COURT STRATEGY

FORMULATING A GRAND STRATEGY

The squash player hoping to improve is constrained by his own level of squash fitness. Squash fitness includes the paramount ingredient of *skill* as well as speed, suppleness, strength, stamina and spirit. Bearing the level of squash fitness in mind, the player should formulate a *grand strategy* which sets realistic yet optimistic goals.

Realistic goals would have to take into account the age of the player and amount of time to be spent on achieving ambitions. The constraints imposed upon an individual by the effects of natural laws also must be incorporated into a detailed plan for success. The structure and function of players' bodies must be taken into consideration. It is thought that Jahangir Khan is the optimum somatotype for squash. He is 5'9" tall, 147 lbs in weight and he has married the racket skills of the Khans with the other vital qualities of flexibility, power and stamina. Conversely, a world-ranked player, such as Gawain Briars who is very tall, would need additional sheer strength to accommodate his longer-than-average levers and would, therefore, probably need to practise lunging movements, really getting down to the ball.

From the grand strategy, macro and micro plans can be extracted to suit the individual needs. Macro plans would usually incorporate the traditional British season, or, if you are an established star, overseas tournaments. The macro plan would include an out-of-season schedule, a pre-season schedule and an in-season programme. Competition events, team events and social events should be taken into account because the player's social well-being is an essential part of preparation. Micro plans would be formulated specifically for a particular championship or using a particular event as match fitness preparation for an important forthcoming event.

SQUASH TECHNIQUE AND TACTICS

A player should be proficient and confident enough in the correct stroke technique to be able to control and direct the ball accurately to any part of the court. The approach to learning correct stroke production and court movement has been described in the first part of the book.

Knowing about basic strategy will help you combine your strokes, minimising weak shots and mistakes and playing attacking shots. For example, you should attack the ball when your opponent is out of position or if he has played a weak or loose shot. This should only be done when you are well-positioned to do so. If you are too close, stretched, rushed, badly-positioned or wrong-footed, attempting to play a winner will be a risk, so a safe shot should be opted for. Having a game plan which will help to minimise errors is another aspect which should be included in an overall approach to successful squash. The tactical aspects of squash are discussed later in this chapter.

How well you play the basic strokes and a basic game determines how well you play and often how successful you are. You must continually make your opponent move around the court attempting to work him out of position or force a weak shot so that a winner can be hit. A good basic game enables you to take control and run your opponent around. This should be a very important part of your overall *strategy*.

The predominant shot in squash, as explained in the text, is the length shot close to the side wall. Here it is being played by Hiddy Jahan against Geoff Hunt. It is in the midst of seemingly uneventful rallies that fitness, concentration and the ability to execute the basic shots perfectly are of paramount importance.

The aim of your strokes should be to move your opponent away from the centre of the court into one of the four corners of the court, whilst you take control of the 'T' position ready to pounce on any weak return. To do this successfully you must eliminate any weak shots or mistakes which you may make so as to deprive your opponent of the chance to play winning shots. This can be done most successfully by keeping the ball tight to the walls and in the back corners. This tactical play becomes more important as you improve from beginner, to club level player, to county level and finally to international level. Have you ever noticed how much better international players execute the basic strokes than club-level players? The strength of Jahangir Khan lies in the fact that he executes the basic strokes, and hence the basic game, so accurately, that he deprives his opponents of any chances, making him invincible.

The combination of good stroke technique, court movement and a sound tactical approach will make you an awesome opponent in any player's eyes.

BACK COURT PLAY

The predominant stroke in the game of squash is the length shot close to the side wall into the back court. Ensure that the ball bounces at least at the back of or behind the service box. If the ball lands any shorter than this, it will not move your opponent sufficiently away from the centre of the court. Moving your opponent into the back corners of the court forces him to try to play an accurate shot in a limited amount of space which will restrict his swing. If his shot is inaccurate or loose, he will be left out of position and you can attack the shot. Your opponent will, therefore, be under pressure in the back corners. Remember to watch the ball and your opponent from the 'T', so you can move quickly into position to play a shot as soon as you know where the ball is going.

The cross-court drive can also be an effective stroke as long as it has enough width to go past your opponent and out of his reach. A stroke with good width is one that is played so that it returns to the back of the court, touches the side wall behind the service box and drops near the back wall. A good opportunity for placing a deep cross-court drive from the back of the court is when your opponent is out of position, poaching in the half of the court from where you are playing your stroke. This usually happens when your opponent is anticipating a straight drive. The opportunity to play a cross-court shot from the front court arises often.

Good length may force a weak boast or short inaccurate shot from your opponent. Good width may also force a weak or loose shot. This is your chance to attack and play a possible winning stroke. Always recover back to the 'T' position after you have played a stroke in anticipation of a return shot. Never stand glued to the floor, gloating over a shot which you think is a winner. You never know, your opponent may surprise you and play a return for which you are not ready.

FRONT COURT PLAY

Another essential ingredient to your basic game is to move your opponent forward in the court as well as deep in the court. The strokes used for this will be the drop shot, the volley drop, the boast, the volley boast, the drive kill and volley kill.

The underlying principle is to move your opponent into the back corners of the court forcing a loose or weak shot, from which you can attack the ball using a boast, drop shot or short kill shot. This will then move your opponent to the front of the court, keeping him under pressure. The ultimate aim is to play a winning shot when he is out of position and which he cannot, therefore, reach. It is important, however, *not* to attempt to play a short shot off an opponent's tight and accurate shot as you will then be at risk of making an error. This is where discipline in your game is such a key factor. You must try to force a loose stroke from your opponent. Never risk finishing a rally early by trying to play a lucky winner off an opponent's accurate shot. If you have to stretch or are not balanced to play a short shot, do not take the risk; the safety of a basic accurate, length shot should be the order of the day. After playing any stroke always recover to the 'T' position.

Susan Devoy against Lisa Opie. This is the final of the British Open in 1984; Opie is left stranded by a delicate forehand drop shot.

If you have taken your opponent forward with a boast or drop shot, attempt to cut his return off by volleying the ball, forcing him back again with an attacking length shot. The more pressure you can put on an opponent by volleying, the better, as this will keep him scurrying around the court, not giving him time to recover his composure or breath. As in all strokes, the placement of the volley is crucial in the winning of a rally. When volleying an opponent's return from the front of the court down the side wall or across the court, always direct the ball to bounce in the service box so that the ball does not rebound off the back wall. This will minimise the time an opponent has to reach the ball from the front of the court. He must play the ball before it reaches the back wall and does not have the cushion of knowing the ball is going to bounce and rebound off the back wall. A cross-court must also have good width.

Always position yourself in a well-balanced stance in the centre of the court so that you can volley a weak return with the minimum of effort. If you have to adopt a stretched and unbalanced position to attempt to play the volley, then do *not* do so. Move into a position in which you can play a deep accurate shot after it bounces. Remember, if there is any risk of playing a weak shot or making an error, *play safe*! This especially applies when playing an attacking shot. If you are not in a good position to do so off a loose shot don't risk it. Discipline yourself and work by playing a basic length game to force an opening from where you will be able to play an attacking short shot safely.

Beware! You cannot build a successful strategy involving front court shots such as boasts and drop shots only. They should be used only as additional shots in your repertoire of deep shots, which are the most important shots. These basic length shots should be the foundations upon which your game is built, introducing short shots as attacking shots to move an opponent around the court. Whenever you are placed under pressure by an opponent, your game loses its rhythm, or you lose concentration, go back to basics and safety. Hit the ball deep and slowly build upon your game once again. *The player with the strongest basic game usually wins.*

'CONDITIONED' GAMES

One of the best ways of improving your basic game strategy is through practice. You need to practise both back court and front court play. One of the most effective practices is for two players to play 'conditioned' games. For example, one player is allowed to play the ball into the back court only, behind the short line. This player can then concentrate on developing good length and width in his strokes, forcing his opponent into the back corners of the court. The other player can play a normal game. Another practice, good for the short game, is where one player is limited to playing shots into the front court, whilst the other player can play a normal game or a deep length game only.

It is, however, essential to concentrate on *one* aspect only at a time.

SERVICE: THE FIRST FORM OF ATTACK

The serve is too often played hurriedly, without thinking, as a means of starting the rally. When serving you have the advantage and should think about playing the stroke accurately, as it is the only stroke where you have as much time as you wish to play it. Your serve should force your opponent to play a difficult and hurried return from the back corner of the court, whilst you move quickly into a balanced position in the centre. An effective serve will force a weak or defensive shot from your opponent giving you an instant opening to play an attacking shot.

Try not to let your opponent volley your service and put you on the defensive straight away. This will almost certainly happen if you serve without taking your time and thinking. One of the most effective services is one which is angled high on to the side wall with little pace, dropping into the back corner. This serve is very difficult to volley accurately. There is, however, a danger of serving the ball out of court or inaccurately so it is advisable in the warm-up period and early stages of the match to obtain the 'feel' of the speed, height and angle at which the stroke should be played, depending upon the court conditions.

If an opponent is playing your high serve successfully by volleying, vary the pace and direction of your serve. Use, for example, a hard flat service either angled into the side wall or straight at the opponent's body.

Do not serve without thinking. Observe your opponent's positioning and ability to deal with your different types of serve. Mix your services, particularly if your favourite serve is proving unsuccessful. If your serve goes out of court, do not let your annoyance or frustration affect your concentration. Concentrate harder and practise your serve outside of matches. Often, if you serve well at the beginning of a match and an opponent has trouble returning the serve (by not being able to volley the ball or by playing a loose return) which you capitalise on, this will psychologically worry or demoralise him. His concentration will be diverted to the worrysome thoughts of his ability to return your serve which will result in a further deterioration in his squash. So the serve can act as a useful psychological weapon as well as giving you a physical advantage.

RETURN OF SERVICE: THE COUNTER-ATTACK

If your first shot off your opponent's service is loose, it gives him the chance of attacking your shot, placing you under pressure immediately. The best and safest return is to play the ball accurately straight down and close to the side wall into the back corner of the court. This will move your opponent into the back court and give you a chance to recover to the 'T' position to begin the building of a winning rally.

The most effective answer to a serve is to take the ball early on the volley. This limits your opponent's recovery time to the 'T' position. Hence you must strike the ball either before it hits the side wall or as it drops off the side wall. In either case you must play the stroke accurately. This can only be achieved using the proper side-on stance, with firmly cocked wrist, balanced body and weight forward on the front foot. Timing is of the essence when playing this stroke and the ball should be hit at a comfortable pace and height. If you cannot play the volley comfortably, do not try and over-extend to play the ball early, sacrificing accuracy and control. Wait for it to bounce! If your opponent moves out of position, poaching on your side of the court, trying to anticipate the straight return of service, play a deep cross-court volley or drive with good width. This will twist your opponent and make him retreat into the opposite back corner.

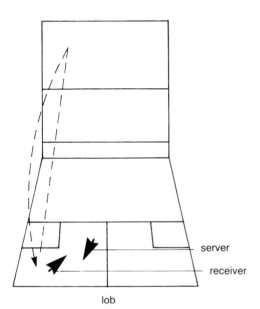

server

receiver

lob

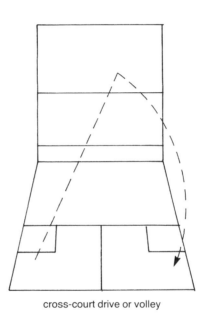

cross-court drive or volley

Return of service: length shots

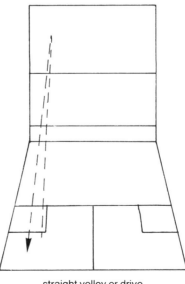

straight volley or drive

If your opponent moves towards the back of the court after serving, as many players tend to do, rather than across to the 'T' position, your return may be a boast or a drop shot in an attempt to catch him flat-footed or pull him forward to the front of the court, as shown in the following diagrams. However, *always* remember to watch the ball after you play your return shot and to move to the centre of the court to take up a balanced position to cover any possible reply.

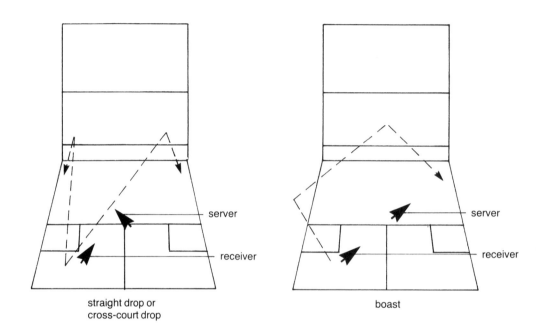

straight drop or
cross-court drop

boast

Return of service: short shots

STROKES TO BE PLAYED FROM THE FRONT OF THE COURT

As a general rule, squash strategy should be based on dominating offensive space. Usually, the closer you are to the front of the court the more advantageous space you possess. Research has indicated that 90% of winning shots are played by the player in front. It should be remembered, however, that some players prefer playing winning shots from other areas of the court, even from traditional defensive space.

1 *Safest shot*: this is the straight drive to the back of the court. Many hours spent practising this stroke will buy you the necessary time to delay the shot and thus deprive your opponent of any advantageous time he may have gained.

2 *Cross-court drive*: if this stroke is played with good width and to a length just behind the service box it will force your opponent to turn and go to the back corners. However a poor cross-court drive can end up in the middle of the court and is then easily punishable.

By playing the straight and cross-court drive you will be keeping your opponent guessing where the ball is going to go.

3 *Lob*: if you are struggling to reach a shot played to the front of the court and have insufficient time to arrange yourself into the classic position, the easiest and safest shot to play is the lob high over your opponent and into the opposite diagonal back corner. The ball should hit the side wall high behind the service box.

The lob can also be a very effective attacking stroke. A high, floated lob is very difficult to volley. It is also a much slower ball than a drive and your opponent has to adjust his timing; this can cause an error. Some of the traditional courts have very high roofs and are extremely cold. This advantageous space should be fully utilised by an efficient lobber.

4 *Drop shot, trickle boast, reverse angle*: if your opponent is loath to return to the 'T' position and stands deep and out of position, a drop shot to the near corner can often terminate the rally. The straight drop is preferable to the cross-court drop because if you miss the cross-court drop the ball returns to the middle of the court, giving your opponent the advantage.

A *reverse angle* is also an effective attacking stroke, but ensure your opponent is hanging back a long way from the 'T', because you are hitting the ball quite near yourself when you play this shot.

A *trickle boast* is yet another scoring threat, once you have added this to your armoury of shots. When you are in the front of the court and, more importantly, in front of your opponent and he is retrieving well, try this stroke as an alternative.

When at the front of the court you must decide whether to play the shot of best effect or whether to introduce deception to test the perceptual motor skills of your opponent. Delaying your stroke by micro-seconds and wrong-footing your opponent gives you more room for error.

Once the game has commenced, the success of the game strategy and tactics will need periodic assessment. In a plan you will have alternatives. Remember, your very carefully laid plans may fail. You may have to modify or revise. This flexibility might even make it necessary to play to somebody's strengths! Quite often the principle of surprise is implemented. It is important never to lose sight of the fact that games are won on unplanned alternatives.

Current training methods result in a feeling of well-being and reduce the need for game strategy. Overload lures the squash player into a false sense of security. The obsession for physical fitness often takes away the importance of a sound game strategy. However, even the best game strategy does not always lead to victory, because in racket sports it is very difficult to jump levels. Matches and their results are the best indicator of squash fitness.

YOUR APPROACH TO SUCCESSFUL SQUASH

Squash is easy from the balcony and advice is easy to give. It is, however, somewhat difficult to translate this advice into playing successful squash. So whilst we all might recognise the problems a player is having during the actual playing of a game or match, many of us are not aware of the 'behind the scene' aspects or approaches which a player should combine to play successful squash.

The physical area

A player's physical condition affects the technical, tactical and mental areas in a game or match. Unforced errors and loose shots due to bad stroke play are accentuated when a player gets tired. His reactions are slower which leads to the mistiming of shots.

Further, a tired body is quickly followed by a tired brain. It is harder to concentrate and keep discipline. A player in this situation often loses his patience whilst waiting for the opening to play an attacking shot, and so makes more mistakes trying to finish the rally too early. Tired players play tired shots, allowing for a greater margin for error. A tired player should rather slow the pace of the game to create time to recover, to regain good concentration and to think. Do not be tempted to finish the rally early by attempting lucky winning shots.

Improving physical condition is described in chapter 4.

The mental area

The first and foremost quality which a player needs if he wants to play winning squash or to be a champion is 'the will to win'. If you have this quality you will be motivated to acquire all the aspects needed for successful squash.

Players often become too nervous and anxious before and during a match and place themselves under additional pressure. This often affects their concentration and discipline whilst playing. The most common fault is that a player has a lapse in concentration and his thoughts begin to wander. His shots will become loose and the mistakes will begin to creep in. The player then often becomes frustrated with his mistakes and his concentration deteriorates further because, instead of concentrating harder on the strokes, he focuses his concentration on his feelings. This leads to the rushing and mistiming of shots.

This nervousness and anxiety can be counteracted with good mental preparation. Good mental preparation will help you concentrate on the important aspects of match play. Further, you will find it easier to discipline yourself and stick to your game plan. A player who loses his discipline in his play will almost certainly lose his patience and concentration. The development of mental attributes is discussed in chapter 5.

4 PHYSICAL TRAINING

Geoff Williams (England) gets in close to Qamar Zaman (Pakistan) to anticipate the famous Zaman drop shot. Zaman, however, seems to be driving the ball close to the side wall to the back of the court.

WHY CURRENT METHODS NEED TO BE REASSESSED

The only way to train for a sport is to play the sport itself. Physical fitness and squash performance are different phenomena. If your goal is excellence at squash, you must spend the bulk of your time playing squash and doing the specific movement patterns on court. By working on technique in carefully-monitored training sessions, the resulting specific conditioning will get you in the best shape for the forthcoming season or event.

The pulse is the most influential monitor available in fitness testing, being the body's most important single indicator of well-being. *If you don't monitor the pulse you can actually become less and less fit even though you are exercising every day.* What happens is that as your technique in squash improves, the skill routines make less demand on your heart resulting in failure to increase your level of fitness. While you are playing squash you are developing motor skills, burning off calories and increasing relevant muscle tone *but*, unless you monitor heart rate (by counting the pulse), you might obey one of the principles of training and graciously decondition in terms of heart and lung fitness. This chart will enable you to work out your training routine. You should aim to work as near as possible to the target heart rate. This is calculated by using the following equation: 220 – age = target heart rate. Work out the heart rate by counting the wrist pulse for 15 seconds and multiplying by four for beats per minute. Remember, working in the training zone is essential, and the no-training zone should only be used for rectifying technique.

The pulse: your fitness guide

WHY YOU SHOULD NEGLECT THE RUNNING SYNDROME

It has become the fashion for squash players to do plenty of running as part of their normal training schedule. Increased mileage rewards them with a rejuventated 'high' and, as a result, too little time is spent on developing racket skills. The increase in cardiovascular recovery rate is easily measurable and the squash player thinks he is improving without even hitting a ball. A vital stage to improving at squash is to realise that there is *negligible* carry over between the sports of running and squash.

With the running boom showing no sign of losing its momentum and traditional keep-fit classes being rechristened 'aerobics', it is important to mention at this stage that squash is aerobic, that is, a highly desirable type of exercise that increases the body's intake of oxygen. The guidelines of the American College of Sports Medicine for the occurrence of effective aerobic conditioning recommend an average heart rate of 70% of maximum or greater for a period of 20 to 30 minutes. Our research indicated an average heart rate of 84% of predicted maximum heart rate was achieved during a squash game. It should be remembered, however, that because of the very nature of the game and its environment your internal body temperature rises from 36°C to 40°C which causes the heart to beat faster anyway. The bending, twisting, lunging movements on a squash court means that breathing activity is poor leading to an oxygen deficiency to the muscles and a resultant elevation in heart rate.

Purposive squash (either doing skill drills under pressure or playing a partner of at least equal ability) will usually ensure effective aerobic conditioning. The sustained work output must be long enough to bring the average heart rate to 70% or more.

When you are running you are continually moving forward, whereas in squash, the movements are sideways, forwards and backwards; jogging overdevelops the hamstring muscles, the calf muscles and the muscles of the lower back. In contrast the muscles on the front of the leg, thigh and stomach become relatively weak. A muscle imbalance is the obvious result.

Whilst running, the trunk muscles are only acting as stabilisers and it has been shown that rotation of the trunk muscles initiates much of the power associated with the squash stroke.

Correct running technique involves standing tall and landing heel first which is contrary to the crouching, bending, reaching movements of the squash player. *Squash players in the perpendicular position never win.* A marathon runner who occasionally dabbles at squash inevitably complains of sore buttocks after his fortnightly game of squash.

Squash is a different sport from running and resulting muscle soreness is indicative of a lack of understanding of specificity in training. Leisure pursuits should not be discouraged but their limitations should be highlighted. Pure endurance training *reduces* both the strength and speed of the muscles.

THE IMPORTANCE OF A TRAINING PLAN

The fundamental aim of a squash training plan is to improve performance since improved performances (actual match results) are the best indicator of squash fitness.

A complete analysis or time-and-motion study of squash must be completed before a training plan can be designed and implemented. Your levels of aspiration must be clearly defined before the regime can be justified. If your goal is the highest level of squash, you will require a more comprehensive programme than the performer who, because of genetic limitations, merely requires noticeable improvement.

The hierarchy of the importance of the individual training factors in squash is not widely known among the squash-loving fraternity. Modern research indicates that the following four components provide a useful hierarchy for training purposes.

SKILL PRACTICES

These should be the predominant feature of any individual training programme. If squash technique is not up to scratch a lot of much-needed energy is wasted. When working on squash technique it would be idealistic to keep the tempo at game speed. This is usually impractical as sometimes isolated *parts* of the stroke action need correcting. Most people find it comparatively easy to develop heart and lung fitness, but retire prematurely from acquiring and developing skills. In the past, improvement in squash can be ascribed to an increased endurance level and an ability to retrieve. We would like to change the trend and greatly improve squash skills.

If you carry out skill practices, a tough match will present no problems, since you will be playing as if it's second nature. Sheer repetition means that you can play a well-grooved stroke almost as if it's a closed skill.

If a skill session is not going according to plan (as is their wont) it is sometimes better to do two shorter periods of practice. The dull colours of a traditional squash court lead to tiredness. It is fundamental to success to concentrate totally during skill practices.

Throughout skill practices, fitness should be monitored and training modified to suit the individual's own requirements.

By simulating match conditions in skill-development sessions, two vitally important aims are achieved:

1 Improving stroking ability under changing conditions.

2 Benefiting physically through increased fitness.

The 'play one more game syndrome' does not work. Don't avoid the problem, tackle it head-on.

STRENGTH AND FLEXIBILITY

Medical research shows that if you train a muscle for strength it
becomes shorter and as a result its range of movement is restricted.
In practice this decreases its ability to utilise its increased force
resources correctly. Therefore, exercises that are designed to train the
strength of a group of muscles should always be followed by
stretching exercises for the same muscle group. It is thus advisable to
group these two components of fitness together.

Strength is important because lack of it affects the power equation:

power = force × speed

However, there is a point beyond which strength does no good.

Squash requires a specific type of strength so the exercises should
be chosen with speed as the main criterion. Maximal strength is not
the order of the day, so 50 – 70% of maximum should be done at a
high speed.

Flexibility in the legs as seen in the wonderfully-agile Chinese
badminton players is much sought after by progressive squash
players. This additional flexibility not only reduces the risk of injury but
gives a greater power range. Analysis of play in championship
matches reveals a colossal amount of forward lunging, bending,
twisting and stretching and fully justifies the importance of flexibility
training.

SPEED

Speed on court is essential because of the stop – start nature of
squash. You need to react quickly to an opponent's shot from a
stationary position, and then move towards the ball with efficiency and
speed. The recovery back to the 'T', must also be done with speed.

Speed on court can be broken into three elements:

Anticipatory speed

This is a prerequisite of success at squash. Prior to making a
movement, hopefully you will be poised on the 'T' with feet at 45° to
the side wall and in a well-balanced position. Your opponent's
philosophy probably revolves around the theme of deception and
disguise. The longer your opponent delays his stroke the more inertia
you have to overcome. It is this stop – start routine which is
particularly tiring. Keeping your eye on the ball is fundamental to
success at racket sports but you may have to glance elsewhere (for
example, at your opponent's body segments) for earlier ideas on
where the ball is going to be hit. Extensive practice of these basic
motor skills gives you spare attention to detect and process other
signals. Apart from vision, we also rely on our hearing for guidance in
performing movements on court. Anyone who has played on a
traditional dungeon court will testify to the relevance of our auditory
receptors as the ball speeds past into the back corner and dies.

There is also a lot of feedback from the proprioceptors in the muscles and joints of our bodies. Thus after initial coaching we *instinctively* know whether our bat, ball and body are in the correct place to play the shot.

Reaction Speed

This can be developed through experience. It is the length of time that it takes to respond to a stimulus and is easily measured in a human performance laboratory. It was previously thought that there was a direct correlation between age and reaction time. The younger you are the quicker your reaction time. However, squash sharpens reflexes. Good anticipatory speed in concert with lightning reflexes will lead to a smooth, balanced and fluid motion which will buy you the necessary time to arrange yourself in the classic position to stroke the ball.

Movement speed

It is not necessary to be able to run like Carl Lewis although it could be useful if your opponent is constantly making you run the diagonal! The aim is to glide around court fluently, ending up in a comfortable well-balanced side-on stance. Ghosting exercises (as described on p. 79) with long rest intervals are a good way of developing movement speed on court. Explosive ghosting exercises from the 'T' position to the four corners with 20 seconds work and 10 seconds rest are a good idea.

ENDURANCE

This is mentioned last because of previous obsession with its importance. Stop-watch analysis of games of squash reveals surprising figures. Matches vary in their intensity from 20 minutes to 2 hours 40 minutes. The time during which the ball is in play until hand-out is called varies from two seconds to five minutes. However, the elapsed time until the combatants are ready to serve (due to collecting up the ball, taking up different positions and appealing to the referee) can vary from three seconds to twenty seconds; this is in a game where play is meant to be continuous. This infers strongly that there is a possibility of oxygen debt being repayed, especially when taking into account the one minute between games and the two minutes between the fourth and fifth games.

A stop-watch analysis indicates that the emphasis placed on endurance is grossly inaccurate. A transfer to increased *flexibility* and *speed training* on court will guarantee improvement.

Lisa Opie playing Martine Le Moignan in the British Ladies Open Final of 1983. Opie is quick off the mark in her attempt to retrieve a drop shot.

ORGANISING A TRAINING PLAN

The preparation of an individual to compete successfully in matches demands the organisation of a year-round training plan. The following programme forms the basis upon which a training plan may be developed by the coach to suit the individual's own needs. Before developing a training plan the following three crucial training principles must be understood.

* *Progressive overload*
  The player must progressively work at a level above which he is accustomed.

* *Specificity*
  Training should be related to specific individual needs.

* *Regularity*
  Gains in skill and fitness are developed over a period of regular practice and training.

DESIGNING THE TRAINING PLAN

Before designing the year-round plan the coach must ask the following questions:

1 What does a match demand of the player?

2 What are the capacities and limitations of the player to meet the demands of matches?

3 What programmes are necessary to:
  – maintain and develop strengths
  – improve upon weaknesses
  – develop new skills and fitness levels

Once the above questions have been answered a training plan may be devised by the coach for the player. The following chart shows a general training plan for the year:

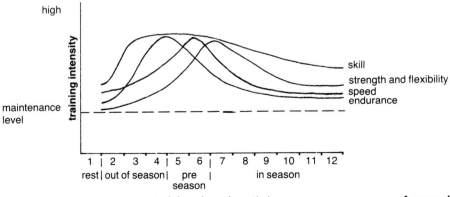

training phase (months)   *A general training plan*

Rest (month 1)

The period immediately following the completion of the competitive season is designated a rest period. A player needs time away from regular practice and training sessions and a psychological break from the continuous demands of training and competition. However, whilst the player should be encouraged by the coach to rest, he should not be completely inactive. The individual may be encouraged to take up another sporting activity or some leisure pursuit. Swimming and cycling are in this instance highly recommended. In these activities your weight is supported by either the water or the bicycle and your overworked joints can get a well-earned rest. Both these sports involve continuous rhythmic movement of large muscle groups and, as a result, in all fitness magazines received a five-star rating for aerobic fitness. But remember, this is the rest month of the calendar so limit your activity to three 20 – 40 minutes sessions per week.

Out-of-season plan (months 2, 3 and 4)

SKILL

An emphasis on the refinement and development of skill is essential in this phase and must not be forgotten as the player involves himself in the fitness training programme.

Strokes need to be practised and developed over a relatively long period. The coach must emphasise correct technique. Gradually, the skill practices need to be executed under simulated match situations. For the development and retention of skill at least three practice sessions per week are necessary.

The coach must never forget the paramount importance of extensive skill practising in the fitness profile.

STRENGTH AND FLEXIBILITY

Strength in weight training is developed with low repetitions using high resistance and muscular endurance is developed with a high number of repetitions using low resistance.

The coach must recognise the importance of training specific muscle groups for a specific purpose as research has shown that there is no transference from general strength to specific strength.

When beginning a programme it is essential that light weights are used to develop the correct technique. Since in the out-of-season phase it is important to develop muscular strength the use of heavy weights with low repetitions can be gradually introduced.

The coach should encourage some strength conditioning for the abdominal muscles (see p. 87) and also some exercises for the back such as lying chest down on the floor and raising the arms and legs off the ground.

Sit-ups should be done in different ways to exercise the four different kinds of abdominal muscle. In the past people have been encouraged by misinformed coaches to do as many as possible of the same type of sit-up. Too many sit-ups one way will weaken the bulk of the stomach muscles and also affects their elasticity or stretch. Further the lower back becomes strained.

The coach must use any back-up service available to him. This is very important in the dynamic area of flexibility training. While he is attempting to get his squash player to incorporate stretching into a life-long routine he must remind him of some of the movements which contort his body into unnatural movements.

SPEED

A programme for speed training should steadily progress in intensity through both the out-of-season and pre-season phase reaching a peak emphasis just prior to the competitive season. Earlier squash coaching manuals recommend repetition 400 metre runs on a circular track. You do not sprint on court. However, to develop speed on court you must still do the specific movement on court ending up in a side-on stance and ghosting the shot. To improve speed you must do this movement pattern more quickly than you would do in a match. A ghosting session lasting 10 to 15 minutes using the four corners would suffice. Because you are developing speed, rest intervals must be substantial.

ENDURANCE

During this phase a strong emphasis should be placed on the *endurance* component of fitness. The type of training should be continuous. The archaic training schedules which are still popular recommend long-distance runs to train the body's basic energy systems. Yes, three months, running will improve cardiovascular respiratory recovery rate, but why not do *sport-specified* endurance training on court? After all, squash takes place on court and does not involve sprinting between two telephone poles or admiring the mountain scenery. To build endurance levels you need to play and train on court for a longer period than the actual tournament match is expected to last. In the early stages you may need breaks every 30 or 40 minutes as the body adapts to the specific training you are giving it. It would be advisable to keep walking quickly during these breaks to keep the heart rate elevated.

It is vitally important during this stage of training to monitor heart rate and work output. The zone for inducing a beneficial cardiovascular training effect in continuous training can be seen on the chart on p. 70

The intensity or length of training sessions may be gradually increased.

Pre-season plan (months 5 and 6)

SKILL

Development still remains the top priority, but practices should now simulate match play. The coach must help the performer to cope with outside influences. Simulated practices present situations where the player will develop skill by being able to make the correct decisions in various differing shot situations. Players respond to feedback, not only concerning their match performances but also with regard to their physical and skill development. Thus, it is advisable to keep a written record on the development of stages of both physical and skill development as well as the results of all matches.

STRENGTH AND FLEXIBILITY

Carry out the same programme as used in the out-of-season months.

SPEED

Here the coach should concentrate on the developing of short, finite, compact movements. A very useful aid for developing this aspect of training is an Automatic Squash Ball Projector. Primarily, it frees the coach from feeding to concentrate on coaching the speed development. The presence of a squash ball is a great motivator and facilitates speed development. Tennis coaches have used this type of aid for years but squash clubs and coaches seem loath to utilise it.

ENDURANCE

As squash consists of stopping and starting movements, interval training seems appropriate at this stage of the year-round plan. Once again, the specific movement patterns on court should be encouraged. Following the continuous exercise programme of the out-of-season phase, an interval training programme of long periods of work for example, 60 seconds with rest periods of 30 – 60 seconds should be developed. Eventually a shorter, faster interval programme should be introduced with the work and rest intervals representing those found in a match such as 20 seconds work and 10 seconds rest.

In-season schedule (months 7 – 12)

During the actual squash season, each of the fitness components should be maintained at a satisfactory level. However, skill development should predominate. Because of the importance of a particular match or tournament certain components of a training programme receive special emphasis. This is commonly known as 'peaking' for performance. Obviously a player who has an intense tournament schedule cannot peak for every tournament. So a player must decide which tournaments are most important to him (or which are the long term objectives) and concentrate on peaking for these tournaments to produce best performances.

In the first two weeks of the build-up to an important tournament there should be an emphasis on practice drills which not only extend the endurance component but concentrate on possible weaker areas of the player's game. This ensures a solid preparation by the player. In weeks 3 and 4, long endurance skill sessions are replaced by practice activities which require players to work at a greater speed level for short periods with longer rest periods. Hence the emphasis is on speed and is commonly known as 'sharpening-up'. During this period the player should also concentrate on the psychological areas of performance. (See also p. 95 – 107.)

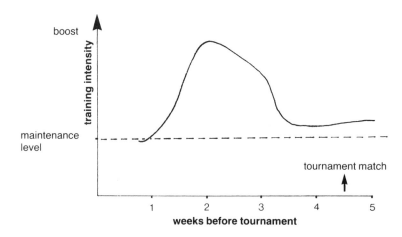

Peaking for a tournament

THE ROLE OF THE COACH IN TRAINING

The concept of all-round fitness has led to coaches clamouring for varied training methods and, as a result, neglecting the concept of specificity. *Variety may be the spice of life but it is not the solution to improvement and winning squash matches.* That is not so say that the coach should not make the training session as interesting as possible. It is just to highlight the fact that, for some reason, coaches engage their players in a flurry of what can only be described as leisure pursuits. This is probably OK as long as the coach realises that there is minimal transfer of training from one sport to another, or uses it in a group coaching session for motivation.

It has always been recognised that a competent coach needs an abundance of technical expertise and that the bulk of his time should be spent diagnosing and remedying faults in technique. Hopefully this will always be the case but what we are suggesting is that these skills need to be augmented by a thorough knowledge of contemporary sports science.

A complete understanding of the body's basic energy systems is a must for any coach attempting to design an extended programme of training. The principles of overload and specificity will remind the coach that squash-specified training is the quickest and safest route to success.

WARMING-UP

Warm-up activities can be employed for two purposes:

1 To reduce the risk of developing injuries to ligaments, skeletal muscles and their tendons.

2 To improve performance.

Warm-up is always one of the areas of least motivation for squash players since they prefer to start playing competitively as soon as the ball is warm.

However, sudden strenuous activity not preceded by a bout of activity of light or moderate intensity may predispose the heart to injury. The cardiovascular system often cannot immediately meet the elevated demands for oxygen at the outset of strenuous exercise. This is because the rate of oxygen delivery from the lungs to the muscles by the cardiovascular system depends upon energy expenditure in the muscle. When there is a sudden increase in energy expenditure in muscles at the outset of strenuous exercise it will take the cardiovascular system a certain amount of time to adjust. Research indicates that warm-up exercises done within the training zone (see p. 70) increase a subject's performance.

The warm-up should be gradual and include the following elements:

1 Stretching

2 Calisthenics

3 Skill warm-up

Stretching

Stretching of the slow tension static type is recommended as opposed to its 'ballistic' counterpart – that is bobbing, jerking or bouncing which can lead to skeletal deterioration. The movement should be gone through slowly and an increased range of movements *coaxed* not forced. Stretching movements should be carried out in two stages:

1 *The easy stretch*
Spend 10 – 20 seconds in an easy stretch at the point where you feel a mild tension. Try to relax the muscle as you hold the stretch. The feeling of tension should subside as you are doing it. If it does not, ease the stretch slightly. The easy stretch loosens tight and stiff muscles.

2 *The developmental stretch*
After the easy stretching of a muscle, stretch a fraction further into what is known as the 'developmental stretch'. Again, hold for 10 – 20 seconds and remember, *no bouncing*. Again, the tension should ease-off slightly. The developmental stretch finely tunes the muscles and increases flexibility.

While stretching, your breathing should be rhythmical and under control. If you are bending forward in a stretch, exhale as you bend forward and then breathe in slowly as you hold the stretch. *Do not* hold your breath while stretching. If a stretch position inhibits your breathing you will not be relaxed. If this happens, ease the stretch slightly so you can breathe naturally.

This part of the warm-up should last only a few minutes and should engage the muscles and joints that are to be used in the subsequent game of squash. The following stretching activities follow the movement patterns of the competitive events as closely as possible. These preliminary exercises increase the range of movement around the joints and should be accompanied by a proportionate increase in strength to further reduce the likelihood of injury. Remember, there is nothing to be gained from increasing the number of repetitions.

Specific stretches

1 A stretch for the lower back, side and top of the hip

a) *Interlace your fingers behind your head and rest your arms on the floor.*

b) *Lift the left leg over the right leg.*

c) *Use the left leg to pull the right leg towards the floor until you feel a good stretch along the side of the hip and in the lower back (see the shaded area). Keep the upper back, back of head, shoulders and elbows flat on the floor. The idea is not to touch the floor with your right knee but to stretch within your limits.*

Repeat the stretch on the other side crossing the right leg over the left leg.

2 Trunk lifts

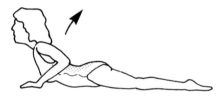

Gently push up with the arms but make sure that the hips do not lift away from the floor.

3 A stretch for the back, shoulder and arms

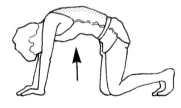 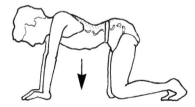

Bend legs under you, reach forward and pull back with straight arms, pressing down slightly with your palms. You should feel the stretch in your shoulders, arms, sides, upper and lower back.

4 A stretch for the tops of the shoulders, triceps and side

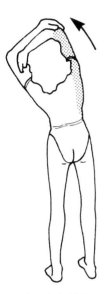

5 A stretch for the muscles along the spine

With arms overhead, hold the elbow of one arm with the hand of the other arm. Gently pull the elbow behind your head as you bend from your hips to the side.

Stand about a foot from a wall with your back towards it. With your feet shoulder-width apart, knees very slightly bent and feet pointed straight ahead, slowly turn your upper body around until you can place your hands on the wall at about shoulder height. Turn in one direction and touch the wall, return to the starting position and then turn in the opposite direction and touch the wall.

6 Stretches for shoulders, arms and wrists

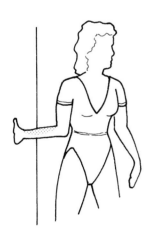

This increases flexibility of the shoulder. Push against the wall and relax. Repeat five times with your playing arm.

This increases flexibility of the shoulder for the backhand stroke. Push against your elbow and relax. Repeat five times with your playing arm.

Dorsiflexion of the wrist. Push against the wall and relax. Repeat five times.

7 Stretches for the hips, legs, feet and ankles

i Ankle stretch

Rotate your ankle clockwise and anti-clockwise through a complete range of motion. Rotary motion of the ankle helps gently to stretch tight ligaments. Repeat 10 – 20 times in each direction.

ii Foot stretch

Use your fingers to pull the toes gently towards you so that the top of the foot and tendons of the toes are stretched. Hold an easy stretch for 10 seconds. Repeat 2 – 3 times.

iii A sitting stretch for the quadriceps

First sit with your right leg bent, with your right heel just to the outside of your right hip. The left leg is bent and the sole of your left foot is next to the inside of your upper right leg. (You could also do this stretch with your left leg straight out in front of you.) Slowly lean straight back until you feel an easy stretch. Use your hands for balance and support (a). Stretch both sides. You can now (after stretching the quadriceps) push your hip over (b). This will stretch the front of your hip and give a good overall stretch to the upper thigh area.

In this stretch position your foot should be extended back with the ankle flexed. Try not to let your foot flare out to the side. By keeping your foot pointed straight back you take the stress off the inside of the knee.

If you experience any problems with this stretch, do not do it. Do exercise 4 instead.

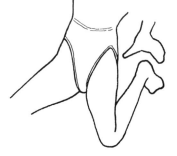 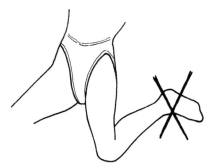

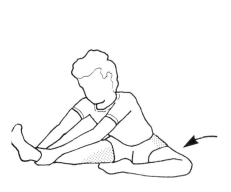

iv A stretch for the hamstrings

Sit with the right leg straight, with the sole of your left foot slightly touching the inside of the right thigh. Slowly bend forward from the hips toward the foot of the straight leg. Hold in the easy stretch position for 10 – 20 seconds. After the easy stretch, hold the developmental stretch. Repeat with the other leg. During this stretch, keep the foot of the straight leg upright with the quadriceps relaxed during the stretch. Slowly bend forward at the waist until an easy relaxed stretch is felt in the back of the leg. Hold for 10 – 30 seconds.

v A stretch for the quadriceps and knee

To stretch the quadriceps and the knee, hold the top of your right foot with your left hand and gently pull your heel toward your buttocks. The knee bends at a natural angle when you hold your foot with the opposite hand. Push your hips forward. Hold for 10 – 30 seconds, then change legs. This is good to use in knee rehabilitation and with problem knees.

8 A stretch for the front of the hips

9 A stretch for the groin area

Move one leg forward until the knee of the forward leg is directly over the ankle. Your other knee should be resting on the floor. Now, without changing the position of the knee on the floor, or the front foot, sink the front of the hips downwards until an easy stretch is felt. This is a good exercise for lower back trouble.

Put the soles of your feet together and hold onto your toes. Gently pull yourself forward, bending from the hips until you feel an easy stretch in the groin. You may also feel a stretch in the lower back.

10 A stretch for the groin and hips

Sit with your feet a comfortable distance apart. Slowly lean forward from your hips keeping your feet upright and your quadriceps relaxed. Do not lean forward with your head and shoulders as this will cause your hips to move backwards placing pressure on your lower back.

11 A stretch for the calf

Stand a small distance from a wall or solid support and lean on it with your forearms, and your head resting on the hands. Bend one leg and place your foot on the ground in front of you keeping the other leg straight. Slowly move your hips forward keeping your back straight. Keep the heel of the straight leg on the ground, with toes pointed straight ahead. Hold an easy stretch.

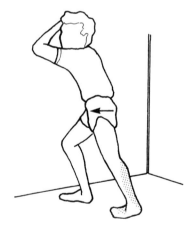

12 A stretch for the neck

Slowly roll your head around in a full clockwise circle, keeping your back straight. Keep your sholders relaxed. Repeat in an anti-clockwise direction. Repeat 10 times in each direction.

Remember, no bouncing whilst carrying out these stretches.

Calisthenics

Calisthenics are active muscular contractions to increase body temperature and are thus an ideal lead into the skill part of the warm-up. Once again, only a few minutes should be spent on these muscular contractions as fatigue shouldn't set in at this stage. When executing a stroke at squash the muscle groups are activated in the following sequence: hips, abdomen, shoulder, upper arm, elbow, lower arm and wrist.

Carry out the exercises in the following order:

1 BENT KNEES SIT-UP FOR ABDOMINAL MUSCLES

Abdominal muscles need exercising at different angles. If you consider your stomach as a hollow cylinder, you will see that doing sit-ups in one direction only will weaken most of the muscles. Do a few sit-ups of the following five types. Six of each should be enough.

It is a good idea to breathe out as you sit up, and breathe in as you come back to the starting position. Do not do these exercises too quickly. Doing them correctly and at a good tempo will improve posture and breathing because the abdominals draw the rib cage and pelvis together. As you are doing these abdominal exercises be aware of using your stomach muscles.

Sit-ups

1 Head touching knees

2 Hands touching knees

3 Diagonal sit-ups. These turn the trunk which is vital for squash

4 Feet elevated

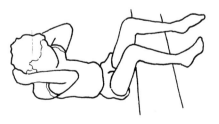

5 Feet and legs elevated. The Americans call this the 'crunch'. By lifting your upper body about 20° – 30°, the abdominals are isolated.

2 PUSH-UPS FOR SHOULDERS, ELBOW AND WRIST

Push ups are an excellent exercise for many parts of the body and are a long-standing method of measuring physical fitness. For squash fitness we advise you do twenty. The exercise should commence with the hands palm down and toes on the floor. The hands should be approximately shoulder width apart and it is important that the back is kept straight. Starting in the up position you should lower yourself until you chin nearly touches the floor and then return to the up position. Breathing out on the resistance part of a push up gives you more oxygen to complete the 20 repetitions.

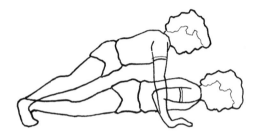

3 SKIPPING FOR LOWER LEG MUSCLES AND WRIST

Although many successful squash players use skipping as an integral part of their training schedules, in this instance we only recommend a couple of minutes of skipping to work the leg and arm muscles prior to the important skill warm up. Rope jumping develops strong calf muscles and increases wrist strength. It is a very useful way of co-ordinating upper and lower body segments. Professional and amateur boxers have trained using a skipping rope for years and squash players have sensed that they need similar movement skills possessed by alert, fit boxers.

   Just a couple of minutes of skipping will improve footwork, balance and explosive leg strength. It sharpens timing, reflexes and can be good fun.

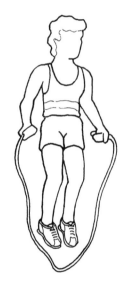

4 HALF-SQUATS FOR THE THIGH MUSCLES

Half squats develop overall leg strength bringing the all important quadriceps into play. Perhaps even more importantly for ambitious squash players, half squats stretch the vital achilles tendon. When doing a half squat you should bend halfway down ensuring your heels are on the floor. Your hips should be fixed and you should be aware of your back alignment.

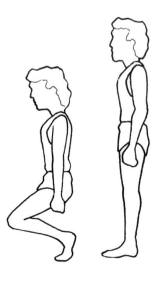

Because two-thirds of the voluntary muscles in the body are in the legs, it is important that the leg muscles conclude the second stage of the warm-up. If you exercise the large muscle groups of the legs, you pump more blood to the heart and force it to push harder to squeeze out the extra load.

Skill warm-up

This is so important because it allows the squash player to develop hand – eye co-ordination in readiness for the match – and particularly for that all-important first game. *How many times have you lost the first game through being a slow starter and only finding your true stroking ability half way through a match?*

Correct warm-up procedure in the above scientifically graduated stages will not only prepare the body for competition but will also warm-up the mind in readiness for match play which is equally important for an optimum performance.

WARMING-DOWN

Despite the benefits to be gained from the correct warm-down procedures very little attention is paid to them by squash players. In fact too many don't even know what they are. Just as you need a warm-up, you need a warm-down. After a match or a pulse-monitored skill session when the heart rate should be hovering around 170 beats per minute for the player in his 20s, it is important to have a gradual phase-out of activity. (For the older player heart rate will not be so high but for any player, hopefully, it will be at least 70% of predicted maximum heart rate.) Some running on the spot or a sequence of stretching exercises will ensure that resting pulse rate is not reached too quickly. Enough blood is needed to flow through the body to make enough oxygen available to clear the lactic acid that prevents the muscles working. Many squash players flop into the sauna after a hard match; this can cause pooling of the blood in the legs and inevitable stiffness and soreness the next day. Further, if you have two tournament matches an hour or so apart, try to keep moving between them.

REST: AN ESSENTIAL PART OF TRAINING

The most difficult job in squash is trying to convince squash nuts that they don't have to train and play all day and every day to improve. Poorly informed coaches sadly lacking sports science backgrounds perpetuate the myth. Playing and training for squash damages the body. You become dehydrated, glycogen levels drop, chemical waste accumulates, muscle fibres become exhausted and, in some instances, damaged and therefore need repairing. This can only be achieved by rest. Heavy on-court training sessions every second day rather than every day would be a good recommended policy. The military notion that you work hard and play hard is out of date.

Overtraining inevitably manifests itself in loss of form as the player attempts to play more and hit his way out of it. This leads to further problems such as sleeplessness and stiffness.

Remember, squash demands a specific type of fitness, which should be monitored. Rest is a component of fitness which allows regeneration to take place, whilst overtraining is a stress state.

SQUASH PERFORMANCE AND NUTRITION

The halcyon days of 'Alf Tupper, The Tough of The Track' are over. Eating fish and chips five minutes before a race and then doing a four minute mile was never really on.

Squash players need to pay more attention to nutrition education for two reasons:

1 Promotion of good health

2 Improving sporting performance

Scepticism abounds when nutritionists and dieticians are mentioned. They work in a dynamic field where what constitutes 'Healthy Eating' changes regularly. However they would be the first to acknowledge that what is known about an individual's food requirements is limited. Despite the proliferation of conflicting information there is still an urgent need for a presentation of simple and accurate information on nutritional guidelines.

The modern squash player's diet needs to take into account the vast increase in nutrient requirements of total calories brought about by practising on court. The body must have enough of all the nutrients which are present in food. So proportionate increases in carbohydrates, proteins, fats, vitamins and minerals will ensure the body's homeostatic mechanisms select the nutrients required. Remember, 'energy intake from food must balance energy expenditure by the body'. An imbalance in this energy balance inevitably leads to obesity and many ensuing problems, including poor performance.

THE IMPORTANCE OF A BALANCED DIET

In the Eastern Bloc countries where sports science has become a way of life, they are quietly adamant that additional vitamin B and vitamin C improves training effectiveness. This is achieved by increasing the body's capacity for work and quickening the recovery process. However, the sports medicine fraternity in this country point out that there is no conclusive evidence backing the call for vitamin therapy, and that the Western diet (if taken from the food groups below) provides a very simple solution to nutritional needs of sports people. If the sports person eats well from the four basic groupings, the nutritional requirements of an active body will be satisfied:

Group 1
cooked cereals
brown rice
wholemeal bread
pasta
popcorn

Group 3
cheese
yoghurt
low fat milk

Group2
fruit & vegetables
salad vegetables
pulses (peas, lentils, beans)

Group 4
lean meats
poultry
fish
eggs
peanut butter

(adapted from the Look After Yourself programme designed by the Health Education Council)

Basically, a balanced diet would comprise the following elements:

1 *Carbohydrates*
These are a highly desirable source of energy for squash players. We now have to deal with counter-acting the results of decades of teaching aimed at reducing carbohydrate intake. Vegetables and whole grain bread sometimes known as complex carbohydrates are good suppliers of vitamins, minerals and fibre. Fresh fruit is an example of a simple carbohydrate. Anything from 50 to 60% of your daily intake should consist of carbohydrates.

2 *Fats*
These are highly concentrated foods rich in vitamins A and D, but also rich in calories. The aerobic squash player will burn fat for energy but the casual, technique-orientated squash player will need less. 15 to 25% would seem prudent.

3 *Proteins*
Your carbohydrates and fats supply energy, releasing protein for tissue repair and growth. 15 to 25% appears to give the right blend to the diet.

A healthy, varied diet includes the need for variety as well as the idea of a higher proportion of healthy foods. There is no one ideal diet for everybody and we should not 'prescribe' what people eat. But we should 'encourage' people to adopt a diet based on national nutrition research. The latest research recommends the following:

* Reduce intake of fats

* Reduce intake of sugar

* Reduce intake of salt

* Increase intake of fibre

Dietary fibre is not digested but has a great affinity for water and as a result makes food residues easier to pass. It seems that lack of it causes many diseases, and therefore it is highly recommended.

WHAT TO EAT AND WHEN TO EAT IT ON THE BIG DAY

Certain foods should be avoided on the day of the tournament. High-fibre or high-fat meals delay gastric emptying. Carbohydrates are highly recommended because they are easily digested and keep the blood sugar levels up.

The timing of the meal is important for two reasons. Firstly, the carbohydrate predominant meal should make sure that the stomach and bowels are empty at the time of the competition. Secondly, enough calories should have been ingested to ensure there are no hunger pangs during the tournament. Many hours of research have gone into this problem; eating the meal 2½ – 3½ hours before the match is recommended. During tight tournament-scheduling squash players should replenish proteins, carbohydrates, fats, minerals, vitamins and water. Once again this is not always simple, so an easily digestable carbohydrate meal is recommended as soon as possible after a match because recent evidence suggests that 'muscle restores its glycogen depots more readily within an hour of depletion'.

There is a great deal of emphasis placed on skilfully arranging the diet to intensify muscle glycogen stores, but this type of diet is most suitable for one-off events such as the marathon. In the week prior to a race the athlete has three days on a normal mixed diet followed by three days on a carbohydrate-rich diet to increase glycogen stores and thus give an optimum performance. This method is fine for one-off races, but a squash player has weekly tournaments and team matches to play; changing the diet *can* cause feelings of fatigue which may hinder maximum aerobic uptake in the long term. It is better to stick to the normal diet.

Fluid intake *during* the matches is much more important. Squash players don't drink enough water between games, unlike their tennis counterparts who, as a result, never suffer dehydration which adversely affects the heart rate and internal core temperature. Since dehydration results in decreased performance the player should take in fluid between games. Plain water is readily absorbed by the stomach, while solutions with a high concentration of sugar and salts are not.

It is also beneficial to take in fluid *prior* to a match. As has been suggested, high carbohydrate meals should be eaten before an important match. During a tournament some 'topping up' can be sought. This can be achieved most readily by drinking a solution containing sugar. The solution however should contain no more than 5% sugar since high sugar levels can delay gastric emptying and prevent the absorption of fluid. 2% sugar solution is recommended, that is 2 grams of sugar to 100 millilitres of water. Soft drinks and fruit juices contain at least 10% sugar.

ELECTROLYTE BALANCE

Many people still believe the myth that salt losses need replacing during matches and tournaments. Research has shown this not to be true. In fit individuals, salt can be lost at the rate of up to 1 gram for every 1 litre of sweat produced. The body requires less than 5 grams for normal functioning. There is ample salt in food for replacement without supplementing your diet with salt. The average daily intake of salt in Western diets is 10 – 15 grams per day. So *reduce* the salt intake, don't increase it.

5 MENTAL TRAINING

HOW TO PREPARE YOUR MIND FOR THAT VITAL MATCH

This section is designed to help the coach better understand the psychological factors affecting the player and to assist the serious player, whether he is a club level player or a top competitive player, raise his performance by adopting a positive and confident frame of mind to compete.

GETTING WHAT YOU WANT FROM YOUR GAME

The most important point of playing squash is to get what *you* as an individual want from the game. If this is beating your clubmates, winning the club championships or winning tournaments, then both the mind and the body need to be tuned towards the task of executing accurate shots and winning points, sometimes over an extended period of time. If your aim is fun and enjoyment, this may be achieved irrespective of competitive success and hence mental fitness will not be such an important factor. Most players, however, gain more enjoyment from their game if they feel that their play is improving. This usually means such players will want to feel confident not only in their skill and physical ability, but also in their mental attitude towards their game. How many times after a game of squash have you heard your fellow clubmates on a winning streak talk in the club bar about how good they are feeling about their game at that moment, or boasting about various shots? Such players mentally feel good, confident and relaxed about their game and hence are getting great enjoyment. It is also noticeable how quiet the losers are, or how many excuses they have for their current losing streak. This leads to their negative mental attitude which will contribute to further losses, more excuses and less enjoyment!

THE MISSING DIMENSION TO YOUR GAME

When Jahangir Khan plays a powerful winning forehand drive, many of us gaze in awe at the manner in which the shot is played. It is executed with seemingly effortless smoothness, speed and coolness

The left-handed Jonah Barrington prepares to serve. Jonah knows about motivation and preparation through his life-long involvement at all levels of the game.

that makes it look easy. When watching Khan and other top players in action, people talk about the player's talent, referring to their skill, physical fitness and agility. What many don't appreciate is, what is occurring in the *mind* contributes a great deal to playing well and making the winning of a match look easy.

Total preparation for competition should include the following four areas:

Technical

Tactical

Physiological

Psychological

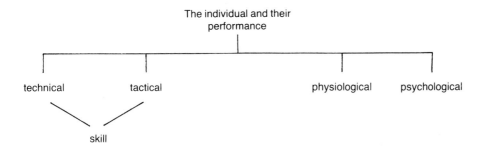

The individual and their performance

technical   tactical   physiological   psychological

skill

Factors affecting a player's performance

There are many instances of players whose performances in match play continually fail to do justice to their skill and physical ability. Many players report that they can perform all the basic squash skills accurately and successfully but not when necessary; namely, when playing a match and needing those crucial points. Afterwards they are left with a feeling of frustration because of the knowledge that the shots in practice can be executed successfully. Many players' performances in match situations are inhibited by extreme muscle tension, the inability to move sharply and quickly, shortness of breath in rallies and nausea. This to many players is commonly known as 'choking' or 'freezing'. When this occurs it is extremely difficult to concentrate on the task of playing squash. You don't have to be a top professional player for this to happen. It can happen to club players in club league matches or even in those fiercely-contested friendly matches poised at a crucial stage.

Sports psychology can contribute in various ways to the above problems and can help in skill practice, training and in the preparation for matches. It can lead to an understanding of specific problems which players may have.

HOW TO COPE WITH NERVES

Many squash players will include some form of fitness training as part of their match preparation. What most players do not include in their training schedules is some form of mental preparation.

The mental attitude that a player brings to the game will affect his performance. Factors such as stress, anxiety, arousal, and tension can have both a positive or a negative effect on performance. Many players get excessively anxious about matches and this can manifest itself in the form of a physical reaction such as: butterflies in the stomach; a parched mouth; and, in some instances, being physically sick. This often happens before that 'big' match, whether it be a league match or a grand final. Another way in which 'nerves' show themselves is the presence of worrysome thoughts. You may be pondering on: reports of how well your opponent is playing; problems with your own game; who will be watching; or how your team place may be affected if you lose. The problem with players experiencing these 'nerves' is that they do not know how to control their anxiety. Important contributory factors to this nervous syndrome and the controlling or remedying of it can best be explained with reference to psychological theory.

Sports psychologists have identified two basic kinds of anxiety. Firstly there is 'trait' anxiety which is a stable personality characteristic which alters little over a period of time. For example, you probably have friends whom you would describe as being generally relaxed and carefree. Secondly, and most importantly to the squash player, there is what is called 'state' anxiety. State anxiety is how you as an individual feel about a particular event. It is a physiological response (for example, those butterflies in the stomach) to what you regard as a stressful event. A particular event may be stressful to you as an individual because of past experiences or your doubtful skill abilities. For example, that vital match in the club championships against player 'A' may be perceived as stressful by you because of unsuccessful experiences against him in the past, or because of a lack of confidence in your skill ability. In such a situation, or where you as a player are expected to beat player 'B', but about whom you are personally unsure, performance is hampered psychologically by excessive 'state' anxiety. This can adversely affect your self-esteem and confidence, for example, you might think 'I am so nervous I will never be able to play my accurate drop shots.' When this happens your concentration is destroyed and your attention becomes focused on your anxiety instead of the task of playing your shots.

At this stage it is essential to point out that anxiety does not always inhibit a player's performance in a match. The secret is being able to arouse your anxiety level to a certain point which is going to aid your performance. Sometimes a player who has a lack of any feelings of tension arousal before a match may not perform well because he is underaroused or 'too relaxed'. On the other hand, a player's performance may be poor if he is too anxious and tense, with the inability to concentrate because of the excessive 'nerves'. The common term for such an occurrence is 'choking'.

Every individual is different in their personality make-up, so just as each player requires an individual training schedule, so too will each player differ in the type of mental preparation and training best suited to his personality make-up. But he can improve his competitive experiences which can be invaluable in overcoming the problems of anxiety and tension. The way in which practice and competitive experience can help the individual to control their anxiety to improve performance shall now be discussed.

PRACTICE AND SKILL REFINEMENT

It is generally considered that individuals perform best under intermediate conditions of stress and least well under high and low levels of stress. Individuals who are generally regarded as having a tense, nervous day-to-day make-up have a low tolerance of competitive stress whilst calm and temperamentally robust individuals can withstand greater degrees of competitive stress. The game of the highly-anxious player tends to be inflexible and easily predictable. He is slow to react in a stressful competitive situation and in tense crucial moments during a game is indecisive and likely to make 'unforced' errors, for example, hitting what should be a winning forehand volley into the tin. For the over-anxious player, the adverse effects of stress upon performance can be minimised if court strategies are over-learned to the extent that they become automatic.

This is also true with respect to the player's stroke repertoire. The strokes which will be vulnerable under the stress of a match are those which have been learnt recently and which have been insufficiently practised. A good example of this is playing a forehand drive off the 'back' or incorrect leading foot when in a match situation. This results in a loose shot or even worse, the player hitting the ball straight back to himself and in so doing giving the stroke and point away. In such a 'pressure' situation, playing the forehand drive off the back foot is the incorrect *dominant response*, which often leads to a deterioration in performance. This occurs mainly because of the lack of confidence in skill ability. It is through practice that correct techniques are rehearsed, reinforced and learned. The mastery of skills can help the player overcome excessive anxiety and have a positive effect on self-esteem and confidence, making the individual more willing to accept competition and matches which are perceived to be challenging.

THE COACH'S ROLE IN PRACTICE AND SKILL REFINEMENT

The gains to be had from the practice of appropriate skills cannot be emphasised enough, especially in the training of all young players. This is where the coach has an important role to play. The coach can direct the player's attention to the important aspects of strategy and play during training sessions. The coach should aim to make many practices as near to the game situation as possible. A vital part of being a good squash player, whether it be at club level or top competitive level, is the ability to decide which shot to play in a particular situation. Unless a player has practice during training sessions in decision-making in game-like situations, he cannot be expected to make the correct decisions in a real game. Further, it is through such practice or training sessions that the player can learn to narrow his attention to concentrating on the task at hand, for example, playing an accurate drop shot.

The coach should bring variety into training sessions by introducing different practices, not relying on a small number of multi-purpose practices. Even if you do not have a coach, you can devise your own variety of practices. If the same practices are used in each training session or if the practice is used for too long at a time, players will get bored and the level of performance will deteriorate. Research has indicated that short practice periods with short rest periods in between, are better than long continuous practices.

If you have a coach, he should have a keen eye on your performance to see that the practice is done correctly with sound technique. Sloppily-performed practices are of no benefit to the player. The coach should also tell the player how well he is performing. When learning a new technique or trying to remedy a fault in technique, the coach should tell the player how their attempted performance measures up to the required standard after each attempt. Feedback is an important factor which contributes to the successful learning of squash.

COMPETITION

For the coach it is important to be aware of the effects of competition on squash performance. The coach must be able to direct the player's attention to the correct and important aspects of play and strategy to be concentrated on, both for matches in progress or for future matches. Hence, a player must have what in psychological terms is known as 'broad' attention, whereby he has the ability to analyse an opponent's performance and type of play, so as to be able to plan a game strategy to counter-act strengths. A player must also have 'narrow' attention during a game whereby he can concentrate on playing an actual shot. Concentration and attention in squash must be able to act like a zoom lens on a camera, capable of wide or narrow focus.

If you make an error, you must be careful that your attention does not become focused on that error, so disrupting concentration. Often, in this situation, your attention narrows but focuses on your *feelings* instead of concentrating on the next shot or rally. Be honest, how many times has this happened to you in a tight match?

Experience of playing matches is very important. Over a number of matches a player gradually builds an extensive repertoire of skills and shots that can automatically be played when the situation demands it. The player also learns to control his anxiety during matches and direct his attention and concentration correctly when playing any shot. Psychological theory suggests that players must be introduced to gradually increasing degrees of stress which they can accommodate in their emotional capacities. Thus, it is important that tournament participation must be appropriate to a player's ability and

Geoff Hunt showing total concentration as he moves to play a backhand volley.

temperament. This is especially important where junior or club players who have just entered the competitive circle are concerned, so as not to destroy their motivation and confidence.

Remember, nerves are a squash player's worst enemy in matches. Practice of skills and the experience of competition can help overcome those 'nerves', and is the key to all success. Keep your concentration on the shots you are playing. Do not give in to the 'enemy' – your feelings and nerves.

PRE-MATCH MENTAL PREPARATION

Pre-match nerves affect most of us before a crucial match. Have you ever experienced any of the following stresses:

– difficulty in controlling pre-match anxiety, for example, problems in falling asleep the night before an important match;

– negative self statements which introduce self-doubt and possible loss in confidence;

– poor concentration and loss of attention in a match resulting in many unforced errors and mistakes?

The following techniques will aid the player in overcoming such difficulties.

WINNING CAN BE ALL IN THE MIND

Mental rehearsal

This is mental simulation of a physical skill. People use mental rehearsal in many situations. For example, have you ever mentally-rehearsed an interview for a job?

Similarly, mental rehearsal can be a useful aid in squash. It is a technique where the player forms a mental image of himself successfully completing the correct performance of the desired task. Mental rehearsal involves the constructive use of the player's imagination to assist in concentration, attention to specific aspects of performance and in building confidence. For example, a player may imagine the preparation, the swing and the striking of the ball and the completion of an accurate forehand drive straight down the wall.

There are some limitations to the use of mental rehearsal. No amount of mental rehearsal will make a player successful if he is not physically prepared for a good performance. Mental rehearsal is not a substitute for physical and technical practice. It should be used in conjunction with physical training and skill practice. This method may not be suitable for very young players who do not have the cognitive ability to utilise correctly the formation of mental images.

HOW TO USE AND PRACTISE MENTAL REHEARSAL

There are two types of mental imagery that can be used in mental rehearsal:

1 The player may form a picture image, as if watching himself on television. This method is useful when using mental rehearsal for the first time.

2 A player visualises himself through his own eyes, successfully performing a shot. He imagines the physical sensations he would feel and the visual display that he would see during the match. For example, try to visualise a situation in a game. Firstly visualise the court and you, the player, in it. Imagine what it feels like holding your racket. Then try to visualise the performance of one shot, for example, a back hand drive. This should involve thinking of the total technique: the grip on the racket; the movement of the feet; the backswing; the point of impact with the ball and the follow-through. Try to feel the muscular tension of your arms and legs during the various phases and also the time taken to complete the stroke. Lastly, imagine the sight of the ball travelling tight against the wall into the back corner of the court. As you become more experienced in the technique of mental rehearsal, you can then add to the situation you are imagining, by visualising an opponent or the pressure under which the shot is to be played in a tense situation. By mentally-practising the execution of successful shots you can build up your confidence. It creates the feeling that you can play accurate and winning shots in any situation.

These two techniques can be used immediately prior to a match as reinforcement and mental practice for the player. It can also be used as a form of mental practice, at training, after a successful match or at any time during the day. Some players like to rehearse in a quiet place with their eyes closed. Others prefer to rehearse in the actual situation in which they are going to participate, for example, on court whilst practising on their own.

Talking and thinking your way to success

Some players talk themselves out of doing well before the match, introducing self-doubt and making excuses afterwards to justify their poor performance. Have you had any of the following thoughts?

'I am not playing well enough at the moment.'

'My shots are not consistent enough.'

'I do not know whether I have completely recovered from injury.'

Appropriate positive thoughts and self-statements must substitute negative thoughts to aid improved and successful performances. For example:

'If I play a basic game, I know I can play well.'

'One mistake does not mean I have lost the game.'

'I have warmed-up properly and have felt no trace of the old injury.'

Another method of avoiding anxiety and negative thoughts and feelings during competition is the use of what is known as 'coping imagery'. This simply means recalling a thought or a memory, of playing brilliantly in a previous match. This can be used to stop thinking about negative feelings.

Progressive muscular relaxation exercises

Regular relaxation counteracts many of the effects of stress and tension. Progressive muscular relaxation exercises involve firstly relaxing the body from head to toe and breathing deeply. Then the player must systematically tense and relax specific muscle groups, for example, neck, stomach and quadriceps. The tension in the muscles should be held for a few seconds and then allowed to drain away by releasing the pressure. This enables the player actually to feel what it is like to have a relaxed muscle or muscles. Many players will find it useful to concentrate on certain muscles which tend to tense up before a match, often the stomach, leg and neck muscles, in order to reduce the discomfort.

The player must ensure when using this relaxation technique that he is not disturbed for 15 – 20 minutes. It is also advisable to find a quiet spot where he can sit comfortably. Once the procedure has been practised, the player can incorporate controlled breathing to the exercise.

MEMORY SERVICE

Thus, mental preparation or mental practice should include:

1 Mental imagery or visualisation and practice of skills and game situations;

2 Imagining playing successful shots in stressful or tense situations which occur during a match;

3 Replacing negative self-statements with positive ones;

4 Using coping images.

5 Muscular relaxation exercises.

Used in conjunction with traditional methods of preparation, these exercises should allow the competitor to achieve the performance of which they are physically capable!

CONFIDENCE-BUILDING – SETTING WINNING GOALS

Continued failure in tournaments not only leads to increased anxiety but also to a loss of confidence. Failure to most of us is depressing and often leads to players forming negative concepts about themselves. Failure can also make a player apprehensive and uncertain about their ability. In this situation, adverse criticism from others is likely to further discourage a player who is playing badly. The regard players have of themselves is not only influenced by their performance in matches and tournaments, but also by the

At the time of writing one man, Jahangir Khan, dominates world squash. Some of the top players have admitted, in private, that they do not think they can beat him. Perhaps Khan's domination can be halted by this man, Chris Dittmar of Australia, simply because he believes he can beat the champion.

expectations of coaches, parents and friends. Everyone involved with a particular player must avoid having pessimistic attitudes for the sake of the player's self-concept and confidence.

The establishment of goals, both short- and long-term provides the player with a supportive structure which builds confidence. The achievement of set goals not only is very satisfying leading to greater enjoyment and self-enhancement for the individual concerned, but also spurs the player on to a new challenge – a higher goal.

Lucy Soutter (setting winning goals?) is seen here playing a forehand drive on her way to winning the Women's World Masters, 1984.

Setting realistic goals

The goals players set for themselves must be realistic. Aiming too high will result in continuous failure and lead to depression and demotivation. This is not to say that goals should be too easy, as achievement then will be relatively meaningless. Goals which a player sets should be challenging. The player must expect some losses on the way to achieving goals, but should not get disheartened by this. Instead he should try and adopt a positive attitude to his own game, learning from his losses.

Goals may be short- or long-term. An example of a long-term goal might be winning the club championships. Part of the means of achieving this should be the selecting of short-term goals. These short-term goals can then be achieved step-by-step in the build-up towards the long-term goal. Examples of a short-term goal might be the achievement of a measurable improvement in cardiovascular fitness or developing greater control in skill. The achievement of such short-term goals can have the effect of building confidence and motivation so that the player will feel that he is now fit enough to sustain a long match or now has better racket control to prevent the opponent from playing attacking shots. Once the initial short-term goal has been achieved, the next progressive short-term goal in the chain to achieving the ultimate long-term goal can be aimed at. These might be winning league matches or ladder challenges.

If a short-term goal is continuously not attained, the cause of failure should be evaluated. Goals can be modified or reassessed if necessary to maintain motivation. Short-term goals can be used by coaches and players to review progress periodically or to measure improvement and progress and plan possible future goals.

Whatever are selected as short-term goals, they should be recorded in a training diary of some sort. Progress towards their achievement can then be monitored in conjunction with physical and skill development as well as results. Failures of goals and match losses should also be recorded to help the player to assess progress completely.

One vitally important aspect of goal-setting is that the player himself must establish his goals. The setting of goals by another person, (for example, a coach) is not advisable since self-selected goals appear to have more meaning for the player concerned. Shared goal-setting is acceptable only if the player has the ultimate choice of goals.

The coach's role

The coach can aid the player in the setting of long- and short-term goals. When dealing with young players or novice competitive players with little experience in goal-setting, it may be necessary for the coach to provide examples of possible goals and to suggest areas of concern which may be apparent, such as in skill development. The coach must also guide the player in setting realistic goals, whilst at the same time letting the player concerned feel that he is contributing to the goals that are set. Positive comments from the coach regarding the setting of goals or the achievement of such builds commitment, motivation and confidence in the player. This can only lead to improved performances!

6 FITNESS AND INJURIES

Squash is a potent explosive sport utilising all the major muscle groups of the body. The vigorous nature of the game means an adequate level of fitness is needed before commencement. Its very dynamism gives it vast scope for injury occurrence and its demand for sudden bursts of increased cardiac output could lead to the ultimate conclusion, if precautions are not heeded. The authors strongly support the philosophy of prevention. Many injuries are *avoidable*. Much discomfort can be prevented by individual action. It is a major duty of all squash advisors to provide the maximum amount of information about injury prevention.

The primary preventive measure to be taken when designing fitness and training schedules is correct *warm-up* technique. Intensive exercise warrants time being spent correctly warming-up the shoulders, neck, back and legs. Warm-up should become a life-long practice and the routines can become graceful as well as functional. (See pp. 80 – 81.)

STRENGTH TRAINING

This is vital for injury prevention. The type of strength important to squash is explosive strength. However, strength for injury prevention is needed to ensure continuity of training. The joints of the body are only as strong as their supporting musculature. Thigh-muscle strengthening is an excellent protective exercise for the knees. The stabilising muscle for the knee is the *vastus medialis*. This is the large muscle on the inner side of the thigh which is most noticeable in soccer players. Any squash player developing knee trouble would be well advised to concentrate on the following strengthening exercises for the inner range.

Roll a towel under your knee and put a weight or sand bag over your ankle. Straighten your knee very hard. Pull your toes towards you. The stabilising muscle for the knee is built up using the final 30° of leg extension.

Wrist strength can add to the total summation of force associated with the squash stroke. Walking around with a squash ball in your pocket and squeezing it at every opportune moment will develop wrist strength. Shoulder strength can be improved by doing the specific exercises outlined in the chapter on training, pp. 69 – 93.

ENDURANCE TRAINING

This is equally as important as strength training. Sports scientists' time-and-motion studies reveal that there are more injuries associated with the last stages of any contest. The prime reason for this is that fatigued muscles can't relax; they tend to remain stiff and are susceptible to tear. This is where specific endurance training comes into its own. The squash body adapts to the stress imposed upon it by the previously outlined training regimes. Squash tends not to ignore any muscles and as a result the blood is shunted to all the millions of tributaries easing the strain on the main cardiac muscle. Squash players need rest or they become overtrained. Sufficient time must be allowed for the body to regenerate or further injury may ensue.

THE IMPORTANCE OF GOOD TECHNIQUE

Promotion of good technique through supervised practice will radically lessen the chances of injury. Modifying poor technique by showing the importance of using the large muscle groups of the shoulder and trunk and mentioning the significance of weight transference will lessen the risk of getting tennis elbow. Hitting the centre of percussion or sweet spot will lessen the amount of tension on impact. Playing with a cocked wrist throughout the whole of the stroke will also help matters. It is vitally important to play the strokes using the correct footwork. If you repeatedly play the forehand drive off the technically correct foot and the backhand drive off the incorrect foot, one of your legs becomes virtually a non-playing limb. Thus, the non-dominant leg is likely to be injured. Muscle imbalance equals injury. Squash, if played correctly in the manner suggested in the technique chapter, does not converge on isolated body parts. If you do the recommended flexibility and strength exercises it can be a complete fitness programme. Reading squash books might be time-consuming but it will show you a *New Approach* which will save wear and tear on the body. A few hours, reading can prove to be a lifetime investment. There could be a huge reduction in the incidence of injuries if suitable equipment were used. Neglect fashion. Proper-fitting, functional shoes are the order of the day. Much time should be spent on selecting an optimum racket weight and choosing a favourable grip size.

Despite however, meticulous preparation and increased knowledge, injuries do occur. The musculoskeletal system does adapt to the stress imposed upon it by our graduated skill and practice sessions. But the *best* way is not the *same* for everybody. Squash players, bodies have different defences when breakdown occurs. You, the individual, need to pace yourself. Find the optimal load of physical and technical training for you.

TREATMENT OF INJURIES

Soft tissue injuries can enjoy a speedy recovery if the ICE method is used:

Ice

Compression

Elevation

At the acute stage, the first-aid treatment should be ice; sports medicine experts insist that the measures taken in the first 20 minutes after injury can make all the difference between success and failure. Ice, either in a commercially available sports-injury pack or wrapped in a wet towel, should be applied directly to the skin for 30 minutes. Forget about ice burns and frost bite. Apply at regular intervals but not continuously. Despite the abundance of information available people still use heat lamps at this stage. This has the opposite effect and actually increases the swelling. You are trying to gain even *compression* on the injury so wrap the ice bag in an elastic material. The injured part should, if possible, be *elevated* above the level of your heart.

Anti-inflammatory drugs can be a great help in getting over a period of pain. Aspirin and its many friends decrease inflammation. Manufacturers recommend taking them at meal times and before going to bed to numb the pain. This is a dangerous practice. Pain is a warning and you should answer your body. It is better to know what damage is being done. A motto to remember: drugs today, gone tomorrow.

Rehabilitation exercises after injury should begin when ICE treatment is terminated. You must progress through the rehabilitation process *gradually* until full movement is restored. If possible, even after application of ice, you should *attempt* to keep full range of motion.

You are ready to play squash only when full flexibility and muscle balance returns. Remember, there are no short cuts – it is better to be safe than sorry.

HEAD-TO-TOE GUIDE TO INJURIES

Eye injuries

Direct trauma injuries to the eyes are not unusual at squash. However, unlike cricket, the wearing of headguards or eye protectors has not caught on. This is rather surprising as the statistics or 'number crunching' of squash show that the bats and balls travel at approximately 100 miles per hour and the squash ball fits perfectly into the orbit of the eye. Perhaps we can learn from our commonwealth colleagues in Canada who offer three types of eye protectors to the squash-loving public.

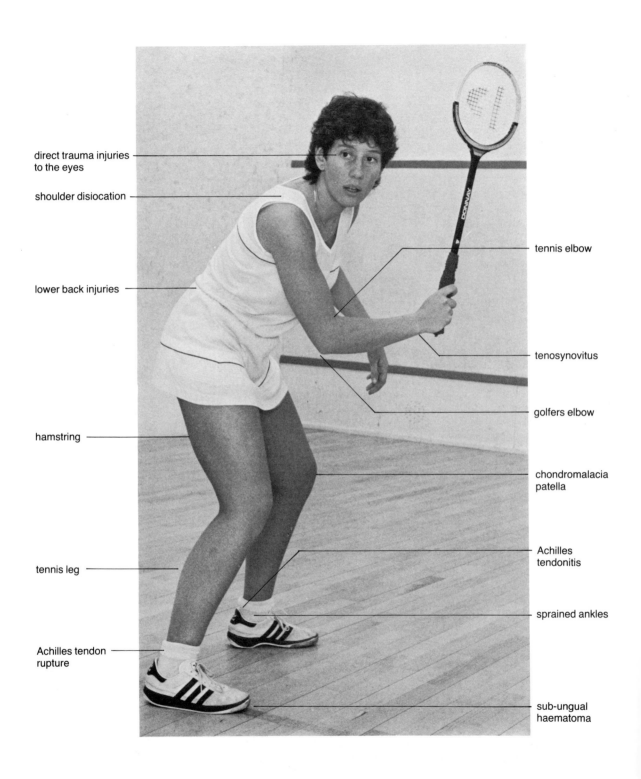

direct trauma injuries
to the eyes

shoulder disiocation

lower back injuries

hamstring

tennis leg

Achilles tendon
rupture

tennis elbow

tenosynovitus

golfers elbow

chondromalacia
patella

Achilles
tendonitis

sprained ankles

sub-ungual
haematoma

The squash player: areas
susceptible to injury

Shoulder injuries

Once these are established they are very difficult to get rid of. It is possible to dislocate a shoulder with a fresh-air shot, particularly if there has been a tendency to dislocate before with ligaments prone to strain anyway. The tendons in the shoulder can become inflamed through over-use or by going straight into a game without warming-up and suddenly flaying the racket at high speed. ICE treatment will help and gentle rhythmical movements of the shoulder joint will alleviate stiffness.

Back injuries

These are just as likely in squash as in other racket sports. Although the maple-sprung floor reduces the shock waves through the ankles, knees, hips and vertebral column, the persistent twisting and turning can cause acute strain, inevitably in the lower back. Strong back muscles and strong stomach muscles *prevent* a muscle imbalance and can therefore cope with these twisting movements better and more efficiently. Order of the day: prevention rather than cure.

Tennis elbow and golfer's elbow

These are experienced by the squash player on the outside and inside elbow respectively. They are classic over-use injuries caused primarily by not playing the shots correctly. However, they are well documented, and many options are open. On discovering Racket Player's elbow, a good method of relieving inflammation and pain is the free application of ice to the affected area for as long as possible. Aspirin as an anti-inflammatory agent will prevent the soreness worsening – but remember the dangers of relying on drugs. For once, rest cannot be freely advocated, because the forearm muscles will tend to waste, thus worsening the condition. This is a dilemma facing squash players because they need to play to maintain fitness yet they need to allow the damaged tissues to heal. Most literature recommends an increase in grip size to reduce the amount of torque in the forearm. This is a dangerous practice because, although it reduces forearm rotation, it affects the stroke leading to poor technique which will cause the same problem. It is also advisable to choose a racket whose weight is commensurate with your strength. Too heavy a racket may prevent access to the ball and cause adjustment of the shot when you are in the hitting area.

A tennis elbow brace acts by reducing the rotation of the forearm and supporting the muscles menaced. It is a tight, elasticated band placed around the upper forearm which neutralises the force. If correctly-placed and fitted this device can restrain tennis elbow, but any joint will only ever be as strong as its assisting musculature. The brace helps to reduce rotation of the wrist and elbow and assists the muscles threatened below the elbow. So again, prevention right from the start is the answer. Ensure there is adequate strength in the muscles of the forearm and upper arm to protect the elbow joint and therefore lessen the likelihood of inflammation and elbow complaints.

Tennis elbow brace

Tenosynovitis

This occurs at the wrist and is an increasing problem. Excessive exercise may be causative but, once again, poor technique is often diagnosed. Recent converts from badminton tend to flick at the ball and the heavier racket causes fluid accumulation and inflammation. Technique adjustment to incorporate the all powerful shoulder muscles and perhaps the use of a lighter all-graphite racket may help.
Treatment initially comprises:

Rest

Ice

Compression

Elevation

Aspirin and gentle massage are also alternatives to be considered. Prevention exercises to build up forearm strength are again recommended.

Knee injuries

The knee, with its remarkable complexities, is the favourite site on the human body for injuries. Rotary motion with vigorous bodily contortions causes the knee to sprain leading to the inevitable diagnosis of a badly-torn cartilage or a parting of the cruciate ligaments at the back of the knee. Corrective surgery is necessary, followed by a gradual build-up of the quadriceps muscles supporting the knee. These are medical problems and orthopaedic surgeons with the backing of physiotherapists should ensure rapid recovery. After traumatic injury the knee capsule is only as strong as its supplementing muscles so carefully-allotted time on strength and flexibility training will be well-spent.

Chondromalacia Patella sometimes known as 'Runner's knee' or 'Housemaid's knee' is also prevalent among squash players. The cushioning material around the knee cap gets damaged every time you twist and turn. The *vastus medialis* muscle should assist the knee cap as it rides up and down its groove. If this muscle is weaker than the other muscles, softening of the knee cap ensues. It is an over-use injury or classic wear and tear injury which has previously been treated by surgery. The recommended treatment these days involves strengthening the large muscles at the front of the thigh (see diagram) and also paying meticulous attention to custom-made squash shoes. The wearing of a *chondromalacia patella* strap is quite popular in the States but this has received considerable opposition from the sports medicine fraternity in England. Whilst recognising the condition is a degenerative process, they believe that persons requiring such an aid should be discouraged from participating in activities which are likely to exacerbate the condition. However, if stopping playing squash is unthinkable, one of these straps must be worn as an aid. An ice pack applied to the affected knee or knees after every match will check the inflammation. If the situation becomes chronic, rest up for a while, but keep doing the quadriceps exercise and your body will tell you when you are ready to play squash again.

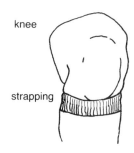

knee

strapping

Chondromalacia Patella strap

Hamstring injury

This is feared by all. How many Olympic sprinters have you seen tear the muscle at the back of the thigh despite taking all the necessary precautions. A reason for this is that these sprinters have bulging quadriceps and the hamstring muscles at the back of the leg are nowhere near as strong. Ice, compression and elevation as usual is the immediate treatment. It may be painful for a few days but usually these indirect trauma injuries are easily manageable. Occasionally these injuries can be a blessing, because they allow the over-zealous squash player to rest and thus recharge his batteries.

Rehabilitation exercises commencing with isometric exercises and followed by cycling on a stationary bicycle are recommended. Running should begin with a trot, building slowly up to half speed and eventually full speed. Remember, gently, gently return to fitness.

Lower leg injuries

'Tennis leg' or a partial rupture of the main upper calf muscle is all too common in squash. The player experiences a violent pain in the back of the leg, often when the game has been going on for some time which cannot be attributed to lack of warm-up! Specific exercises for the calf will lessen the chances of getting this injury. (See stretches for the calves on p. 86.) This injury is most common among the 'geriatric' squash players and that tends to suggest that a reduction in flexibility and strength is causative. Once again ICE is the orthodox treatment, followed by a quiet return to correct warm-up procedure.

The most famous of all lower leg injuries is a complete rupturing of the *Achilles* tendon. People who have experienced this injury will tell you of the echo of the gun shot as they clasp their lower leg. It results in six to nine months of comparative inactivity and all the frustration that goes with it. Mental health is affected because your squash-trained body needs its 'daily dozen'. How do you insure yourself against this evil demon? The answer, as ever, lies in paying even more attention to correct warm-up technique. An *Achilles* tendon stretch (which is similar to the calf stretch) must be inserted into the programme.

The *Achilles* tendon is the largest tendon in the human body but it is located in an area of the body which is a long way from the main cardiac muscle. When it 'goes' it is unable to heal fast because of the ineffective blood supply from the heart. Treatment for this particular type of traumatic injury to the *Achilles* tendon appears to be surgical repair or plaster cast.

Achilles Tendonitis is an ever-increasing problem which physiotherapists are attributing to the raised firm heel tabs on many modern squash shoes. This heel tab produces localised swelling. Either changing to a softer heel tab or removing the existing one will fight the injury.

Foot and ankle injuries

These keep the squash doctor busy all the year round. Without an anatomy lecture it would be difficult for the every day squash player to fully understand the complexities and workings of the 28 bones all held together by the supporting ligaments.

With the running boom came the 'podistrists' (specialists in feet care). They basically believe that ligament strains and tendon strains produced in the whole foot are transferred through the knee, hips, to the vertebral column. You can see the relevance to squash. Thus careful consideration must be given to squash shoe choice. The shoes should have a pad on the tongue to prevent excessive forward movement of the foot. Sliding forward causes *sub-ungual haematoma,* which is a blackened big toe under the nail.

Sprained ankles occur because the lateral ligaments go when the weight goes outwards over the foot. Once again, shoes are often to blame. A squash player needs shoes with firm soles and which are sturdy where the uppers meet the sole.

The treatment for this in the first 48 hours is ICE, followed by the normal physiotherapy practice of ultrasound and massage. For players who consistently turn their ankles over, the use of a 'wobble board' might be the answer. This is sometimes termed 'proprioceptive training' and it is an attempt to get the foot, ankle and knee to work in unison. Other strengthening exercises such as turning of the ankle clockwise and then anti-clockwise by drawing an imaginary circle with the foot may prove useful.

So, in insuring your body against injury, remember the following points:

1 Strength training – joints are only as strong as their complementary muscles

2 Endurance training – fatigued muscles are susceptible to injury

3 Good technique – saves wear and tear

4 Good equipment – sound and sensible not flimsy and fashionable

5 When injury occurs – ICE treatment first

INDEX